1977-78 EDITION
ARTHUR FROMMER'S

DOLLAR WISE GUIDE TO CALIFORNIA AND LAS VEGAS

By RENA BULKIN

Sponsored by *TWA*

Copyright © 1977
by
THE FROMMER/PASMANTIER PUBLISHING CORPORATION
All Rights Reserved

Published by
THE FROMMER/PASMANTIER PUBLISHING CORPORATION
380 Madison Avenue
New York, New York 10017

Distributed by
**SIMON AND SCHUSTER
A GULF+WESTERN COMPANY**
1230 Avenue of the Americas
New York, New York 10020
671-22724-6

Distributed outside the USA and Canada by
FLEETBOOKS
c/o Feffer and Simons, Inc.
100 Park Avenue
New York, New York 10017

Distributed in Canada by
P J PAPERBACKS LTD.
330 Steelcase Road East
Markham, Ontario L3R2M1

All opinions, judgments and statements of fact appearing in this book are those of the author alone, and not Trans World Airlines.

Manufactured in the United States of America

CONTENTS

INTRODUCTION	A DOLLAR-WISE GUIDE TO CALIFORNIA	1
CHAPTER I	GETTING THERE	9
	1. Traveling To California	9
	2. Traveling Within California	12
CHAPTER II	SAN FRANCISCO	14
	1. Getting Around	15
	2. Hotels	20
	3. Restaurants	31
	4. Sights	55
	5. San Francisco After Dark	67
CHAPTER III	AROUND SAN FRANCISCO BAY	77
	1. Angel Island	78
	2. Oakland	78
	3. Berkeley	80
	4. Muir Woods	83
	5. Tiburon	84
	6. Sausalito	86
CHAPTER IV	THE WINE COUNTRY	90
	1. Napa Valley	90
	2. Sonoma	94
	3. Fort Ross and Timber Cove	98
CHAPTER V	DAY TRIPS SOUTH FROM SAN FRANCISCO	100
	1. Marine World/Africa U.S.A.	100
	2. Marriott's Great America	101
	3. San Jose	102
	4. Santa Cruz	104
CHAPTER VI	HIGHLIGHTS OF NORTHERN CALIFORNIA	108

	1. Little River	108
	2. Mendocino	109
	3. Fort Bragg	110
	4. Avenue of the Giants	111
	5. Yosemite National Park	112
	6. South Lake Tahoe	116
CHAPTER VII	**SOUTH ALONG THE SHORE**	**127**
	1. Monterey	128
	2. Carmel	135
	3. Big Sur	140
	4. San Simeon	144
	5. San Luis Obispo	146
	6. Santa Barbara	153
CHAPTER VIII	**LOS ANGELES**	**168**
	1. Getting Around	169
	2. Hotels	172
	3. Restaurants	193
	4. Sights	222
	5. Nightlife	237
CHAPTER IX	**DISNEYLAND AND ENVIRONS**	**245**
	1. Anaheim	245
	2. Buena Park	248
	3. Santa Ana	251
CHAPTER X	**PALM SPRINGS**	**253**
	1. Where to Stay	254
	2. Where to Dine	256
CHAPTER XI	**FROM MALIBU TO NEWPORT BEACH**	**258**
	1. Malibu	259
	2. Redondo Beach	260
	3. Marineland	262
	4. San Pedro	262
	5. Long Beach	263
	6. Catalina Island	264
	7. Newport Beach	264
CHAPTER XII	**THE BOTTOM LINE: SAN DIEGO**	**269**
	1. Things to Do and See	270
	2. Where to Stay	274
	3. Where to Dine	277

	4. La Jolla	278
	5. An Excursion to Tijuana	280
CHAPTER XIII	**LAS VEGAS**	281
	1. Getting There	282
	2. Getting Around	282
	3. Food, Fun and Shelter	282

MAPS

CALIFORNIA	3
SAN FRANCISCO	16
SAN FRANCISCO BAY	79
NAPA VALLEY VINEYARDS	92
THE REDWOOD EMPIRE AND WINE COUNTRY	95
SOUTH LAKE TAHOE	117
GREATER LOS ANGELES	170
BEVERLY HILLS	175
HOLLYWOOD	225
SAN DIEGO	271
LAS VEGAS: THE MAJOR ACCESS ROADS	283
LAS VEGAS	286

Introduction

A DOLLAR-WISE GUIDE TO CALIFORNIA

EUREKA! (I HAVE FOUND IT!) is the motto of the State of California —and people have been echoing that sentiment since 1542, when navigator Juan Rodriguez Cabrillo in fact did find it. The first permanent settlers were the Franciscan fathers who came from Spain to convert the heathen as part of Spain's plan to colonize California. They persevered, taming the vast and savage land as well, and erecting a chain of 21 missions extending almost 600 miles from San Diego to Sonoma. The famous Mission Trail, begun in 1769 with the San Diego Mission, grew into El Camino Real (The Royal Road), which can be followed to this day.

It was almost a century later that the next wave of immigrants found their way to California—half-a-million Forty-Niners from clear around the world lured by the cry of "Gold!" Many of those who came for gold stayed to find their fortunes farming the millions of acres of virgin soil.

With the planting of orchards and vineyards—first sown by the mission padres—came great numbers of Mexican, Chinese and Japanese laborers to tend them. Still more immigrants arrived from distant shores with the discovery of oil in the 1890s. And in the 1930s it was dreams of a land of milk and honey that prompted "Okies" by the thousands to leave their dust-storm-ravaged lands behind and head for California.

By this time, of course, the movie industry (itself a New York emigrant) was firmly rooted on West Coast soil, and Hollywood hopefuls were flocking to California to pursue glittering stardom.

Of course, not everyone who came to California found the rainbow's end. Very few of the prospectors of 1849 unearthed a gold mine (the daily profit of the average speculator was about $1). Only a relatively small number of aspirants ever struck oil, achieved stardom or found the Promised Land. But that reality has not daunted California's incredible growth. One out of every 11 Americans lives here, making it the nation's most populous state. Following a deep-rooted American tradition, people are still heading West to the Golden State—tourists and settlers, dreamers and speculators, spiritual seekers and political idealists—all lured by the sunshine, the wide-open spaces, the laid-back, free and easy lifestyle, and most of all, by California's magical ability to assume the shape of any dream.

FROM THE REDWOOD FORESTS TO THE L.A. FREEWAYS: Pack up your own dreams, and we can guarantee you'll run no risk of disappointment. California is a tourist mecca overflowing with attractions sufficient to satisfy and surprise the most jaded of visitors.

A land of almost excessive natural beauty, it contains Mount Whitney, at 14,500 feet the tallest mountain in the contiguous United States. Death Valley, not far away in the Mojave Desert, is the lowest point in the entire Western Hemisphere—almost 300 feet below sea level. Four-hundred miles of towering trees make up the majestic "Redwood Empire." Visitors can marvel at the picturesque vineyard regions of the Napa Valley and Sonoma, explore quaint, historic towns like Monterey and Carmel, discover delightful beach resorts from Santa Cruz to Santa Barbara—and still not have seen the greater part of California.

There are more miles of coastline—1,264 to be exact—than in any other state except Alaska. Perhaps the most breathtakingly beautiful vista in the world is from the road that winds along the Big Sur Coast—yet it's only one of many awe-inspiring California sights.

The results of human effort in California are equally impressive—and as diverse. Los Angeles and San Francisco are both "typical" of California, yet they share no apparent similarities. Los Angeles presents a glamorous, often ostentatious face. Criss-crossed by an astonishing number of freeways, it sprawls on seemingly forever. It's the home of the stars, stomping grounds of wealthy jet setters, right wingers, and every faction of the lunatic fringe—a colossal, Technicolor ode to modernity, chic, sophistication and success.

Four-hundred miles up the coast and a world away is mist-enshrouded San Francisco—draped delicately over steep hillsides, small, enchanting, elegant. It's everyone's favorite city (did you *ever* meet anyone who didn't like San Francisco?), where the old (like cable cars) is carefully preserved, and where the worst of the new (like freeways) is publicly decried.

Sporting enthusiasts in particular will find there's too much to do in just one trip to California. Facilities abound for everything from skiing to hang-gliding, the wide spectrum encompassing fishing, boating, golf, tennis, surfing, hiking, horseback-riding, mountain-climbing, even skate-boarding.

Then, of course, there are the "special" attractions of California. They range from Disneyland (one of scores of amusement-park extravaganzas) to Hearst Castle, to across-the-Nevada-border gambling centers at Lake Tahoe and Las Vegas (both of which are included in this book).

All of this, along with much, much more, is why so many tourists come to California, and why so many never leave—now *that's* the risk the tourist runs in coming out to California.

INTRODUCTION 3

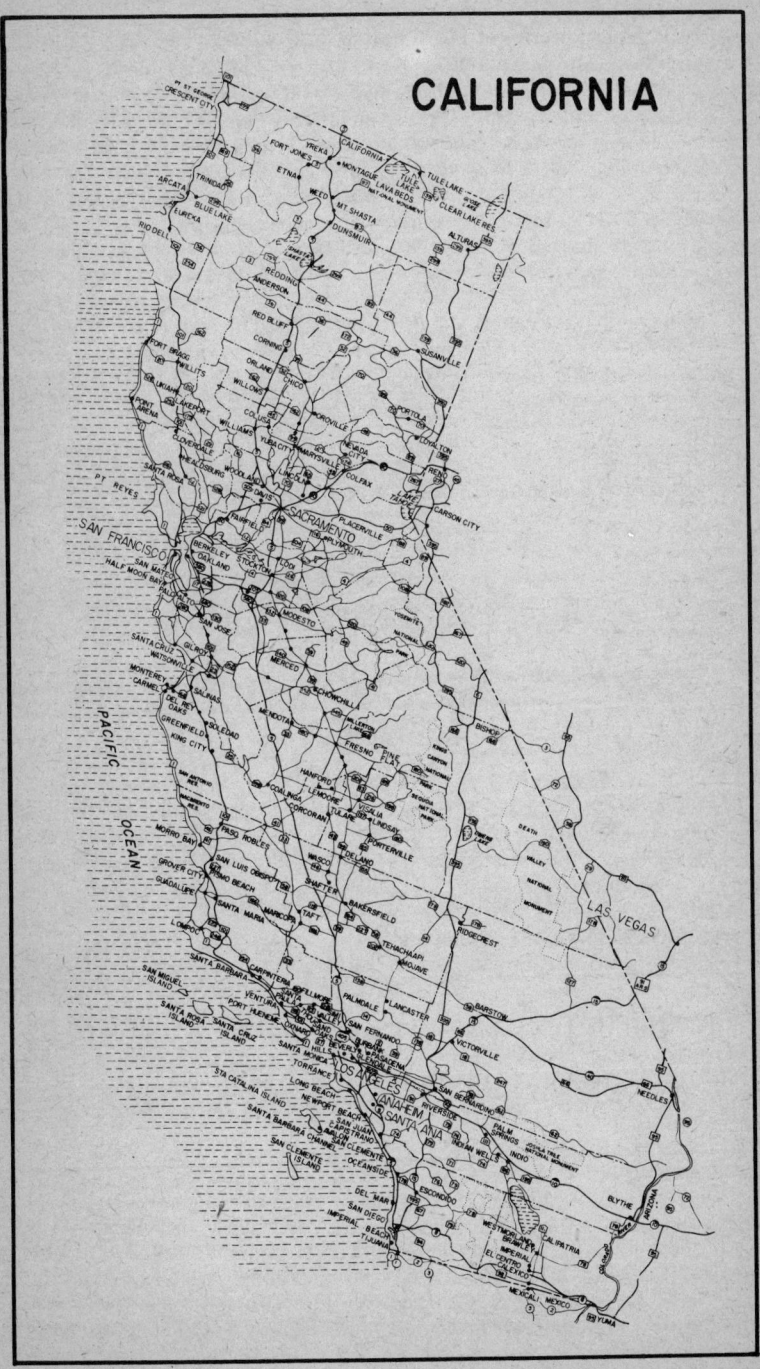

4 DOLLAR-WISE GUIDE TO CALIFORNIA

ABOUT THIS BOOK: In brief, this is a guidebook giving specific, practical details (including prices) about hotels, restaurants, nightlife, sightseeing attractions and other tourist-related activities throughout California and Las Vegas. We've tried to open up some new realms for you to explore, to give you the data you need to make a vacation into an adventure. Establishments in all price ranges have been described, from the luxurious Beverly Wilshire in L.A. with its Dior-designed rooms, to a little bath-in-the-hall budget hostelry in San Francisco. No restaurant, hotel or other establishment has paid to be included in this book. What you read are entirely personal recommendations, carefully checked out and judged by the strict yardstick of value. If they measured up—gave good value for your money—they were included, regardless of price range.

You'll find that the majority of listings are geared neither to the super-rich nor to the best-things-in-life-are-free contingent. Rather, the book is aimed at the dollar-wise, middle-income traveler who wants occasionally to splurge and occasionally to save, but always to get maximum value for his or her dollar.

California Telephone Area Codes

Anaheim	714	Palm Springs	714
Berkeley	415	San Diego	714
Big Sur	408	San Francisco	415
Buena Park	714	San Jose	408
Carmel	408	San Luis Obispo	805
Fort Bragg	707	San Simeon	805
La Jolla	714	Santa Barbara	805
Los Angeles	213	Santa Cruz	408
Monterey	408	Sausalito	415
Napa Valley	707	Sonoma	707
Newport Beach	714	South Lake Tahoe	916
Oakland	415	Yosemite	209

Telephone numbers with 800 as the area code may be dialed toll-free from anywhere in the U.S.

CALIFORNIA HOTELS: As a state that yearly receives millions of visitors, California is well prepared for the onslaught with the best accommodations situation we've ever seen. In just about every city, we found a large selection of superb hotels, motels and inns in every price range and category.

For the Frugal

We've covered all kinds of hotels, but we want to make a special recommendation here for the traveler who is on a particularly tight budget. The no-frills **Motel 6** chain, charging $8.95 for a single room, $10.95 to $11.95 for a double, has motels in over 60 key California locations, including Anaheim, Lake Tahoe, Monterey, Oakland, Napa, San Jose, Santa Barbara—even posh Palm Springs. All units have black and white TV, air conditioning and bath, most have a swimming pool, and they're almost all centrally located, next to some luxury hotel in whose plush coffee shop you can enjoy your morning bacon and eggs. For a listing of all Motel 6 locations, write to Motel 6, Inc., 1888 Century Park East, Los Angeles, California 90067.

First Come Is NOT First Served

To reiterate, tourists flock like lemmings to California shores. We've seen enormous conventions of Shriners, Rosicrucians and once even (shudder!) I.R.S. employees fill an entire city of hotel rooms. Particularly in summer, you're taking a big chance, and certainly lessening your options, if you don't book ahead. Don't waste hours of precious vacation time hunting down hotel rooms, when a simple call or two in advance will take care of business. Be a smart lemming, and you won't drown in a sea of tourists and conventioneers.

AVERAGE MONTHLY TEMPERATURES (F)

Los Angeles		San Francisco	
January	55.8	January	50.7
February	57.1	February	53.0
March	59.4	March	54.7
April	61.8	April	55.7
May	64.8	May	57.4
June	68.0	June	59.1
July	73.0	July	58.8
August	73.1	August	59.4
September	71.9	September	62.0
October	67.4	October	61.4
November	62.7	November	57.4
December	58.2	December	52.5

CALIFORNIA CLIMATE: The two words "California climate" create a phrase about as meaningless as any we've ever heard. There ain't no such animal. Climate here varies from the sizzling Palm Springs desert to the cool mountain regions, and factors like the cold Humboldt current and the warm Japanese current swirling about don't make things any easier. Regional generalizations follow.

As far as weather is concerned, Southern California (an area encompassing San Diego to San Luis Obispo) has no one particular tourist season. The climate doesn't vary too much, though the summer months are the warmest and there is a rainy season from January to May. After that don't even bother packing your umbrella. When it rains in summer, Southern Californians go outside to look at the novelty. Be warned that when the sun goes down the air is cooler, so pack some warmer apparel for nocturnal adventures. The Los Angeles monthly temperature chart above will give you a fair indication for the entire region.

Up north, the climate is even trickier. In San Francisco, for instance, the mercury rarely dips below 40° or rises above 70°. When the latter occurs Bay Area residents go into a tropical stupor and mutter darkly about a "heat wave," while astonished New York tourists consider the weather balmy. Anyway, San Francisco seldom gets more than a few hottish days every summer, and a warm jacket or coat is a *must*—much more important than your bathing suit. Coastal regions north as far as Mendocino and south to about Santa Cruz are fairly close to San Francisco in climate, give or take a few degrees. Once again, check the average monthly temperature chart for San Francisco below.

Areas further east of the coast get progressively warmer, unless they're in the mountains—like South Lake Tahoe, where, for instance, April temperatures will be anywhere between 1° and 74°!

In the coastal area between San Luis Obispo and Santa Cruz, things might vary in either direction.

In summation: When you go to sunny California, take some warm clothes along.

AN INVITATION TO READERS: Like all the Dollar-Wise Guides, *Dollar-Wise Guide to California* hopes to maintain a continuing dialogue between its writer and its readers. All of us share a common aim—to travel as widely and as well as possible, at the best value for our money. And in achieving that goal, your comments and suggestions can be of tremendous help. Therefore, if you come across a particularly appealing hotel, restaurant, store, even sightseeing attraction, please don't keep it to yourself. We'll send free copies of the next edition of this book to readers whose suggestions are used. And the solicitation for letters applies not only to new establishments, but to hotels or restaurants already recommended in this guide. The fact that a listing appears in this edition doesn't give it squatter's rights in future publications. If its services have deteriorated, its chef grown stale, its prices risen unfairly, whatever, these failings should be known. Even if you enjoyed every place and found every description accurate—that, too, is good to know. Send your comments to Frommer/Pasmantier Publishing Corp., 380 Madison Ave., New York, N.Y. 10017.

THE $10-A-DAY TRAVEL CLUB: Before you begin your journey West, perhaps you'd like to learn about a device for saving money on all your trips and travels. We refer to the now widely known $10-a-Day Travel Club, which has gone into its 13th successful year of operation.

The Club was formed at the urging of numerous readers of the $10-a-Day Books and the Dollar-Wise Guides, who felt that the organization of a $10-a-Day Travel Club could bring financial benefits, continuing travel information and a sense of community to budget-minded travelers in all parts of the world. We thought—and have since learned—that the idea had merit. For, by combining the purchasing power of thousands of $10-a-day'ers, it has proved possible to obtain a wide range of exciting travel benefits—including substantial discounts to members from auto rental agencies, restaurants, sightseeing operators, hotels and other purveyors of tourist services throughout the United States and abroad.

In order to make membership in the Club as attractive as possible—and thus build a Club large enough to achieve the above goals—we have agreed to offer members immediate benefits whose value exceeds the cost of the membership fee, which is $8 a year.

And thus, upon receipt of that sum, we shall send all new members, by return mail (book rate), the following items:

(1) The latest edition of any *two* of the following books (please designate in your letter which two you wish to receive):

Europe on $10 a Day
England on $15 a Day
Greece on $10 a Day
Hawaii on $15 & $20 a Day
India (plus Sri Lanka and Nepal) on $5 & $10 a Day
Ireland on $10 a Day
Israel on $10 & $15 a Day
Mexico and Guatemala on $10 a Day
New Zealand on $10 a Day
Scandinavia on $15 & $20 a Day
South America on $10 & $15 a Day
Spain and Morocco (plus the Canary Is.) on $10 & $15 a Day
Turkey on $5 & $10 a Day
Washington, D.C. on $10 & $15 a Day

Dollar-Wise Guide to California
Dollar-Wise Guide to England
Dollar-Wise Guide to France
Dollar-Wise Guide to Germany
Dollar-Wise Guide to Italy
Dollar-Wise Guide to Portugal
(Dollar-Wise Guides discuss accommodations and facilities in all price categories, with special emphasis on the medium-priced.)

Whole World Handbook
(Prepared by the prestigious Council on International Educational Exchange, the Handbook deals with more than 1,000 programs of student travel, study and employment throughout the world.)

Where to Stay USA
(By the Council on International Educational Exchange, published in cooperation with the American Revolution Bicentennial Administration, this extraordinary guide is the first to list accommodations in all 50 states that cost anywhere from 50¢ to $10 per night.)

(2) A copy of **Arthur Frommer's Guide to New York**—a pocket-size guide to hotels, restaurants, night spots and sightseeing attractions in all price ranges throughout the New York area.

(3) A copy of **Surprising Amsterdam**—a 192-page pocket-size guide to Amsterdam by Arthur Frommer.

(4) A one-year subscription to the quarterly Club newsletter—**The Wonderful World of Budget Travel**—which keeps members up-to-date on fast-breaking developments in low-cost travel to all areas of the world.

(5) A voucher entitling you to a $5 discount on any Arthur Frommer International, Inc. Tour booked by you through travel agents in the United States and Canada.

(6) Your personal membership card, which, once received, entitles you to purchase through the Club all Arthur Frommer Publications for 1/3 to 1/2 off their regular retail prices during the term of your membership.

These are the immediate and definite benefits which we can assure to members of the Club at this time. Even more exciting, however, are the further and more substantial benefits (including, in particular, a comprehensive grant of reductions and discounts on travel accommodations and facilities in numerous areas), which it has been our continuing aim to achieve for members. These are announced to members at frequent intervals throughout the year, and can be obtained by them through presentation of their membership cards. Equally interesting has been the development of the Club's newsletter, which has now become an eight-page newspaper, and carries such continuing features as "The Travelers' Directory"—a list of members all over the world who are willing to provide hospitality to other members as they pass through their home cities; "Share-a-Trip"—offers and requests from members for travel companions who can share costs; advance news of individual and group tour programs operated by Arthur Frommer International, Inc.; discussions of freighter travel; tips and articles on other travel clubs (air travel clubs, home and apartment exchanges, pen pals, etc.) and on specific plans and methods for travel savings and travel opportunities.

If you would like to join thousands of other travelers from all parts of the world who are now members of this exciting organization and participate in its exchange of travel information and hospitality, then send your name and address, together with your membership fee of $8, to: $10-a-Day Travel Club, Inc., 380 Madison Avenue, New York, N.Y. 10017—and remember to specify which *two* of the books in section (1) above you wish to receive in your initial package of members' benefits.

A WORD OF WARNING: We've made every effort to get accurate prices for all the establishments listed here. But unfortunately costs change—these days more than ever—and they rarely go down. So we must include the disclaimer that all prices in this book are subject to change. Enough said. Now let's start planning your trip—California, here we come.

Chapter I

GETTING THERE

**1. Traveling To California
2. Traveling Within California**

HOW YOU GET TO the Golden State, and how you get around it, obviously depend on where you're coming from, how much you want to spend, how much time you have and similar considerations. What follows is information on the various options, including some unusual ones.

1. Traveling To California

BY AIR: There are several airlines connecting most major American cities with San Francisco and Los Angeles. Using as an example a New York departure point, and **TWA** as our chosen airline, the following fare options are available:

Regular round-trip coach fare via TWA between New York and San Francisco/Los Angeles is $412 for adults; $274 for children ages two to 11 when accompanied by an adult.

Night Coach

This is the least complicated of the discount fares. The only difference between it and the regular round-trip coach fare is that you fly at night, on designated flights, usually after 9 p.m. (If you remember that there is a three-hour difference between New York and California time, this is really like leaving at 6 p.m.). There's no restriction in the amount of time you stay, and tickets may be purchased one way or round trip. Round-trip fare between New York and San Francisco/Los Angeles is $330 for adults; $220 for children ages two to 11 when accompanied by an adult.

Discover America Excursion Fare

This is a special Bicentennial fare offered on a limited number of seats per flight through May 31, 1977 (hopefully, it will be continued after that date). This ticket is good for a minimum stay of seven days and a maximum stay of 30. Reservations must be made at least 14 days in advance of your flight, with tickets purchased no later than ten days after your reservations are confirmed (whichever comes first). Round-trip fare for adults between New York and San Francisco/Los Angeles is $350 in peak season, from June 1 to September 15 ($330 the rest of the year); $206 the year round for children ages two to 11 when accompanied by an adult.

It's also possible to go Night Coach on the Discover America Excursion Fare during the off-peak season, in which case the round-trip fare is $309 for adults; $206 for children ages two to 11 when accompanied by an adult.

Tour Basing Fare

This fare can be used only in conjunction with tour packages, such as TWA's Fly-Drive packages (about which more follows), and it has departure-time limitations and black-out periods (e.g. major holiday periods). There's also a minimum-price requirement for the land package ($65 to Los Angeles and San Francisco), and a minimum/maximum requirement on length of stay (two to 30 days). The round-trip fare for adults is $309.

Packages

TWA offers three types of packages that you can use with tour-basing fares: fly-drives, on-your-own vacations and escorted motorcoach tours. We're presenting the bare outlines below, but there are almost endless variations on the three basic categories. If you're interested in a package, it's advisable to discuss the many options with a travel agent, who can find the plan that most perfectly fits your needs. Remember that the tour-basing fare is good for 30 days; you can purchase land arrangements for any part of your trip and do the rest on your own.

Fly-Drive: Not only can you save up to 25% on coach fare when you purchase a fly-drive package, but the land arrangements are convenient, economical and incredibly flexible. A car is waiting for you when you arrive at the airport in California. And you'll be issued interchangeable hotel vouchers (good at all hotels participating in the program you choose) for every night of your trip. That means you can have TWA or your travel agent make all your reservations in advance. Or if you prefer a looser itinerary, make them yourself en route.

An example of a fly-drive is the popular **Hertz Multiple-Choice Hotel Package.** Let's assume a couple is planning a two-week trip during off-peak season from New York to San Francisco or Los Angeles, staying at Holiday Inns along the way and renting a Ford Pinto. The round-trip tour basing fare will be $309 each. The car with unlimited mileage and hotel room combined will cost only about $20 each per night. If they decide to splurge and stay at a luxurious Sheraton or Hyatt (both participating hotels) one night, they merely pay an extra supplement for that night. And extra car rental days can be purchased independently of hotels.

On-Your-Own Vacations: These are free-style vacations in which you purchase a land package of hotel vouchers along with sightseeing attractions and some other extras. A good example is the eight-day **California Double Bill** package, which costs $354 per person (plus airfare), and takes in San Francisco, Monterey, Pismo Beach, Los Angeles and Disneyland. It includes first-class hotel rooms with bath each night, baggage handling, tips and taxes, eight meals, and transfers between airports and hotels. Among the highlights: two Gray Line tours (one day, one night) of San Francisco; a Bay cruise; tour of Hearst Castle; a day in Disneyland with a book of tickets; "Glamor tram" ride through Universal Studios.

Escorted Motorcoach Tours: These really offer the utmost in relaxed travel. From arrival to departure, everything—hotel registration, baggage, sightseeing, etc.—is efficiently handled for you by a friendly and knowledgeable guide. You just sit back and relax in the air-conditioned comfort of your motorcoach. Most popular of this category is the 14-day **California Circle**, which costs $774 per person (plus airfare), and takes in Lake Tahoe, Yosemite, Bakersfield, Palm Springs, San Diego, Los Angeles, Santa Maria, Monterey and San Francisco.

Additional Notes

TWA flies to San Francisco/Los Angeles from the following cities: Albuquerque, Amarillo, Atlanta, Baltimore, Boston, Chicago, Cincinnati, Cleveland, Columbus, Dayton, Detroit, Harrisburg, Hartford, Indianapolis, Kansas City, Las Vegas, Louisville, Miami, New York, Oklahoma City, Philadelphia, Phoenix, Pittsburgh, St. Louis, Tampa, Tucson, Tulsa, Wichita and Washington, D.C. Service from Denver is to San Francisco only.

Night coach flights are available to San Francisco/Los Angeles from Atlanta, Boston, Chicago, Kansas City, New York, Philadelphia, Phoenix, Pittsburgh, St. Louis, Tucson and Washington, D.C.

Keep in mind that all fares quoted above are subject to change.

BY BUS: Both **Continental Trailways** and **Greyhound** bus lines encompass every major American city and many less-than-major cities in their vast transportation networks. Both charge the same fares, and offer occasional excursion sales. For instance, regular New York to Los Angeles or San Francisco round-trip fare is $270.20, but once in a while there's a 20-day excursion ticket available for $157.

Depending on how you take to bus travel, and how many places you want to visit, Greyhound's **Ameripass** and Continental Trailways' identical **Eagle Pass** can provide terrific savings. These passes offer unlimited travel between all route cities for a fixed price during a given time period: 15 days for $165, 30 days for $225 and 60 days for $325.

BY TRAIN: Amtrak, the nation's most complete long-distance passenger railroad network, connects 484 American cities, over 30 of them in California. By train, in coach, round trip between New York and San Francisco is $325; $346 between New York and Los Angeles.

However, like the bus companies, Amtrak has something called the **U.S.A. Rail Pass,** which offers 14 days of unlimited travel for $165, 21 days for $220 and 30 days for $275. And there's an added benefit here: for another $35 per stop, at about half the cities reachable via Amtrak, you can get a Hertz rental

12 DOLLAR-WISE GUIDE TO CALIFORNIA

car and overnight accommodations for up to four persons in a room at a Holiday Inn.

Amtrak also has excursion fares, family plans and other money-saving fares. Call them for details and further information.

RIDE CENTERS AND DRIVEAWAYS: An unconventional and inexpensive method of getting yourself to the coast is the increasingly popular ride center. A typical organization of this ilk is **Manhattan's Original Ride Center**, 200 West 72nd Street, Room 37 (tel: 212/799-9170). Using converted Greyhound buses, they offer trips to Los Angeles and San Francisco every week in summer (via Denver) and every other week the rest of the year (via St. Louis) for just $69 one way. The trips take between 72 to 76 hours of continuous driving and are recommendable mostly for the young and young at heart. The atmosphere on the bus is relaxed and laid back (literally laid back, since all the seats are torn out and everyone just lounges around on mattresses). People sing, play guitar and generally have a good time.

The Original Ride Center also handles driveaways: you register for a car, and when one becomes available you put down a $75 deposit and are given $25 for gas (you pay the rest of the gas—your only expense). When you deliver the car on the West Coast, your deposit is refunded.

Yet a third self-explanatory service they offer is called "drivers meet riders." There's no fee or obligation to the rider, save what you work out with the driver.

The Manhattan Ride Center is one of several such organizations that operates out of New York, and advertises weekly in *The Village Voice*.

Check underground newspapers in other cities to find local ride centers.

2. Traveling Within California

BY CAR: In every chapter of this book, easy-to-follow driving instructions have been provided, and the San Francisco and Los Angeles chapters contain data on car rentals. Of course you'll want to pick up a good map of the state before you start your trip and keep it handy in the glove compartment. In addition, a glance at the mileage chart on the next page will give you a quick idea of distances between various California cities.

BY AIR: Although national airlines like TWA fly between Los Angeles and San Francisco, there are two local airlines providing service at reasonable prices to many California cities.

Pacific Southwest Airlines (PSA) connects Fresno, Hollywood/Burbank, Lake Tahoe, Long Beach, Los Angeles, Oakland, Ontario, Sacramento, San Diego, San Francisco, San Jose and Stockton.

Air California flights encompass Lake Tahoe, Oakland, Ontario, Orange County, Palm Springs, Sacramento, San Diego, San Francisco and San Jose.

Pick up a brochure for either airline at any major hotel, airport or Chamber of Commerce of any California city.

BUS AND TRAIN: Once again, Greyhound and Continental Trailways can provide bus service to just about anywhere you want to go in California, and Amtrak has trains serving over 30 California cities.

Distances by Car from San Francisco to:

Oakland	13	Avenue of the Giants	240
Muir Woods	17	Yosemite	193
Tiburon	18	South Lake Tahoe	209
Napa Valley	46	Monterey	130
Sonoma	45	Big Sur	156
Marriott's Great America	45	San Simeon	224
San Jose	48	San Luis Obispo	266
Santa Cruz	74	Santa Barbara	332
Mendocino	125	Los Angeles	460
Fort Bragg	166		

from Los Angeles to:

San Diego	137	Las Vegas	298

Chapter II

SAN FRANCISCO

1. Getting Around
2. Hotels
3. Restaurants
4. Sights
5. San Francisco After Dark

THERE ARE THOUSANDS OF quotable quotes about San Francisco, from Georges Pompidou's approbatory tribute—"Your city is remarkable not only for its beauty. It is also, of all the cities in the United States, the one whose name, the world over, conjures up the most visions and more than any other incites one to dream"—to the pithy praise of Francis Ford Coppola: "I kinda like this place."

Most people do. The only negative sentiment we've ever heard uttered about San Francisco dates back to the 16th century, when the English navigator Sir Francis Drake wrote in his ship's diary: "Anchored here in a stynkinge fogge."

"Fogge" notwithstanding, this 47-square-mile peninsular city exerts a compelling charm, comprised of open-air fish markets at the Wharf, Victorian houses, exotic ethnic districts (from whence springs a lauded international cuisine), quaint, bell-clanking cable cars and sudden, breathtaking glimpses of the ocean and Golden Gate Bridge from atop a steep hill.

The hills at first seem of an impossible steepness (bring comfortable shoes), but you'll soon find yourself enjoying the exercise, the views and the camaraderie of fellow mountaineers. And as someone once said, "When you get tired of walking around San Francisco, you can always lean against it."

GETTING YOUR BEARINGS: San Francisco is a town to walk in. The hub of the city is **Union Square,** flanked by Geary, Post, Powell and Union Streets. Named for a series of violent pro-Union demonstrations staged here in Civil War days, today it is an impeccably manicured 2.6-acre park, planted with palms, yews, boxwood and flowers. You'd never know you were sitting on top of a huge underground garage, capable of housing over 1,000 automobiles ($3.70 for 24 hours).

This compact area is the logical setting for many of San Francisco's hotels. From Union Square, it's an easy walk to **Chinatown's** gateway at Bush Street and Grant Avenue.

Adjoining Chinatown is **North Beach** (where Columbus crosses Grant), home of San Francisco's Italian community and a slightly passé bohemian outpost similar to New York's Greenwich Village; the scene has moved elsewhere, but the atmosphere lingers on. A lively nightlife district with entertainment ranging from jazz clubs and espresso bars to sleazy topless joints, North Beach offers many tourist attractions—a beach, however, is not one of them.

Head on in the same direction, and you come to the **Embarcadero,** one of the world's largest and busiest ports. Slightly to the west lie **Fisherman's Wharf** and **Aquatic Park.**

Union Square is equally convenient to the **Financial District,** to the northeast; and a few blocks south of Union Square is **Market Street,** the city's seemingly endless main artery.

Golden Gate Bridge

No description of San Francisco would be near complete without mention of the Golden Gate Bridge, the most beautiful bridge in the world—a 1.7-mile-long span of spidery bracing cables and lofty red-orange towers. As beautiful to look at as to look out from, the Golden Gate can be enjoyed from many vantage points of the city, and can be crossed by bus, car, foot or bicycle. Every year an average of 28-million vehicles pay 75¢ to cross it (southbound only; no toll for northbound traffic), and millions of pedestrians enjoy the terrific views.

Bridge-bound Golden Gate Transit buses depart every half hour during the day for **Marin County,** starting from the Transbay Terminal at Mission and First and making convenient stops at Market and Seventh, at the Civic Center, and along Van Ness and Lombard Street. Call 332-6600 for schedule information.

Oakland Bay Bridge

Less celebrated, but nonetheless important, this 8¼-mile silvery giant links San Francisco with Oakland, her neighbor across the Bay. You can drive across the bridge (toll is 50¢ coming into the city, nothing going out). Or you can catch a Transbay Terminal (Mission at 1st Street) bus, and ride to downtown Oakland for 60¢.

1. Getting Around

San Francisco is easier to get around than most large American cities we've visited. For one thing, most attractions are in walking distance of your

16 DOLLAR-WISE GUIDE TO CALIFORNIA

SAN FRANCISCO: TRANSPORTATION 17

hotel and of each other. And the public transportation is excellent, varied and efficient.

Most of San Francisco's public transport is operated by the Municipal Railway, better known as **the Muni.** For detailed information, call 673-MUNI or consult the bus map and routings at the front of the Yellow Pages in the San Francisco telephone book.

The city's public transport is one of the greatest bargain buys in America. Fares are a uniform 25¢ to every point covered by the 693-mile network of streetcars, buses and cable cars. Only the Express buses, which run during rush hours and stop only at major intersections, charge an extra nickel. Transfers are free.

The Muni also issues special 50¢ **tour passes** good for 24 hours of unlimited riding on Sundays and holidays (purchase them from the cable-car conductor). On top of that, there's the **Downtown Shoppers' Shuttle,** which costs 10¢ and runs up and down Market and Mission Streets daily between 10 a.m. and 3 p.m., easily recognizable by the yellow flags flown on the cars. Senior citizens can ride the Muni at any time for a nickel by showing their Senior Citizen's card; the disabled can also ride for 5¢ if they show a Medicare Card.

San Francisco bus and streetcar drivers are usually cheerful, courteous and helpful. They're not equipped to make change, so have correct fare ready for deposit when you climb aboard.

STREET CARS: There are four lines, lettered J,K,L and N, and they all run up and down Market Street past the Civic Center, where they branch off in different directions.

BUSES: Some 58 different bus lines go to virtually every point on the San Francisco map.

CABLE CARS: Ever ride a national landmark? A century-old San Francisco tradition, cable cars were named a national historic landmark in 1964.

With no engines, cable cars are hoisted along by means of a steel cable permanently moving at a speed of 9½ miles an hour. The cars move when the gripman (not driver) pulls back a lever which closes a pincer-like "grip" on the cable. Though 9½ miles per hour may sound like a snail's pace, it doesn't feel that way when you're slamming around curves on San Francisco terrain that turn this ride into a veritable roller coaster. The conductor contributes to the excitement by hollering "heeeeeere we go!" and "Hold on tight for the curve!" at appropriate moments.

A typical San Francisco sight is the crew manually reversing the cars on a turntable at Powell and Market Streets—always with a crowd of willing helpers. And clanging bells are as essential a part of the San Francisco symphony as the hooting of fog horns.

The two types of cable cars in use hold a maximum of 90 to 100 passengers in theory; in practice it's as many as can get a toehold somewhere.

There are three lines in all. The most scenic—and exciting—is No. 60, which follows a vertical and lateral zigzag course from the corner of Powell and Market Streets over both Nob Hill and Russian Hill to a turntable at gaslit Victorian Square in front of Aquatic Park. Ghirardelli Square is less than a block away.

18 DOLLAR-WISE GUIDE TO CALIFORNIA

The No. 59 Powell-Mason line leads from the corner of Powell and Market Streets in the center of the shopping district up over Nob Hill and down again into the lively hubbub of Fisherman's Wharf.

And the No. 61 route, stretching from the foot of California Street in the financial district to Van Ness Avenue, cuts through Chinatown and crests Nob Hill.

TAXIS: As everywhere else, this is an expensive way to get about, particularly in light of a recent fare rise which sent the rates skyrocketing to $1 when the meter starts (for the first ninth of a mile) and 20¢ for each 2/9 of a mile thereafter.

If you need one though, it's not too hard to find a cab here. And if you call one, you pay no extra charge. Herewith, a few sample numbers:
   Yellow Cab: 626-2345
   Veteran's Cab: 552-1300
   De Soto Cab: 673-1414
   Luxor Cabs: 673-4040

BART: We love to travel on BART (it stands for Bay Area Rapid Transit)—a super-modern, high-speed rapid transit rail network that connects San Francisco with Oakland, Richmond, Concord, Daly City and Fremont. Run by a computerized system right down to the ticket gate, BART offers a ride with the feel of a sci-fi adventure.

Its coaches are 70 feet long and designed to represent the last word in public transport luxury: carpeted floors, tinted picture windows, automatic air conditioning and recessed lighting. They hit a top speed of 80 miles an hour (average, including stops, is 42 miles an hour), and the aforementioned computer system monitors and adjusts speeds and maintains safe spacing.

Minimum fare is 25¢, and extra costs depend on distance ($1.45 from Fremont to Daly City is the highest BART fare). Information boards at all stations show the fares to all other stations. And large maps in the stations and trains make this simple system extra-easy to use.

BART tickets can be purchased in any amount from 25¢ to $20 at the station or at local banks; your ticket is good indefinitely, until its value is used up.

If you're continuing your journey by local bus in the East Bay, get a free AC Transit transfer from the white machine in the station. Bus route and schedule information can be found in free "BART and Buses" folders in the stations.

BART operates Monday through Friday from 6 a.m. to midnight. Children under five ride free; children five through 12 and handicapped persons can purchase a red ticket worth $6 for $1.50.

Even if you have no real reason to ride BART you might want to try this computerized subway for the experience. Remember, nothing can go wrong, can go wrong, can go wrong, can go wrong, can go. . . .

CARS & CAR RENTALS: Driving around hilly San Francisco requires some special instruction. For openers, always remember that cable cars have the right of way, and don't argue with them unless you want to end up as a junk sculpture. Also, on wet days their tracks tend to be slippery and should be avoided.

SAN FRANCISCO: TRANSPORTATION 19

Pedestrians also have right of way and the cops back them to the hilt. So for the sake of your pocketbook, follow the example of local drivers and wait courteously while the foot traffic crosses.

And though the steep hills are part of the city's charm, don't forget when parking on a grade always to jam your front wheels against the curb, put on the hand brake and put your car in gear. Otherwise, your car might join the hundreds of yearly runaways, which is not so charming.

You don't need a car to explore most of San Francisco, and in crowded areas like Chinatown it's a handicap. But if you're going further afield, you may want to utilize one of the many car rental firms in the area. Sample rates are offered below:

Hertz: International Airport and 433 Mason Street (tel: 771-2200). Compacts: $14.95 plus 15¢ per mile for 24 hours. Standard cars: $16.95 plus 17¢ per mile for 24 hours. Pintos are rentable for $13.95 a day, with no mileage charge, but they must be returned to the renting location.

Avis Rent-a-Car: International Airport and 675 Post Street (tel: 885-5011). Compacts: $13.95 a day and 17¢ a mile for 24 hours. Standard cars: $15.95 plus 17¢ a mile for 24 hours. Special "See America" rates of $126 a week for compacts with unlimited mileage in California. Avis also has weekend rates beginning Friday noon and ending Monday noon—$18.95 for a compact, $20.95 for a standard; no mileage charge in either case.

Pacific: 322 Mason Street (tel: 692-2611). Airport pick-up can be arranged. Compacts: $9 plus 10¢ a mile for 24 hours. Weekly rates from $90 plus 10¢ per mile, with 500 miles free each week.

National: International Airport and 500 Post Street (tel: 474-5300). Compacts: $13.95 plus 14¢ a mile for 24 hours. Standard cars: $15.95 plus 16¢ a mile for 24 hours. Vacation special: one week with 1,000 free miles (unlimited mileage if car is returned to San Francisco) is $129 for a compact, $146 for a standard.

Budget: 349 Mason Street (tel: 776-3588). Minis (VW, Pinto, etc.): $13.95 a day with 100 free miles for one day and unlimited mileage for two days or more. Standard cars: $22.99 with 100 free miles a day.

TOURIST INFORMATION: Questions about any aspect of San Francisco tourism can be fully answered in German, Japanese, French, Chinese, Spanish and Italian—not to mention English—by the cheerful experts at the **San Francisco Visitor and Convention Bureau**, 1390 Market at Polk Street (tel: 626-5500). In fact, it's well worth your while to write in advance of your trip—they'll send you an invaluable packet of literature, including a tourist map and a three-month calendar of events. When in town, dial 391-2000 any time of the day for a recorded description of current cultural and sporting events.

A second source of assistance and information is the **Visitors Information Center** of the Redwood Empire Association, 476 Post Street (tel: 421-6554), just a half block off Union Square. The walls are lined with racks of informative brochures, and the charming staff will help you plan tours of San Francisco and points north. Their invaluable free *Redwood Empire Visitors' Guide,* updated annually, is chock-full of detailed information on everything from Sonoma County farm trails to favored fishing areas in the entire northern region. Stop by and pick one up.

2. Hotels

One of the world's great hotel cities, San Francisco has 45,000 rooms for visitors, and is constantly adding more—19 hotels, motels and major additions to existing properties have opened since 1970.

The wide variety of high-quality facilities, however, is matched by the large volume of tourist and convention traffic (about 2½-million visitors per year) flocking to San Francisco. Especially in peak season—from late May to late September—it's foolish not to make prior reservations.

San Francisco boasts a dozen hotels in the international luxury class—a cross section of these, from the old-world traditional and the super-modern, comprises our first two categories, deluxe and upper bracket, the latter a shade less expensive and luxurious than the former. The bulk of our selections falls in the moderately priced range, with doubles approximately in the $25 to $35 area, some more, some less. The hotel section concludes with budget listings for those traveling on limited funds.

But all these hotels have one thing in common. They come up to our exacting standards of comfort, hospitality and cleanliness. Most (though not all) are in the downtown area. There's something to suit just about every taste and pocketbook—read carefully and you'll find what you're looking for.

Remember: there is a 6% tax on all hotel bills in San Francisco, which must be added to the prices we've quoted.

THE DELUXE HOTELS: The Stanford Court, Powell and California Streets (tel: 989-3500; 800/227-4736). Housed in the former Nob Hill mansion of multimillionaire Leland Stanford, this gracious establishment has made few concessions to the modern world. High tea is served in the lobby lounge every afternoon, service is in the old-fashioned European tradition, and such touches as a fresh rose on your breakfast tray, hand-milled soap and heated towel racks provide a sense of well-being most elusive these days. Even the carriageway entrance is under a lofty stained-glass dome.

The distinguished interior is a masterpiece of restrained elegance. Japanese Imari bowls and jardinières from the lobby of the Grand Hotel in Paris overflow with fresh-cut flowers. Baccarat chandeliers from a Loire chateau, Carrara marble and objets d'art from the Rothschild estate are complemented by countless fine paintings, French provincial and Empire antiques and reproductions. Indeed, the only artificial materials used in the hotel are in the phones and light switches!

In each of the 402 guest rooms, a reproduction of a classic French armoire serves as a desk and a discreet hideaway for the color TV (there's a second TV and an additional phone in the bath/dressing-room area). The rooms feature hand-crafted rattan furnishings, exquisitely patterned carpeting, canopied beds, marble bedside tables and original wall lithographs of early San Francisco scenes. Rates range from $40 to $70 single, $55 to 85 double, $100 and up for suites.

The Cafe Potpourri, a delightful dining area encompassing three intimate cafes, serves breakfast, lunch, dinner and high tea. Not your typical hotel coffee shop; the menu here offers the likes of fresh poached salmon, salade Niçoise, and perhaps praline ice cream pie or brie cheese for dessert.

The hotel also houses a fine gourmet restaurant—Fournou's Ovens, the domain of chef Marcel Dragon, who previously served for six years as executive chef of San Francisco's famed L'Etoile. Open nightly for dinner, Fournou's offers a warm French provincial ambience in which succulent specialties like roast rack of lamb ($9.95) emerge from massive tiled oak-burning open-hearth ovens. The antiques which decorate the restaurant walls and grilled balcony levels—including authentic 18th-century French armoires and chests—were collected from five continents. The floors are terra-cotta tile, the beamed ceilings of substantial mahogany. The wine cellar downstairs maintains 88 bins just for the use of Fournou's regular clients who wish to keep their own wines on hand—though, of course, a fine selection is available for all. You might begin your meal here with little snails in clay pots covered in delicate pastry ($3.50) or with a bowl of cream of artichoke soup with hazelnut ($2). Roast boned duckling with green peppercorn and kumquat sauce ($9.50) is another oven specialty. Oven-roast potatoes and fresh vegetable du jour are served with all entrees. Soufflé glacé Grand Marnier is a truly memorable dessert.

In a similar class and setting stands the elegant **Mark Hopkins,** No. 1 Nob Hill (tel: 392-3434; 800/621-1155), where some of the suites even feature grand pianos! It occupies one of the most ornate and extravagant Nob Hill homes built by railroad tycoons in the 1870s, the gabled and turreted Mark Hopkins mansion. In its 50 years of operation, the Mark has been headquarters for distinguished visitors and celebrities ranging from Haile Selassie, Prince Philip, King Hussein and Eleanor Roosevelt to Frank Sinatra, who maintained a suite here for years.

When the hotel opened its doors in 1926, it was (with 20 stories) the highest point in San Francisco, and each room was designed to offer an expansive view. Guests can choose rooms of either classical or contemporary decor; all are beautifully furnished and have sumptuous baths and huge closets. Thoughtful extras include an electric shoeshine machine, a new soft bathrobe to wrap yourself in, and the morning paper delivered daily to your door.

For dining there's the stately, oak-paneled Nob Hill Restaurant, specializing in steaks and seafood; the Vienna Coffee House, for simple meals, delicious pastries and excellent cappucino: and the Club Grill, appointed in the manner of a private English club. Most notable, however, is the renowned Top of the Mark, a glass-walled room offering a panoramic 360-degree view of the city along with lunch, dinner or cocktails.

Rates at the Mark Hopkins are $35 to $57 single, $45 to $70 for doubles and twins. Suites begin at $90 and ascend rapidly.

Cross the cable-car tracks and you'll find yourself at the magnificent stone and marble carriage entrance to **The Fairmont,** at California and Mason Streets (tel: 772-5000; 800/527-4727), a third Nob Hill hostelry where old-world luxury and graciousness are still alive and well. The historic main building with its opulent lobby contains 340 rooms and 40 distinctive suites. The adjoining tower, which opened in 1961, added 200 more rooms and 20 suites.

There are six restaurants to choose from: The Tonga, offering dancing on a boat deck along with Oriental and island specialties; a 24-hour coffee shop; the flower-bedecked Brasserie, featuring continental cuisine and music nightly; the Fairmont Crown—29 stories high and reached by an outdoor glass elevator —wherein lavish buffet luncheons and dinners are this establishment's counterpart to the Top of the Mark: the award-winning Canlis, where international fare is gracefully served by kimono-clad waitresses; and the Venetian Room, an elegant supperclub featuring top-name entertainment (see Nightlife section). In addition, there's live dixieland jazz nightly in the New Orleans Room, and you might enjoy cocktails or high tea in the Lobby Lounge, a sundae or a sandwich at The Sweet Corner, an ice cream parlor.

Guests are pampered with nightly turn-down service, extra pillows, an electric shoe polisher, oversized towels and custom-made soap, among other little conveniences. Room decor is richly traditional.

Rates in the Fairmont's main building are $30 to $52 single, $45 to $67 double or twin. In the Tower, singles go from $59 to $69, doubles from $74 to $84.

The **Hyatt Regency,** No. 5 Embarcadero Center (tel: 788-1234; 800/228-9000), takes us not only to another section of town from the above-mentioned listings, but also into another century—the ultra-modern 20th. Even if you don't stay here, do come by to ogle this amazing seven-sided pyramid hotel and its spectacular lobby. A babbling brook meanders through the vast central court. Longer than a football field, it's lined with 150 live trees, and 15,000 potted ivy plants hang from the lofty balconies which ascend 17 stories. Daylight filters down from the skylight roof, casting a rosy glow. The centerpiece (the only unfortunate note, in our opinion) is an enormous aluminum sculpture rising four stories over a huge reflecting waterfall pond. Arrangements of flowers, live birds in cages, eating areas scattered here and there, and strolling musicians complete the picture.

Off the lobby are five glass cylinder elevators, each highlighted by 500 tiny lights. One of these will whisk you, at a speed of 500 feet per minute, to the Equinox, a revolving rooftop restaurant which provides a complete sweep of San Francisco scenery every 50 minutes. There are six other restaurants as well—these all located off the lobby—plus a nightclub and several cocktail lounges.

As for the rooms, over two-thirds offer bay views. They're done in monochromatic color schemes—rich earth tones set off by splashes of red, blue or green. Custom-designed modern furnishings are softened by elm burl and cane accents, brushed-bronze hardware and sheer draperies. Above the beds are impressionistic San Francisco seascape murals. Each room has a dressing area with make-up and full-length mirrors, and there's a choice of six first-run movies on your color TV ($3.90 per).

Singles range from $55 to $62, doubles from $70 to $77, suites begin at $85.

Hyatt on Union Square, on Stockton Street between Post and Sutter (tel: 398-1234; 800/228-9000), is another new member of the Hyatt chain, and though it's less spectacularly innovative than the Regency, it is quite handsome and exceedingly well located.

Champagne draperies and awninged windows give the hotel an inviting regal appearance when viewed from the street. Inside, the ultra-modern decor has an almost theatrical quality of hushed elegance. The 700 rooms, restaurants, many shops and facilities are housed in a three-story forebuilding and a 35-story tower, fronted by a lovely brick courtyard. Bedecked with potted trees and flowers, the courtyard is the setting for Ruth Asawa's bronze fountain sculpture, the design of which imaginatively depicts the city's familiar landmarks.

Your room at the Hyatt will be spacious and contemporary, with beige shag rugs, off-white and mirrored walls, beds with high backboards, and gold, brown or royal-blue drapes and spreads. Sliding doors open onto a railed parapet. The carpeted baths have marble sinks. And, once again, there are first-run movies available on your color TV.

Business people will appreciate the free limousine service to the financial district weekday mornings.

A good inexpensive restaurant, What This Country Needs ("is a good soup kitchen"), overlooks the courtyard on the ground floor. It's a most pleasant place to partake of hearty and healthy fare like homemade soups, sandwiches on nine-grain bread and homemade desserts. We're very partial to the Plaza Restaurant, also overlooking the courtyard, and featuring a stained-glass skylight dome overhead. The rugs are green, and grassy-green velvet drapes grace lofty arched floor-to-ceiling windows. With bamboo chairs, marble-topped tables, an abundance of potted palms—even a fountain—it's like dining in a delightful European garden, and the continental fare is quite good. You can also watch the sunset, enjoy cocktails, or take lunch or dinner comfortably ensconced on a plush and private tufted leather and velvet banquette at Hugo's One-Up, 36 stories skyward. Great view, very romantic.

Rates at the Hyatt are $48 to $60 single, $63 to $75 double, with higher rates, generally, for rooms on upper floors.

Since 1904, the centrally located **St. Francis,** Union Square (tel: 397-7000; 800/228-3000), has welcomed thousands of prominent guests from royalty to theatrical luminaries. Rebuilt after massive damage from the 1906 earthquake, the hotel's latest expansion—the addition of the 32-story Tower—brought room capacity to 1,200. Sporting five glass-enclosed elevators, the Tower is topped by a fine rooftop restaurant, Victor's, offering first-rate continental cuisine and an extensive wine selection in posh surroundings. The Penthouse, open for lunch, cocktails and dancing, adjoins.

Rooms throughout are quietly elegant, with cream-colored walls, very attractive furnishings and all modern appurtenances from color TV to electric blankets. Rooms in the original building have unusually high ceilings.

And though, to the best of our knowledge, Howard Hughes never owned this hotel, he no doubt would have approved their practice of washing all the coins in the cashier's office every day.

The St. Francis has its own garage, charging $5.50 per 24 hours with in-and-out privileges.

Rates in the main building are $35 to $53 single, $45 to $68 double. Tower rooms range from $51 to $65 single, $66 to $80 double.

The **Sheraton Palace Hotel,** 639 Market Street at New Montgomery (tel: 392-8600; 800/325-3535), opened in flamboyant style over a century ago with a royal banquet (costing $5,000,000) for Lt. General Phillip Sheridan, fresh from his success in the Franco-Prussian War. Hailed as the showplace of the western world, the largest, finest hotel on earth, it promptly became the place to stay. Though its former grandeur has been surpassed over the years by other establishments, the Sheraton retains its place as a venerable San Francisco institution and a landmark that is a vibrant link to the city's past.

Not to be missed is Sunday brunch in the opulent Garden Court. It has been called "the most beautiful dining room in the world," and its leaded-glass dome overhead, elaborate chandeliers and splendid Italian marble columns create the perfect setting in which to experience the grace and luxury of a bygone era. A string quartet plays chamber music, and the buffet is an elaborate feast proffering the likes of roast shoulder of lamb in apricot sauce, quiche lorraine, glazed ham, etc. The cost for this sumptuous buffet is $7.95 per person. There are four other restaurants off the lobby, including the Pied Piper, an elegant wood-paneled affair that boasts a Maxfield Parrish mural.

Guest rooms and suites are housed on the eight upper floors. They're quite luxurious, furnished traditionally but with all modern conveniences, including first-run movies on your color TV.

Rates are: $35-$45 single, $42-$52 double or twin. Suites begin at $65.

The Clift, Geary and Taylor Streets (tel: 775-4700; 800/854-3380), is a highly personalized 400-room hotel emphasizing excellence of service, quiet but unimpeachable style and total comfort. It's the familiar haunt of discreet and knowledgeable travelers who care more about quality than flashy digs or the number of celebs in residence. The Clift is the kind of place where the staff remains unchanged year after year and guests' names and preferences are remembered.

Spacious accommodations are furnished with pieces selected for comfort and elegance. All rooms have oversized beds and pillows, color TV, and extension phones in the bath. Fine grades of linen and toweling are used, and attractive prints grace the walls. Room service is available around the clock.

There's only one restaurant, the prestigious Redwood Room, designed by architect Albert Lansburgh in 1934 (he also did the San Francisco Opera House). The dining room is paneled in 2,000-year-old redwood burl (the bar, also, is of redwood), and three 18th-century crystal chandeliers hang majestically overhead. At night, the Redwood Room is wonderful by candlelight. Roast prime rib, carved and served at your table, with Yorkshire pudding ($10.95), is the house specialty.

To live in quiet comfort away from the parvenus will cost singles $38 to $56, doubles and twins $50 to $68.

Last, but certainly not least, of San Francisco's deluxe hostelries—with 1,800 rooms the largest hotel west of Chicago—is the **Hilton,** Mason and O'Farrell Streets (tel: 771-1400). Unique features here include an outdoor heated swimming pool (a statusy frill in usually chilly San Francisco), and convenient free guest parking on floors five to 11 in the main building. Connecting doors from the parking area lead directly into guest rooms.

Ideally located and adjacent to the Airline Terminal, this miniature city houses five restaurants. They include the Chef's Table for plush and formal dining complete with a strolling violinist and elaborate continental fare served on fancy Lenox china with 12-carat-gold trim; Henri's, the requisite rooftop restaurant offering superb views along with buffet lunches and dinners ($5.95 and $10.50, respectively); and Kiku of Tokyo, a serene Japanese restaurant utilizing a pleasing combination of raw woods, bamboo and rattan to create a traditional decor.

Of course, shops, airline offices, tour desks, etc. abound in the busy lobby, usually bustling with conventioneers.

Guest rooms are large and modern in typical Hilton tradition. All rooms face outside and offer views through floor-to-ceiling windows. Tower rooms, of course, offer the best views. Each floor has a slightly different decor; reproductions of great masterpieces grace the hallways throughout. First-run movies are available on your color TV.

Singles in the main building are $31 to $52; twins and doubles, $42 to $63. Tower singles go for $45 to $62; doubles, $56 to $73.

THE UPPER BRACKET: On the scene for nearly half a century, the superbly located **Sir Francis Drake,** Sutter and Powell Streets (tel: 392-7755; 800/ 327-1313), puts the accent on unobtrusive service and tasteful surroundings. The exquisite lobby sets the elegant tone, with richly carpeted marble floors, marble and mirrored walls, 30-foot-high vaulted ceilings with gold-leaf trim and crystal chandeliers.

The hotel's Carving Board restaurant is the scene of nightly Elizabethan pageantry, complete with strolling minstrels and serving wenches. A similar menu prevails in Drake's Tavern, where Olde English ambience is highlighted by armor dating back to Drake's time. And there's dinner and dancing nightly, as well as cocktails and a buffet lunch, on the Starlite Roof, 21 stories up.

The 415 rooms are handsomely furnished. First-run movies are available on the color TV. Single rooms are $32 to $50; doubles and twins, $40 to $58.

SAN FRANCISCO: HOTELS

Just across from the Drake is an exceptionally bright and pretty **Holiday Inn,** 480 Sutter Street at Powell (tel: 398-8900). It's just oh-so-pretty, with hallways sporting grass-green carpeting and flowered silver foil decorator wall covering; even the garage roof has been made into an attractive rock garden.

Rooms are light, cheery and spacious, with large bay windows. White walls and flower-print spreads and draperies are enlivened by wood furnishings painted in glossy primary hues. Of course, all the expected conveniences are on tap, right down to the first-run movies on your color TV.

A rooftop restaurant is seemingly a San Francisco hotel prerequisite; this one's on the 30th floor and is called The Veranda. The ambience is pure garden party—more grass-green carpeting, sunny yellow tablecloths, white rattan and bentwood chairs, drapes gathered tentlike overhead, an abundance of leafy and flowering plants, even a fountain. Buffet lunch here is only $3.95; Sunday brunch, $5.25. There's a pubby eatery on the premises, too, The White Elephant, complete with framed fox-hunting prints on the walls and items like Beef Wellington on the menu.

Rates are seasonal: September 7 through May 31, singles are $36 to $41; doubles, $43 to $47. The rest of the year, add about $6 to those figures. Rooms on lower floors are less expensive.

You can't miss the imposing **Jack Tar,** Van Ness Avenue and Geary Street (tel: 776-8200; 800/227-4730)—its blue, white and brown checkerboard exterior extends a city block. With 400 rooms spread over eight stories, this bustling modern hotel, emphasizing convenience and extensive facilities, is popular with families and conventioneers. Parking is free for registered guests, the lobby abounds with shops, and there's even a swimming pool, children's playground and shuffleboard court.

Rooms are spiffy and attractive in a contemporary mode, and offer conveniences like bedside remote control of the color TV and a message light on the phone.

Continental food is served at the Cosmopolitan Restaurant, popular for its lavish buffets.

Rates are $30 to $41 single, $35 to $46 double or twin.

A unique kind of luxury accommodation is offered at **Miyako,** 1625 Post Street at Laguna, in Japan Center (tel: 922-3200; 800/228-3000)—a first-class Japanese Hotel. Here your room, decorated in shades of gold and subtle autumn hues, will feature shoji screens, wood paneling, golden birds on the wallpaper, delicate watercolors or scrolls, bronze lampstands in the shape of a lotus and a *tokonoma*—an alcove for flowers, a bowl or perhaps a statue of the Buddha. Rooms also have direct-dial phones, clocks, AM-FM radios, color TV and whatever other accoutrements of modern living you might expect.

Most of the bathrooms have Japanese sunken tubs, wherein you'll find instructions on how to take a Japanese bath; a packet of special powder, which turns the water a tranquil green, adds refreshing fragrance and softens the skin. There are showers, too, for those not in the mood for a ritual bath.

Two rooms and two suites—our favorites—are entirely Japanese in decor. Here you sleep on the floor on Japanese beds called *futons*—downy silk quilts laid out on tatami mats. In the suites there's even a bamboo and rock garden in your room. Ceilings are wood paneled and there are fusuma screens and shoji panels. The Japanese won't touch these rooms (they prefer the hotel's most American-style accommodations), but we think they're exquisite and romantic.

There's a restaurant downstairs, the East-West, which looks out over sunken gardens. The breakfast menu here is gold for the rising sun, the orange lunch menu denotes midday sun, and the dinner menu is red to represent sunset. As the name of the restaurant would indicate, both Japanese and

American dishes are served. Choose your weapons—fork and knife or chopsticks.

Single rooms here are $31 to $40; doubles and twins, $41 to $45. Japanese rooms (reserve far in advance) are $35 single, $45 double; Japanese suites, $75 a night.

MODERATELY PRICED ACCOMMODATIONS: With its white-awninged facade, the **PSA San Franciscan,** 1231 Market Street at Civic Center (tel: 626-8000; 800/227-4747), looks like an elegant beach-resort hotel. Previously the Whitcomb, it was one of the first hotels to be built in San Francisco, dating back to the turn of the century. For a period after the earthquake it served as the City Hall, and the jail cells used in those days are still here in the basement. PSA, a California intrastate airline, took the place over about five years ago and began a massive $3-million renovation. They scraped through six layers of paint to get to Philippine mahogany wood hallways, and $41,000 worth of stained glass was discovered—totally intact—concealed by fake ceilings.

The flamboyant lobby is authentically Victorian, with marble floors, pillars and balustrades, an antique clock, sculptured ceilings, crystal chandeliers, and stained-glass skylights and panels. About three-quarters of the rooms have been redone (ask for them), and they are, unequivocally, the prettiest rooms in town. The walls are delicate pastel colors. Furnished with white wicker, they have high ceilings, lovely paintings on the walls, polished cotton drapes and bedspreads. Some of the bathrooms are as large as the average living room; all have big tubs with antique brass fixtures, marble-top sinks and gilt-framed mirrors. Rooms contain Princess phones, color TVs and full-length door mirrors, too.

Three restaurants to choose from at PSA—Beppino's, an Italian *ristorante* with stained-glass windows, ancient Italian banners hung from vaulted ceilings and a huge stone fireplace; the Black Bart Saloon, sporting real Old West cowboy-movie decor and featuring intimate dining in a Wells Fargo stagecoach; and a cheerful coffee house for quick service.

Single rooms here are a reasonable $24 to $32; doubles and twins, $28 to $38. Spacious family suites accommodating four persons are $34 to $38. Our highest recommendation.

The **Commodore International,** 825 Sutter Street at Jones (tel: 885-2464), receives guests in a warmly old-fashioned pale green lobby adorned with lots of plaster curlicue trim and a big grandfather clock. Hallways, lit by antique cut-glass lanterns, are freshly painted white, with thick red carpeting and glossy black doors—very Old West. The 150 rooms all have large baths with tub or shower, built-in wall TVs (half of them color), big walk-in closets, heavy carpeting and attractive floral-print drapes and spreads. A coffee shop and cocktail lounge are on the premises. Rates at this conveniently located, quiet and friendly little hotel are $18 to $26 single, $22 to $34 for doubles and twins.

The **Oxford Hotel,** Mason and Market Streets (tel: 775-4600), is a friendly, family-owned hotel. In the business for three generations, the Haase family runs a tight ship and takes pleasure in making guests comfortable. The 114 rooms—all of which have outside exposure—are neat and clean, all with color TV, switchboard phones and bath with tub and shower. Parking is $2 a day. Sam's Brauhaus, a richly oak-paneled cafeteria, with a turn-of-the-century carved oak and mahogany bar and stained-glass lamps overhead, is in the hotel. Corned beef and cabbage, goulash, knockwurst and the like are served up at lunch and dinner along with steins of draft beer. Nothing costs over $3. Single rooms are $16 to $23; doubles and twins, $19 to $25; family rooms accommodating four persons, $25 to $30.

Billing itself as San Francisco's "*little* elegant hotel," **The Rafael**, 386 Geary Street off Mason (tel: 986-2000), provides quite luxurious accommodations at moderate prices. One-hundred-and-fifty rooms occupy 12 stories, and the door to each is individually hand-painted, making for very cheerful hallways. Each interior is uniquely attractive. Most rooms have striped vinyl or fabric wall covering and shag carpeting; all have two phones, color TV, AM/FM radio, clock and make-up mirror. The Pam Pam East restaurant and cocktail lounge adjoins. It's open around the clock and is so popular you might have to wait for a table whatever the hour.

Single rooms at the Raphael are $24 to $36; double or twin rooms, $34 to $46.

The **Hotel Stewart**, 351 Geary Street (tel: 781-7800), is an old-timer on the Union Square scene. But the big bonus here is that it is connected to the spanking-new Handlery Motor Inn, whose facilities—like the large heated swimming pool—can be used by guests at the Stewart. Rooms are clean and pretty, mostly done in autumnal color schemes, have baths with tubs and/or showers, and sport color TVs with first-run movies available. Within the hotel is the popular Highland Room, for cocktails in a Scottish setting (red plaid walls, etc.), and Mannings Cafeteria, quite elegant for a cafeteria and reasonably priced, too.

Singles are $22 to $32; doubles and twins, $26 to $36. Parking is $4 per night at the Handlery garage.

As for the adjoining **Handlery Motor Inn**, 260 O'Farrell Street at Powell (tel: 986-2526), it offers all the above-mentioned facilities plus a sauna. And although the gleaming mosaic tile exterior is off-putting and the lobby merely functional (it's just a registration desk), the rooms are truly large and luxurious. They include such frills as bedside remote control of the color TV (with movies available, once again), electric shoe polishers, dressing rooms with make-up mirrors, and balconies. Rates are $33 to $39 for singles, $39 to $44 for doubles and twins. That's a little high for our moderately priced category, but with free parking thrown in it's really quite a good deal.

Well located and heartily recommended is the **Hotel Canterbury**, 750 Sutter Street near Taylor (tel: 474-6464; 800/227-4788), a popular hostelry with lots of Old San Francisco charm. The bustling lobby contains a grandfather clock, one terrarium and two aquariums, and there are usually a few folks seated in wicker chairs by the fireplace sipping cocktails and watching the passing scene. A lot of the scene consists of the crowds coming and going to Lehr's Greenhouse, a lush garden restaurant that is one of the most popular eateries in town (see Restaurants, below).

The hallways have an Old West look. Rooms are large and very attractive —freshly carpeted with colorful floral-print spreads and gold velvet chairs. They all face outside, have color TV, radio, coffee-maker, direct-dial phone, and bath with tub and shower. First-run movies on the TV are free! There's a rooftop sundeck and a coffee shop off the lobby. And the staff is multilingual and most friendly and attentive.

Singles are $22 to $28; doubles and twins, $26 to $37.

Built in 1924, the 17-story **Hotel Californian,** Taylor and O'Farrell Streets (tel: 885-2500), offers an ideal location and accommodations that have been carefully maintained and frequently refurbished. The gracious lobby has a beamed and stenciled ceiling, ornate columns, elegant draperies and a charming brick fireplace. The rooms sport floral-pattern drapes, chenille bedspreads, leather armchairs and blond wood furnishings. All have TV—some color—and a tub/shower combination bath.

A beauty parlor and barber shop are on the premises, and so is a really good Italian restaurant, Goveia's, with its somewhat schizophrenic decor—half pizza parlor, half elegant *ristorante*. Attractive oil murals and paintings adorn the wood-paneled walls, and tables are candlelit, but there's a jukebox and lots of plastic flowers, too. The ambience is pleasant enough, however, and chef Peter Quartaroli is devoted to the excellence of his cuisine, utilizing fresh produce and homemade pasta in his delicious preparations. Dinner entrees begin around $4.

Room rates at the Californian are $22 to $27 single, $28 to $32 double or twin.

In deference to San Francisco's many Japanese visitors, the 17-story **Drake Wiltshire**, 340 Stockton Street (tel: 421-8011), just across from the Union Square Hyatt, has added some Eastern touches. The gift shop is Japanese, and sauna and shiatsu massage are available to guests. Rooms are large and homey, decorated in a 1950s mode with blond wood furnishings and chenille bedspreads. All have radios, TVs (mostly color) and shower/tub combination baths.

Simple, inexpensive meals—char-broiled steaks are the specialty—can be had at the Charcoal Room off the lobby; cocktails are served in the Cameo Lounge.

Single rooms are $18 to $22; doubles and twins, $22 to $30.

Conveniently located in San Francisco's such-as-it-is theater district, **The Bellevue**, at Geary and Taylor Streets (tel: 474-3600), is a popular and well-maintained establishment. Off the elegant lobby—replete with gold and crystal chandeliers—a magnificent carpeted staircase simply begs for a dramatic descent. Rooms are attractively furnished and have shag carpeting, tile baths with tub and shower, direct-dial phones, color TVs and radios. The Yum Yum Coffee Shop (open 24 hours) and the Belle Tavern cocktail lounge are on the premises, as are men's and women's hair salons, a garage and a car-rental service.

Rates are: $22 to $32 single, $26 to $36 double or twin.

Ironically, since it's located at the gateway to Chinatown, the **Beverly Plaza Hotel**, Grant Avenue at Bush Street (tel: 781-3566), has made considerable effort to court Japanese visitors. Brochures and guidebooks in Japanese can be obtained in the lobby, and the Midori Restaurant has a Japanese decor and staff. The menu, however, ranges from sukiyaki and sashimi to a ham omelet with hash browns and a toasted English. And American guests can also get home-style fare at the Roppongi Restaurant and Bar.

Rooms are bright and colorful, with matching floral-print drapes and spreads, color TVs with movies available, and direct-dial phones color-coordinated to your room decor. Other facilities include a handy electric map in the lobby (like the ones in the Paris Metro), and a Ping-Pong room—perhaps one concession to the Chinatown locale.

The friendly staff and concerned management here are noteworthy. Room rates—very good value for the money—are $20 to $22 single, $22 to $28 double and twin.

Under the same ownership, but exhibiting no pull to the East, is the **Hotel Cecil**, 545 Post Street, between Mason and Taylor (tel: 673-3733), offering a superb location, comfortable accommodations and a friendly staff. Furnished in "flea-market homey," the rooms are pretty and clean, with a bit of an old-fashioned country-inn look. They have cheerful tile baths, switchboard phones and black and white TVs.

In the lower lobby, you'll find a Ping-Pong room, television lounge, ice machine and other coin machines dispensing snacks and candy. If you feel like a little sun, there's a redwood deck and cabana with patio furniture on the seventh floor. A writing desk is situated in an adjoining plant-filled sunroom, where light streams through a skylight. And in the morning, free coffee and tea await you in the lobby. Parking in the adjacent garage is $3.50 a night.

Single rooms are $20 to $22; doubles and twins, $22 to $25.

Step into the lobby of the **Hotel Beresford,** 635 Sutter Street at Mason (tel: 673-9900), and you'll find yourself in a Victorian drawing room with gaslight lamps, flocked wallpaper, and a gilt-framed portrait of Lord Beresford overlooking the scene. This delightful European-style hostelry is the homiest in town, from the flowerboxes adorning the street windows to the friendly staff proferring good old-fashioned service. There's a writing parlor off the lobby with wicker furniture, desks and a color TV.

Rooms have white drapes, white Valley Forge bedspreads, stippled shag rugs, baths with tubs and/or showers, TVs (some color) and direct-dial phones.

The White Horse Taverne, here, reputedly an authentic replica of its 18th-century Edinburgh namesake, contains an antique bedwarmer and an ancient crossbow hung over the fireplace. A congenial pub, the White Horse also offers home-cooked breakfasts and lunches, sending out its own fishing boats for the day's catch and serving fresh produce from the hotel's out-of-town gardens.

If you like European charm—and who doesn't?—this well-located hotel is a good choice. Rates for singles are $20 to $22; doubles and twins, $24 to $26; family rooms accommodating four persons are $34.

Similarly charming and well situated is the **Cartwright Hotel,** 524 Sutter Street at Powell (tel: 421-2865), a cozy little place where the management takes pride in its reputation for comfort and efficiency—a pride that is reflected in every nook and cranny. Rooms sparkle with cleanliness—even the doorknobs and phone are polished to a high shine. There are eight floors of accommodations, all with pretty print spreads and drapes, shag carpeting, large baths, direct-dial phones, color TVs and light switches that glow in the dark. No dining facilities here, but continental breakfast is available, and 22 restaurants are within a block of the front door. Single rooms are $18; doubles and queens, $22 to $24; family suites, $40 to $45.

Under the same ownership is the **Bedford,** 761 Post Street, between Leavenworth and Jones (tel: 673-6040), an equally attractive and homey property. Pretty and quaint, the Bedford has an Early American feel. The high-ceilinged lobby—very pleasant with grass-green carpeting and furnishings, and crystal chandeliers overhead—looks like it was fashioned out of Wedgwood. Rooms are cheerful and spacious, with color-coordinated drapes and quilted chintz bedspreads, nice prints on the walls, color TVs and direct-dial phones. The Bedford does have a restaurant, La Brochette, with a garden decor. The pubby Pewter Mug bar adjoins.

Rates at the Bedford are $17 to $20 single, $22 to $28 for doubles and twins; family suites are $40 to $48.

The **El Cortez Hotel,** 550 Geary Street, near Taylor (tel: 775-5000), as the name and the arched entranceway indicate, is distinctly Spanish in flavor. The attractive, high-ceilinged lobby has white stucco walls, a ceramic tile floor and graceful pillars. The 170 rooms are actually apartments, with kitchenettes, dressing rooms, tub and shower baths, color TVs and radios. They're also Spanish-style, as are the stucco-walled hallways.

Surprisingly, the hotel's restaurant is not Spanish but French, and very elegantly French at that. Modeled after the hunting lodge of an actual French country estate, La Mère Duquesne has quaint wallpaper, brass chandeliers, lots of antiques and hunting trophies. Complete lunches begin at $3.50, dinners at $6.50, and there's a large wine selection.

The rates: singles go for $20 to $21; doubles and twins, from $23 to $27.

A cheerful and friendly little hotel, the **Somerton**, 440 Geary Street (tel: 474-4411), is located on San Francisco's theater row. Many permanent guests here, so only about a third of the 200 rooms are available to tourists, but these are clean, colorful and freshly painted. All rooms have switchboard phones, and sinks with hot and cold running water. Those with baths also have a color TV. Parking is available nearby and costs $3 a day, with in-and-out privileges. Rooms without bath (ample bath and toilet facilities are in the hall) are $10 single, $12 double. Rooms with bath are $20 single, $24 double, $28 twin and $35 for family suites sleeping four.

Built in 1924, the seven-story **Manx**, 225 Powell Street, between Geary and O'Farrell (tel: 421-7070), has been well cared for and frequently refurbished over the years. The cream-colored lobby has lots of old-fashioned charm, with stately marble pillars, comfortable furnishings, an intricately carved ceiling, marble reception desk and globe chandeliers overhead. The very attractive accommodations are done in cream and coffee colors, featuring pretty print spreads and drapes and fine wood pieces and headboards. Baths are large, with tub and shower combinations in each. Your room will have a color TV with first-run movies available, direct-dial phone and radio. There's a coffee shop, cocktail lounge, newsstand, sightseeing desk and beauty salon; ice and Coke machines are on every floor. Rates are $22 to $24 single, $25 to $30 for doubles and twins.

In nearly a half-century of operation, the **Mark Twain**, 345 Taylor Street at O'Farrell (tel: 673-2332), has undergone many incarnations. Originally the Linden, it was purchased in 1933 by the brother-in-law of the owner of Nob Hill's prestigious Mark Hopkins and christened Mark Twain. The Handlery chain bought the place in the '50s and called it the Don, for David Handlery's son of that name. And then in 1973 a former public relations executive named Will Rogers bought the hotel, renamed it Mark Twain, and refurbished it in what the San Francisco *Chronicle* labeled "Nouveau Steamboat" decor.

Turn-of-the-century furnishings and photographs grace the lobby and bedrooms, and there are little riverboats above every room number. Rooms are simply furnished, very clean, and all have coffee-makers, phones and black and white TVs. An unusual extra (perhaps Rogers is a Telly Savalas fan) is the complimentary lollipop left on your bed each day when the maid cleans up. Other bonuses include an attractive rooftop sundeck with chaise lounges and plants, a coffee shop and a tiny saloon that has a jukebox, pinball machine and Christmas decorations that once went up and never came down.

Rates are $18.50 to $22.50 for a single, $20.50 to $26.50 for doubles and twins.

There are 13 clocks in the lobby of the **Sutter Hotel**, 191 Sutter Street at Kearny (tel: 781-3060; 800/227-4248), keeping concerned guests up to the minute re correct time in Bombay, Tokyo, London, Montevideo and Sydney, among other places. But even if you don't care what time it is in Uruguay, you will care for the attentive staff and pretty, colorful rooms here. Decorated with a definite flair, they have bentwood and rattan furnishings, ceramic lamps and wall-to-wall carpeting. All rooms contain color TVs and large baths (with tubs or showers) attractively papered in striped vinyls. Many also have coffee-makers.

Single rooms cost $16 to $23; doubles and twins are $22 to $30. There's parking at a drive-in garage on the premises ($2.50 for 24 hours).

SAN FRANCISCO: HOTELS & RESTAURANTS   31

BUDGET HOTELS: We can't say enough good things about the **Hotel Regent**, 562 Sutter Street, between Powell and Mason (tel: 421-5818). This 120-room, seven-story hotel is a true budget find. Located on a lovely street in the heart of downtown, the Regent has lots of early California charm. The lobby is Spanish-style, with a terra-cotta and ceramic-glaze tile floor, carved and hand-stenciled beamed ceiling and a grillwork entranceway. Even the steps leading to the second floor are faced with ceramic tiling. The same motif prevails in the very pleasant dining room, where hearty four-course dinners are just $2.95 to $4.25.

Almost half of the guest rooms have sizable private baths, while the rest use the immaculate hall baths (painted a cheery pink). Rooms are simply and attractively furnished—very homey—some overlooking the street, others facing a tree-lined rear courtyard. Half the rooms have TVs, and about half of those are color. All have switchboard phones. Service is excellent and friendly to a fault.

Rooms with a bath and color TV begin at $14 single, $18 double and $19.50 twin. Bathless rooms begin at $8.50 single, $13.50 double, and $14.50 twin. From October to June, weekly rates are available (stay for seven days and pay for six). Highly recommended.

A centrally located **YWCA**, 620 Sutter Street (tel: 775-6500), provides eminently suitable accommodations for women of 18 or over (girls under 18 must be accompanied by a legal guardian). You're allowed to stay a maximum of two weeks, and you should make a reservation with a deposit at least 20 days in advance. Rooms are comfortable, though decor could easily be described as "no frills." All have running water, and rooms with bath are available; phones are in the hall. Facilities include a large indoor swimming pool and a full-time recreation program. Cut-rate tours are offered. Amorous ladies take note: No male visitors allowed at this proper institution.

Rates with bath are $10 for singles, $15 for twins, and $21 for triples. Without bath, rates are $7.50 single, $12 twin.

The downtown area also has a **YMCA Hotel**, 351 Turk Street, between Hyde and Leavenworth (tel: 673-2312), and—good news—it's open to men, women and families. It has a large oak-paneled lounge with comfortable leather chairs and writing desks. Upstairs, the rooms are plain, but adequate. Many rooms have private baths, but they're difficult to obtain, so if you want one, reserve well in advance. Otherwise, you can use the immaculate hall baths. Guests have access to the swimming pool and gym facilities, and the desk is knowledgeable about tourist attractions. Women's accommodations are on a separate floor. The only drawback is the location—very convenient and central, but in the "Tenderloin" district, not one of the city's showcases. If the sight of a girl in the doorway at night shocks you, stay elsewhere.

Rooms with bath are $10 single, $13 to $14 twin. Rooms without bath are $6.50 to $7.50 single, $10 double, $15 triple and $20 for four persons.

3. Restaurants

Only New York can match the quality, quantity and ethnic variety of eateries in what Trader Vic (he lives here) once called "the city that knows chow" (a variation on President Taft's tribute to San Francisco—"the city that knows how").

What's your dining pleasure: Indonesian rijsttafel, Filipino chicken in adobo sauce, West Indian curried goat, Russian piroshky or a chopped liver on rye? From acclaimed (and pricey) gourmet French cuisine to budget Basque, San Francisco has a place to please every palate. And the special savor of dining out in San Francisco is enhanced by California wines, which are excellent and less costly than imported labels.

In the upcoming section we've selected over 50 of the city's 3,000-or-so restaurants, and ranged them according to price bracket, subdivided by nationality. We could easily add another hundred worthy establishments, but that would fill the whole book. Be sure, too, to consider the hotel restaurants recommended throughout the previous section.

LUXURY RESTAURANTS: For a splurge of gastronomic excellence during your visit, choose one of the following venerables. Several are highly acclaimed internationally, and charge prices that such fame denotes. Each provides a dining experience par excellence—a romantic and memorable evening made up of sumptuous cuisine, distinguished service and ambience.

French and Continental

Ernie's: 847 Montgomery Street, between Pacific and Jackson (tel: 397-5969). Dinner from 6 to 11 p.m. nightly. Reservations recommended.

San Francisco's most prestigious and elegant restaurant, Ernie's proffers distinguished continental fare in suitably plush surroundings. The decor is elaborate Victorian, the intimate parlor and massive mahogany and stained-glass bar so exquisite, it would be a shame not to enjoy a quiet drink before dinner. At any rate, Ernie's is an experience to be slowly savored. Many of the furnishings in the red-flocked dining room originally adorned San Francisco's extravagant turn-of-the-century mansions.

And unlike most restaurants in this category, where the quality of the haute cuisine is only matched by the icy hauteur of the staff, the maitre d' and waiters at Ernie's are actually polite and friendly.

The menu is à la carte, and every dish is excellent. You might begin with a galantine de canard, which is duck in terrine ($4); escargots bourguignon ($4.25); cream of lobster soup ($2.75) or perhaps a Belgian endive salad ($3). Our favorite entrees include salmon trout in a pastry shell with sauce beurre blanc ($8.50); entrecôte au poivre made with green peppercorns and flamed in brandy ($12.50); and faisan pôelé Saint Hubert—pheasant in wild game sauce ($20 for two). Of course you'll order one of Ernie's fine wines to complement your meal, and who could resist the sumptuous desserts? So expect your total bill to be at least $50 for two—a worthy splurge.

La Bourgogne: 320 Mason Street off O'Farrell (tel: 362-7352). Open for dinner 5:30 to 11:45 p.m. Closed Sunday. Reservations recommended. La Bourgogne is one of the country's top-ranking restaurants, offering superbly prepared French cuisine in an ornate setting. Guests are seated on gold-tufted leather banquettes, a lovely vase of roses gracing every table. Gold satin wallpaper alternates with smoked mirrors, and elaborate crystal and bronze chandeliers overhead provide a warm and flattering glow. Service is impeccable, and once again friendly—evidently San Franciscans do not share New Yorkers' masochistic desire to be snubbed and scorned by waiters in better restaurants.

All lobster dishes are prepared with live Maine lobster, and fresh Dover sole is flown in from France. Quenelles de brochet Nantua—mousse of pike with fresh lobster sauce ($3.75)—is an excellent hors d'oeuvre selection. Or throw caution to the winds and order the Royal Iranian Beluga caviar ($12). Specialties include homard (that's the aforementioned lobster) à la Pompadour ($14.50); roast duck Tahitien ($18.50 for two) and piccata of veal à l'ancienne ($10). We can never pass up an accompanying order of haricots verts au beurre

($1.75)—French string beans are an art. An extensive wine list is, of course, available.

L'Orangerie: 419 O'Farrell Street, between Taylor and Jones (tel: 776-3600). Dinner from 5:30 p.m. to 1:30 a.m. Closed Sunday. Reservations recommended.

L'Orangerie flourishes under the brilliant ownership and management of Roselyne Dupart, who not only oversees the gastronomic excellence of the establishment, but is also responsible for the impeccably tasteful interior. The cocktail lounge evokes the library of a European country estate. Its warm ambience provides the perfect setting to while away the rest of a lovely evening with after-dinner liqueurs and good conversation.

There are several dining areas. The main room has a garden decor, with orange trees in the doorway and white latticework over green felt walls. The Topaz Room, modeled after a 16th-century hunting lodge, has a brick fireplace, coffered ceiling and medieval tapestries on the walls. And the Blue Room is classically French—delicate blue and green flocked wallpaper, plush powder-blue velvet furnishings and crystal chandeliers. Tables are elegantly appointed with silver candlesticks, Limoges china and one or two fresh roses.

You might begin with an hors d'oeuvre of quenelles de poisson—fish mousse in clam sauce ($3.75). Coq en pâté—chicken with goose liver and truffles ($18.50 for two)—is a highly recommendable entree, as is selle d'agneau forestière—lamb with French forest mushrooms ($9.50). For dessert don't fail to order the soufflé Grand Marnier ($4)—a culinary delight which will provide you with wistful memories for weeks after.

Moroccan

Marrakech: 417 O'Farrell Street, between Taylor and Jones (tel: 776-6717). Open for dinner Monday through Saturday, 5:30 p.m. to 1:30 a.m. Reservations recommended.

Located downstairs from L'Orangerie, also owned, managed and designed by the talented Madame Dupart, Marrakech is, quite simply, our favorite restaurant anywhere. So much for superlatives; on to enthusiastic description.

The exotic interior is entered via a hexagonal room with Moroccan tile and intricately carved mahogany walls. A marble reflecting pool, roses floating on the surface of the water, is the centerpiece. The dining areas are carpeted with Berber and Oriental rugs; seating is also covered with rugs and an abundance of plush-velvet cushions and pillows in earth tones; the lofty ceiling is a pale blue sky punctuated by cheerful hand-painted beams. Light filters down through cut-brass lamps, creating yet another pattern. Large straw bread baskets are strewn about near the round brass and inlaid Mogador tables.

The meal is a ritual feast—don't eat all day in preparation—served by waiters in maroon Zouave costumes and fez (they look rather like Shriners) and hostesses in flowing djelabbas. It begins when a hostess brings out a brass pot and basin filled with hot water. She washes and dries your hands, and you keep the towel to use as a napkin. You'll need it, since the entire meal is eaten with your hands—no plates or silverware are supplied!

There are three complete dinners to choose from (at $12.75, $13.75 and $14.75), and all begin with a piquant Moroccan salad scooped up with hunks of homemade bread. Then come several entrees, which might include chicken with lemons, lamb with honey and almonds (exquisite), or hare and raisins. It's all twice as tasty and twice the fun pulling off bits of meat with your fingers. The entrees are followed by a delicious couscous with vegetables, easily a meal in itself. Fresh fruits and mint tea (poured from a height of several feet in good Moroccan tradition) are the finale.

As you lounge, satiated, over tea or after-dinner drinks (it's perfectly okay to recline on the cushions), the hostess once again washes your hands and sprays you with refreshing rosewater.

Praise Allah—this is a blissful and romantic dining experience.

Greek/French

L'Odeon: 565 Clay Street, between Montgomery and Sansome (tel: 434-2345). Open 11:30 a.m. to 11 p.m., Monday through Friday; 5 to 11 p.m. on Saturday. Reservations recommended.

Greek/French? Admittedly an unusual category, but, you see, owner Peter Zane is Greek, which accounts for many Greek items on an otherwise French menu. (We won't delve into the reasons for murals of ancient Rome on the walls.) The mix seems to work, however, for L'Odeon is highly esteemed for its sumptuous cuisine, and has won decorator awards for its posh interior.

An irresistible appetizer is the avocado à l'Odeon with sour cream and caviar ($6). We're also partial to the wilted spinach salad ($5.50 for two). Entrees range from rack of lamb sauteed in tarragon and Nemea wine sauce ($8.75) (a specialty) to roast chicken à la Plaka, which is stuffed with rice, pine nuts, raisins in herbs and cognac ($12). An inexpensive choice is moussaka with bechamel sauce ($5.50). Other than the baklava ($1.25), the desserts are French, with several flambée selections. If dinner here is beyond your budget, try L'Odeon at lunch, when many entrees are in the $3.75 to $4.50 range.

Indian

India House: 350 Jackson Street, between Battery and Sansome (tel: 392-0744). Open for lunch 11:30 a.m. to 2:30 p.m. weekdays; for dinner 5:30 to 10:30 p.m., Monday through Saturday.

The ambience of India House is fittingly exotic, complete with leopard skins and mounted hunting trophies adorning the walls, candles in winding snake holders, gold curtain room dividers, strains of Indian ragas in the background, and turbaned Sikh waiters. Photographs of India further enhance the setting.

The menu ranges over various regions but stresses the cuisine of the north, making a few concessions, such as romaine salad, to Western palates. Curries (instruct waiter as to desired hotness) are served with rice, the above-mentioned salad and a sambal (condiment) tray on which you'll find grated coconut, ground peanuts, chow-chow, raisins, onion chutney, sweet pickle relish, quartered limes and mango chutney. Our favorite listing is for khorma ($7.75), described with Winnie-the-Pooh pomposity as "a rather more important lamb curry." The royal feast for two ($21.50) includes the rice, salad and sambal tray, as well as samosas (meat filled pastries), tarkari (curried vegetables), dahl (curried lentils), Bombay duck, chapattis (Indian bread), papadums (seasoned wafers), raita (a yogurt and cucumber mix), achaar (hot pickle), dessert, tea and coffee. Beer, wines and specialty drinks served in Indian brass goblets; English pewter tankards are also available.

Luncheon entrees range from $3.25 to $4.95.

Polynesian

Trader Vic's: 20 Cosmos Place, off Taylor between Post and Sutter (tel: 776-2232). Lunch Monday through Friday from 11:30 a.m. to 2:30 p.m.; dinner nightly from 5 p.m. Reservations recommended.

Yes, Virginia, there is a real Trader Vic, and at the San Francisco branch of this exotic chain the old trader himself, Victor Jules Bergeron, though now retired, is frequently in residence. Some quotes from the great man: "When I started the restaurant business, I did everything to keep customers. I sang and I even let them stick an ice pick in my wooden leg." On the South Seas decor: "It intrigues everyone. You think of beaches and moonlight and pretty girls without any clothes on. It is complete escape, relaxation."

We couldn't describe the mood better. Trader Vic's outdoes all others in creating an ambience of South Seas enchantment—lush jungle foliage, authentic Polynesian batiks, spears, sculpture and artifacts, big-game trophies and skins bagged by the Trader himself, peacock chairs, even a palm-frond canoe overhead, and endless bamboo and rattan.

The menu is enormous—order one of the potent rum concoctions to sip while you peruse at leisure (order a second and you won't care if they serve you a Big Mac).

There are lots of hors d'oeuvres, the most intriguing of which is Malossol caviar with blini and sour cream ($12). A more "conventional" start would be bongo bongo (cream of pureed oyster) soup ($2). A whole page is devoted just to accompanying vegetables and salads. One hundred entrees include Malay peanut chicken ($6.25), a wide variety of curries served with nine condiments ($6.25 for most), Trader Vic's special oyster flambé ($7), Szechuan beef ($5.25) and breast of peach blossom duck ($6.75). Save room for one of the 29 exotic desserts. The luncheon menu, though extensive, is simpler and a bit less pricey.

EXPENSIVE RESTAURANTS: Just a shade less grandiose than the bastions of haute cuisine we've looked at up till now, the following restaurants are nonetheless elegant and delightful in every respect. In general, they offer meals in varying price brackets, and with a careful perusal of the menu you needn't spend a king's ransom. All offer superb cuisine and a suitable atmosphere in which to enjoy it. If your budget doesn't stretch to dinner, try lunch where it's available—same chef, same dishes, lower prices. Also, notice that some spots serve a full dinner early in the evening for the price of an entree later on.

Continental

Lehr's Greenhouse: 740 Sutter Street near Taylor (tel: 474-6478). Open 11:30 a.m. to 11:30 p.m. daily. Reservations imperative.

Three full-time gardeners are required to maintain this glass-roofed tropical garden, where diners relax under a leafy bower of vines, hanging ferns and palm fronds. There are fountains, peacock chairs and wicker gazebos amidst the banana trees in this carefully planned jungle. The carpeting is grass-green Astroturf, big pots of anthurium grace the tables, and recordings of bird sounds are heard in the background (the Health Department doesn't permit live birds). Not surprisingly, Lehr's is one of the most popular places in town.

Some sample entrees are shrimp creole with rice ($5.25), brochette of filet mignon ($6.75) and roast rack of baby lamb ($9). Selections from the salad bar are included in the price of entrées. For dessert choose a pastry from the cart ($1.25). Prices are lower, and the crowds a bit thinner, at lunch. Sunday brunch (a sumptuous all-you-can-eat buffet served from 9:30 a.m. to 2:30 p.m.) costs $6.25 and is a mob scene, but very "in."

Jack's: 615 Sacramento Street at Montgomery (tel: 986-9854). Open from 11:30 a.m. to 9:30 p.m. weekdays, Sundays from 4 to 9:30 p.m. Closed most holidays. Reservations suggested.

A venerated San Francisco institution, Jack's has been catering to a discriminating clientele since 1864 (note the Hundred Year Club certificate on the wall). Located in the heart of the financial district, it exudes an aura of old and established wealth. A sea of white linen, gold-embossed walls, wooden Thonet chairs, a potted palm here and there comprise the dignified but unpretentious decor.

The continental menu lists entrees from as low as $3 (ravioli or spaghetti), ascending to $22 for the rack of spring lamb for two with potatoes boulangère. And the complete dinner (served from 5 to 9 p.m. only) is a terrific buy at $8.75. It includes soup, salad, entree (perhaps boeuf bourguignon with pilaf), vegetable, and a choice of desserts ranging from plain sherbert to sumptuous banana fritters with brandy sauce. The food is always excellent, and the service impeccable. Jackets and ties are required apparel for men.

Chinese

The Mandarin: 900 North Point in Ghirardelli Square (tel: 673-8812). Open from 11:30 a.m. to 11 p.m. daily. Reservations recommended.

Located in the Woolen Mill Building, the Mandarin is the domain of gracious owner/hostess Madame Cecilia Chiang, who runs the restaurant as a great lady would run her home. Her Northern Chinese cuisine is quite the best in town, the setting as elegant, we're told, as her palatial childhood home in Peking. Reminiscent of an ancient Chinese temple, the rich interior is accented by quarry floor tiles, burnt orange carpeting and Mandarin furnishings. The focal point of the dining area is the Mongolian Fire Pit, where guests can barbecue their own dinners or have the chef do it for them. Nearby is a centerpiece sculpture—a carved cherrywood lotus blossom in a blue tile receptacle. The ceiling is lined with haige twigs and supported by heavy rough-hewn beams. The walls are exposed brick or covered in pale green silk; exquisite paintings, priceless antiques and forbidden-stitch embroideries (using stitches allowed for the court only) from Madame Chiang's home complete the decor.

A complete dinner, of which several are available, includes hot and sour soup, almond chicken, oyster-sauced beef, ham fried rice, jasmine tea and cookies ($7.50). For each extra person taking part in the meal another dish is added.

If ordering à la carte, an appetizer of chiao tzu—grilled meat-filled dumplings served with vinegar and hot pepper oil ($2.25)—is heartily recommended, as is a cauldron of sizzling rice soup ($4.75). Smoked tea duck, baked to crispness in ancient ovens over burning tea leaves ($9.50) and Mongolian beef—slices of lamb or beef grilled quickly over the fire pit, served in hot Mandarin buns ($6.50)—are specialties. You might finish up with Mandarin glazed apples or bananas, dipped in batter, glazed with candy syrup and plunged into ice water at your table to crystallize the coating ($4.75).

Complete lunches are $3.95 to $5.25.

Imperial Palace: 919 Grant Avenue, between Washington and Jackson (tel: 982-4440). Open 11:30 a.m. to 1 a.m. daily. Reservations essential.

For haute cuisine Cantonese-style, the magnificent Imperial Palace—as elegant as the name implies—is the preferred choice. Entered via imposingly tall Chinese red doors, the interior is papered in gold with alternating black panels framing ancient Chinese paintings. A velvet-lined showcase displays Ch'ing Dynasty antiques. Large bouquets of flowers are judiciously placed, and red roses enhance the beautifully appointed tables. Lighting is provided from cut-glass candle lamps and gold and crystal chandeliers above. Strains of Chinese music can be heard in the background.

Prints of ancient Chinese paintings on rice paper adorn the elaborate menu. You might begin with a crabmeat puff—wrapped fillings of crabmeat and cheese, deep fried ($4.50). For your entree, perhaps the squab Macao style—marinated in wine and deep fried ($8.50); tossed chicken Imperial—shredded fried chicken with onions, parsley, chopped almonds and spices ($7.50); or fresh prawns in a crystal glaze sauce ($6.50). Exotic desserts include flaming black leaf lichee ($4.25) and almond delight pudding ($1.75). A complete dinner including soup, appetizer, two entrees, rice, tea and cookies is $8.50 per person, and a comprehensive wine list is available. Prices are considerably reduced at lunch.

Armenian/Middle Eastern

Bali's: 310 Pacific Avenue, corner of Battery (tel: 982-5059). Lunch Monday through Friday 11 a.m. to 2 p.m.; dinner Tuesday through Saturday 6 to 10:30 p.m. Reservations recommended.

Reams have been written about Bali's and its colorful owner a Manchurian-born Armenian, Armen Baliantz. Nureyev, the Francis Ford Coppolas, James Caan and Kathryn Crosby were just a few of the guests at the party she gave when Bali's moved to its Pacific Avenue location. And roast suckling pig, half a dozen pheasants, a steamboat of roast beef and 24 pounds of Iranian caviar were just a few of the dishes surrounding a swan centerpiece carved from a 300-pound block of ice. Of course, the Stolichnaya flowed freely.

Bali's—a romantic candlelit hideaway, is San Francisco headquarters for visiting ballet dancers, Russian emigrés, celebs and others who enjoy the superb dishes and intimate ambience. Dinners are served upstairs, where photos of dancers (with good pal Nureyev prominent) are displayed on the exposed brick walls, carved Indian sheeshamwood panels on the windows create a cozy feeling, and soft light filters through cut-brass lamps overhead.

The menu is limited to three perfectly prepared items: rack of lamb as prepared by the shepherds of Kazbek for holiday celebrations, marinated in pomegranate juice ($8.95); shish kebab deluxe from the ancient Armenian recipe of Ararat, with tomatoes, peppers and onions ($8.95); and steak deluxe ($9.95). All entrees are served with tossed green salad, spiced vegetables and fruits, pilaff, panir (Armenian cheese), lavash (Armenian bread) and coffee or tea. There are two desserts: baklava ($1) and plombir ($1.50)—ice cream served with fresh fruits and cream. Fine wines are of course available. It is a memorable feast.

Luncheon, served downstairs, features items like salade Niçoise ($3.25), piroshki with soup or salad ($3.50), or a simple Baliburger served on French bread with fried potatoes ($2.50).

Caravansary: 310 Sutter Street, between Stockton and Grant (tel: 362-4640). Open for lunch from 11 a.m. to 3 p.m.; for dinner from 5 to 10 p.m. Closed Sundays.

Armenian chef Setrak Injaian is the culinary genius in residence at this downtown oasis. It's a family tradition— his father was chef for King Abdullah of Jordan. And his expertise in the kitchen is enhanced by the restaurant's delightfully tasteful decor—light and airy, with fine Oriental rugs strewn on a pine plank floor, judiciously placed plants, ferns and small trees, good paintings, oak cabinets and bar, shelves of bric-a-brac and handsome brass chandeliers overhead. The gold-clothed tables are beautifully set with colorful floral-print napkins wound into whimsical shapes, candles aglow in orange holders and baskets of lavash bread.

All dinner entrees are served with meza (a cold platter of Middle Eastern delicacies including feta cheese, dolma, tabuleh, hummos, eggplant, etc.), tossed green salad and pilaf. Mouth-watering entrees include geras—boneless breast of chicken with wild rice, pine nut and raisin stuffing, baked in dark rum and cherry sauce ($6.95); or charcoal-broiled fish, in season, served with lemon butter and capers ($7.95). A glass of house wine is 85¢, and a different fine coffee is featured each day. For dessert a rich homemade mousse served with fresh fruit ($1.10) is our choice.

Caravansary is also a marvelous place for an inexpensive and elegant lunch. The Orient Express is our favorite menu item: two Aram sandwiches (roast beef, cream cheese, tomatoes and lettuce rolled in lavash bread) and a wedge of quiche served with green salad, fruit and cheese ($3.75).

A second Caravansary is located at 2263 Chestnut Street at Steiner (tel: 921-3466).

Italian

North Beach Restaurant: 1512 Stockton Street, between Union and Green (tel: 392-1587). Open seven days from 11:30 to midnight. Reservations suggested.

When Lorenzo Petroni and chef Bruno Orsi started the place, they vowed to serve the finest *cucina Toscana* possible. And how they do! They prepare their own fresh pasta daily (highest honors to the fettuccine), use only fresh vegetables and quality meats, hang and cure their own prosciutto hams and serve the finest California wines.

The decor is cheerful and unpretentious; you know the place has a lot of class, but it's intangible; no Louis XV chairs or crystal chandeliers—you just feel it. But the mood is flamboyantly Italian; women can expect frank ogling and admiration. North Beach is also something of a celebrity haunt; John Denver threw a party in the wine cellar recently.

But who cares about ambience and admiration here? It's the food we come to revel in. Complete dinners include antipasto, mixed green salad, soup du jour, pasta della casa con prosciutto sauce, fresh vegetable, dessert and coffee. With an entree of veal scaloppine marsala, such a dinner will cost you $8.25; $10.50 for scampi della casa, $8.50 for salmon steak alla Perelli. Entrees are also available à la carte. For dessert, a zabaglione ($4 for two) is a supreme joy.

Very reasonable at dinner, the North Beach is even less expensive at lunch, when a complete meal is $4.50.

Seafood

Tadich Grill: 240 California Street, between Battery and Front (tel: 391-2373). Open 11:30 a.m. to 8:30 p.m. Monday through Saturday.

Established in 1849—along with the Gold Rush—the Tadich Grill is a venerated old California institution. Entered via massive copper doors, the interior is substantial. A mahogany bar, with rows of gleaming glassware on display, extends the entire length of the restaurant. On the wall is an old wooden clock with Roman numerals. Tables, draped in no-nonsense white linen and provided with a big plate of lemon wedges, are ranged along the wall, separated into intimate dining areas by heavy mahogany partitions. (We imagine discreet business deals are more frequent than romantic trysts in these private compartments.) Lighting is provided by gleaming brass wall lamps and overhead lighting fixtures of the kind found in public-school classrooms.

The food is excellent. For a light meal you might try one of the delicious seafood salads, like shrimp or prawn Louie ($5.25), with a glass of wine (only 50¢), fresh sourdough bread and butter. Hot entrees include baked avocado with shrimp diablo ($5.50), baked casserole of stuffed turbot with crab and shrimp à la Newburg ($6.50), and char-broiled lobster tail with butter sauce ($10.50). A side order of big, tasty French fries (50¢) is hard to resist, as is the homemade cheesecake (90¢) for dessert.

Japanese

Benihana of Tokyo: 740 Taylor Street, between Bush and Sutter (tel: 771-8414). Open for lunch weekdays from noon to 2 p.m.; dinner nightly from 5 to 10 p.m.

The well-known Benihana chain, which features teppanyaki (at table) hibachi-style cooking at its best, has a conveniently located branch in the heart of downtown. If you've ever dined at a Benihana you know that the decor is always authentic, and the "performance" awesome. The chef wheels a cart full of raw food to the table and methodically cuts, trims, chops, fries and flips the food onto your plate with a dazzling display of rapid knifework. Each chef has his own style, but all wield knife and fork with the expertise of a samurai swordsman.

All dinners come with rice, green tea, hibachi shrimp appetizer, soup, salad, vegetable and dessert. Prices vary according to the entree you select: hibachi chicken is $6.95, sukiyaki steak with vegetables $7.95, hibachi steak or filet mignon $8.95.

Bush Garden: 598 Bush Street, corner of Stockton (tel: 986-1600). Open for lunch weekdays from 11:45 a.m. to 2 p.m.; dinner Monday through Saturday from 5:30 to 10:30 p.m. Reservations suggested.

The strains of Japanese music greet you as you enter Bush Garden, along with the gentle splashing of a waterfall fountain. These very Japanese touches are designed to create the proper tranquil mood before dining. We suggest you reserve one of the 23 intimate tatami rooms with shoji-screen and grass-papered walls. The rooms are simply adorned with a Japanese scroll and perhaps a vase of flowers. They're most conducive to long, leisurely dining—preferably prolonged by much sake. If you're not used to sitting on the floor, you will find wells under the table for your legs, and you can ask for a back rest. If sitting on the floor—under any conditions—is out, request one of the intimate booth areas, constructed of pine and bamboo, downstairs, where a 200-year-old samurai warrior's outfit is on display.

The specialty here—a veritable Japanese feast—is the kaiseki dinner ($11.50). It includes suimono or miso soup, sunomono (cucumber salad), zensai (an hors d'oeuvre), tsukemono (pickled tidbits), sashimi, beef and lobster teriyaki, assorted tempura, rice, dessert, green tea and a fortune cookie. Slightly less elaborate but nonetheless complete dinners can be had for $6 and up; you can also order à la carte. Full lunches are available for $2.50 to $2.95.

Mingei-Ya: 2033 Union Street, between Webster and Buchanan (tel: 567-2553). Open for dinner Tuesday through Sunday. Reservations suggested.

Mingei-Ya means "folk-art restaurant," so it's not surprising that many simple hand-crafted creations are part of the decor—uchiwa fans, rice tubs, straw stools, umbrellas, kites, basketry, even the pottery, napkins and utensils used in serving your dinner. The interior is most pleasant, designed to look like a Japanese country inn, with plum-colored walls and tatami rooms overlooking a miniature garden containing a shishidoshi fountain; it's lit by paper lanterns at night. A room with tables and chairs is also provided for less nimble diners.

Complete dinners include soup, hors d'oeuvres, tsukemono (pickled tidbits), rice, bancha tea and dessert. Prices vary according to entree selected. The specialty is o-mizu-taki—ribbons of prime beef with vegetables, mushrooms and bean cake flavored with a special sauce ($7.75). A terrific before-dinner cocktail, sure to enhance your meal (and everything else) for the rest of the evening is the Mingei-Ya sunrise ($2.75): a 14-ounce ceramic mug filled with rum and apricot liqueur, topped with a burst of sun in the form of a brandy-soaked apricot rising from a white froth cloud. A small Japanese paper lantern is inserted to "help you find your way."

Australian

Down Under: 619 Taylor Street, between Sutter and Post (tel: 771-4378). Open for lunch weekdays and dinner Monday through Saturday. Reservations suggested.

When Down Under (named originally for its cellar location) opened its doors about a decade ago, it had nothing whatsoever to do with Australia. However, employees of Qantas and the Australian government offices—which happened to be located around the corner—immediately dropped by to check the place out. Owners Jim and Don Somerville were amused and began catering to the homesick Aussies, first just serving Australian beer, then, little by little, plastering the walls with line drawings of kiwi birds and koala bears, boomerangs, photos of aboriginals and a framed copy of Waltzing Mathilda. The number of kangaroos in the decor kept pace with the increase in Australian clientele, and today San Francisco is one of the few towns in America that can boast an Australian restaurant.

The bar, which contains a pong machine and is tended by a chap from Liverpool, is always lively. A steak and lobster tail dinner is $8.25; veal scaloppine with fresh mushrooms is $5.75, teriyaki steak $6.50 and mahi-mahi $5.25. All entrees come with potatoes, a fresh vegetable and selections from the help-yourself salad bar. Luncheon entrees are $2-$3 cheaper.

We don't have any idea what people eat in Australia, so we can't judge authenticity, but the food at Down Under is very good, and the ambience jolly.

Hungarian

Budapest West: 3011 Steiner Street, off Union (tel: 921-2141). Open Tuesday through Saturday 5:30 to 10:30 p.m., Sunday to 9:30 p.m.

Homey and *gemütlich,* in the manner of Hungarian restaurants, Budapest West is housed in a white-trimmed blue, Victorian building, fronted with hedge trees in large wooden barrels. Nine pots of geraniums are neatly lodged in the front window. Tables are appointed in white linen, set off by vases of flowers, red napkins and candles aglow in red holders. A carved oak cabinet displays wine racks and decorative plates; a bar of dark, varnished wine barrels separates the two dining areas.

Salads—like the cucumber and sour cream ($1.10) or beet root in horseradish and caraway dressing (75¢)—are served, Hungarian style, with your entree rather than before it. Beef goulash with buttered dumplings and red cabbage is $5.95; chicken paprika and sour cream, also with buttered dumplings is $4.75; a traditional stuffed cabbage, filled with smoked ham, pork and seasoned rice, cooked in sauerkraut and cream, with layered potatoes, is $5.25. Assorted cakes and pastries are $1.10 to $1.35.

A good buy is the early-dinner special—homemade soup or salad, entree and coffee for $4.95, served between 5:30 and 7 p.m.

MODERATELY PRICED RESTAURANTS: The following choices are in the moderate price range that most of us prefer when dining out. Yet many offer a great deal of "atmosphere," along with affordable prices, and we've covered almost every cuisine imaginable, from steaks and chops to Vietnamese.

Chinese

Tao Tao: 675 Jackson Street, corner of Grant Avenue (tel: 982-6125). Open 4 to 11 p.m. Closed Thursdays.

Upstairs and downstairs, the walls at Tao Tao are lined with enlarged reproductions of Arnold Genthe's enchanting photographic record of turn-of-the-century Chinatown. Worth a visit for the exhibit alone, Tao Tao also offers a relaxed and cheerful ambience and an excellent selection of Cantonese delicacies. We like to dine upstairs under the handsome gold ceiling with dragon designs, where gold-painted, carved-wood room dividers depict scenes of ancient China.

The back page of the menu is devoted to gourmet preparations (24 hours advance notice required), the most intriguing being shark's fin in soup and gravy, which costs a whopping $85! However, you can stop in any time for paper-wrapped chicken ($5.25), fried shrimp ($3.25), almond duck ($3.50), or gah ming yeong—finely cut beef with Chinese vegetables and toasted rice noodles ($3.35).

Shanghai Low: 532 Grant Avenue, between Pine and California (tel: 982-2007). Open from noon to 11 a.m. Closed Tuesdays.

The oldest (established 1913) and most traditional in decor of Grant Avenue's many Chinese eateries, Shanghai Low has been operated by the Low family for several generations. One flight up, the main dining room is called the Celestial Terrace Room. It has two picture windows, one overlooking Saint Mary's Square, the other framing bustling Grant Avenue. The interior is impressive: the bar is situated under a Chinese canopy; gold-embossed and grass-paper walls are hung with embroidered antique tapestries and inlaid mother-of-pearl mirrors with hand-embroidered inserts.

We love the exotic atmosphere; the food, however, is somewhat geared to those who prefer the fried rice, chow mein and eggroll variety of Chinese cookery, though many more sophisticated items are listed. A full dinner of egg flower soup, chicken chow mein, sweet and sour pork, fried prawns, fried rice, tea and cookies is $6. From the à la carte menu, you might order diced chicken with almonds ($3.50), Chinese sausage ($2.75) or fried prawns with halved walnuts ($4.75). Special lunches are $1.75. The menu thoughtfully provides instructions on how to use chopsticks, and your place mat will tell you which Chinese year you were born in. A good Chinatown choice for family dining.

Yet Wah: 1801 Clement Street at 19th (tel: 387-8040). Open seven days from 11:30 a.m. to 11 p.m.

So popular is Yet Wah's delicious and reasonably priced Mandarin fare that it has sprouted two more Clement Street locations, at #1829 and #2140. (These are open 4-11 p.m.) The original restaurant is simple in decor, with cream-colored walls, colorful Chinese lanterns overhead, candlelit tables and a red lacquerwork screen behind which the crowds line up nightly. It's really very pleasant—always lively and buzzing with conversation.

A $5.85 dinner for two includes sizzling rice soup, su mi (deep-fried won ton), Mandarin beef over snow, almond press duck in sweet and sour sauce, phoenix and dragon (a shrimp and chicken dish with mushrooms and snow peas), rice, tea and cookies. Ordering à la carte, you might begin your meal with an order of kuo teh (six crispy pot-stickers) or fried fish balls in plum sauce ($1.75). Entrees include kubla lamb—lamb slices in spicy Szechuan brown bean sauce and scallions ($3.30); princess garden chicken salad—shredded chicken with lettuce, nuts, green onions and Chinese parsley, served with fun see noodles ($4.10); or fried duck with banana or mandarin orange sauce ($4.10). Everything sounds so good (with the notable exception of a dish called "ants on tree"—it's diced pork with vermicelli noodles and green onions) that it's difficult to decide just what to order; even "ants" are scrumptious. Best to go with a bunch of friends and order a wide choice of entrees. Domestic and Chinese wines and beers are available to complement your meal.

Yenching: 939 Kearny Street, between Columbus and Jackson (tel: 781-9712). Open 11:30 a.m. to 10 p.m. Closed Tuesdays.

Owned and operated by the very capable Madame Liu, who hails from Sandung Province in Northern China, Yenching has been delighting knowledgeable Bay Area residents with Mandarin and Szechuan specialties for over 15 years. It's a large, comfortable place, offering little in the way of decor. The food, however, is first-rate.

Complete dinners range in price from $10.90 for two to $75 for the 12-course Peking duck banquet which serves eight. A la carte, we once again advise an appetizer of pot stickers ($1.75), though very adventurous diners might want to split an hors d'oeuvre plate ($12 for a medium portion)—assorted cold cuts of abalone, shrimp, ham, spiced beef and shredded jellyfish, thousand-year-old eggs are extra! More conventional palate-pleasers include large fried prawns with green onions in ginger sauce ($4.25), sauteed shrimp in sweet and sour sauce with golden sizzling-rice crust ($4.25), or Mongolian beef—thin slices sauteed with green onions and garnished with long-grain rice ($3.80). A portion of glazed apples or bananas for dessert will add $3.25 to your check, but one dish is enough for two persons.

Ya Su Yuan: 638 Pacific Avenue, between Kearny and Grant. Open 11:30 a.m. to 10 p.m.

This is a little hole-in-the-wall with no particular decor, but it does offer authentic Mandarin cuisine and is popular with local Chinese. Prices here are a little lower than at our other listings: mu shi pork is $2.50, pot stickers are $1.50 for an order of six, and a very tasty cashew chicken dish is $3.50.

The Pot Sticker: 150 Waverly, off Washington Street (tel: 397-9985). Open seven days from 11:30 a.m. to 10 p.m.

We've been advocating the ordering of pot stickers for several paragraphs, now—and this pleasantly modern Mandarin restaurant specializes in them. A pot sticker, as it's no doubt time we explained, is a pan-fried, thin-skinned dumpling stuffed with seasoned meat or vegetables—and it does, yes, tend to stick to the pot. Here you can order several varieties of the dumplings, as well as other delicious Mandarian dishes.

We especially like the decor—unusually spartan for a Chinese restaurant: exposed brick walls hung with attractive Chinese paintings and scrolls and globe lights overhead.

The $4.25 dinner includes sizzling rice soup, pot stickers, cashew chicken, sweet and sour spare ribs, mandarin fried rice or steamed rice, cookies and tea. A la carte, you might order Szechuan prawns ($3.95), chicken sauteed in hot bean sauce ($2.95), or just gorge yourself on a variety of dumplings ($1.50 to $1.75 a plate). Leave some room for yummy ginger ice cream for dessert.

Italian

Tommaso's: 1042 Kearny Street, between Broadway and Pacific (tel: 398-9696). Open Wednesday through Saturday 5 to 11 p.m.; Sunday 4 to 10 p.m.

Francis Ford Coppola (certainly a mavin) is an enthusiastic habitué of this boisterous and utterly delightful Italian trattoria. Tables with cheerful yellow cloths and vases of flowers are set in intimate alcoves; oil murals of Neopolitan scenes decorate the walls. But the center of attention is Mama Crotti, expertly tossing huge hunks of garlic and mozzarella onto the pizzas and sliding them into a long brick oak-burning oven with a long wooden spatula. The pizza's great; we like the super-deluxe version: mushrooms, anchovies, peppers, ham, cheese, chicken, sausage, basil and garlic ($6 small, $7 large). Less jaded palates will be satisfied with any of 18 other varieties. A basket of hot homemade bread accompanies entrees like veal scaloppine marsala ($5) and chicken cacciatore ($5)—also oven baked. Homemade manicotti ($4.25) and a chilled broccoli salad with olive oil and lemon ($1.50) make an excellent meal. Of course, you need at least a half-bottle of soave ($3.50) or chianti ($4) with such a feast, and you'd do well to order homemade cannollis ($1.25) and a pot of Italian roast coffee ($1.25) for dessert.

Caffe Sport: 574 Green Street, between Grant and Columbus (tel: 981-1251). Open Monday through Saturday 11 a.m. to 2 a.m.

Decorative plates, plants, sausages, trinkets, dolls, flags, mirrors and other such oddments (many varnished to a high gloss) are hung from the ceiling and glued to the walls to create a decor best described in *New West* Magazine as "a masterpiece of contemporary Sicilian rococo." The Caffe Sport is a great favorite of Italians, bohemians and neighborhood folk, who revel in the lusty Sicilian ambience and the hearty free-hand-with-the-garlic cookery. Those with delicate appetites, temperaments or digestive systems should read no further; the rest proceed with gusto.

Owner-chef Antonio, who is also responsible for the interior design, presides in the kitchen, his undershirt flapping over an ample beer (or is it pasta) belly. His sauces are laced with raw chunks of garlic, his portions are generous and delicious. The calamari, prawns and clams, sauteed in garlic and olive oil and laced with white wine is $7.50. Get a large salad with it ($3.50), plus a bottle of wine ($3.50), and you have enough to amply feed two. Another favorite is the pasta rustica alla Carrettiera—hollow rigatoni noodles al dente, smothered in parmesan cheese, cream, small bay shrimp and thick red tomato sauce ($4). Fresh crusty bread and butter come with all entrees. For a late-night snack you might order the $3 antipasto—also enough for two. Finish off your meal with a cannolli ($1) and perhaps a belch, which would not be inappropriate here.

Seafood

Sam's Grill and Seafood Restaurant: 374 Bush Street at Kearny (tel: 421-0594). Opened Monday through Friday from 11 a.m. to 8:30 p.m.

Very similar in style to the previously described Tadich Grill, Sam's also has an old mahogany bar, intimate booths separated by heavy mahogany partitions (though here there's even a curtain you can draw for greater privacy), school-room lights overhead and big plates of lemon wedges on every table.

Maybe they copied the idea; newcomer Sam's came on the scene almost 20 years after Tadich's—in 1867. Anyway, we're partial to both establishments.

Entrees at Sam's include fresh salmon Newburg ($4.50), fried deep-sea scallops with tartar sauce ($4.65), and deviled crab à la Sam—a specialty ($4.90). There are many non-seafood offerings as well: half a broiled chicken is $2.75; accompanying side dishes include creamed spinach (65¢) and or potatoes au gratin (90¢). A glass of house wine is 75¢, and there's perplexing array of desserts. What to choose? A wedge of camembert (80¢), fresh strawberries and cream (90¢), French pancakes with lemon and sugar or jelly (90¢) or with anisette ($1.50), or perhaps the traditional homemade cheesecake (90¢)?

Maye's Oyster House: 1233 Polk Street, between Sutter and Bush (tel: 474-7674). Open 11 a.m. to 10:30 p.m. Monday through Saturday; 2 to 10 p.m. on Sunday.

Established the same year as Sam's (1867), Maye's is another San Francisco landmark. In over a century, the Croatian ownership has remained unchanged and the secret family recipes have been handed down from generation to generation. The decor also is largely unchanged; it's nothing much to look at, but it's comfortingly substantial and authoritatively established with big brown leather booths and ship-wheel chandeliers overhead. Once again, the fresh seafood is top quality, and prices are exceedingly reasonable.

R.B. Read, author of San Francisco's *Underground Gourmet,* notes that the oysters on half shell (six for $3.50) are so fresh "they react to a squirt of lemon juice." The great buy here is a complete dinner; priced according to entree selected, it includes soup, salad or seafood cocktail, pasta with mushroom sauce, dessert and beverage. Such a dinner with an entree of broiled calamari is ($5.85); $7 for baked creamed crabmeat with noodles au gratin, $8 for poached salmon in egg sauce. All entrees are also available à la carte. Non-seafood entrees, like charcoal-broiled French lamb chops ($5.25) or cold roast turkey with potato salad ($3.50), are also listed. A glass of Heineken's with your meal is $1.

Crêpes, Quiches and Omelets

The Magic Pan: 341 Sutter Street near Stockton (tel: 788-7397). Open Monday to Thursday 11 a.m. to 10 p.m.; Friday and Saturday 11 a.m. to midnight; Sunday from 11 a.m. to 9 p.m.

Large and airy, with one wall of windows overlooking a garden courtyard, this is one of the prettiest restaurants in the Magic Pan chain. Like the others, the decor here is French provincial, with parquet floors, antique cupboards, oak tables, framed French prints on the wall, well-placed hanging plants and big baskets of dried flowers. Up front is a spacious bar with comfortable couches, where a harpsichord player entertains at cocktail hour and on Friday and Saturday nights. The crêpe wheel is positioned at the door to the dining room, and you can watch the chef at his delicate work.

Crêpes are stuffed with a variety of delicious fillings: ratatouille ($3.30), creamed chicken topped with parmesan ($4.25), beef bourguignon ($4.75). Crêpe dinners give you a combination—like the steak kobab on a skewer served with a fresh mushroom crêpe (in bechamel sauce) and a spinach salad ($5.50). Hearty soups (95¢ a bowl), avocado, spinach or melon salads—ask for the house sweet/sour dressing—($1.20 to $1.35) and wines (95¢ a glass) are also available. Dessert crêpes are most tantalizing, including the likes of a southern praline crêpe—vanilla ice cream wrapped in a crêpe, covered with bubbling hot praline sauce, spiced whipped cream and toasted pecans ($1.75). The Magic

Pan is also popular at Sunday brunch for items like the crêpe benedict, maple butter crêpes and bacon, and chicken livers stroganoff, all under $3.

There's another Magic Pan at 900 North Point in Ghirardelli Square.

Salmagundi: 442 Geary Street near Taylor (tel: 441-8800). Open daily from 11 a.m. to midnight.

Situated in the heart of the theater district, and flanked by three Jewish restaurants, Salmagundi offers a chic alternative to chopped liver and pastrami. Ultra-contemporary in decor, it's furnished with white wrought-iron and bentwood chairs, matte white tables, an occasional high table with rattan stools, lots of plants, wicker baskets, macramé hangings and framed woodcuts on the walls. In the back there's a Spanish-tiled fountain, and windows look out on lush plantings. There's always good background music—light jazz, classical or whatever. Crowded at lunch and dinner, bustling with excitement after theater, Salmagundi takes on a casual coffee-house ambience during off hours—people hang out drinking wine or cappucino, playing backgammon, writing letters or reading *War and Peace*.

Every day three different choices of soups, salads and omelets, and one kind of quiche, are offered. Quiches, soups and omelets are served with a fresh oven-baked roll and butter and a small salad; ordered separately, salads come with just the roll. Among the soups ($2.50), the changing daily menu might list "al fresco avocado." Barbary Coast bouillabaisse, Ukranian beef borscht or English country cheddar; salad choices ($2.75 to $3.50) might include Niçoise, wilted spinach, King Kamehameha crab and Bombay chicken salad; omelets ($3) have a variety of fillings and toppings, from the Pondicherry—filled with chutney and topped with sour creato the classic Val d'Isère, stuffed with sauteed fresh mushrooms and creamy Gruyère cheese, garnished with parsley. As for the quiches ($2.60), they've gone the way of the pizza, and though you might find a simple quiche Lorraine listed occasionally, more often it's bedecked with spinach and nutmeg, shrimps and tomatoes, or even chicken livers and water chestnuts. The indecisive can order a combination plate—soup, salad, roll and quiche for $3.35. Wine and beer are 70¢ a glass; homemade desserts, 50-80¢.

There's another Salmagundi at 355 Bush Street in the financial district.

La Quiche: 550 Taylor Street, between Post and Geary (tel: 441-2711). Open 11:30 a.m. to 2:30 p.m. for lunch, 5:30 to 9:30 p.m. for dinner. Closed Sundays. Reservations suggested.

There is only one quiche lorraine say the trio of owners, Jean Ouyen, Claude Cassuto and Simon Charbonnier, who valiantly strive for and achieve classic purity in their cuisine. The decor is equally classic. La Quiche is a charming little bistro such as you might find on a Paris side street. The 20 or so tables are draped in red oilcloth with fruit motif. Hanging copper pots and a shelf of decorative plates adorn the beamed walls, and there are lace curtains in the windows.

Meals are accompanied by crusty loaves of homemade French bread (the authentic baguette) and fresh butter in little ceramic pots. The quiche (exceptional, with the lightest crust ever), a salad ($2.75), a glass of wine (85¢), homemade chocolate mousse with real creme Chantilly ($1.10) and a pot of expresso (60¢) makes an excellent lunch or dinner. Thirty delicious crêpes with scrumptious fillings ($2.75 to $4) are also available at both meals. Dinner specials, served with soup, salad, bread and coffee, might feature boeuf bourguignon ($5.95) or chicken sauteed in Riesling Wine ($5.95). At lunch, entrees served with French bread and coffee include chicken in cream and mushrooms ($2.95) and a very tasty salad Niçoise ($3.50).

La Quiche is a must.

Indian

Anjuli: One Embarcadero Center, at the corner of Battery and Sacramento (tel: 788-1629), third floor. Open for lunch Monday to Saturday 11 a.m. to 2:30 p.m.;dinner nightly from 5:30 to 9:30.

Specializing in tandoori and thali dinners, Anjuli offers North Indian cuisine in an exotic setting. Especially cozy are the intimate dining rooms behind beaded curtains where you sit on plump cushions at a low table. In the main dining area there are regular chairs and tables; carved sandalwood screens serve as partitions, brass candle lamps and flowers grace each table. There are many plants around.

Food is served thali-style by sari-clad waitresses and turbaned waiters. That means a great many dishes (here nine courses) are served on a shallow plate or thali. All dinners include pulav (fried rice cooked with vegetables), naan (Indian bread), vegetable, dal (lentil soup), salad, raita (yogurt and cucumbers), chutney, papad (lentil wafers) and gulab jaman (fried milk balls in cardamom syrup and rose water). The above thali feast with an entree of tandoori murg—baked chicken marinated in yogurt and spices—will cost $5.50 —with curried jumbo prawns, $5.95. You can also order à la carte. Eating with your fingers is encouraged, the menu contending that using implements is as unsatisfactory as making love through an interpretor.

Vietnamese

Vietnam-France: 1901 Divisadero Street, corner of Pine (tel: 567-9443). Open for lunch Monday through Friday; dinner nightly.

Mademoiselle Ngan Dang defected from Hanoi to the West several years ago, bringing her culinary skills and a new cuisine to San Francisco, and establishing this charming bistro-like restaurant. Vietnam-France has red and white checkered tablecloths, a long red candle on every table. One wall is exposed brick, the others dark wood paneling. Pots of ivy are placed here and there, and some orange lamps add a warm glow. Tapes—perhaps Edith Piaf or Vietnamese music—are played in the background. The place attracts a knowledgeable crowd of diners, all adept with their chopsticks.

An order of cha gio (Vietnam's answer to the eggroll but much more delicate) is $2.50. Our favorite entree is chicken with Vietnamese herbs and lemon-grass roots ($3). Also recommended: pork stuffed in boneless duck with sweet and sour sauce ($5.50) and charcoal-broiled beef brochette ($3.50). All entrees come with soup and rice. For dessert, fried banana flambee is $1. A Coors with your meal is 70¢.

Lunch is extremely inexpensive and qualifies for our budget category.

Jewish

David's: 474 Geary Street at Taylor (tel: 771-1600). Open from 8 a.m. to 1 a.m. Sunday through Thursday, till 3 a.m. Friday and Saturday. Reservations suggested.

"Mary Hartman, Mary Hartman" has just ended, and you're dying for a pastrami on rye. You don't have to return to New York. Just head on over to David's, where a lively crowd of theater-goers will be taking apart the evening's performance over the blintzes. The decor? It's not important, though pleasant enough with white brick walls, indirect lighting and Formica tables. Here you come for the food.

A complete dinner, including appetizer, soup, entree, dessert and coffee ($6.50), served with a basket of bagels and freshly baked bread, is a great buy for those unafraid of heartburn. A la carte entrees include delicious cheese blintzes smothered in sour cream and laced with jam ($3.50), and sweet and sour stuffed cabbage with potatoes ($5.75). Don't overlook the appetizers: herring in cream sauce ($1.75); gefilte fish with matzoh or challah ($1); and chicken liver in schmaltz ($2.10). Sandwiches come on rye or Siberian soldier's bread and include everything from hot pastrami ($2.25) to Russian caviar ($9). Desserts are homemade and delicious.

If you're really keen on Jewish cookery, you can stay at David's adjoining hotel and get a 10% discount on all meals at the restaurant. There are 45 rooms, all with phone, TV, radio and bath. It's simple and immaculate. Singles are $16, doubles $18 to $22.

Basque

Izarra: 1775 Polk Street, corner of Washington (tel: 771-4034). Open for lunch 10:30 a.m. to 3:30 p.m. Monday through Friday; dinner 5 to 10 p.m. Monday through Saturday.

H. B. Read, San Francisco's restaurant guru, reverently suggests that to eat Basque is "to break the bread of the spirit: to ingest not knowledge . . . but primary wisdom." We noticed no difference in our store of wisdom, or lack thereof, upon leaving Izarra, but we were happy and satisfied. The charming proprietress, Marie-Antoinette Ansola, takes great pride in the excellence of her cuisine. It's a pretty little place, light and airy with a white latticework ceiling, stucco walls hung with travel posters, white-curtained windows, red-clothed tables bedecked with fresh flowers in Perrier bottles, and lots of hanging plants.

The price of your entree includes soup, salad, fresh vegetables and coffee. There's beef bourguignon ($5.25), duckling sauté with cherry sauce ($7), and perhaps escalope de veau with mushrooms and cream sauce ($6.50). At lunch, tasty salads, omelets and burgers are under $2, and entrees like trout meunière with rice and a vegetable are $3. A glass of wine is 75¢, and the dessert to order is the homemade Basque almond cake (75¢)—delicious!

Mexican

Tortola: 1237 Polk Street, between Sutter and Bush (tel: 673-2636). Open Tuesday through Saturday from 10 a.m. to 10 p.m.

For over 40 years the Scarpulla family has been offering a unique variety of Mexican hacienda cookery. Their secret recipes, originally obtained from the early Spanish Dons, are the early-California fiesta foods combining the best elements of Spanish and Mexican cuisine. The menu items sound like those at other Mexican restaurants, but they're very different—not as heavy, more delicately prepared and spiced.

We like the way Tortola looks, too—not ornate, but with an air of unmistakable authenticity. Heavy wrought-iron chandeliers are suspended from the peaked, beamed ceiling; large framed oils of the Spanish missions decorate the mahogany-paneled walls. Diners sit in roomy high-backed Philippine mahogany booths with deep red leather seats.

Specialties include the plato de oro—a stack of corn cakes, filled with ground chicken and beef, refried beans, onions, a piquant sauce, melted cheese, peppers and tomatoes ($4.25); pollo al jerez—panfried chicken smothered with sherry wine and served with Spanish rice ($5.75); tostada de Camaron with shrimp, avocado and sour cream ($4.75). Combination plates are $4.65 to $5. This distinctive cuisine is not to be missed.

Nicaraguan

Rancho Nica: 3147 22nd Street, near Mission (tel: 282-2898). Open Tuesday through Thursday from noon to 10 p.m.; Friday, Saturday and Sunday from noon to midnight.

The decor is authentic "South American funk"—plastic orange chairs, a hokey mural of mountains on the wall, pinball machine and blaring jukebox. Two tables are enclosed in a little bamboo and rattan booth decorated with fishnets. The ambience is festive and fun.

The food comes in huge portions, and it's very good. The beef soup ($1.75) has big chunks of beef and corn-on-the-cob in it. You can order an entree of "old Indian (stuffed)" for $3.50—it's a thin slice of beef filled with ground corn, eggs, milk, cheese and spices; or perhaps banana slices with pork and cheese ($3). Broiled barbecued spare ribs are $3.50, fried perch $4. All of the above are served with rice and salad. Original libations are concocted from cocoa bean and milk, ground corn, barley, corn and cocoa, or tamarind—any of these cost just 50¢, so indulge your curiosity. Mexican entrees are also available.

Peruvian

Pabellon Espagnol: 3115 22nd Street, between Mission and Van Ness (tel: 285-0690). Open Monday, Wednesday and Thursday 4 to 11 p.m.; Friday and Saturday 4 p.m. to 4 a.m.; Sunday 1 p.m. to 1 a.m.

One thing about Pabellon Espagnol's cheery decor—there's a lot of it: tables draped in red oilcloth, red velvet curtains fringed in gold, and on the bright yellow walls, oil paintings, mirrors decorated with pictures of bullfighters, travel posters, a rug depicting flamenco dancers, etc. The jukebox is very Latin, the food is great, and all in all, this is a charming and pleasant place to eat.

It's imperative that you order the papa rellena appetizer—a baked potato stuffed with ground meat, eggs and raisins, topped with a black olive ($1.25). An excellent and authentic paella is $5.75; Peruvian specialties include anticuchos—marinated barbecued beef hearts ($3.50), and saltad de Mariscos—prawns, scallops, squid and fish sauteed with fresh tomatoes, onions and spices ($5). A delicious salad, rice and hot homemade bread are served with all entrees. A glass of wine or beer is 65¢, Sangria—the house recipe—is 75¢. Finish up with espresso and an excellent flan (it has an orange flavor)—75¢.

Brazilian

Casa Brasil: 731 Bush Street, between Mason and Powell (tel: 397-8717). Open Monday through Saturday from 5 to 10 p.m.

Reflecting its downtown location, Casa Brasil is much more elegant in tone and decor than our previous South American listings. It's a charming, candlelit little place, with bright green tablecloths, fresh flowers on every table and cafe curtains on the front window. White and pine-green walls are adorned with a few Brazilian artifacts and travel posters. Brazilian music is played at a reasonable decibel level in the background.

All entrees are served with soup, toast and butter, as well as a dish of ground yucca-root flour which you sprinkle on your food like parmesan. Favored entrees include feijoada—black beans and marinated meats in a savory sauce with rice and collard greens ($4.10); and chuleta de porco, which you may have realized translates to cuts of pork, these marinated in lemon sauce, served with rice and roast potatoes ($4.95). A glass of wine with your meal is 85¢, but you might want to try a non-alcoholic Brazilian beverage called guaraná (55¢)—it tastes like carbonated apple cider and complements this cuisine very well. Desserts are very sweet—banana pudding with brown sugar (85¢) and the like. They're best taken with strong Brazilian coffee (50¢).

Japanese

Michikusa: 417 Grant Avenue at the foot of Chinatown (tel: 986-3489). Open for lunch Monday through Friday from 11 a.m. to 2 p.m.; dinner nightly from 5 to 10 p.m.

A bit of an anomaly in Chinatown, Michikusa offers authentic Japanese cuisine and excellent service to a largely Japanese clientele and a handful of Western cognoscenti. Up one flight from the street, it's simply and attractively decorated with Japanese prints, fans and kites, rice-paper screens on the windows. Tables are separated by delicate beaded curtains.

A hot towel is brought to you at the beginning and end of the meal in the Japanese tradition. And whether you know enough to ask for it or not, a raw egg in a bowl is served with your sukiyaki (dip the pieces in it). It happens to be a terrific sukiyaki, by the way, and costs only $3.85; beef teriyaki is $4.50, shabu shabu is $3.75, and okisuki (Japan's version of bouillabaisse) is $3.85. All the above entrees come with soup, salad, rice, tsukemono, dessert and tea. Luncheon entrees are $2.25 to about $3 and come with Japanese pickles, rice and tea.

Yumiko's Tempura House: 2339 Clement Street, between 24th and 25th Avenues (tel: 387-5090). Open for lunch and dinner every day except Monday.

Simplicity and understatement are the keynotes of the elegant decor at Tempura House—a lovely pine-plank cabin with yellow paper lanterns suspended from a slanted ceiling, raw pine walls and tables. The decor consists of a few tasteful photos and Japanese prints on the walls, a plant here and there, an antique split bamboo shade (200 years old) over the front window. There's a tatami room in back. The restaurant is named for owner Harou Abe's seven-year-old daughter, whose other honors include being chosen to greet Hirohito during his U.S. visit.

Tempura (deep-fried vegetables or shrimp in a light flour and egg batter) is, of course, the specialty. A combination order of shrimp tempura and fried chicken or chicken teriyaki is $3.25; shrimp tempura with fried salmon or beef teriyaki, $4.10. All orders include soup, rice and excellent tea. A salad on the side is just 30¢, a bottle of sake $1.20. Tempura House is highly recommended.

Indonesian

A Bit of Indonesia: 211 Clement Street, between 3rd and 4th Avenues (tel: 752-4042). Open 5 to 11 p.m. nightly except Mondays.

Set aside some enchanted evening to dine at this cozy, candlelit restaurant, the most popular of San Francisco's Indonesian eateries. The pretty interior does evoke "a bit of Indonesia," with batik cloths and flowers on every table, one wall lined with shelves of Indonesian wood carvings, others hung with oil paintings of *Ramayana* themes or Indonesian villages.

We recommend that you order the rijsttafel ($14.50 for two), a full Indonesian banquet. It contains two lumpia (eggrolls with peanut sauce), nasi kuning (rice cooked with spices and coconut milk), steamed rice gado-gado (vegetable salad in peanut sauce), sate lembu (char-broiled marinated beef), ayam panggang besengek (spiced barbecued chicken), kari Jawa (beef simmered in Javanese curry), vegetable, roasted coconut and tea or coffee. A bottle of San Miguel beer with the meal is 90¢. If you still have room for dessert, how about banana fritters topped with fresh whipped cream (30¢)? If the rijsttafel is too steep for your budget, you can order any of its parts in larger portions à la carte at prices between $2.25 to $4.20.

Philippines

Mabuhay: 836 Kearny Street, between Jackson and Washington (tel: 421-3320). Open Monday through Saturday from 11:30 a.m. to 9 p.m.; Sundays 3 to 9 p.m.

Reflecting the influences of Chinese, Indonesian, Spanish and Portuguese cookery, Filipino cuisine is unique indeed. San Francisco has several Filipino restaurants, of which Mabuhay (it means *ciao* in Tagalog) is the best.

The decor is certainly not belabored—tropical murals of the Philippines and one peacock chair (the others are an eclectic assortment, possibly gleaned from someone's kitchen) create the "exotic" setting. However, you'll soon forget the lack of island decor if you begin your meal with a piña colada or masarap—a concoction of rum, banana liqueur and fruit juices. The traditional appetizer is lumpia—Philippine eggrolls ($1.90 for a plate of four). We like the fried shrimp in batter ($4); sinigang isda—a rich tamarind-flavored fish soup with greens ($2.60); and the ginger beef ($2.90). Unusual desserts include breadfruit, coconut or avocado ice cream. San Miguel beer is 90¢ a bottle. The great buy at Mabuhay is the five-course lunch for $2.50: pork or chicken in adobo (vinegar and spice sauce), sauteed flank steak with fresh onions, Filipino chow mein, chicken with vegetables, and dessert.

Under the same ownership, and offering the same menu, is **Mabuhay Gardens,** 443 Broadway at Montgomery (tel: 956-3315). Open from 6 p.m. to 1:30 a.m. Wednesday through Sunday, this restaurant also throws in a floor show and dancing to live music at no extra charge.

Natural Foods

Shandygaff: 1760 Polk Street at Washington (tel: 441-1760). Open daily from 11:30 a.m. to 11 p.m.; till midnight Friday and Saturday nights.

Under the tent-like ceiling at Shandygaff, with plants everywhere, strains of classical music and tantalizing aromas filling the room, the very air seems fresher. Of course, the fact that diners are asked not to smoke helps. This is one of the most delightful of health-food eateries, serving gourmet fare in an exquisite setting. Delicious breads and desserts are baked on the premises, and only the finest natural and organic ingredients are used in all preparations.

Our favorite dinner entree is the Northpoint cioppino—fresh fish and shellfish in a rich broth of tomatoes, peppers, onions, garlic, spices and olives ($5.95). There's a large selection of tasty salads, from Indonesian, with sweet and sour dressing and toasted peanuts ($3.35), to the more conventional Niçoise ($3.95). A vegetarian lasagne is $4.75, quiche with vegetables $4.50. Even the wines are unpasteurized and made from organically grown fruits; they include plum, pear, apricot, brambleberry, peach and loganberry (90¢ a glass). A rich and satisfying blend of South and Central American coffees is served, as are about 20 choices of tea from jasmine to Love Potion #9. And you couldn't tell the desserts—carob silk pie, carrot cream cake, etc.—from the real sugar-laden, tooth-rotting McCoy.

Shandygaff is a perfect choice for long, leisurely lunches, dinners or Sunday brunches.

Creole

Le Creole: 1809 Union Street, corner of Octavia (tel: 921-1132). Open daily for lunch and dinner.

Strikingly decorated in black and white—black oilcloth over white linen tablecloths, black bentwood chairs and ceiling, white painted brick and shuttered walls hung with photos of New Orleans—Le Creole is intimate and charming. Candles glowing from red glass holders, ferns and potted plants, and red carnations on every table provide a counterpoint. It's all very pretty, and the New Orleans cuisine is excellent.

The complete table d'hôte dinner is $6.40 to $6.80. It starts with chicken gumbo, a basket of hot French bread and tossed salad with Creole, vinaigrette or Roquefort dressing. There's a choice of six entrees, among them the traditional jambalaya (a spicy combination of diced ham, shrimp and rice), roast beef in wine sauce and rosemary, and ramekin of crabmeat. A glass of California burgundy, rosé or chablis comes with your meal, and so does tea or coffee. For dessert there's a choice of tomato spice cake or whiskey pudding, but an extra 25-50¢ gets you pecan or sweet potato pie topped with whipped cream. If you choose a chicken, crab or shrimp gumbo entree with the dinner, it's only $4.50, and all the above entrees are also available à la carte. Luncheon entrees are just $1.65 to $3.

West Indian

Connie's: 1909 Fillmore Street, near Japantown (tel: 563-8755). Open 5 to 10 p.m. Wednesday through Sunday; till 11 p.m. Friday and Saturday. Reservations suggested.

Proprietress Connie Williams hails from Trinidad and the cuisine she serves reflects the cultural mix of that island, featuring East Indian, West Indian and African specialties. It's a large, cheerful place, the walls haphazardly roller-painted in all different directions and colors, further adorned by a variety of oil paintings and prints of Caribbean scenes (including, for some reason, a Gauguin).

Dinner includes soup, salad, entree and dessert, not to mention Connie's delicious homemade coconut bread. There are only three entrees; curried lamb ($4.65), curried beef with eggplant ($3.90) and Caribbean chicken with rice and Congo peas ($3.90). The African dinner ($3.90) of coocoo (a corn mush, shrimp and meat casserole) and baked fish must be ordered 24 hours in advance. On weekends curried goat ($4.65)—don't knock it if you haven't tried it—and a delicious hearty gumbo ($3.65) are available. Portions are large; desserts, like the almond-flavored pound cake, are also homemade. The house wine is 60¢ a glass, $1.75 for a small carafe.

Steaks and Chops

The Butcher Shop: 2348 Polk Street at Union (tel: 771-5544). Open daily from 5 to 11 p.m.

Friendly and relaxed, with a quasi-Victorian decor, the Butcher Shop draws a young and attractive crowd. The ambience is romantic—softly lit by candles and gaslamps, with vases of flowers on tables draped in red-and-white-checkered oilcloth. Classical music plays in the background, large fans revolve slowly overhead, and the walls are hung with U.S. Department of Agriculture steer grade illustrations. A few antiques and hanging plants complete the picture.

All entrees are served with a salad, potatoes, vegetables and a basket of hot homemade whole wheat bread. Pan-fried chicken or ground sirloin is $3.95. Ascending the price scale, prawns are $5.50, top sirloin $7.50 and a full pound of New York strip steak $8.50. Homemade desserts—posted on a blackboard—are likely to include cheesecake and carrot cake with icing, both 95¢. A glass of wine is 75¢.

BUDGET MEALS: The following are for those of you who haven't got too many coins jingling in your jeans. Nothing prosaic, these low-cost eateries range from Chinese to Salvadorean, and are worth investigating even by better-heeled travelers.

American

Tommy's Joynt: Corner of Van Ness and Geary Streets (tel: 775-4216). Open daily from 11 a.m. to 1 a.m.

Outside it's pure carnival with brightly painted walls depicting oversized edibles, signs proclaiming world-famous sandwiches, and 22 flags that are purely decorative fluttering in the wind. Inside it's funk-and-junk time: old hockey sticks, mounted moose and buffalo heads, a statue of a lion guzzling Löwenbräu, stuffed birds, a Santa Claus mask, a notice declaring "No Rickshaw Parking," etc., etc., etc. There's an old upright piano ("This piano for your pleasure; play it if you know how") and a TV going full blast at all times to add lots of noise to the general confusion.

The food is cafeteria-style and high in quality. Buffalo stew ($2.84), stronger and gamier than beef stew, is a specialty; beef burgundy is $2.69, a big turkey leg $2.29. Salads are about 60¢; delicious cheesecake is priced the same. Beer comes in 78 varieties, listed alphabetically by national origin—from Australia to Switzerland. Average price is $1.20 a bottle.

The Noble Frankfurter: 529 Powell Street, between Bush and Sutter (tel: 989-6533). Open for lunch and dinner till 10 p.m. Other branches at 1900 Polk Street, 3159 Fillmore Street and 4109 24th Street.

Casual and funky, the centrally located Powell Street branch is light and airy, with plants suspended from a skylight roof, red-and-white-checkered oilcloth tablecloths and a much-played jukebox. It's kind of a hangout, where people sit and read the paper, converse or maybe play checkers. Service is cafeteria-style, and choices range from Coney Island kosher-style (75¢) to Polish kielbasa (85¢) to a spicy Sicilian sausage (90¢). Homemade chili comes in two portion sizes (90¢ and $1.25), potato salad and slaw are 50¢, a large order of French fries is 70¢. A nine-ounce glass of wine with your weiners is just 60¢. Help yourself to as much mustard, ketchup, sauerkraut and relish as you like.

Mexican

La Victoria: 2937 24th Street, corner of Alabama (tel: 824-9931). Open daily from 10 a.m. to 10 p.m.

This most authentic and least costly of Mexican eateries is entered via an aromatic bakery-cum-grocery where fresh-from-the-oven breads and pastries, plaintains, chiles, cactus leaves, chayote, mangoes, hot sauces and the like are attractively displayed. The interior consists of two small rooms divided by an open kitchen with hanging plants over the counter. Mexican travel posters and a plaque of the Virgin enshrined in plastic flowers adorn red cement-block walls, the floor is covered in red linoleum, and the tables are bright yellow Formica. During the day it's very sunny, at night La Victoria is lit by candles.

The menu is in Spanish only, and entrees range from about $1.20 to $2.35. Two burritos, tacos or enchiladas with rice and frijoles (beans) cost $1.70; orden birria, an order of beef with chiles and sauce, is $2.35; menudo grande, a large serving of hunks of tripe with fresh lemon, chopped onions, fresh oregano and red chile, is $1.70. Other specialties include fried pork skin with chile verde ($1.95) and scrambled eggs with chorizo sausage ($2.35). Have a bakery-fresh pan dulce (25¢) with your coffee.

Chinese Tea Lunch

Yank Sing: 671 Broadway, between Stockton and Grant (tel: 781-1111). Open daily from 10 a.m. to 5 p.m.

Chinese tea lunch, known as *dim sum,* is a branch of Chinese cookery which consists of many varieties of hot and cold delicacies—buns, steamed dumplings, meatballs, and pastries stuffed with meat, fish, vegetables or sweet fillings.

The atmosphere at Yank Sing is always bustling, with waitresses carrying plate after plate of delicious goodies to your table. Don't grab everything that's offered; wait for the ones that appeal. Plum sauce, chili sauce and mustard enhance the flavor of your dim sum. Most dishes at Yank Sing cost 65¢, and you get two or three items to a plate. Among the daily offerings, you might be served shrimp wrapped in dough, pork balls, curried chicken dumplings, paper-wrapped chicken, rice rolls, fried taro-root dumplings, mushrooms wrapped in dough, bean-curd rolls, stuffed beancake, stuffed green pepper or a mixture of rice, mushrooms and sausage wrapped in bamboo leaf. Dessert dim sum include puffy doughnuts, coconut with lotus bean and egg custard.

This delightful culinary experience is best shared with several friends.

Hang Ah Tea Room: 1 Hang Ah Street, off Sacramento (open daily from 10 a.m. to 3 p.m.) is another good spot for dim sum meals.

Basque

Elu's: 787 Broadway, between Powell and Stockton (tel: 986-9646). Open for dinner from 5 to 9:30 p.m. nightly except Monday.

The *New York Times* called Elu's a "mama and papa bistro, where you can eat a decent table d'hôte with the house red wine for *deux fois rien.*" We concur.

This is the real thing: Euzdaki is spoken at the bar, Basque and Spanish tunes fill the air, and Mr. and Mrs. Elu live upstairs and rent out rooms. There's a print of "Guernica" over the bar—the only notable item in an otherwise just-off-the-boat decor. It's just marvelous!

Paella ($4.25) is the specialty. Otherwise, different dinners are featured nightly. Typically, the Saturday night feast begins with shrimp-potato salad, served on a relish plate with salami slices, green onions, etc. Next comes homemade vegetable soup, creamed sweetbreads, roast leg of lamb, mashed potatoes, ice cream and coffee. The whole feast costs just $4.25.

Russian

Miniature Bakery and Restaurant: 431 Clement Street, between 5th and 6th Avenues (tel: 752-4444). Open 8 a.m. to 8 p.m. every day except Monday.

Mr. and Mrs. Krainer operate this aptly named hole-in-the-wall with doleful Slavic solemnity. However, their grim demeanor, the total lack of ambience, and the slow service are not only tolerated by a devoted clientele, but hailed as an important element of the Miniature's mystique. The food is terrific and authentic. Entrees include selianka—a flavorful and spicy stew of pork sausage, cabbage, meat, olives, peppers, etc. ($3); pelmeni—like ravioli filled with meat and topped with sour cream ($2.80); and zrazal—a Russian hamburger with mushroom stuffing ($2.70). Full dinners, including soup, salad, coffee and dessert, begin at $4.30. Lots of people come here for hearty snacking on piroshky—a puffy doughnut-like pastry filled with meat, fish or cabbage (55¢); borscht (80¢); or delicious homemade pastries—meringues with chocolate cream, Napoleons, cream rolls, etc. The traditional drink is tea, served in a glass, though wine (60¢ a glass) and beer ($1) are available.

Salvadorean

Coatepeque: 2240 Mission Street, between 18th and 19th (tel: 863-5237). Open Friday through Tuesday from noon to 8:30.

Leave it to San Francisco to harbor a Salvadorean restaurant (it's in Central America, in case you're wondering), and it's a gastronomic delight to boot. The decor is nil—Formica tables, yellow walls—but it's not unpleasant. The menu, printed in English and Spanish, lists entrees varying in price from $1.40 to $3.50. Specialties range from Salvadorean-style steak to chorizo with egg to stuffed peppers; all are $2.25 and come with rice and beans. You might get a side order of fried bananas, cream and beans, or homemade corn tamales with sour cream. A side of avocado salad is $1.40; prawn soup, 95¢. Several trips are needed to properly explore this unique menu.

Snacks and Sandwiches

The Wildwood: 517 Sutter Street near Powell (tel: 397-0884). Open from 7 a.m. to 4 p.m. Monday through Saturday.

Light and cheery, this downtown cafeteria has a garden ambience, with fern-pattern wallpaper, butcher-block tables adorned with dried flowers, lots of hanging plants and green Astroturf carpeting.

The menu features sandwiches and salads. We like the healthful combinations on nine-grain bread the best: avocado, tomato and sprouts ($1.50), peanut butter, banana and honey ($1.25) and the like. Salads are of a similar ilk—avocado stuffed with tuna or chicken salad ($1.95) is one example. There's some rather good carrot cake for dessert, and wine and beer are available.

And In Conclusion

Just Desserts: 1469 Pacific Avenue, between Hyde and Larkin. Open from 11 a.m. to 10 p.m. Monday through Thursday, till midnight Friday and Saturday. Closed Sunday. Another location at 248 Church Street, between Market and 15th.

The perfect finale for a meal or a restaurant section, Just Desserts is a delightful place to indulge in rich chocolate fudge cake, banana nut cake with butter cream icing and laced with raspberry jam, strawberries with fresh whipped cream, creamy cheesecake or apple tart à la mode with Bud's (everyone's favorite) ice cream. All are homemade with natural ingredients, except for demon sugar. Prices range from 20¢ to 75¢. Fresh-ground coffee and herbal spice teas are also served.

4. San Francisco Sights

San Francisco is chockablock with sightseeing adventures, many of which can best be enjoyed on foot. Chinatown, Japantown, Fisherman's Wharf, the Cannery, Ghirardelli Square and the like make San Francisco a stroller's paradise, and while you're checking out these attractions, you can savor the unique and charming atmosphere of the city.

In the upcoming pages, we've detailed daytime activities, including those mentioned above, as well as parks, museums and excursions.

We'll begin with an area of major importance in the San Francisco tourism picture:

CHINATOWN: Head for Grant Avenue at Bush Street, where an ornamental green-tiled archway, crowned by a symbolic dragon, marks the entrance to the biggest Chinese stronghold this side of Taiwan. Here begins an eight-block labyrinthine array of pagoda-roofed buildings, dragon-entwined lamp posts, exotic shops and food markets, renowned restaurants, temples and museums. A little history follows.

The early-comers from Canton reached San Francisco during the Gold Rush of 1849. They called the city Gum Sun Dai Fow—"Great City of the Golden Hill." Today their numbers have swollen to an estimated 70,000, though some local Chinese sources set the figure at more than 100,000.

Banding together in one tiny area of the city was not totally a clannish choice of these immigrants: they were partly forced into it by anti-Oriental prejudice. It became, as ghettos will, ridden with vice, and until the earthquake of 1906, Grant Avenue (then Dupont Street) was known as "the wickedest thoroughfare in the States." Only after devastation swept away the strings of bordellos, gambling dens and opium parlors, was it given a new name—and a new image.

Along with vice, the earthquake swept away another old Chinatown symbol—the Tong hatchet men, so named because they actually dispatched their victims with an ax. Originally formed as protective societies, because "pigtail-baiting" was a favorite pastime of San Francisco hoodlums, the Tongs evolved into criminal associations. Like the Mafia families, they were frequently at war with one another. During their heyday, around the turn of the century, they left the pavements of Chinatown as scattered with corpses as the gang wars were to leave Chicago some years later. Today, however, the Tongs are gone, and, in fact, Chinatown is one of the safest neighborhoods in America. And it's packed with interesting sights, which we've detailed below.

At the corner of Grant Avenue and California Street, having survived the earthquake and a fire in 1966, is **Old St. Mary's Church.** The city's first cathedral, it was erected in 1854 of brick brought around Cape Horn and granite cut in China. Above the clock dial, its red-brick facade bears this warning: "Son Observe the Time and Fly from Evil." Diagonally across is **St. Mary's Square,** a tranquil, flower-filled retreat, over which an imposing, 12-foot statue of Sun Yat-Sen, by sculptor Beniamino Bufano, presides.

The tiny **Chinese Historical Society of America,** at 17 Adler Place, just off Grant Avenue, houses a collection of regional Chinese artifacts, Gold Rush relics and sepia-toned 19th-century photographs of early arrivals.

Open from 1-5 p.m. Tuesday through Sunday, the museum has exhibits ranging from tiny slippers for the bound feet of aristocratic ladies, to gadgets and pipes used in opium dens.

The **Chinatown Wax Museum,** 601 Grant Avenue at California Street, preserves in wax the early history of the Chinese in California. It contains 31 exhibits and 115 figures. Scenes include the travels of Marco Polo, the original fortune-cookie factory, the opium war, the Chinese opera—even the gangland murder of "Little Pete," Chinatown's Al Capone, in a barber shop. The museum is open daily from 10 a.m. to 11 p.m. Admission is $1.50 for adults, $1 for children six to 12, under six free.

At 838 Grant Avenue, you'll come to the **China Trade Center,** an arcade of shops and restaurants, which is fun to visit.

For a peek at Chinese nightlife, have a drink at the **Ricksha Lounge,** tucked away at 37 Ross Alley, between Grant and Stockton. The street is a dark little cul-de-sac that has been used as the locale of several movie thrillers. The Ricksha is an intimate, beautifully designed (and slightly expensive) meeting place of local showbiz celebs (even including, occasionally, Frank Sinatra). There's a very sophisticated piano bar.

One more suggestion. If you've had your fill of bustling crowds, exotic wares, mountains of souvenirs, etc., you might want to take a break and stop in at a Chinese movie. Most of the theaters are on Mason and Jackson Streets, off Grant Avenue, and many have English subtitles. There's usually a double feature—a classical costume drama and a very Hollywood-style epic, or at least some Hong Kong studio's idea of one. Both are highly entertaining. Tickets average about $2.75.

Chinese New Year

One of the most exciting festivals celebrated anywhere in America, Chinese New Year occurs sometime in late January or February, depending on the fullness of the moon. The merry-making lasts a full week, and celebrations spill onto every street in Chinatown, transforming the square into noisy and exciting fairgrounds. The finale is the "Miss Chinatown USA" pageant parade, an incredible mix of marching bands, floats, barrages of fireworks, and a wonderful block-long dragon writhing in and out of the crowds.

Guided Tours

Gray Line offers a **Chinatown by Night** tour, which takes you first on a bus ride through downtown San Francisco (also encompassing Ghirardelli Square, Fisherman's Wharf and the Cannery). Then on to a walking tour of Chinatown with a Chinese guide to explore the temples, the Wax Museum, etc. You are given some time for shopping. The price is $6.25 for adults, $4.60 for children. The **Chinatown Dinner Tour** is much the same, but it also includes a multi-course Chinese dinner. Adults pay $12.50, children $10. For information phone 771-4000.

Somewhat more elaborate is a Chinese-run operation—**Ding How Tours,** 111 Waverly Place (tel: 981-8399). A taxi picks you up from—and delivers you back to—your hotel. On the 3½-hour tour, you'll dine at a Chinese restaurant, watch Buddhists and Taoists at worship in the same temple, visit a fortune-cookie factory, attend a reception at a private association (with family-style tea and delicacies), explore an art gallery, Oriental herb shop and clothing shop, visit a Chinese theater, take a cable-car ride to the top of Nob Hill and admire the panoramic view from the Crown Room of the Mark Hopkins Hotel. In between you get an explanation of the Chinese language, a lecture about Chinese culture, and a demonstration of Oriental painting.

The tours cost $13.25 for adults and $11.25 for children; without dinner, $7.50 for adults and $6.50 for children.

SAN FRANCISCO: SIGHTS   57

JAPANTOWN/JAPAN CENTER: Set in and around Japan Center, a $15-million showcase completed in 1968, **Nihonmachi** (Japantown) is as slickly modern as Chinatown is ancient and exotic. The focal point of the city's Japanese business and cultural activities, the area abounds in Japanese art galleries, bookstores, restaurants, hotels and shops displaying a fascinating array of products from Japan.

You get there by taking the No. 38 (Geary Street) bus. The Center occupies three blocks bounded by Laguna, Fillmore, Geary and Post Streets. It is one mile west of Union Square.

Many of the shops and facilities here—including an academy which teaches Japanese flower-arranging, brush-painting, tea ceremony and calligraphy—are housed in three commercial buildings with staircases built around beautifully landscaped gardens. Two of these buildings are linked by the **Webster Street Bridge,** 135 feet long and lined with shops, a restaurant, a Japanese doll-making school and art galleries—including one that exhibits works from the Avery Brundage Collection of Asian Art.

The **Miyako Hotel** (see our Hotels, above) offers traditional Japanese accommodations.

Kabuki Hot Springs, 1750 Geary Boulevard (tel: 922-6000), acquaints visitors with the pleasures of the traditional Japanese bath and shiatsu massage. Facilities include the furo (big tub), whirlpools, saunas, steam cabinets, and showers. The works, including massage, is $18.

The hub of the Center is the 30,000 square-foot **Peace Plaza,** landscaped with Japanese gardens and reflecting pools. A graceful *yagura* (wooden drum tower) spans the entrance to the Plaza, and its focal point is the five-tiered, 100-foot-high **Peace Pagoda.** Designed by world-famous Japanese architect Yoshiro Taniguchi, the Pagoda was a gift of friendship and goodwill from the people of Japan. Atop the highest tier is the *kurin,* a nine-ringed spire symbolizing great virtue. The Pagoda is illuminated at night, and an eternal flame, brought from the Sumiyoshi Shrine in Osaka, burns above the reflecting pool.

Recently, Buchanan Street between Post and Sutter was turned into another mall area. Here shops and flowering plum trees line a cobblestone walkway designed to resemble a meandering stream. The mall is graced with two fountains by Ruth Asawa.

The Center is also the scene of numerous Japanese festivals and events. These include: **Sakura Matsuri** (Cherry Blossom Festival), held for seven days in April; **Aki Matsuri** (Fall Festival), in late September; **Tanabata** (Star Festival), held the weekend closest to July 7th; **Bon Festival,** a Buddhist celebration held one or two days in mid-July, its high point being a community dance with 500 costumed dancers; and the **Mochi-Pounding Ceremony,** held one Sunday in the latter part of December, an unusual event that culminates in the making of rice cakes. Colorful occasions, these are often beautifully costumed affairs with music, dance, demonstrations of everything from martial arts to doll-making and flower-arranging, and exhibits ranging from bonsai trees to dog shows.

In addition to festivals, programs featuring traditional Japanese entertainment and activities are held each Saturday afternoon, beginning at 1:30, from June through September.

FISHERMAN'S WHARF AND VICINITY: Take the Hyde and Beach cable car from Powell and Market Streets to the end of the line. Disembark at **Victorian Plaza,** a gaslit replica of a turn-of-the-century park that is the center of ocean-oriented activities stretching from the Maritime Museum at the western edge of Aquatic Park to the *Balclutha* moored at the eastern end of the Wharf.

Rows of fishing boats, fresh-seafood stalls and restaurants, fishermen mending nets and unloading catches, and similar scenes create a festive atmosphere. People jam the area, browsing through the street stalls selling handmade jewelry and craft items, and there are any amount of street musicians, puppet shows, magicians, ventriloquists, even an automatic human jukebox—deposit a coin, a flap lifts and out pops a man's head, a trumpet and the requested tune.

About 3 a.m. every morning, the fishing fleet sails out through the Golden Gate—a very picturesque sight if you happen to have insomnia. In the afternoon, the boats return and sell their catch to the stalls and restaurants. That's the time to buy a paper cup of crab or shrimp cocktail (usually about $1). However, no need to sustain yourself on snacks—there are about 20 restaurants to choose from, including one founded by "Yankee Clipper" Joe Di Maggio at 209 Jefferson Street.

But eateries are just part of the Wharf's attractions. Here are some others you won't want to miss:

Museum of the World of the Unexplained

This fascinating and unusual museum explores the mysteries that have puzzled man from the beginning of time, from primitive man's superstitions to today's renewed interest in the occult. You'll see experiments in ESP, exhibits on flying saucers, the Bermuda Triangle, the prophecies of Nostradamus, Aztec human sacrifices, voodoo and alchemy. A disembodied head will address you, and you'll see a tiny skull which appears to be resting on a column—until you try to touch it, at which point your hand goes right through the skull.

Many of these mystifying tricks and props are on sale at the museum shop. The museum is open seven days a week. Summer hours are 9 a.m. to 11 p.m., till midnight on Friday and Saturday; winter hours are 10 a.m. to 10 p.m., also until midnight on Friday and Saturday. Admission is $3 for adults, $1.50 for children. The price of your ticket is also good for admission to our next listing.

Ripley's Believe It or Not Museum

This unlikely compilation of exhibits from the Ripley arsenal (at 175 Jefferson Street) includes the world's smallest violin; a shrunken head from Ecuador; a replica of "Man of Chains" (an ascetic who, clothed in 670 pounds of chains, dragged himself through the streets of Lahore, India as an act of self-mortification); the Lord's Prayer on a grain of rice, and so on. Open Sunday through Thursday from 9 a.m. to 11 p.m.; Fridays and Saturdays 9 a.m. to midnight.

Balclutha

At Pier 43, Fisherman's Wharf, lies the *Balclutha,* a typical British merchant ship of the late Victorian period. Launched in Scotland in 1886, *Balclutha*'s maiden voyage was around Cape Horn to San Francisco. During her early trading years, she rounded Cape Horn 17 times carrying rice, wine, hardware, nitrate and wool. In 1899 she was put under the Hawaiian flag carrying lumber from Australia and coal from Newcastle, and in 1902, under the Stars and Stripes, began a new career in the Alaska salmon trade.

Wrecked in 1904, she was refitted and renamed the *Star of Alaska.* By 1930, when she made her final voyage north, she was the last square-rigger left in the salmon trade. From here the old girl went Hollywood—renamed the *Pacific Queen,* and used as a background for motion pictures. But by 1954, she had had it. Plans were afoot to dismantle the old vessel, when she was bought by the San Francisco Maritime Museum Association and restored to her original name and state.

Today she enjoys yet another incarnation as a playground for nautical-minded youngsters, who can spin her wheel, squint at the compass and climb into the foc's'le. The hull contains an exhibit of windjammer lore and some fascinating exhibits of the old Barbary Coast.

Visiting hours are from 9 a.m. to 11 p.m. daily. Admission is $2 for adults, $1 for children 12 to 17, free for kids under 12 accompanied by an adult. Admission includes a recorded tour.

San Francisco Maritime State Historic Park

More historic ships are docked for inspection at Hyde Street Pier, near Ghirardelli Square. They include the *C.A. Thayer,* a wooden-hulled, three-masted schooner, designed and built to bring lumber to rapidly developing turn-of-the-century California cities; the *Wapama,* a wooden-hulled steam schooner built in 1915, designed to replace the likes of the *Thayer;* the *Eureka,* a 78-year-old paddle-wheel ferryboat; the *Alma,* the last remaining San Francisco Bay scow schooner; and the *Hercules,* a huge ocean-going steam tug built in 1907.

Ships can be boarded from 10 a.m. to 6 p.m. daily. Admission for all the ships is 75¢ for adults, 25¢ for children.

The Enchanted World of San Francisco

This kid-pleaser at Mason and Jefferson Streets is a tunnel ride (via miniature cable car) through the history of San Francisco from the Gold Rush to the 1915 Panama-Pacific Exposition. You travel past 14 scenes and 150 animated characters. Open daily in summer from 9 a.m. to midnight; till 10 p.m. in winter. Admission is $1.50 for adults, 75¢ for kids six to 12, under six free.

The Wine Museum of San Francisco

Now something for us grown-ups. Up a short flight of steps at 633 Beach, the Wine Museum traces the history and development of wine. Most of the exhibits are from the Christian Brothers and Alfred Fromm collections—contemporary and historical wine-related works of art. Another major feature is the Sichel glass collection spanning nearly 2,000 years and including drinking vessels from the Roman era to the present.

Admission is free. Regrettably, there's no tasting room. The Hyde Street cable car goes right to the door. Open Tuesday through Saturday 11-5, Sunday 12-5.

Maritime Museum

Walking west along the shore from Victorian Plaza, in the opposite direction from the Wharf, you come to a modernistic building that looks like a huge ship at dock. Once the "Palace for the Public," a huge bathing casino, it now houses the treasure trove of sailing, whaling and fishing lore that makes up the Maritime Museum.

In addition to the finest collection of marine photography on the Pacific—over 70,000 pictures covering the whole subject of West Coast shipping from the Gold Rush to present day—the museum also has wonderful ship models, including a huge one of the *Preussen,* the only five-masted full-rigged ship ever built. Lining the walls are the wooden figureheads favored by the old windjammers, wrought-iron caps, truss bows and other examples of the shipsmith's art. The huge anchor of the man-of-war *Independence* towers above the visitor. There's much more—all extremely interesting.

The museum is open daily from 10 a.m. to 5 p.m. Admission is $1 for adults, 50¢ for kids ages 12 to 18. No admission is charged the first Saturday of every month.

Bay Cruises from the Wharf

One of the best ways to see San Francisco is to leave it—just for a while, to enjoy a short cruise around the bay. The following leave from Fisherman's Wharf:

Harbor Tours, Inc., 43½ Fisherman's Wharf (tel: 398-1141), offers a magnificent cruise around San Francisco Bay. The cost is $3.50 for adults, $1.50 for kids aged six to 12.

The Red-and-White Fleet (tel: 398-1141) runs a 1¼-hour tour, also starting from Pier 43½, aboard deluxe sightseeing vessels with a passenger capacity of 400-500. There are open-air decks and glass-enclosed lower decks, and a snack bar dispenses hot dogs, sandwiches, coffee and souvenirs. The round trip takes in the Presidio, Sausalito, Angel Island, Alcatraz, as well as many other sights, and passes under the Golden Gate and San Francisco-Oakland Bay bridges.

Frequent departures begin at 10 a.m. year round (weather permitting). Adults pay $3.25; juniors aged 12 to 17, $2.25, children five to 11, $1.25, under five free.

Gold Coast Cruises (tel: 775-9108) start at Pier 45. Their two-hour cruises follow a similar route to the above, but take in even more sights—and you can see them from the comfort of theater-loge seats within a glass-enclosed lower deck. There's an open-air deck, too, and a complete snack bar.

Daily departures at 10:30 a.m., 1 p.m. and 3:30 p.m. from Memorial Day through October. Adults pay $4, children five to 12 pay $2, and under-fives are free.

ALCATRAZ ISLAND: A mile and a half out from Fisherman's Wharf, the Bay's once grim bastion, The Rock, has emerged from over a century of isolation. Its history dates from 1775 when the island was discovered by a Spanish explorer who christened the place "Isla de los Alcatraces" (Island of the Pelicans) after its original inhabitants. When the Americans came, they drove off the birds, transformed the rock into a fortress, later an army prison, and finally into the nation's most notorious penitentiary.

The final transformation came in the '30s—America's gangster era—when the likes of John Dillinger and "Pretty Boy" Floyd seemed to bust out of ordinary jails with toothpicks. An alarmed public demanded an escape-proof citadel, and the federal government chose Alcatraz Island on which to erect it.

It seemed an ideal choice. The Rock was surrounded by freezing cold water, with currents strong enough to defeat even the strongest swimmers. At a cost of $260,000, the old Army cages were transformed into tiers of tiny, toolproof, one-man cells, guarded by machine-gun towers, heavy walls, steel panels and electronic metal detectors.

Stern prison rules included no talking, no canteen, no playing cards, no privileged trustees or inducements to good behavior. One of the prisoners said it was like living in a tomb. Into that "tomb" went Al Capone, "Machine Gun Kelly," "Doc" Barker, "Creepy" Karpis, and other big-time criminals. All were broken by Alcatraz, except those who died trying to escape.

But even though Alcatraz was successful in its intended purpose, in many ways it created as many problems as it solved. Its cells were intended to hold 300 convicts, and there simply weren't—happily—that many incorrigible heavies around. So more and more small fry (ordinary car thieves, burglars, forgers, etc.) were sent up just to maintain the population—petty crooks who could just as well have been sent elsewhere at a fraction of the cost. For the expense of maintaining Alcatraz was immense; by the 1950s the money required to keep a single inmate on The Rock could have housed him in a luxury hotel suite.

So when three inmates seemed to stage a successful escape, tunneling out with sharpened spoons (no trace of them was ever found, and likely as not they drowned), the federal government took the opportunity to order the prison "phased out." On March 21, 1963, the Rock's last inmates—27 pale men in wrist and leg shackles—were transferred to other federal penal institutions.

For the next ten years The Rock remained empty, inhabited only by a caretaker, his wife and an assistant. And for a while a protest group of American Indians took it over.

Then in 1973, the National Park Service opened it to the public, running conducted tours from the San Francisco waterfront. Today great numbers of visitors flock to see the island's grim cells and for   tions, to explore the main prison block with its steel bars, the claustroph   .ne by five feet) cells, mess hall, library and "dark holes" where recalcitrants languished in inky blackness. If you've ever had an urge to experience instant hysteria, the "deep six" is the place. Just ask the guide to close one of the steel-plated doors behind you.

To take the tour make reservations (phone 398-1141 and specify time and date) as far in advance as possible. Only 150 are taken on each tour, and there are always large groups of disconsolate standbys waiting on the windy pier.

The ferry leaves Pier 41 about every 40 minutes between 9 a.m. and 4:20 p.m. daily, bound for the 1½-hour guided tour of The Rock. The park rangers tailor their tours to individual groups, because almost everyone reacts differently on their first exposure to a prison haunted by the ghosts of so many notorious criminals. Most visitors *do* wish to experience being locked in a cell, for enough time to imagine what it was like for men who spent years—sometimes the majority of their lives—within these walls.

One exhibit displays military and prison artifacts along with photographs spanning the years of occupation.

Important note: Wear comfortable shoes and a heavy sweater or windbreaker—it can be very cold. And make sure the kids hit the rest rooms on the ferry going over. The only rest rooms on the island are at the landing, and once you start out on your 1½-hour hike, that's it.

The ranger-guided tour is free; round-trip ferry fare is $2 for adults, $1 for children five through 11, under five free.

GHIRARDELLI SQUARE: On the north waterfront, between Fisherman's Wharf and the Golden Gate entrance to San Francisco Bay, is Ghirardelli Square—a streamlined beehive of terraces, shops, theaters, restaurants, cafes and other diversions.

Originally a chocolate factory built by an Italian immigrant, Domingo Ghirardelli, the property was set on 2½ acres which included the old Woolen Mill Building. When, in the early '60s, the chocolate company decided to sell the plant and relocate, a group of prominent San Franciscans, fearing the site might be acquired for high-rise office buildings, purchased the property with the idea of converting the fine old buildings to a contemporary use. A talented group of architects, landscape artists and designers was hired to restore and transform the factory to the entertainment center that it is today.

There are about 15 eateries in the complex, among them an authentic Delhi/Bombay-based Indian establishment that only recently opened branches in the United States (**Gaylord's**), as well as excellent Chinese (**The Mandarin**), Japanese (**Ginza Suehiro**) and Mexican (**Señor Pico**), restaurants. Our personal favorite is the one called **Ghirardelli Chocolate Co.**, a manufactory and soda fountain where you can watch chocolate being made and purchase the rich results at the candy shop. The soda fountain dispenses irresistible and gooey sundaes—like the "Golden Gate Banana Split" ($1.85), which has a base of three flavors of ice cream topped by three syrups and a banana bridge rising above great gobs of whipped cream.

Here, too, there's a cinema, a Japanese art gallery and over 50 shops where you can buy or browse through Persian rugs, Dutch imports, kites of all nations, handmade Greek pottery, hand-sculptured glass items, music boxes, Japanese cultured pearls and much more. There's something for everyone. And, as at the Wharf, street entertainers are out in profusion.

During the summer, Ghirardelli Square is open Monday through Saturday from 10 a.m. to 9 p.m., 11 a.m. to 6 p.m. on Sundays. The rest of the year it's open 10:30 a.m. to 6:30 p.m. Monday through Thursday, 10:30 a.m. to 9 p.m. Friday and Saturday, and Sundays 11 a.m. to 6 p.m.

Want some more of the same? Proceed to a newer version of the above formula, known as—

THE CANNERY: The defunct Del Monte produce plant, two blocks to the east of Ghirardelli Square, made an equally dramatic comeback as The Cannery in 1967. Attorney Leonard V. Martin, obviously inspired by what could be done with a chocolate factory, acquired the pre-earthquake Del Monte cannery at the foot of Columbus Avenue in 1962 and gave it a multimillion-dollar face lift. A great effort was made to preserve The Cannery's early San Francisco exterior of weathered sienna brick with arched entrances and windows. A flower-filled courtyard with gnarled olive trees was added, and this became the setting for much entertainment, both organized and impromptu, including The Cannery's star street performer, a sprightly character called Toad the Mime.

The centerpiece of this three-story compound is the Ben Jonson Restaurant, its interior a 100-foot-long gallery that was originally part of the mansion built by Queen Elizabeth I for her ambassador in France. Of course, there are the requisite number of boutiques and restaurants packed into the complex.

When you're ready to leave, just hop a cable car at the corner of Hyde and Beach or Bay and Taylor; both lines return to Union Square.

EMBARCADERO CENTER: Yet another area for leisurely strolling and browsing is the Embarcadero Center, situated in the financial district on 8½ bayside acres between Wall Street West and the Ferry Building. The hub of activity is just outside the **Hyatt Regency** (be sure to check out the lobby while you're here). Noon is the best time to go—that's when all the street merchants have their stalls set up to catch the lunchtime trade. Most feature handmade items—leather goods, macrame, copper-enameling, jewelry—and sometimes even paintings and sculpture.

You can stop at the Hyatt's outdoor cafe for rest and refreshment. Then continue strolling about and take in the **Vaillancourt Fountain** (made of 100 concrete boxes), as well as the many sculptures scattered throughout the area. These range from a three-foot Bufano bear to an eight-story steel abstract by Willi Gutmann. Many Bufano animals are situated on the open deck of the **Alcoa Building,** from whence you can cross one of the pedestrian bridges to the **Golden Gateway,** a $150-million waterfront renewal program of townhouses, apartments, shops, courtyards and fountains.

GOLDEN GATE PROMENADE: Opened in 1973, this 3½-mile shoreline footpath, providing access to the Presidio and Fort Mason, has been called the most spectacular walk in the United States. Approach is from **Fort Point** —built in 1863 to protect San Francisco from the Confederate Army (made quite a success of it, too!). Now it's a military museum, open from 10 a.m. to 5 p.m. daily, and free guided tours are offered.

From Fort Point you meander along a rocky beach, past the fishermen at Fort Point dock, past the Coast Guard lifesaving station and on to a sandy beach beside Crissy Field Landing Strip. Further along: the decorative waterfront plaza of the municipal water treatment plant; the St. Francis Yacht and Marina breakwater: Fort Mason, and, finally, **Aquatic Park.**

En route you might consider exploring the **Presidio Army Museum** (open 10 a.m. to 4 p.m. Tuesday through Sunday), established in 1777 as a Spanish garrison. Now a 1,500-acre headquarters for the Sixth Army, it is a center of historical research, housing artifacts and memorabilia from the Presidio's past. A second detour might be the **Palace of Fine Arts,** with its Exploratorium (details coming up).

The easiest way to begin this walk is to board a Golden Gate transit bus from Market and Seventh or from one of its stops along Van Ness Avenue, and get off at the bridge toll-gate plaza. To return, simply hop the cable car at its turntable in Aquatic Park.

GOLDEN GATE PARK: Now the largest manmade park in the world (three miles long by a half-mile wide), Golden Gate is a far cry from the windswept wasteland of rolling sand dunes acquired by San Francisco back in 1868. The original plan was for a great public park to compare with the one then being developed in New York by Frederick Law Olmsted. Mr. Olmsted was invited to look at the proposed site and he declared it hopeless. But year after year, park superintendent John McLaren (an indomitable horticulturist and forester whose motto was "trees and more trees") continued planting trees and shrubs, gradually taming the shifting sands. When he died in 1943, after 56 years of service, the park was an unbroken expanse of forest and glen, green lawns, bridle paths, lakes and flowers.

You reach Golden Gate Park by taking a No. 38 bus on Geary Street to 10th Avenue then changing to a No. 10, which lets you off at the **Music Concourse,** where band concerts are held nearly every Sunday and holiday afternoon. (Other musical events—Broadway shows, jazz, country music, operas, ballets, etc.—take place on summer Sunday afternoons at 2 p.m. in **Stern Grove,** Sloat Boulevard near 19th Avenue; admission is free.)

Not far from the Concourse nestles the **Japanese Tea Garden**, created in 1894 for the California Midwinter International Exposition, and kept on as a permanent attraction. Entered through a hand-carved gateway, it's an enchanting five-acre Oriental garden of bamboo-railed paths, bonsai trees, rock creations, reflecting pools filled with goldfish, pagodas, torii statues and Oriental art objects including a Japanese bronze Buddha that dates from 1790. There's a Japanese tea house where kimono-clad waitresses serve aromatic blended teas. If you come in late April, you'll see the cherry blossoms in bloom, not just in the Tea Garden but throughout the park; Japan recently donated 700 cherry trees to the Golden Gate as a Bicentennial gift.

Near the tea garden is **Stow Lake**, where you can rent a rowboat or peddleboat for a leisurely ride to the island in the center of the lake. The area near the lake is ideal for picnicking.

Other notable park features include:

The **Conservatory**, Main Drive near Arguello Boulevard, with tropical plants and a continuous flower show in bloom.

The **Strybing Arboretum**, South Drive at 9th Avenue, open from 8 a.m. to 4:30 p.m. (10 a.m. to 5 p.m. weekends and holidays), which covers almost 70 acres and has in its collection over 5,000 species of plants, trees and shrubs.

The **M. H. De Young Memorial Museum**, the **California Academy of Sciences**, and **Asian Art Museum** (about which more later in this section).

The **Golf Course** (next to the archery field), a nine-hole course for which no reservations are required. Weekday green fees for non-residents are $1.75 for the first round, 75¢ for a second round. On weekends and holidays it's $2 a round.

And then there are football and baseball fields, soccer pitches, bowling greens, tennis, handball and basketball courts, horseshoe pits, bicycle, equestrian and hiking trails, track facilities—even a vast enclosed pasture (near John F. Kennedy Drive) where herds of buffalo roam. What's more, you can picnic anywhere in the park.

The best way to navigate the park is on a bicycle; shops at 640 and 672 Stanyan Street, at the east and west entrances to the park, respectively. Both charge $1 per hour rental fee weekdays, $1.50 weekends.

MISSION DOLORES: Founded in 1776, this was one of the original 21 missions established throughout California by Father Junipero Serra. The Mission (believed to be the oldest structure in San Francisco) was erected in what was then wilderness, the city later growing up around it. The name Dolores was taken from a nearby lake, long since filled. The architecture combines Moorish, Mission and Greek styles; the altar and decorations are from Spain and Mexico. Its adobe walls are four feet thick, its hewn roof timbers lashed with rawhide. There's a statue of Father Serra in the Mission garden, where many prominent pioneers are buried.

Open from 9 a.m. to 4:30 p.m. in summer, 10 a.m. to 4 p.m. from November through April. Admission is 25¢ for adults, free for children. You can reach the Mission by taking the "J" streetcar up Market Street to the corner of Church and 16th Streets, then walking back one block to Dolores Street.

SAN FRANCISCO ZOOLOGICAL GARDENS AND CHILDREN'S ZOO: Modeled after the innovative Hagenbeck Zoo at Sellingen near Hamburg, the S.F. Zoological Gardens are one of the largest in the country, comprising over 95 acres. Most of the animals are kept in wonderfully realistic landscape enclosures, guarded by cunningly concealed moats. The zoo is home to over 1,000 animals and birds, including such rarities as pigmy hippos (about as large as a very overweight pig), musk oxen and some seldom seen gorillas.

You can take a motorized train tour of the grounds: adults ride for 60¢, children for 30¢. Open daily from 10 a.m. to 5 p.m. Admission is $1 for adults, 50¢ for children six to 16, free for kids under six. Unaccompanied kids under 16, however, pay $1.

Adjacent to the Zoological Gardens lies the **Children's Zoo**, a seven-acre glade dedicated to the pleasures of the young. Baby animals from the main zoo are raised here, and there are naturalistic trails to follow, barnyard and exotic animals to pet and feed. Admission is 25¢ for children 15 and under, 50¢ for adults. Open daily in summer from 10 a.m. to 5 p.m., and weather permitting the rest of the year.

To get to the zoo take the L streetcar from downtown Market Street to the end of the line.

WELLS FARGO HISTORY ROOM: Filling a large ground-floor area of the bank's headquarters, the History Room houses hundreds of relics and photographs from the Wells Fargo's whip-and-six-shooter days. The centerpiece is the Concord stagecoach, proudly identified as the Wells Fargo Overland Stage —the 2,500-pound buggy that opened the West as surely as the Winchester rifle and the Iron Horse.

There are samples of the treasure Wells Fargo carried—to wit, gold nuggets and coins from the fabulous Mother Lode mines—and mementoes of the men who were after it.

Open banking hours, 10 a.m. to 3 p.m., Monday through Friday. The Bank is located at 420 Montgomery Street at California. No admission is charged.

THE CABLE CAR BARN: Strictly speaking, this is the powerhouse and repair shop of the cable-car system, in full workaday operation. But at a cost of $250,000, the city's Public Utilities Commission has restored its original 1878 gaslight look, painted the interior in carnival colors, installed a spectators' gallery, and added a museum of cable-car relics that look like bits of Rube Goldberg machinery.

The quaint brick car barn stands at Washington and Mason Street. You can stand on the mezzanine gallery and watch the massive, groaning and vibrating winders thread the cable on which the car runs through a huge figure eight and back into the system via slack-absorbing wheels.

Among the displays are 57 exact scale models of all cars used on various lines and a fascinating stereopticon show of turn-of-the-century San Francisco (insert 25¢). You'll also see the granddaddy of them all—the first cable car, invented by Andrew S. Hallidie in 1873. At the centennial celebration in 1973, it actually rolled once more, tracing its original route and bearing the Mayor and other celebrities.

The museum is free; open from 10 a.m. to 6 p.m. daily.

THE EXPLORATORIUM: Housed in the Palace of Fine Arts, this mind-boggling museum is organized around the theme of perception. Over 400 exhibits on sight, light, color, sound and related subjects demonstrate, often dramatically, how human perception works. Almost all of the exhibits require visitor manipulation, button-pushing or tinkering, and this participation, of course, makes it lots of fun. It's an Alice-in-Wonderland world. You see a bust of a statue in three dimensions; try to touch it and it isn't there. Parrots move without moving. Another exhibit lets you design abstract art using sound.

Admission is free, though a contribution is suggested. Open Wednesday to Sunday 1 to 5 p.m.; also Wednesday evenings from 7 to 9:30 p.m. To get here, take the No. 30 bus on Stockton Street or the No. 2 bus on Sutter.

THE CALIFORNIA ACADEMY OF SCIENCES: At this famous complex of buildings, located on the Music Concourse in Golden Gate Park, you can view a Fijian cannibal fork, weigh yourself on the moon or join an Arctic Eskimo on a seal hunt. It's actually a cluster of widely differing museums. Taking them one by one, we have first:

The **Steinhart Aquarium,** home of more than 14,500 specimens of fishes from all over the globe, as well as invertebrates, amphibians, reptiles and aquatic mammals.

Morrison Planetarium, presenting seven different shows a year, exploring black holes, neutron stars, quasars, pulsars, UFOs and other puzzles of the universe. Exhibits in the **Astronomy Hall** and the **Hohfeld Hall of Space Science** further probe cosmic mysteries.

In the new **Wattis Hall of Man** the concept of ecological anthropology—how human societies have related and adapted to their environments—is explored. Exhibits deal with evolutionary history and creative responses of man to each of several environmental situations (arctic, temperate, tropical and desert), and displays range from gems, insects, birds and mammals native to North America and Africa, to pre-Columbian art and gastroliths from the stomachs of dinosaurs.

The California Academy of Sciences is open daily from 10 a.m. to 5 p.m. (9 a.m. to 9 p.m. in summer). Admission is 50¢ for adults ages 18 to 64; 25¢ for those 12 to 17; all others admitted free. Planetarium shows are $1.50 for adults, 50¢ for persons under 18. For further information and show times, call 752-8268.

M. H. DE YOUNG MEMORIAL MUSEUM: The grandaddy of California museums, the M. H. DeYoung Memorial had its origin in the California Midwinter International Exposition of 1894. At the end of the exposition, the Fine Arts Building was turned over to De Young, a newspaper publisher who had served as Director General of the fair, for the purpose of establishing a permanent museum.

Located on the Music Concourse of Golden Gate Park, the museum contains 200,000 square feet of exhibit area. Paintings, sculpture and decorative arts, as well as period rooms, illustrate the cultures of the Western world from the time of ancient Greece and Egypt to the 20th century. Various collections contain works of Fra Angelico, Goya, Rubens, El Greco, Van Dyck, Poussin and Rembrandt, among others.

The museum is open from 10 a.m. to 5 p.m. daily; admission is free.

THE ASIAN ART MUSEUM: Until recently part of the M. H. De Young Memorial museum, the Asian Art Museum houses the Avery Brundage collection of over 6,000 Oriental art treasures. The scope of the exhibits is dazzling, spanning some 60 centuries of Oriental history, beginning with the earliest Chinese bronzes, pottery and ceremonial objects, and extending through the great ages of Chinese art. One of the world's largest and most comprehensive

SAN FRANCISCO: SIGHTS & NIGHTLIFE

collections of jade is on display here. Arts of Iran, India, Afghanistan, Turkey, Syria, Tibet, Nepal, Pakistan, Korea, Japan and Southeast Asia are also well represented.

Frequent conducted tours are given daily and are highly informative. The collection is in a wing of the De Young Museum. Open 10 a.m. to 5 p.m. daily. No admission.

MUSEUM OF MODERN ART: The Museum of Modern Art, McAllister Street and Van Ness Avenue, opened at its present headquarters in 1935. It was avant-garde then, and it still remains a leader in the field.

Up-to-the-minute, the museum recently "documented"—by means of the artist's drawings and collages, slides, video presentations and photographs—the well-publicized and controversial installation of Christo's "Running Fence."

The permanent exhibits are strong on impressionism, surrealism and other major schools of the late 19th and early 20th centuries, including works by Dali, Picasso, Matisse and Monet. A wide range of Mexican painters is also represented.

A new floor of gallery space, opened in June of 1976, is devoted mainly to prints and photography. And an important new acquisition was the gift by Clyfford Still of 28 of his paintings.

In addition to permanent and changing exhibits, the Museum also organizes many artistic and cultural events. A film program, Tuesday and Friday nights and Sunday afternoons, presents contemporary and historical film classics (admission $1). In addition there are lectures, concerts, dance performances, poetry readings, conceptual art events and many activities for children.

Admission is free. Open Tuesday to Friday 10 a.m. to 10 p.m.; Saturday and Sunday 10 a.m. to 5 p.m. For further information on museum shows and events call 863-8800.

CALIFORNIA PALACE OF THE LEGION OF HONOR: Intended as a memorial for America's fallen of World War I, this beautiful museum is an exact replica of the Legion of Honor Palace in Paris, including the inscription "Honneur et Patrie" above the portal. Rising classically white and pillared from a hilltop, the building is Athenian in architecture, but the collection housed within is French, with special emphasis on the 18th and 19th centuries. Among the artists represented are Corot, Degas, Fragonard, Manet, Monet and Renoir. There's a comprehensive Rodin sculpture collection, as well as some splendid period rooms, like a Louis XVI salon.

Although the collection is all French, traveling exhibits range from contemporary Russian art to turn-of-the-century posters. And the museum runs a series of auxiliary attractions, such as classical music concerts on Sunday afternoons.

Location is in Lincoln Park. To get there take a No. 2 Clement bus from downtown Sutter Street to 33rd and Clement. Admission is 75¢ for adults, 25¢ for children 12 to 18, free for senior citizens. Open from 10 a.m. to 5 p.m. daily.

5. San Francisco After Dark

The Bay City is a great town for bars—plush bars, laid-back hangout bars, singles bars, Latin bars and neighborhood bars. Discotheques come in the same categories, and more.

There are enough quality theatrical, concert, ballet and operatic productions to sustain the most culturally minded visitor. And enough bare pulchritude on one North Beach block to sustain the most salacious.

Everything, in fact, for everyone. The gamut follows.

THEATER: The **American Conservatory Theatre (ACT)**, which made its San Francisco debut in 1965, has been heaped with praise, and even compared to the British National Theatre and the Comedie-Française. ACT offers solid, well-staged and brilliantly acted productions, with some emphasis on the classics, but offering a sufficient number of new and experimental works to keep its repertoire exciting and contemporary. A recent season, for instance, included *Desire Under the Elms, Equus, Tiny Alice, Merry Wives of Windsor,* and *Peer Gynt.*

Some plays are staged at the **Geary,** 415 Geary Street (on San Francisco's little theater row), others at the **Marines' Memorial Theatre,** 609 Sutter Street. Performances are simultaneous, not alternating, and telephone reservations for both theaters can be made by calling 673-6440. Tickets range from $5 to $7.50 for matinees (Wednesday and Saturday) to $6 to $9.50 for evening performances.

The Curran Theatre, another theater-row resident at 445 Geary Street (tel: 673-4400), concentrates mainly on musicals, often Broadway musicals coming from or going to New York. Recent productions included *A Chorus Line, The Wiz, Pacific Overtures,* and *The Baker's Wife.*

Tickets for matinees (Wednesday and Saturday) are $4.25 to $10.75; Monday through Thursday evenings, $4.25 to $12.75; Friday and Saturday nights, $5.50 to $13.75.

Little Fox Theater, 533 Pacific Avenue (tel: 434-4738). Once a fabulous motion picture palace with Wurlitzer organ rising from the orchestra pit and an elaborate rococo interior, the Little Fox borrowed some of the trappings and most of the atmosphere from the old days. The lobby contains all the furnishings from the ladies lounge!

The current owner of the theater is Francis Ford Coppola, who bought the place in 1975.

The Little Fox seems to specialize in long runs: after ages of *You're a Good Man Charlie Brown,* and six years of *One Flew Over the Cuckoo's Nest,* the Peanuts gang is back with *Snoopy,* which has been going since December of 1975.

Tickets are priced from $5.50 to $8.50, with a $1 discount to students. Fifteen minutes before curtain time, there is what is known as the "Student Rush," when tickets for students go for exactly half-price!

The On-Broadway Theatre, 435 Broadway (tel: 398-0800), once a meeting hall, is a gracious old building in the center of the Broadway morass of topless clubs. Light fare and musical revues are featured, and at the time of this writing, Jon Hendricks' very enjoyable *Evolution of the Blues* has been going for several successful years. Tickets are priced at $4.50 to $8.50, and drinks are available in the lounge.

Club Fugazi, 678 Green Street, near Columbus (tel: 421-4222), is not, strictly speaking, a theater. A 64-year-old North Beach landmark, it's more like a nightclub, with tiny candlelit tables, very high ceilings and a rotating mirrored globe overhead.

For about two years now, they have been presenting a fully orchestrated musical production that is so funny, original and utterly delightful we hope it runs forever. It's called, of all things *Beach Blanket Babylon Goes Bananas.* At this writing the Fugazi does not know how long the show will run, or what is next on the agenda. If you're lucky enough to catch *Beach Blanket* still going, don't miss it. And otherwise, hopefully the Fugazi will be replacing it with something of equal quality.

Shows are at 8:30 p.m. Wednesday and Thursday nights (tickets $5); 8:30 and 11 p.m. Friday and Saturday nights ($6); and Sunday nights at 7:30 ($5). One-price tickets mean first-come, first-served seating.

OPERA, SYMPHONY AND BALLET: San Francisco's magnificent **War Memorial Opera House**, built in 1932, is the focal point for most of the city's classical music productions, and the quality of the performances is on a par with those you might see in New York or London. The trouble is getting tickets. The ten-week opera season, beginning in September, is just too short for everyone to get tickets—even at prices ranging from $6 to $25. It's a good idea to get your name on the mailing list before your trip and order tickets in advance. To do this write to Opera Box Office, Opera House, San Francisco 94102. For phone reservations (lotsa luck) dial 431-1210.

The **San Francisco Opera Company** is actually a five-part company, with each branch offering something a little different from the others. They include:

The **San Francisco Opera Company** itself, which features celebrated guest stars like Joan Sutherland and Dorothy Kirsten. Staging and direction are a wonderful blend of traditional effects and avant-garde innovations. The company has presented 18 U.S. premieres by composers such as Richard Strauss, Britten and Shostakovich, and provided American opera debuts for the likes of Birgit Nilsson, Leontyne Price and Renata Tebaldi.

The **Spring Opera Theater** produces contemporary operas and standard works, inclining strongly to performances in English and fresh approaches to staging and interpretations. It provides a showcase for many young professionals in a recognized opera company. Housed in the Curran Theatre, 445 Geary Street (tel: 673-4400), the Spring Opera Theater has a short season, just three weeks in April. Ticket prices are reasonable.

Western Opera Theater offers top-quality "street opera" in English to low-income communities around the country—a feat made possible by the mobility of its specially designed portable stage and lighting equipment. In May, at the end of its road tour, the company's entire repertoire is repeated at the Palace of Fine Arts, Bay and Lyon Streets. Admission is $1 per person; tickets go on sale about three weeks before each performance. Call 861-4074 for ticket information.

The **Brown Bag Opera** offers 40-minute noontime productions geared to the typical lunch hour of office and factory workers. Audiences are encouraged to bring a lunch (or purchase one at the auditorium) and eat during the performance. The series is designed to offer opera at a minimal cost (50¢). Performances are held in varying locales; call 431-1210 for information.

The fifth part of the San Francisco Opera Company is the **Merola Opera Program,** which selects 15 to 20 audition finalists to participate in a ten-week period of performance and study, including a full-scale performance at Stern Grove during the summer.

Also based in the Opera House is the **San Francisco Symphony Orchestra,** currently in its 66th annual season, which lasts from December to May. This nationally admired ensemble is the cornerstone of the Bay City's cultural life. Once again, tickets are somewhat limited because of heavy subscriptions, so it's good to purchase in advance. Tickets are sold at symphony box offices in the

Opera House (tel: 431-5400) or at Sherman Clay & Co., 141 Kearny Street (tel: 781-6000).

The San Francisco Symphony also plays for the **Pops Concerts,** a nine-concert series conducted by Arthur Fiedler, in the Civic Auditorium, Civic Center, during July and August.

In summer you can enjoy the Symphony while sitting under the trees at Stern Grove, 19th Avenue and Sloat Boulevard, during the **Midsummer Music Festival.** The season opens mid-June and consists of ten programs comprising jazz, ballet, symphony, musicals, etc., on Sunday afternoons. No charge for performances.

And to round things out, in November the Symphony's **Chamber Orchestra** presents a two- to three-week series in various concert halls. Tickets at the Opera House symphony box office.

The **San Francisco Ballet** troupe is the oldest in the United States, and many say it is the best. It has two principal seasons: from December to February and during the spring, beginning in late May. Usually performances are at the Opera House, but sometimes they're elsewhere. Call the Opera House or Sherman Clay Box Office for information.

COCKTAILS IN THE SKY: A good place to "get high" prior to an evening on the town, or after one, is at any of the city's plush skyline bars. Most stay open till about 2 a.m.

The loftiest is the **Carnelian Room,** 779 feet up, on the 52nd floor of the Bank of America building, 555 California Street. It's open for dinner (about $14) and cocktails nightly, and neither hills nor high-rises interfere with its glorious outlook.

The plushest, however, is the Fairmont Hotel's **Crown Room,** 29 stories up. It's reached by the "Thermometer," a glass-enclosed elevator which glides up and down the tower's east side. (Acrophobics can avail themselves of an inside lift.) The center section of the room is on a slowly revolving platform, furnished with comfy tufted gold-leather banquettes to sit on while you enjoy the panoramic backdrop. Sunday buffet dinners—featuring a different nation's cuisine each week—are $9.50. Drinks average $2.25.

Originally a private penthouse on the 19th floor of the Hotel Mark Hopkins, the **Top of the Mark** is a nostalgia-loaded cocktail lounge and a popular rendezvous spot for San Francisco's well-heeled denizens. Libations average $2.50.

The **Starlight Roof,** 21 stories skyward, at the Sir Francis Drake Hotel, Powell and Sutter Streets, throws in dancing to a combo along with the view. There's no cover charge, and you can trip the light fantastic from 9 p.m. until 1 a.m. Sunday through Thursday; until 1:30 a.m. Fridays and Saturdays. Regular mixed drinks are $1.50. A recent facelift here expanded the view by replacing the northwest wall with glass.

Henri's Room-at-the-Top—the top of the Hilton tower, that is—also has a band and a marble dance floor as well. The dance combo swings into action at 9 p.m. nightly, in a cage suspended above the dance floor; on fine nights the roof is rolled back for dancing under the stars. It's very elegant. A cover charge of $1.50 goes into effect at 9 p.m. Drinks average $2.25.

More skyline views at **The Penthouse** and **Victor's,** both on the 32nd floor of the St. Francis Hotel tower. The former is for drinks and dancing, the latter for delicious French dinners in an English library setting. The Penthouse has a three-piece combo playing mellow rock from 5 to 9 p.m. nightly; from 9:15 p.m. to 1:15 a.m. a really good rock band playing top-40 numbers. Hustle lessons are available. There's no cover or minimum and drinks are $2.75. Between Victor's and the Penthouse, there's a view of every area of the city.

And finally, there's **One Up** at the Hyatt on Union Square (35 stories), with an adjoining discotheque called **Inoui**; **The Veranda** on the 30th floor of the Union Square Holiday Inn; and the revolving **Equinox** at the Hyatt Regency.

FLOOR SHOWS AND DANCING: The most glamorous club in the city, drawing the biggest names, is without a doubt the Fairmont's **Venetian Room**. This is the kind of place where you might see Joel Grey, Peggy Lee, Tony Bennett, Jose Feliciano or Patti Page. The decor leans to heavy draperies and lots of gold in the color scheme, with scenes of gondoliers around the arches at one end. The cover charge varies from $10 to $15, depending on the artist appearing. Weeknights are usually less expensive. Drinks go for about $2.25.

The entertainment fare at **Sinaloa Cantina/Restaurant**, 1416 Powell Street, just off Broadway (tel: 781-9624) couldn't be more different from the above. A dark, candlelit Latin club, the Sinaloa dishes up Mexican food (quite good, too); after dinner, you can stay for the show without paying an extra thing. It takes place every Friday, Saturday and Sunday night—a complete Latin-style revue of dancers and singers. There's also a dance floor. No cover charge. Most drinks are $1.75.

DANCING TO LIVE MUSIC: For dinner, dancing and your first tango in Frisco, head for the **Tonga Room** in the Fairmont Hotel. Built around what used to be the hotel's swimming pool, the Tonga Room has a South Seas decor complete with thatch-roofed tables and a tropical storm bursting over the pool at random intervals. The band plays in the middle of a lagoon on a roofed barge, and dancing is on what was once the quarter deck of a three-masted schooner. Dinners are Chinese/Polynesian. No cover charge. Dancing begins at 9 p.m.

Live music for dancing—rock musicians, boogie blues bands and "uncrowned kings of jazz" (which means good unknowns)—is the nightly offering at **Slats**, just off Union Street at 3111 Fillmore. The enthusiastic crowd tends to be under 30. The decor is rustic, with milk-can bar stools and some unusual pictures that look like stained glass but are actually made of caulked wood. Open nightly from 6 p.m. to 2 a.m. There's a $1 cover charge every night and a one-drink (about $1.25) minimum.

Woodstock, 951 Clement Street, corner of 11th Avenue, alternates live music with the disco variety nightly from 7 p.m. to 2 a.m. The ambience is of the flashing-lights school, the crowd is youngish (21-30) and the music is top-40s. Dancing begins nightly at 9 p.m.; Friday and Saturday nights there's a $1 cover and a one-drink minimum per set (about $1.25).

Just across the street, at 950 Clement, is **Jolly Friars**, a larger operation centered around a circular open-hearth fireplace with a big copper flue. It's a very warm and comfortable setting, with wood-paneled and stone walls, stained-glass windows, large wine casks over the bar, a peaked ceiling with slatted beams and lots of seating around the fire. The crowd (in the 21-35 age group) is mellow, the music top-40s and featuring groups with names like Post Raisin Band. There are some pinball machines and electronic games here, too. Music begins nightly at 9 and goes to about 2 a.m. No cover or minimum weeknights; Friday and Saturday, $1 cover and two-drink minimum.

DISCO DANCING: Boasting the biggest elevated dance floor in Northern California, **Broadway Power and Light Co.**, 688 Broadway, between Columbus and Stockton, is very dark and very loud. Whatever is "in" is what "J.J. the D.J., the boogie man from New York" is going to be playing. He'll be handling the usual lighting effects, too. If you work up an appetite on the dance floor, you can get anything from a full meal to a sandwich or tacos. Mixed drinks are $1.50 and there's no minimum. Open nightly from 7 p.m. to 2 a.m. Admission is $1; Friday and Saturday nights, $2.

Probably the most popular disco in town is **Dance Your Ass Off,** at 901 Columbus, where the light show ($40,000 worth of equipment) is dazzling, the floor pulsating with bumping, bobbing, boogeying bodies. The philosophy here is to keep up a frenzied excitement at all times—an atmosphere that is helped along by the mixed bag of San Francisco types who patronize the place—whites, blacks, Chicanos and a sprinkling of celebs and androgynous types. It's not a place for the uptight—the crowd and dancing are of the hang-loose, no-inhibition variety. The action begins nightly at about 10:30.

Much more intimate is **Disco 2001,** named not for the famous movie, but for its location at 2001 Union Street, corner of Buchanan. Candlelit, with exposed brick walls, 2001 has a bit of European ambience (owners are from Germany and Switzerland), and caters to a mellow late-20s to mid-30s age group. In addition to the requisite disco tunes, the D.J.s here occasionally throw in a Jacques Brel or Aznavour selection. A large screen projects TV programs with no sound, another screen features a changing slide show—these in addition to the standard light show effects.

Upstairs, there's a very attractive steak restaurant, the **Mother Lode,** with exposed brick archways and wood-paneled walls, where entrees, including home-baked bread and salad bar selections, cost $4.50 and up. There's also a backgammon room upstairs, which you can use even if you don't have dinner.

Disco 2001 is open from 8 a.m. to 2 p.m.; Friday and Saturday nights there's a $1 cover.

The walls of the **Pierce Street Annex,** at 3148 Fillmore Street, off Union, are lined with caricatures of local customers expressing risqué (actually they're downright dirty) sentiments in balloon captions. Open till 2 a.m. nightly, the Annex is always mobbed with wall-to-wall singles of the up-and-coming-executive, advertising-agency variety. The rock music is a little mellower than at some other places. There's no cover, but there is a one-drink minimum (average drinks are $1.25).

More of the same types hang out at **Ripples,** One Embarcadero Center, a disco bar where the singles scene is in full force and it's very easy (hard not to) connect with attractive members of the opposite sex. At this writing Ripples is about to undergo a total transformation in decor so we won't describe, but they will keep one unusual item, which men can see for themselves in the men's room. Dancing begins nightly at 8 p.m., and the music is good hard rock.

The poshest disco in town is **Alexis,** a basement hideaway at 1001 California Street, across from the Mark Hopkins Hotel. The decor is medieval, with Russian tapestries, mounted hunting trophies and zebra skins on the walls, and a large fireplace. This is *not* the kind of place you go in your faded jeans—evening gowns are more like it, and men arriving without ties or jackets will be given same and expected to keep them on. Surprisingly, for all the plush private-club Nob Hill ambience, there's no cover charge or minimum. The music is pretty-good-quality rock, though they occasionally do a little Frank Sinatra or Tony Bennett. A very attractive blonde D.J. in an evening gown will take requests, and also teach the hustle if asked. For a change of pace, go through the door to the elegant cocktail lounge, where a chanteuse, strolling violinist and pianist entertain in elegant surroundings.

Alexis is open Friday and Saturday nights only, from 10 a.m. to 2 a.m. Drinks are $2.50.

PUBS AND BARS: To begin with the unusual, there's **Edinburgh Castle**, 950 Geary Street, near Polk, a Scottish pub complete with live bagpipe music on Friday and Saturday nights. On Tuesday nights Highland dancers add to the atmosphere. The front window is filled with Guardhouse collectables, Scottish coats of arms hang from the ceilings, the bartender is from Edinburgh, and the juke box is heavy on Scottish airs. Of course there's a dart board, and the fare is the likes of fish and chips ($2) with Scottish draft beer (65¢ a half-pint) to wash it down. It's lots of fun, open till 2 a.m. nightly.

For sardine-packed singles action, there's no place like **Perry's**, 1944 Union Street at Buchanan. The clientele includes many over-30s and tends to successful lawyers, businessmen, stewardesses—what New Yorker's would call an Upper East Side crowd. There are several dining areas (the bar action is up front) all very charming with accoutrements like blue-and-white-checked tablecloths, candlelight, brick flooring, ivy climbing the walls and hanging plants. Posted menus list simple fare like hamburgers (they're good) for $2.95 and beef stew for $3.50. On the walls are framed newspaper clippings of events like the moonwalk, movie posters and other memorabilia. Drinks are priced from $1.20. If you don't meet anyone you can always browse through magazine-rack periodicals like *The Village Voice, New Yorker* or *Women's Wear Daily*.

Hip, laid-back and comfortable, **Spec's**, 12 Adler Place near the intersection of Broadway and Columbus, is more or less an artist bar. More or less, because the clientele is diverse, but that's always the case at artist bars. Glass-fronted cupboards are filled with San Francisco memorabilia and items given to Spec (who is usally behind the bar, by the way) by sailors who frequent the place. Unpredictability is the greatest asset of an evening here. Open from 4 p.m. to 2 a.m. nightly.

In a vaguely similar category is **Vesuvio Cafe**, 255 Columbus, between Broadway and Pacific, across the street from that famous haunt of the beat generation, the City Lights Bookstore. A note in Vesuvio's matchbook cover says: "The customers in this bar are entirely fictitious. Any resemblance they may have to actual persons is purely coincidental." We agree. On our last visit about half the customers were wearing weird greasepaint masks and sequins on their faces, and a few were in their underwear—but no one took any notice. The decor consists largely of paintings and photos of nude women, with stained-glass lights overhead. Drinks are a low 85¢, beer 50¢, and even cigarettes are just 50¢. Open 6 a.m. to 2 a.m., 365 days a year.

Low-key and comfortable is the ambience at **McGreevy's Fish Market**, 1981 Union Street off Buchanan. The interior is rustic, with wood-paneled walls, plank-wood floor, blue-and-white-checked tablecloths, bentwood chairs and the requisite number of plants and stained-glass lights overhead. The crowd is mid-20s to mid-30s, the jukebox good, and only premium booze is used in the drinks ($1.10 average). Seafood dinners ($4.95 to $6.95) are served 5 to 11 p.m., weekends till midnight. Open nightly till 2 a.m.

A perennial favorite, the inspiration for scores of imitators, is **Henry Africa's**, at the corner of Van Ness and Vallejo. Owned by a former French Legionnaire of the same name, this was the original Tiffany-lamped, hanging-ferned, stain-glassed, antique-filled San Francisco singles bar. And it's still the only one that has toy trains running around on tracks over the bar and portraits of Stanley and Dr. Livingstone on the wall. A campy jukebox runs from Nat King Cole to the Andrews Sisters. There's a restaurant in the back called **Doidge's.** Open from 11 a.m. to 2 a.m. daily, Henry Africa's is usually packed from six on. Generous drinks are priced at $1.25.

Almost identical in decor, and, in fact, the previous location of the above pub, is **Lord Jim's,** at 1500 Broadway near Polk. The crowd is the same, too—semi-affluent, semi-hip—but the atmosphere is a shade less frenetic. Owner "Spiro" is in the habit of presenting single roses to attractive women, which never fails to elicit a favorable response from those who merit the honor. One of the reasons for Lord Jim's popularity is the great booze—only premium liquors are used and the average drink is just $1, Irish coffee 75¢. It's also very comfortable. Open nightly till 2 a.m.

Menus are attached to cricket bats, and photos of cricket and rugby teams line the walls at **Thomas Lord's,** an English-style pub at the corner of Union Street and Buchanan. Popular and easygoing, Lord's best feature is its comfortable leather couches in front of a blazing fire. Popular and easygoing, this is an unfrenzied place to hang out and meet people. Open till 1:30 a.m. (except Sunday and Monday nights, when the doors close at 11:30), Lord's charges $1.10 for mixed drinks or bottles of English beer.

MOSTLY FOR MUSIC: For ambience, you can't beat the **Rusty Scupper,** 475 Francisco, between Mason and Powell, just a few blocks from Fisherman's Wharf. It looks like an elegant ski lodge, with high ceilings, natural wood walls hung with macrame, deep orange shag rugs, and enormous flourishing plants. The bar and bandstand are up a flight of stairs in a candlelit room with trees growing up to a skylight and comfortable chairs and couches around a woodburning fireplace. There's great folk rock on Wednesday through Saturday evenings, and sometimes new talent auditions Monday and Tuesday nights. Dinner is served downstairs; the menu printed on a wooden oar emphasizes steak and seafood entrees in the $6 range. Drinks are $1.25 to $1.55; no cover or minimum. Entertainment begins at 8:30 p.m

Dixieland fans flock to **Earthquake McGoon's,** 630 Clay Street, off Montgomery, where veteran trombonist Turk Murphy proffers the best New Orleans jazz in the west. We like to sit up in the balcony overlooking the stage amidst World's Fair memorabilia beginning with the 1876 Centennial. You can dance to the music, but most people just listen. In the basement is the **Magic Cellar** cocktail lounge, where the former property of a stage wizard called "Carter the Great" is on view, and magic shows are presented at regular intervals. The band plays Tuesday through Saturday nights from 9 p.m. to 2 a.m. There's a cover charge of $2, which admits you to both levels of entertainment. Drinks cost $2 and there's a two-drink minimum.

Somewhat misleadingly named, **El Matador,** 492 Broadway near Kearny, was once the property of Barnaby Conrad, the famous bullfighting author. The decor still retains a Spanish feel, but the music is provided by big-name jazz artists and groups—people like Mose Allison, Cal Tjader, Oscar Peterson, Cedar Walton and Kenny Burrell. Open Tuesday through Saturday from 9:30 to 2 a.m. A sliding cover (depending on who's appearing) ranges from $3 to $7. There's no minimum; drinks average $2.50.

The Coolidge-era decor at **The Red Garter,** 670 Broadway at Stockton, ranges from an eclectic selection of elaborately framed paintings from the '20s to Coolidge for President posters. The Red Garter Banjo Band, wearing traditional strawboaters and striped coats, produces music on strings, bagpipes, gut buckets, saws and washboards. Heaps of peanuts on every table; throw the shells on the floor. No cover or minimum except on Friday ($1) and Saturday ($1.50). Beer is $1.25 a stein, $4.25 a giant pitcher. Hard drinks are $1.75. Open nightly.

For serious listening to quality jazz, **Reunion**, 1823 Union near Laguna, is a Bay City favorite. Owner/manager Tony Lewis and his trio play occasionally, but the fare varies from Brazilian-Latin-salsa to big names like the Kai Winding Trio. Dancing is allowed, but most people just listen. The interior is attractive, with weathered barnwood walls, natural brick floor, old-fashioned globe chandeliers and Tiffany-style lamps overhead. Reunion is open till 2 a.m. nightly, with music going from 9 p.m. to closing. There's a one-drink minimum at all times ($1.25 to $1.75) and a $1 cover weeknights, $2 weekends.

Similar sounds and more barnwood walls at the **Last Day Saloon**, 406 Clement Street between 5th and 6th Avenues. The music runs the gamut of jazz, rock, folk rock, Latin and salsa. It's a pretty place with shag-carpeted floors, large pots of hanging plants, and flowers on the rough wood tables. When there are big names, like Jules Proussard—a well-known Bay area jazz saxophonist and flutist—there's a $1.25 cover; otherwise not. And there's always a one-drink minimum ($1.25). There's music Wednesday through Saturday from 9:30 p.m. to 1:30 a.m.

Bonnie Raitt, Blood, Sweat & Tears, Maynard Ferguson, Carmen Mac-Rae, Herbie Mann and Mose Allison are just a few of the performers who have played at the **Great American Music Hall**, 859 O'Farrell Street, between Polk and Larkin. The interior of this turn-of-the century building is a great open square under carved plaster cupids on the ceiling, with gilded mezzanine boxes supported by huge marble pillars. The cover runs between $4 and $7.50, depending on who's appearing. Snack food in the $2 to $4 range is available, beer is $1, mixed drinks $1.65. The Hall is open from 8 p.m. to 2 a.m., five to seven nights a week; this varies, so call 885-0750 before starting out.

A MIXED BAG: Warm and woody, with 80-year-old barnwood walls, **Holy City Zoo**, 408 Clement Street, between 5th and 6th Avenues, offers a mix of comedy and music. (There is, by the way, a place called Holy City, California, and the sign outside comes from the town's zoo.) On Monday nights anyone who so desires can audition—three songs or 15 minutes, whichever comes first. Tuesday is amateur night for comedians; Wednesday through Saturday professional musicians play—mostly folk rock and country rock à la Cat Stevens, John Denver, etc. And Sunday nights there are professional comedians. Open Wednesday through Sunday from 6 p.m. to 2 a.m.; Monday and Tuesday nights from 8 p.m. There's a one-drink minimum per set (drinks begin at 75¢) and a $1 cover if a well-known performer is appearing.

At **The Coffee Gallery**, 1353 Grant Avenue, between Green and Vallejo, entertainment varies from comedy to poetry, with an emphasis on music—blues, jazz and occasionally folk or country. There are usually art exhibits on the walls, too, and when we were last at the Gallery a conceptual show was in progress. Inexpensive soups, sandwiches and salads are available; beer is only 45¢ and wine 60¢. When there's a big-name performer, a cover charge of $1.50 is levied, and very rarely, a one-drink minimum. To find out what's happening call 397-3751. Open daily from 11:30 a.m. to 2 a.m.

Housed in a building that has been a speakeasy, a church, a theater, a Russian restaurant, a topless joint and a recording studio, **The Boarding House**, 960 Bush Street at Jones, is currently reincarnated as a nightclub/restaurant. Performers here have included Arlo Guthrie, Lily Tomlin, Ronee Blakeley, Esther Phillips and Patti Smith. Downstairs is a restaurant called **Magnolia**

Thunderpussy serving three entrees nightly as well as hearty sandwiches and homemade soups and desserts. There are two shows nightly at 9 and 11 p.m.; ll:30 on weekends. Admission is $3.50 to $5, and there's no minimum. Beer costs 75¢, wine starts at $1.

The most mixed of our mixed bags is the **Intersection**, a block above Washington Square at 756 Union Street. In the basement is a coffee house cum art gallery, while upstairs a theater showcases local acting groups. Theater groups perform Wednesday through Saturday, with "donations" ranging from $1 to $3.50. Sundays are set aside for funky films and "liberated" vaudeville, which cost $2, while Mondays are devoted to poetry in the coffee house and are free. Thursday nights comedians come to try out new material in the coffee house; Friday nights there are about ten professional comedians working down there; both nights the donation is $2. Open 6:30 to midnight seven nights a week.

PIANO LOUNGES: Ornately decorated in Gothic style with peach mirrors and lots of gilt trim, **Baron's Lounge**, corner of Powell and O'Farrell Streets, features a series of singers at the organ-piano bar. Drinks begin at $1.40, and Baron's is the home of the "Earthquake Special"—a potent $4 concoction of rum, vodka, gin, Hawaiian Punch, orange juice, pineapple juice, cream and brandy, among other things! Open nightly; music begins at 9 p.m.

The **Curtain Call**, 456 Geary Street, between Mason and Taylor, is less curlicued and more sophisticated. Located in the theater district, it catches not only the after-show crowd, but also various and sundry performers. The whole place has an exciting theatrical air, and audience contributions frequently have a professional touch. Sometimes well-known personalities—even Marlene Dietrich—have belted out a few numbers just for the fun of it. Needless to say, the Curtain Call is always packed. Open Monday through Saturday, the piano bar begins at 10 p.m. and keeps going till 2 a.m.

CHAMPAGNE DINNER CRUISES: During summer months, a lovely way to enjoy a lazy evening is on a cruise. Four Saturday night Bay cruises depart at 7:30 p.m. from Pier 43½ at Fisherman's Wharf. A price of $20 per person includes champagne, a hot buffet dinner and dancing to live music provided by a three-piece combo. Another choice is the Thursday night Tiburon cruise, same departure time and place, which costs $15 per person. There's a shipboard champagne party and dancing to live music en route to Tiburon, a full-course dinner at your choice of one of five Tiburon restaurants, and a romantic return cruise to San Francisco. For reservations contact **San Francisco Dinner Cruise Co.**, 1714 Stockton Street (tel: 391-2137).

Chapter III

AROUND SAN FRANCISCO BAY

1. Angel Island
2. Oakland
3. Berkeley
4. Muir Woods
5. Tiburon
6. Sausalito

WITH SAN FRANCISCO as your base, you can explore nearby areas that range from the vineyards of Napa Valley, to the ancient redwood forests, to sun-drenched missions and one of America's greatest universities. All these destinations—and many more—can be seen in day trips from San Francisco, and are reached in a few hours, at most, by car or public transport. We'll begin with some fascinating forays in and around San Francisco Bay, traveling counter-clockwise. In the next chapter, we'll investigate the Wine Country, and in Chapter V, we'll see what's to the south. First, then, a short and delightful excursion to:

1. Angel Island

Half the fun is getting there. **Red & White Ferries** (tel: 398-1141) make the trip from Pier 43 four times a day between 10 a.m. and 4 p.m., daily during summer and on weekends and holidays the rest of the year. Round-trip fares are $3.25 for adults, $1.75 for children five to 11, free for children under five.

This 730-acre island is a state park, popular for bicycling, hiking, fishing and picnicking. To get an overall view of the island, take the **Elephant Train** —a guided tour in an open-air coach that costs $2 for adults, $1 for children five to 11. Or rent a bike on the island and explore on your own. There are picnic sites with tables, benches, barbecues and restrooms at **Ayala Cove**, where you land, and at **West Garrison**. If you like hiking, 12 miles of trails lead you around the island and to the peak of **Mt. Caroline Livermore**, 776 feet above the bay.

One more possible activity: if you feel like digging in the dirt, know that it's rumored pirates and smugglers once hid treasures on the shores of Angel Island.

2. Oakland

The name Oakland derives from the oak groves in which the city's first homes were constructed in the mid-19th century. Today a sprawling industrial port town of 350,000 (the largest East Bay city), Oakland is no longer a few homes in the forest. But what the city lacks in charm is made up for in its many outstanding attractions.

First and most central, in the heart of downtown, is **Lake Merritt**, a 155-acre body of saltwater that is Oakland's favorite recreation spot. Part of the lake is a refuge for ducks and other waterfowl; in winter the bird count sometimes goes as high as 5,000, and birds banded here have been traced as far away as Siberia.

The lake is encircled by Lakeside Park, which is the setting for **Children's Fairyland.** Entered via the home of the "Old Woman Who Lived in a Shoe," Fairyland features over 60 nursery-rhyme rides and attractions, as well as puppet shows, magic shows, live animals, clowns, dancers, musicians and storytellers. It's open spring and fall from 10 a.m. to 5:30 p.m. Wednesday through Sunday, the same hours every day in summer, and 10 a.m. to 4:30 p.m. weekends only in winter. Admisson is 75¢ for adults, 50¢ for kids.

On the west shore of Lake Merritt you can rent rowboats, sailboats and canoes.

Adjacent to Lake Merritt, four blocks east of Highway 17 at 10th and Oak Streets, is the **Oakland Museum,** which opened in 1969. Its intended purpose is to document California's development through art, history, natural sciences and special exhibitions. The Gallery of California Art includes works ranging from the late 1600s to the most contemporary works by Californians. The Cowell Hall of California History exhibits the artifacts—clothing, tools, furniture, machines, etc.—that man used to shape his environment in the state from the Indian era to the present. Environmental and conservation themes are stressed in other galleries. The museum is open daily, except Monday, from 10 a.m. to 5 p.m. and Friday till 10 p.m. No admission is charged.

At the end of Oakland's Broadway lies **Jack London Square,** an area of landscaped malls, shipping wharves, marina docks and some of the city's finest restaurants and shops. The square is dedicated to the writer, a bust of whom overlooks the scene. At 50 Webster Street, about a block away, stands the **First and Last Chance Saloon,** built about a half-century ago from the remnants of an old whaling ship. London did some of his writing and much of his drinking

SAN FRANCISCO BAY

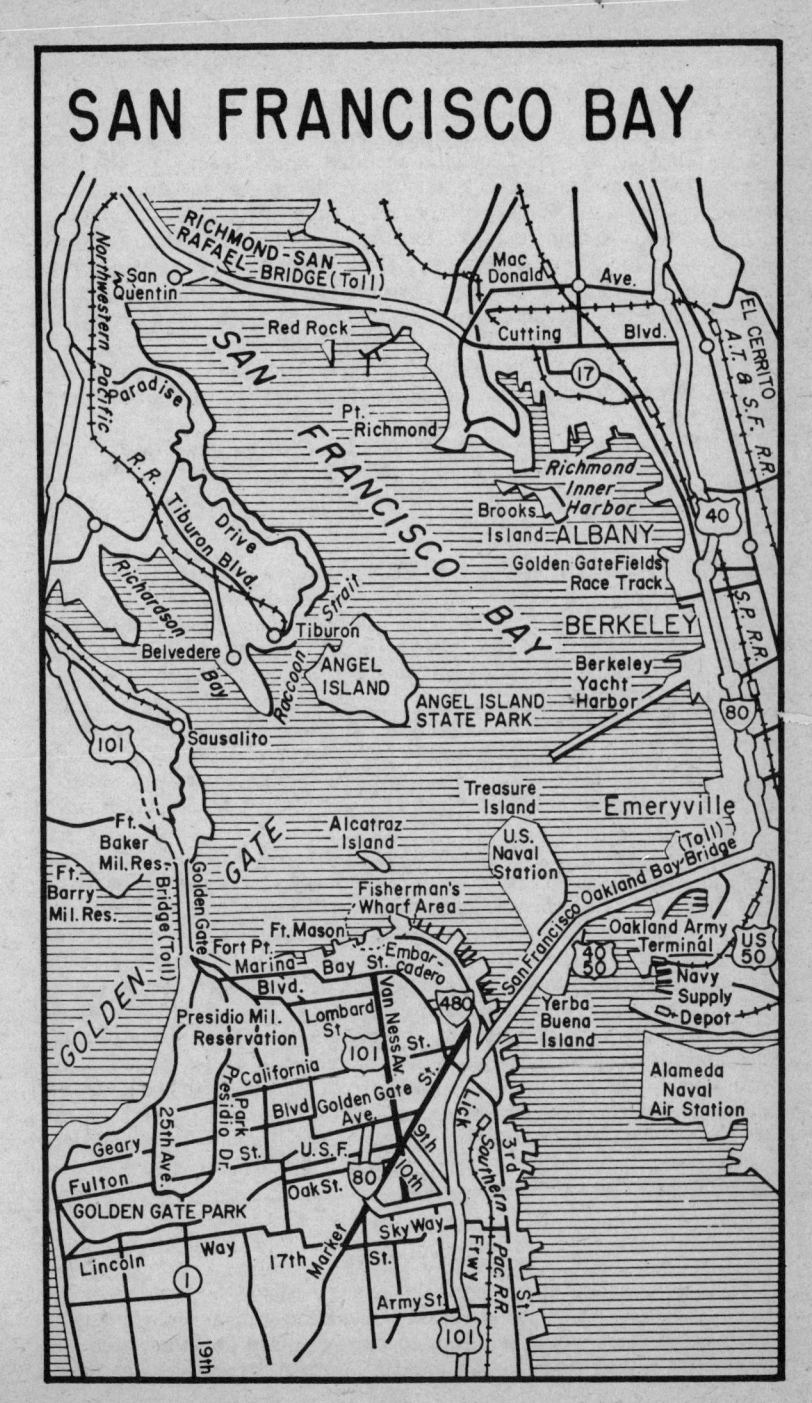

here (Robert Louis Stevenson is also supposed to have been a habitué). The corner table London used has remained as it was 60 years ago, and his photos and other memorabilia abound.

A very pleasant way to see Jack London Square is to take the **Champagne Supper Cruise** that sails from Clay Street Pier every Friday at 8 p.m., May through October. The cruise includes champagne and dancing on the boat, dinner at your choice among six restaurants in the Square, and time for some sightseeing. Cost is $12.50 plus tax and tips. Phone 441-5205 for reservations.

Oakland is also home to hundreds of birds, reptiles and mammals which roam freely in the 500-acre **Oakland Zoo** in Knowland State Park. For an overall view take the 1,250-foot-long chair lift that takes you high up over the African Veldt where animals graze in a natural setting. There's also a Baby Zoo where children can feed and pet nearly 200 animals.

For maps and more detailed information on Oakland's attractions, stop in at the **Chamber of Commerce** at 1939 Harrison Street, across the street from Lake Merritt.

To get to Oakland, you can drive over the Oakland Bay Bridge, take a direct bus from the Transbay Terminal (Mission and 1st Streets) for 60¢, or take BART from Powell Street to Oakland City Center (75¢).

OAKLAND RESTAURANTS: Because Oakland is a port city, many of her restaurants are along the shore, offering spectacular marine views and fresh seafood. Just such a place is the **Sea Wolf**, 41 Jack London Square (tel: 444-3456), named after the author's famous novel. One wall of windows affords a delightful view of the boat-filled estuary. Very romantic at night when piano music fills the air and tables are draped in white linen, adorned with fresh flowers and lit by brass candle lamps. Seafood entrees include a superb bouillabaisse served with hot garlic bread ($7.25). A complete dinner, including cheese dip, Boston clam chowder, sole meunière, vegetable, potato, strawberry shortcake and coffee, is just $6.50. Open 11:30 a.m. to 10 p.m. Sunday through Thursday.

Oakland also boasts a restaurant situated in a 3½-acre roof garden, the **Mirabeau**, 344 20th Street, on the third floor of the Kaiser Building (just across the street from the Chamber of Commerce). Very elegant, with gold draperies and tablecloths, this fine French restaurant looks out on an exquisite garden of flowering and leafy trees, petunias, foot bridges, floral beds and beautifully manicured lawns surrounding a large pond. Chef André Mercier is a well-known caterer for San Francisco society, and he has also cooked at the White House. Lunch is very reasonable here, with entrees like salmon quiche or trout amandine with potage or salad just $4. A complete $10 dinner might include pâté maison or quiche Lorraine, an entree of roast duckling with chestnuts and wild rice, a salad, chocolate mousse and coffee. A gourmet specialty is pheasant Vladimir ($19 for two) served in sour cream and vodka sauce with wild rice. Open for lunch weekdays from 11 a.m. to 2:30 p.m.; dinner Tuesday through Saturday from 5:30 to 10:30 p.m.

3. Berkeley

The compleat college town, Berkeley has achieved both fame and notoriety from its university, which has produced Nobel Prize winners and activists in about equal numbers. You're not likely to see any student riots these days, but you will see plenty of students—about 30,000 of them are currently enrolled.

Nestled in the Berkeley hills, the university's 720-acre campus and surrounding activities are the city's major attractions.

To get to Berkeley from San Francisco, take the bus from the Transbay Terminal (fare 60¢); it leaves every 15 minutes and goes right to the University. BART will also take you to Berkeley for a fare of 85¢.

The main drag here is **Telegraph Avenue,** lined with coffee shops, a wide variety of eateries, bookstores, head shops and the like. Currently, the three most popular student hangouts (subject to change any minute) are:

Larry Blake's, Telegraph Avenue at Durant, a mom and pop operation run by Larry and Leona Blake for close to 40 years. Students love the downstairs Rathskeller, dark and atmospheric, with pinball machines, foosball, a pool table and a very good jukebox. About ten kinds of hamburgers are available ($1.40 to $2.45), as well as more serious items like ratatouille provençale ($2.95), which comes with soup or salad, French bread and butter, beverage and ice cream. Liquor is also served here. Open from 11 to 2 a.m. Wednesday through Saturday, till midnight the rest of the week.

Kips, 2439 Durant (off Telegraph), abounds in student-hangout ambience and would probably not appeal to anyone over 25. The main floor features cafeteria service and lots of roomy wooden booths. The upstairs portion is dimly lit, with heavy beamed ceilings, a jukebox, unfinished butcher-block tables and a pervading pizza-booze aroma. Low-priced burgers and pizza are the principal fare, with beer and wine available. Open daily from 11 to 1 a.m.

Perhaps the most popular gathering place is **Oleg's,** 1974 Shattuck Avenue, off University, furnished with a Salvation Army assortment of comfortable chairs and couches leaning towards the tufted-red-leather look. Vaguely Victorian in feel, the decor consists of funk-and-junk antiques and paraphernalia: antique baby carriages, boots, mounted animal heads, musical instruments, old photographs and Mary Hartman lamps. In the back is a large room under a skylight roof—usually open in good weather—with a very colorful jungle scene painted on the walls. It all comes together to create a charming and comfortable hangout. Ibiza-type paella ($6.95) is the specialty, but the menu (as eclectic as the decor) also lists moussaka ($4.95) and a Mexican plate (both $4.95). The "Album of Libations," AKA wine list, is a complex affair, complete with old photos and elaborate descriptions of drinks. Oleg's is open from 11:30 to 2 a.m. daily.

The hub of student activities is where Telegraph Avenue runs into the University campus at **Bancroft Way.** Here you'll find student-run stalls selling jewelry, felafel, craft items or whatever. Right across from you is the **Student Union.** Go to the information desk on the second floor and get yourself a map of Berkeley, a local paper and a brochure outlining a campus walking tour, which you can take on your own or with a guide at 1 p.m. Monday through Friday; it's free and takes about 45 minutes.

Just off Telegraph Avenue on Durant stands the **Abbey Mall,** a shopping complex that opened in 1970 and contains an intriguing mixture of art, souvenir, gadgetry, knick-knack and bookstores to explore.

For Berkeley day and night doings, pick up the *Berkeley Barb* (25¢); it has reams of announcements concerning everything from documentaries on Tibetan Buddhism to folk concerts to chamber music, not to mention where to get an expert "French massage" and so forth.

Other than university-related activities, which can easily fill an entire day, you might want to visit the **Berkeley Marina Yacht Harbor,** a two-million-dollar aquatic sports development on the Berkeley shore of San Francisco Bay, where several hundred private boats and yachts are anchored. The fishing pier extends 3,000 feet into the Bay; it's open 24 hours daily, free to the public, with no license required. There are sandy beaches, picnic areas, trails and lookout points—mostly it's a lovely, tranquil place to be.

WHERE TO EAT: If you really want to get the feel of student life, you can eat on campus in the building directly behind the Student Union Building. The least expensive food is available downstairs in **The Cafeteria**, where lunch is served from 11:30 a.m. to 1 p.m. weekdays. Upstairs at **The Terrace** you can get breakfast, snacks and lunch. Also on this level of the building is the light and airy **Golden Bear Restaurant** with indoor and outdoor dining areas. The specialty here is hamburgers accompanied by salad-bar selections ($2).

At the **Lion of India**, 2438 Telegraph Avenue, turbaned owner Magh Singh forewarned, "We are all sick here." Visions of leprosy and plague passed briefly through our minds, and then we realized what he had actually said was, "We are all *Sikh* here." Relieved, we proceeded to enjoy an excellent shrimp curry ($3). Curry entrees—vegetable, chicken, lamb, etc.—are in the $2.25-to-$3.25 range, and include soup or salad, roti (Indian bread), rice and chutney. And desserts are much more interesting than the usual Indian-restaurant fare —like ice cream topped with gulabjamun (sweet milk balls in rose-water syrup) and whipped cream (85¢). Open seven days from 11 a.m. to 11 p.m.

At 2428 Telegraph stands **Don Paquin's Mexican Restaurant**, an unpretentious little eatery where you sit at long tables on colorful red, blue, yellow, pink and green wicker-seat chairs. The usual taco, tamale, enchilada combinations are in the $2.60-to-$3.75 range, the latter a veritable feast. All items are also available à la carte. Open 11:30 a.m. to 8:30 p.m. Monday through Saturday.

At 2393 Telegraph is **Darvish**, an exotic two-level establishment with a large and varied menu ranging from felafel ($1.65), Indian curries ($3.25 to $3.50) and shish kebab ($3.95), to a bacon, lettuce and tomato sandwich ($1.50) or hot shrimp with melted cheese on an English muffin ($2.50). Super, equally eclectic desserts include a hot fudge sundae ($1), baklava (65¢) and chocolate fondue with fresh fruit ($1.50). It's particularly nice to dine upstairs in the candlelit Tangier Room, seated on cushions at low tables. The ceiling is hung, tent-like, with Indian fabrics, the walls are patterned into minaret-shaped arches, and there's Middle Eastern music in the background. Open daily 11:30 a.m. to midnight.

Under the same ownership, and serving equally excellent food (both establishments serve homemade bread and desserts), is **Cafe de La Rue**, 2399 Telegraph. Provincial, with funky overtones, La Rue has terra-cotta floors, heavy wood-beamed ceilings, wood-paneled walls adorned with French art nouveau posters and some large graphics of cattle, and shelves of potted plants in the window. The cuisine is French, with a large sprinkling of other good things. Crêpes stuffed with various goodies are $1.55 to $2.95; Cornish hen glazed with orange, honey and saffron sauce, topped with crushed walnuts and served with rice, salad, fresh-baked bread and butter, is $3.75. Salads, sandwiches and desserts are all first-rate as well. Highly recommended. Open seven days from 9 a.m. to 11 p.m.

A few blocks from the campus hubbub is **Chez Panisse**, 1517 Shattuck Avenue, between Cedar and Vine (tel: 598-5525), an exquisite raw wood and stucco cottage entered via a brick terrace filled with flowering potted plants. The provincial interior is equally charming; downstairs the walls and peaked beamed ceiling are of redwood, with ivy entwined around the beams. A blazing fireplace, art deco lamps, brass candle holders and beautiful floral arrangements further enhance the decor. Upstairs the oak bar is adorned with potted plants a.m. to 11 p.m.; bar is open till 1 a.m. Sunday through Thursday, till 2 a.m. on weekends.

Yet another seafood-with-a-view eatery is **The Dock,** 25 Main St..., where you climb wooden steps hung with overflowing planters to the upstairs dining room. One wall is given over to a brick fireplace, which is lit if the weather warrants. Beneath the raised outdoor dining deck is a dock for yachts and other craft. From the deck and the window-walled dining room, you get terrific marine views. A complete dinner with an entree of coquille St. Jacques (a combination seafood plate laced with a light curry sauce) is $6.95. Weekdays The Dock is open for brunch, lunch and dinner from 11 a.m. to midnight; Saturday and Sunday it opens at 10 a.m. The Dock has an admirable policy of selling bottled wine at retail prices, without the usual restaurant mark-up.

Tiburon is liveliest on Sunday afternoons, when weekend boatmen tie up at the open docks of the waterside restaurants and there is much drinking, laughter and general conviviality. For over 50 years now, the traditional place to tie up has been **Sam's Anchor Cafe** at 27 Main, a long-lived tavern with two 110-foot piers and a large wooden deck which is filled to overflowing with blithe Sunday spirits from early on. There are two pianos on the premises on which customers work out occasionally, as well as three pinball machines and a pong machine. Sam's special is a casserole of filet of sole stuffed with crabmeat and baked in wine sauce ($5.95), served with soup or salad, and sourdough French bread and butter. Open daily from 10 a.m. to 10 p.m.; from 9 a.m. on weekends.

Another popular hangout is **39 Main,** named for its address. Warmly decorated with deep-red carpeting, wood-paneled walls and black leather chairs, 39 Main usually has a fire blazing at night. On Sunday afternoons from 3 to 8 p.m., and Monday nights from 8 p.m. to 1 a.m., there's a Dixieland band on the open deck. While you're enjoying the Monday night music, you can also dine very cheaply on the spaghetti dinner special, served with garlic bread ($1.25)—the sauce is a secret old family recipe. On Sundays, only hamburgers and liquor are served. Tuesday through Saturday a lot of the action centers around the dart board, and entrees like broiled salmon steak ($5.25) and deep-fried jumbo prawns ($5.50) served with salad, baked potato and vegetable are available. Open daily from 9:30 a.m. to 2:30 a.m.

At 41 Main is **Tiburon Tommie's,** a Polynesian restaurant with all the South Seas decor that such establishments generally abound in—bamboo stick and rattan ceilings, lots of netting, a jungle of hanging plants, vines, etc. As we go to press, Tiburon Tommie's has just changed ownership, so there may be some alterations coming up. Presently it's open from 10 a.m. to 2 a.m. daily, serving the likes of cashew nut chicken ($3.75) and Mandarin duck ($2.75), not to mention potent concoctions like the Royal Tahitian Pineapple—rums, peach brandy, passion fruit, lemon and lime ($3.25).

Across the street at 16 Main is a delightful little place called **El Bórro,** serving authentic and delicious Mexican cuisine. The decor in the two cozy dining areas consists of rattan grillwork screens, an eclectic selection of photos and paintings, large colorful clusters of paper flowers, and some Mexican pottery, bark paintings and other artifacts on the walls. Further south-of-the-border ambience is added by large wrought-iron sconces on the walls. The chicken in mole sauce ($4.95) is excellent; another good choice is arroz con pollo—Spanish rice and chicken seasoned with saffron and cooked in wine ($4.9S). Soup or salad, rice, beans, tortillas and coffee are served with entrees. A nice surprise on the menu is pecan pie for dessert (75¢). Open from noon to 2 p.m. for lunch, 5 to 10:30 p.m. for dinner; closed Mondays.

Sweden House, 35 Main, has a plant-filled outdoor terrace overlooking the bay for al fresco dining. Inside, the walls are done in yellow-and-white-checked gingham and hung with heavy copper pots and pans, rolling pins, neat little prints and tapestries. There are fresh flowers on every table and dotted Swiss cafe curtains on the windows. And if that's not enough quaint charm for you, the waitresses are in ruffly pinafore aprons. Stop in for a Scandinavian open-face sandwich ($1.50 to $2.75), coffee and dessert; there are so many of the latter that they're not listed on the menu, rather they are temptingly displayed in a glass case—chocolate rum balls, tarts, baked Florentines, mocha meringues and all. All bread and desserts are baked on the premises. Open 9 a.m. to 5 p.m. every day except Monday.

FINAL LIBATIONS: After a leisurely browse down Main Street and a relaxed meal at one of the above establishments, head over to the **Tiburon Vintners,** behind the parking lot at the end of Main Street. This century-old frame building with its twisting iron staircase is an outlet for the premium wines produced on the wine-growing estates of Sonoma and Windsor Vineyards in Sonoma County. The winery specializes in table wines, many of them priced at just $3 per bottle. You can sample them in the wine-tasting room—just enough to get nice and mellow for the ferry ride back to San Francisco. Open daily from 10 a.m.

6. Sausalito

Even more "consciously quaint" than Tiburon—and making no attempt to hide it—is Sausalito, a picturesque-as-all-get-out seacoast village just eight miles from downtown San Francisco. Its lovely harbor is filled with vessels of all shapes and sizes, and its streets are lined with restaurants, art galleries, hip boutiques and shops wherein the arts of candle-making, pottery, glassblowing and scrimshaw are practiced. What other little town can boast eight goldsmiths? But we forgive Sausalito its pretensions; a slightly Bohemian, completely nonchalant and very relaxed adjunct to San Francisco, it has scenery and sunshine and lots of very real charm, both because of, and in spite of, its efforts in that direction.

You can get to Sausalito by car via the Golden Gate Bridge and Highway 101 (or by the Golden Gate bus—75¢). But once again we advise the ferry, departing from Pier 1 at the foot of Market Street from 7:50 a.m. to 8:15 p.m. weekdays, from 10:25 a.m. to 8:20 p.m. Saturdays and Sundays. For more precise information call 332-6600.

SHOPPING IN SAUSALITO: The town's main street, running along the water, is **Bridgeway;** this, along with one or two side streets, is where most of the action is. What everyone does in Sausalito is, shop, stroll and browse. Here follows a roundup of the more interesting establishments to explore:

Along Bridgeway

First stop should be 777 Bridgeway, a complex of 40 shops known as the **Village Fair,** all open daily from 10:30 a.m. to 5:30 p.m. Housed in an old warehouse (it was also, at one time, a Chinese gambling hall), the Fair includes a glassblower, caricaturist, a terrific candle store, a Mexican boutique and a shop for nuts, teas and spices.

Even further up, at #795, is **The Quest Gallery,** specializing in things Eskimo: sculptures, masks, woven hangings and other artifacts. Quest also sells the works—macrame, jewelry, pottery, etc.—of local artists.

Up a flight of stairs at #759 is **Scrimshaw**, "purveyors of carved whales' teeth, harpoons, paintings and prints and all manner of graphics on subjects nautical, books, carvings, intricate models of sailing craft, cannons, curiosa of interest to ladies, sea chests, macrame, casks and other objects, all under the auspices of a well met and personable management." And, yes, they also sell scrimshaw carvings.

Also appropriately upstairs, but not too high up, is **High as a Kite** (#691), which imports paper and fabric kites from all over the world. Not only can you buy a kite here, but the owners of the shop will be happy to take you across the street and give you kite-flying lessons on the green.

Shelby Galleries (#673) has a changing exhibit of local art, as well as local craftwork—cloisonné, scrimshaw, etc. They also feature an extensive collection of American Indian jewelry, primarily from the Hopi, Zuni and Navaho tribes.

If you should happen to inhale as you're passing **Ole's Bakery** (#669), you'll find yourself drawn into the shop as though moved by a power greater than your will, commanding you to order a Dutch crunch roll, hazelnut and buttercream tart, or perhaps a macaroon with brandy cream. Don't try to resist.

Ethereal and romantic women's fashions are designed from antique lace and patchwork at **Opening Thursday**, #559. Antique fabrics also decorate the walls and ceiling at this charming shop.

Princess Street

Go back along Bridgeway a bit, turn left on Princess and check out **Pegasus** (#30),—designers extraordinaire of leather jackets, pants, skirts and clothing of every description, ready or custom-made. It's first store along a crooked mall called **Princess Court**.

A little further along is **Davidson's Gold Jewelery** (52), selling exquisite reproductions of pre-Columbian gold jewelry. The authentic pieces are made in Bogota using the lost-wax process; they are set with antique stones that are from 1,200 to 2,000 years old.

You might also want to sift through the goods at **Sausalito Salvage** (#19), a thrift shop which might have any sort of bric-a-brac, clothing and oddments that people have seen fit to donate to charity.

There's much more awaiting the serious browser here. For a complete listing, pick up a copy of *The Foot Peddler's Guide to Sausalito* (25¢) in any of a number of stores, or explore on your own.

DINING AND DRINKING IN SAUSALITO: By now you're no doubt famished and foot-weary, and the shopping bags are getting a little heavy. Sausalito has an abundance of dining choices, from snack bars and coffee shops to swank gourmet restaurants.

Most unique is **Valhalla**, at Second and Main (tel: 332-1792), owned by Miss Sally Stanford, ex-madam and author of *A House is Not a Home*. She took possession of Valhalla in 1946, but it had been going since 1870, serving liquor uninterruptedly right through Prohibition with none other than Baby Face Nelson tending bar! Movie-goers of the '40s saw Valhalla in *Lady from Shanghai*, starring Rita Hayworth, and Jack London wrote *The Sea Wolf* in one of the upstairs rooms. The furnishings are plush bordello Victorian, with floral carpets, big sofas, beaded curtains, large gilt-framed mirrors and a needlework sampler expressing the sentiment "What is a Home Without a Mother." Two walls are windowed to allow glorious views of the bay. A piano player entertains nightly except Sunday. Specialties include chicken Kiev with rice pilaf ($6.50) and crab legs with wild rice au gratin ($9.75). Since meals here can get a little pricey, you might want to go at lunch when you can have eggs benedict with truffles ($4.95) or rainbow trout amandine ($4.75). Valhalla is open for lunch Tuesday through Sunday and for dinner nightly.

A delightful place to dine is **Soupcon**, 49 Caledonia Street (tel: 332-9752), a tiny establishment with just enough room for an antique oak country cupboard in which luscious desserts are displayed. Luncheon fare, served 11:30 a.m. to 2:30 p.m., consists of homemade soups; tasty sandwiches—like turkey, avocado, tomato and jack cheese ($2.80); salads; and the aforementioned desserts. At dinner, 5:30 to 10:30 p.m., continental entrees might feature prawns Malabar with onions and green olives ($6.45) or broiled steak Dijon ($8.85), both of which come with soup or salad, hot garlic bread, vegetable and rice or potato. Be sure to leave room for a generous wedge of carrot cake with rich creamy icing ($1.25). A glass of wine is 75¢. So small is Soupcon, you'd best make reservations. Closed on Sunday.

The best bay views in town are from **Ondine's**, 558 Bridgeway (tel: 982-1740). Enter via imposing white doors, and then proceed up a gold carpeted stairway to a dining area with elegantly appointed tables. The expansive and spectacular view provides most of the decor and creates a delightfully tranquil ambience. A specialty here is boneless squab Montmorency ($10)—a plump whole squab stuffed with wild rice and served with port wine sauce and cherries. If you come before 8 p.m. a complete dinner, including potage du jour, salad, entree, dessert and coffee, is $7.75 (for broiled salmon) to $12 (for lobster casserole). Ondine's is open daily from 5:30 to 11 p.m. Reservations are essential.

More terrific views at **The Spinnaker**, 100 Spinnaker Drive (tel: 332-1500), just off Bridgeway near the ferry landing. Diners sit on comfortable tufted leather banquettes facing picture windows overlooking the bay. Fir-trunk columns, the bark removed, then stained and varnished, add a natural note to the elegant nautical decor. Dinner, served from 5 to 10 p.m. daily, Sunday from 2 p.m., includes soup or salad, ice cream or sherbert, and coffee. Prices vary according to the entree you select: sole meunière is $6.85, Cornish game hen à la Kiev $7.25, scallops sauté $7.50. You can also order à la carte from a more extensive menu at lunch or dinner. Open daily from 11 a.m. to 11 p.m.

For Japanese fare head over to **Benkei**, 45 Caledonia Street, where the multi-talented owner, Ms. Seihi Sakima, has created a tasteful environment using bamboo, rice paper, rattan, and her own ceramics and batiks. The leather-bound menu (covers also done by Ms. Sakima) offers full dinners, including sunomono (cucumber and crab salad), tsukemono (pickled tidbits), soup, rice and dessert, for $6.95 with an entree of sukiyaki, prawn and vegetable tempura, or beef teriyaki; $5.75 for chicken teriyaki. Open for dinner only, from 6 to 10 p.m., Monday through Saturday.

One of Sausalito's prettiest right-on-the-bay eateries is **Scoma's**, 588 Bridgeway (tel: 332-9551). Recently redecorated after a fire, Scoma's is very homey with gray wood-paneled walls and well-selected antique furnishings. A scrumptious cioppino, meaning shellfish stew ($5.95), and linguine and clams in cream sauce ($3.95) are among the seafood-Italian-style entrees at this very charming establishment. Open nightly for dinner. Reservations are recommended.

For beer and conversation, stop in at the local hangout—the **Bar With No Name**, 757 Bridgeway, a combination coffee house and tavern with oak wainscoted walls, comfortable cushioned wicker and bamboo chairs, and stained-glass panels here and there. In the delightful garden out back you can relax amidst vines and plants hanging from a slatted wood arbor above. The No Name attracts chess players, local artists, yacht skippers, poets and, of course, tourists. Drinks start at $1.

And finally, if you're still hanging around Sausalito at nightfall, the place to go is **Gatsby's**, 39 Caledonia, where musical groups play anything from jazz to bluegrass and deep-dish Chicago pizza is the house specialty. Open daily till 2 a.m., Gatsby's has a $1 cover charge Friday and Saturday nights.

A HOTEL CHOICE: If you care to spend the night, the **Sausalito Hotel**, 16 El Portal (tel: 332-4155), next to the park between Bridgeway and the bay shore, is a Victorian hideaway par excellence. All of the rooms are furnished in turn-of-the-century antiques—beds with massive carved headboards (including one that once belonged to General Grant), elaborate dressers, plush armchairs, gilt-framed mirrors and all the rest. The hotel is popular with celebrities who want a retreat undisturbed by TV, radio or phone—recent guests included Joe Cocker and Sterling Hayden. Of the 15 rooms, five come without private bath. These are $25 a night; rooms with private bath are $35. Rates include parking.

Chapter IV

THE WINE COUNTRY

1. **Napa Valley**
2. **Sonoma**
3. **Fort Ross and Timber Cove**

YOU'RE ABOUT TO ENTER the wine country, one of the most uniquely lovely and fascinating areas of California. Some of the wineries date back to the days of the Franciscan fathers, who planted the first vines as they built their missions. Of course, in those days, all the wine was—ostensibly—for sacramental use. Today the many wineries of this picturesque district are giving stiff competition to France. A drive through the wine country, stopping for tours here and there, and a picnic lunch en route, is one of the most delightful outings we can imagine.

A similarly enjoyable day can be spent exploring historic Sonoma, which sprang up around the last of the missions. More wineries here, too, if you've not yet quenched your thirst. Then take a slight detour west from Sonoma and visit Fort Ross, founded by the Russians in 1812 (did you know the Russians once occupied parts of California?).

The combination of exquisite scenery and interesting sights throughout the areas coming up make this chapter's offerings especially recommendable for inclusion in your itinerary.

1. Napa Valley

Nestled in the coastal mountain range some 50 miles north of San Francisco, this fertile valley has close to 25,000 acres of vineyards, and it produces most of California's superior wines. To get there from San Francisco, head north on Route 101, turn east at S-37 and proceed to Route 29, where the greatest concentration of wineries open to visitors is located. The **Napa Chamber of Commerce,** 1900 Jefferson Street, will provide you with maps, a listing of antique dealers and other information. Or pick up some literature right in San Francisco at the **Wine Institute,** 165 Post Street between Grant and Kearny.

The best time to visit Napa is during September and October when the grapes are being harvested. But any time of year the very air seems intoxicated in this area of unparalleled scenic beauty. As you drive along Route 29, you'll see welcoming signs beckoning you to one winery or another. Almost all offer free tours and lavish free samples of their product. Two or three tours are the most you'll want to take, and we've recommended the ones we think are more intriguing or picturesque. If you find the lecturers at these a little pedantic, be assured that the situation is much the same or worse at the other vineyards. The tours are nonetheless interesting, and the tasting is lots of fun.

THE WINERIES: Make your first visit to **Beaulieu** (the name means, quite aptly, beautiful place), founded in 1900 by Georges Latour, who began his vineyard with the finest cuttings from France. During Prohibition, this clever Frenchman built up a nationwide business in altar wines while others were forced to close. When Repeal came he was one of the fortunate few with well-aged wines on hand. In the early '30s Latour brought over a young Russian enologist (wine scientist), who helped him to produce a sensational Cabernet Sauvignon—a wine for which Beaulieu is still famous. This winery offers one of the most comprehensive tours (including a movie and slide show at the end of all), daily from 10 a.m. to 4 p.m. The tour takes about 40 minutes, after which you can sample at least three wines in the tasting room, and purchase same if you so desire.

Most wineries instruct as to proper tasting procedure: begin with the lightest white wines, go on to rosés, reds and finally sherries and dessert wines—sparkling wines come last.

Just north of St. Helena, you'll come to a castle-like sandstone building set imposingly against a hillside. This is **The Christian Brothers Greystone Winery.** A Napa Valley landmark, dating from 1888, Greystone houses the Christian Brothers' principal aging cellars and complete facilities for the production of their champagne and other sparkling wines. The building is entered via an impressive Roman arch. Behind wrought-iron gates, in the massive cellar, you'll see row upon row of oak casks, each with a capacity of about 2,000 gallons; these are part of the original winery equipment. A similar array of casks extends the length of the building to the south; these are redwood tanks, each with a 5,000-gallon capacity. On the second floor the type and arrangement of cooperage (casks) is duplicated. Casks and tanks on these two levels combined have a total capacity of 1,800,000 gallons! The beautifully paneled ceiling on this floor is hung with 19th-century-style lighting fixtures, and turn-of-the-century hand presses and crushers are on display. Also exhibited here are nearly 500 corkscrews from different countries, assembled by cellarmaster Brother Timothy, a member for 46 years of this ancient Catholic teaching order. The third floor is given over entirely to champagne production. Thirty-minute tours leave every 15 minutes daily from 10 a.m. to 4:30 p.m., followed, of course, by a tasting session.

Practically next door is **Charles Krug,** founded in 1861—a classic old Napa estate set in a shady grove of oak trees on beautifully landscaped grounds. Krug was one of the first California winegrowers to produce wines by other

NAPA VALLEY VINEYARDS

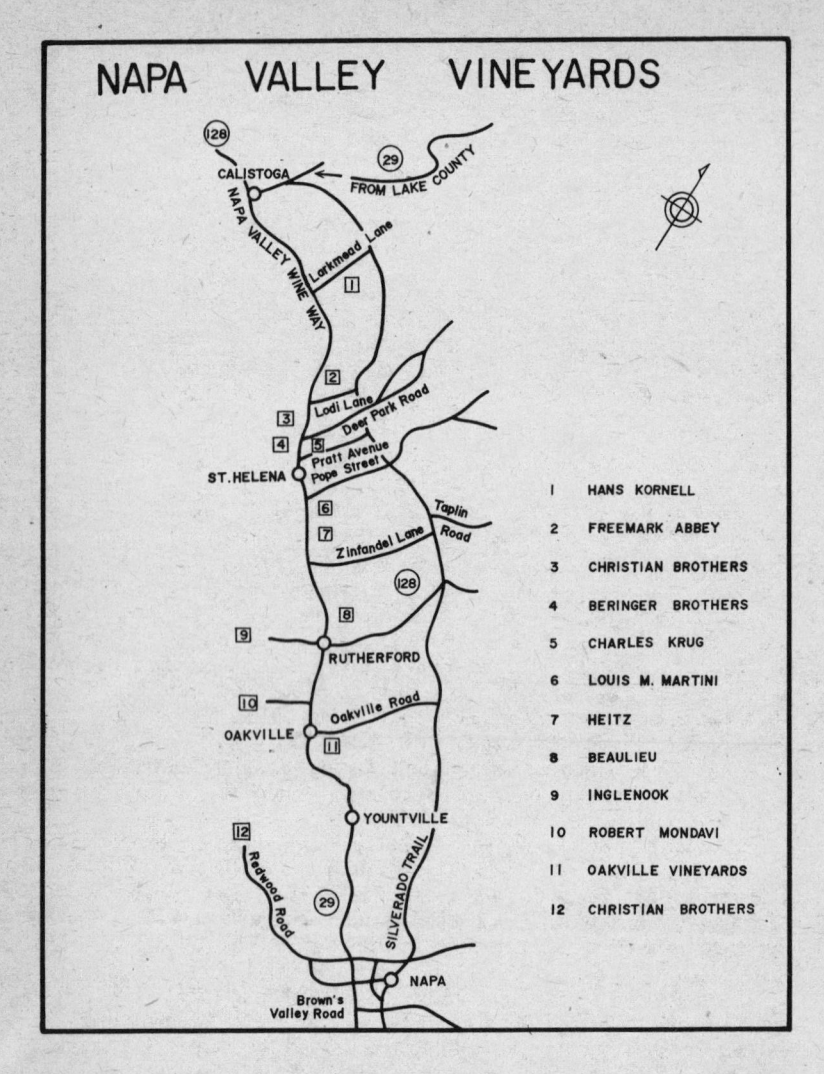

1. HANS KORNELL
2. FREEMARK ABBEY
3. CHRISTIAN BROTHERS
4. BERINGER BROTHERS
5. CHARLES KRUG
6. LOUIS M. MARTINI
7. HEITZ
8. BEAULIEU
9. INGLENOOK
10. ROBERT MONDAVI
11. OAKVILLE VINEYARDS
12. CHRISTIAN BROTHERS

than the primitive Spanish methods introduced by Father Junipero Serra. Two of his original stone buildings remain the core of the present winery, and the one-time coach house holds small cooperage for aging select wines. Since 1943 the winery has belonged to the Mondavi family. Winemaker Peter Mondavi believes that the human element is as important as modern equipment: "The old-timers believed the quality of the man's wine depended on his own quality and character. A little bit of himself goes into every bottle. To gain lasting fame, a winemaker must be a poet, a philosopher, an honorable man, as well as a master craftsman."

Krug's ably led winery tour shows you the crushers, fermenters, tanks (both redwood and steel), aging cellars and bottling lines, ending up in the tasting room. Tours are given at regular intervals daily from 10 a.m. to 4 p.m.

Completely visitor-oriented, and therefore one of the most interesting for our purposes, is **Sterling Winery,** six miles north of St. Helena. Established as recently as 1969, Sterling is housed in a white stucco Mediterranean-style structure, with monastic overtones like stained-glass windows, archways, carved doors, fountains and carillon towers containing bells cast in 1740. Set high on a wood-fringed hill, it's reached via gondola (park your car at the bottom of the hill), which takes you over fields of yellow poppies and wildflowers. A $2 parking fee can be put toward the purchase of wine.

Visitors are left on their own to peruse the carefully labeled exhibits and watch the work in progress. At your own pace, you can walk through the bottling operation, see the giant stainless-steel fermenting tanks, the grape-crushers and cooperage rooms. Quotations from the famous are posted here and there, like this gem from Lord Byron: "Let us have wine and women, mirth, and laughter, sermons and sodawater the day after." After exploring the winery you proceed a short distance up the hill to a tasting room, where you can sit at tables indoors or out, and a guide will pour the wines and discuss them with you. Open daily from 10:30 a.m. to 5 p.m.

OTHER THINGS TO DO: While you're in the area, there are a few other activities you can take in while sobering up for the drive back to San Francisco.

Literary buffs won't want to miss **The Silverado Museum,** 1347 Railroad Avenue, a block east of Main Street, in St. Helena, devoted to the life and works of Robert Louis Stevenson, author of *Treasure Island, Kidnapped,* etc. It was here that Stevenson honeymooned in 1880, at the abandoned Silverado Mine. Over 200 rare items include original manuscripts, letters, photographs, portraits of the writer and the desk he used in Samoa. Open daily from noon to 4 p.m., except Mondays and holidays, the museum is about a 15-minute drive north from Sterling. No admission charge.

As far back as anyone remembers, **Old Faithful Geyser** on Tubbs Lane in nearby Calistoga (a left turn off Route 29 a short drive north of the Sterling Winery) has been spouting 60-foot showers of steam and vapor about every 40 minutes. The performance takes about three minutes, and a visit will teach you a lot about the origins of geothermal steam. There's an admission charge of $1 for adults, 50¢ for children under 14; under six free. The geyser area is open from 8 a.m. to sundown daily.

Also in Calistoga, off Route 128 on Petrified Forest Road, is the **Petrified Forest,** an entire forest of gigantic redwoods that turned to stone through the infiltration of minerals in the volcanic ash that covered them after the eruption of Mt. St. Helena. In addition to trees, you can also see petrified worms, snails, clams, nuts and leaves in a museum on the premises. Open daily from 9 a.m. to 6 p.m. in summer, 10 a.m. to 5 p.m. the rest of the year. Admission is $1.50 for adults, free for children under ten.

The **Hurd Candle Factory,** in Freemark Abbey (up above Christian Brothers in St. Helena), has an open workshop where the public can observe a demonstration hive and the actual handcrafting of beeswax candles. Candles, wine, food items, books about the area and other merchandise can also be purchased here—it's sort of a country store.

In Yountville, a small town in the southern part of Napa Valley, off Route 29, is the wine country's answer to Fisherman's Wharf and the Cannery. **Vintage 1870,** a four-building complex that was originally (1870) a brick winery, contains over 30 shops, art galleries and eating places. Here you can buy anything from crewelwork to African beads, and in bad weather you might want to lunch on a curried chicken sandwich with white wine at **Chutney**

Kitchen. Usually it's more appealing to buy some wine, bread, cheese and sausage (all available at shops here) and make a picnic of it. We're sorry to see this kind of touristy development in Napa, but it's most popular and looks like it's here to stay.

Antiquers should refer to the aforementioned Chamber of Commerce listing.

STAYING OVER: If you'd like to stay in the area, you might consider **camping** at nearby **Lake Berryessa.** An excellent base for your explorations of Napa, it has boating, swimming, water-skiing and fishing facilities. Details from the Chamber of Commerce.

Less rustic types who would like to spend more than a day in the area might consider the **Wine Country Inn,** two miles north of St. Helena at 1152 Lodi Lane (tel: 707/963-7077). A New-England-style inn, it has 14 rooms, many with fireplaces and balconies, all furnished in antiques. Double rooms, including continental breakfast, are $33 to $35.

2. Sonoma

Though not far from Napa Valley, Sonoma, 45 miles north of San Francisco, is of sufficient historical interest to warrant a day's sightseeing all its own. To get there, just take Route 101 north, make a right at State 37, a left at 121, then head north on Broadway, following the signs.

Centuries before Europeans colonized the area, it was inhabited by the Pomo and Miwok Indians. It wasn't until the 19th century that world powers—Spain, Mexico, Russia and the United States—began to converge in the Sonoma region. During the 1830s and 1840s one man, General Mariano Guadalupe Vallejo—a brilliant Mexican army officer—was given 44,000 acres in nearby Petaluma Valley and charge of the mission at Sonoma. Vallejo's far-reaching civil and military powers brought him immense wealth and undisputed rule of the area as long as California was in Mexican hands. By 1846 he had increased his personal holdings to 175,000 acres; in that same year, however, American frontiersmen under John C. Fremont captured the area and arrested him. He was soon released and he later served as Mayor of Sonoma in 1852 and 1860.

Many aspects of the town, including the approach via a wide boulevard, Broadway, and the central Plaza are still here as Vallejo laid them out originally. He left his mark everywhere, as you'll see when you explore Sonoma's major attractions, all of which center around the **Plaza**—today a lovely city park and the setting for City Hall. The Plaza is also the location of the **Bear Flag Monument,** which stands adjacent to the exact site where a band of adventurers raised the crude Bear Flag. Symbolizing the end of Mexican rule, the Bear Flag was later to become the state standard.

Major historical landmarks and attractions are detailed below. For a complete listing, an easy-to-read map and a listing of antique shops in the area, make your first stop the **Chamber of Commerce,** conveniently located at 461 First Street West.

CASA GRANDE: General Vallejo's first home, this Mexican-style adobe was one of the grandest residences in California when it was built in 1836. In its heyday this Spain Street house was the center of social and diplomatic life north of San Francisco. Eleven Vallejo children were born here, and it was here that Vallejo was arrested in 1846. Unfortunately, the main wing of the building was destroyed by fire in 1867, and only the Indian servants' wing remains today.

SONOMA 95

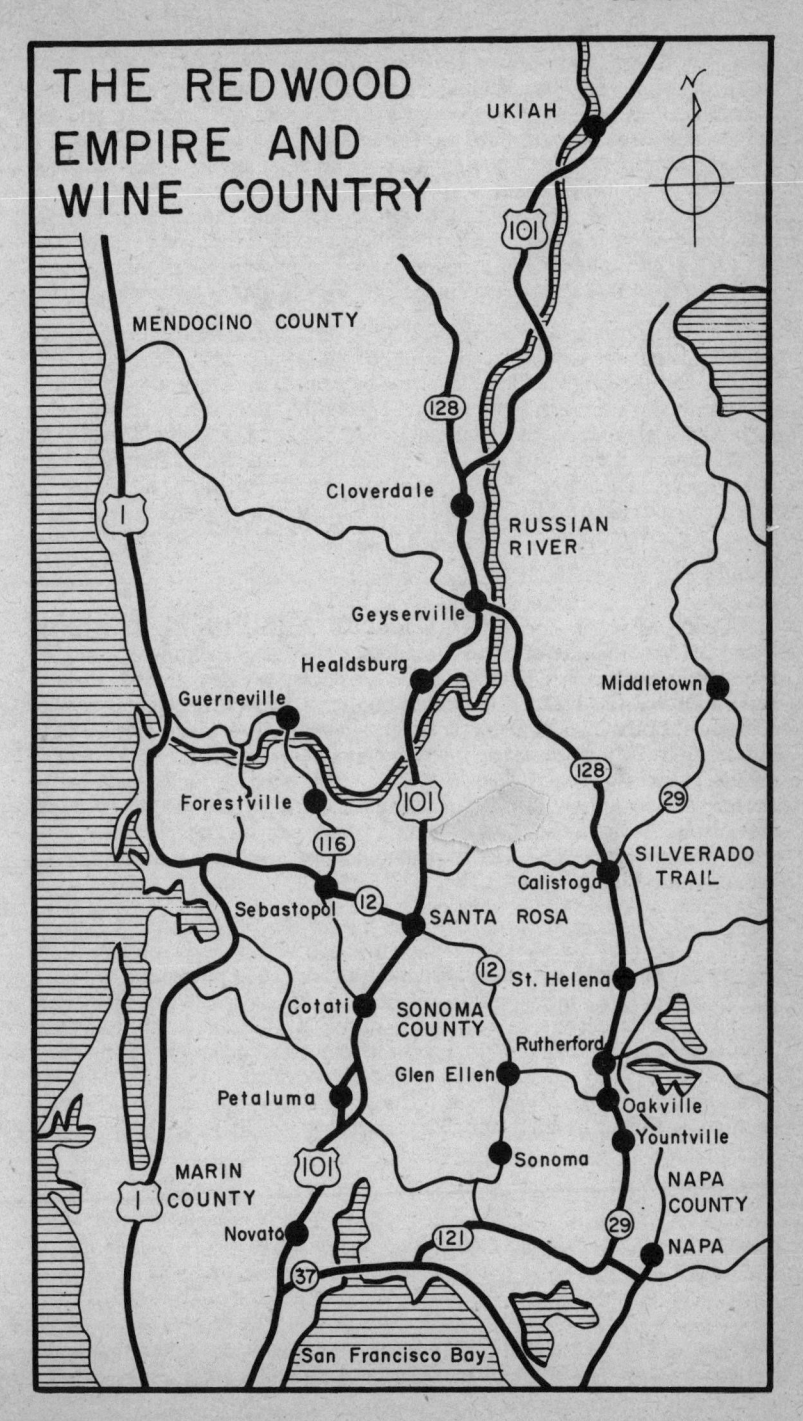

THE REDWOOD EMPIRE AND WINE COUNTRY

VALLEJO HOME: In 1850, Vallejo purchased some additional property about a half-mile northwest of the Plaza on which to build another estate, called, in Latin, **Lachryma Montis** (mountain tear). Grapevines, a wide assortment of fruit trees, and other foliage and shrubbery were planted, and the quarter-mile driveway was lined with roses and cottonwood trees. An arbor-shaded pathway encircled a pool, and a number of fountains further enhanced the carefully tended grounds. The Victorian-style house went up in 1852, its interior decorated with crystal chandeliers, lace curtains and elaborate furnishings imported from Europe. General Vallejo and his wife lived here for over 35 years. Today the buildings, grounds and interior—furnished with many of Vallejo's personal effects—are maintained as closely as possible to the original.

SONOMA BARRACKS: Erected in 1836 by (you guessed it) General Vallejo, on Spain Street facing the Plaza, this wide-balconied, two-story adobe was built to house the Mexican Army troops. In the years 1835 to 1846, over 100 military expeditions set out from Sonoma, most with the aim of subduing hostile Indians. Following the military takeover by the Bear Flag Party, and the subsequent raising of the Stars and Stripes, Sonoma continued to be an important U.S. Army post. In still later years the building served as a winery, store, law office and private residence, until it was purchased in 1958 by the state and partially restored.

MISSION SAN FRANCISCO SOLANO DE SONOMA: Founded in 1823, this was the last of the 21 missions founded in California by Father Junipero Serra. The first building was a temporary wooden structure; later a low adobe wing was added for living quarters. This latter building, which stands east of the chapel, is the oldest in Sonoma. The Mission reached peak prosperity in 1830 when nearly 1,000 Indian converts were in residence. The present chapel was constructed in 1840 and furnished by Vallejo as a parish church. After later incarnations as a hay barn, winery and blacksmith shop, the Mission became a state monument in 1903 and was restored. It houses many mission artifacts as well as watercolors of mission scenes throughout California by Virgil Jorgensen.

SWISS HOTEL: Over at 16 West Spain Street, facing the Plaza, this adobe was yet more living space for Don Salvador Vallejo. Later it was used as a hotel and restaurant, and meals are served here to this day. The furnishings are Eastlake, and the decor is of the ye-olde-inn variety. A menu on the wall from 1936 proffers a full dinner from appetizer to dessert for just $1. Full-course dinners today are $4.25 (for ravioli or spaghetti entree) to $9.50 (for lobster). Dinner begins at 5 p.m. Wednesday through Saturday; Sunday, food is served from noon. Closed Monday and Tuesday.

BLUE WING INN: This 1840 hostelry, at 133 East Spain Street, was erected by General Vallejo to accommodate travelers and emigrants who needed a place to stay while they built their Sonoma homes. It was purchased during Gold Rush days by two retired seafaring men who operated it as a hotel and store. Notable guests included John Fremont, Kit Carson, Ulysses S. Grant; notorious guests included the bandit Murieta and "Three-fingered Jack." It now houses an antique shop and folk-art shop which are open Wednesday through Sunday from noon to 5 p.m.

TOSCANO HOTEL: Among the most interesting sights in the Plaza area, this wood-frame building next to the barracks looks almost as if the guests and staff just walked out suddenly one day leaving everything behind. In the parlor downstairs a game of cards in progress is laid out on the table. Bedrooms upstairs have period furnishings, rag rugs, lovely quilts, shaving stands, pitcher and bowl for washing up, and antique tortoise-shell dresser sets which include button hooks. On exhibit are some teensy clothes that were traveling salesmen's samples. Free guided tours are given Tuesday from 11 a.m. to 1 p.m.; Saturday and Sunday from 11 a.m. to 4 p.m.

NASH-PATTON ADOBE: This house, built in 1847, is where one John H. Nash was taken prisoner for refusing to surrender his post as alcade. The adobe was restored in 1931.

LUNCH BREAK: For gastronomical rather than historical intake, stop in at the **Sonoma Cheese Factory,** 2 Spain Street, where a long display case is filled with every variety of Italian meats imaginable and 101 kinds of cheese. They'll by happy to put it into a sandwich for you, which, along with a small bottle of wine, will make a great picnic lunch. Picnic tables can be found in the Plaza park.

WINERIES: Sonoma, like Napa Valley, is wine country. If you're planning a trip to Napa as well, you'll get enough of winery tours without these. Otherwise two to visit are **Sebastiani,** 389 4th Street East, and **Buena Vista** at the end of Old Winery Road. The former was founded in 1904 by Samuele Sebastiani and is still operated today by his son and grandson. You can see the original crusher and press, as well as the largest collection of oak barrel carvings in the world. One tank here holds 590,000 gallons of wine—If you drank a bottle a day it would last for 800 years! If you don't want to take the tour you can go straight to the tasting room, where you can sample all 27 wines—on the condition that you stay more or less sober doing it. Open 10 a.m. to 5 p.m. daily.

Buena Vista, slightly northeast of Sonoma, was founded in 1857 by Count Agoston Haraszthy, the Hungarian emigré who is called the father of the California wine industry. A close friend of General Vallejo, Haraszthy journeyed to Europe at his own expense in 1861 and returned with 100,000 of the finest cuttings from European vineyards, which he made available to all winegrowers. An official California landmark, the winery is still housed in the original massive stone buildings. Open daily 9 a.m. to 5 p.m. Tasting takes place in a tunnel carved into the limestone hills (originally dug so that the wines could be stored at a constant cool temperature). Picnic grounds adjoin.

JACK LONDON STATE PARK: A ride to nearby Glen Ellen, about seven miles northwest along State 12, takes you to Jack London State Park, where the famed author lived until his death at the age of 40 in 1916. Here you can see the ruins of **Wolf House,** which London planned but never occupied—a magnificent rustic home of natural wood and stone. On August 22, 1913, a few weeks before the Londons were to move in, an arsonist destroyed the building. The house of **Happy Walls,** where London's wife Charmian lived for many years after his death, now is a veritable London museum, filled with the author's possessions, mementoes and artifacts the couple brought back from their travels in the South Seas. A room on the first floor is fitted out as London's office used to be, with his desk, typewriter and other items. Not far away, under a huge red lava boulder on a wooded knoll, are London's ashes. Open 10 a.m. to 5 p.m. daily.

TRAIN TOWN: The **Sonoma Gaslight and Western Railroad,** a meticulous miniature model of a diamond-stack 1875 locomotive, is located a mile south of the city on Broadway. Everything at Train Town is built to the same one-quarter scale, including a depot, freight office and other business buildings. The train runs a 1½-mile track through a manmade landscape of cedars, hills and valleys, and around a small lake. About midway in the 15-minute trip, a stop is made at a miniature Old West mining town, Lakeville. Passengers can debark and explore, peeking into the windows of a Wells Fargo express office, depot, Victorian bungalow, stores, fire station and newspaper office. Trains leave daily every 30 minutes from 10:30 a.m. to 5:30 p.m. June 17 through Labor Day; Saturdays, Sundays and holidays, weather permitting, the rest of the year. Adults pay $1.50; kids two to 17 pay $1; under two free.

3. Fort Ross and Timber Cove

Now a state historic park, Fort Ross, 13 miles north of Jenner on State 1, was once a North American outpost of the Russian empire. It was over 150 years ago, during the "fur rush" days, that Fort Ross was dedicated by the Russian-American Fur Company on the name-day of Czar Alexander I.

The history of Russian imperialistic designs on California (which helped prompt the Monroe Doctrine) actually dates back to 1740, when Russian explorer Vitus Bering brought news that Alaska was teeming with sea otters, for whose pelts the Chinese Mandarins would pay up to $250. Bering's countrymen founded the Russian-American Fur Company and by 1799 had taken possession of Alaska. They soon decimated the otter herds of Alaska, and sent ships southward for supplies and to scout out new sources of prey. One of these expeditions, headed by Manager Ivan Kuskof, landed at Fort Ross in 1812. In two years they shipped home 200,000 otter skins from the area.

California at the time was more or less administered by Mexico. The Russians conveniently disregarded Mexican rule and made a trade with the peaceful Pomo coastal Indians: two axes, three blankets and a pound of beads for 1,000 acres.

At first, Fort Ross prospered. So highly did the Czar value this California colony that in 1821 he issued an imperial order denying the coast north of San Francisco to all except Russian ships. Mexico rose from apathy and sent one of its officers, Mariano Guadalupe Vallejo, up to the area with a few soldiers and orders to contain the Muscovite threat. Two years later President James Monroe promulgated his historic Doctrine forbidding the American continent to foreign despots.

But it was neither the Americans nor the Mexicans that caused Alexander's minions to pull back. It was, rather, the work of the otter and the gopher. The limitless herds of otter, indiscriminately slaughtered, were just about extinct by the 1830s. And to make matters worse, gophers (described by the Russians as "hordes of underground rats") began to destroy crops. From a glittering prize, Fort Ross was turned into a liability to the Imperial crown. That fall, Captain Johann Sutter paid $30,000 for the land and the buildings and the Muscovites sailed home, writing an end to Russia's colonial expansion in America.

World/Africa U.S.A., less than an hour's trip south on Route 101 by car or via Greyhound bus (departures every half-hour from Market and 7th Streets). Combining a uniquely innovative zoo and aquarium, Marine World/Africa U.S.A.'s inhabitants range from killer whales to golden eagles, flamingos and hippopotami.

To get acquainted with the grounds, make your first ride the **Jungle Raft Safari.** Seated on a rubber raft with a thatched roof overhead, you'll float very close to zebras, ostriches, rhinos, goats, lions, llamas, tigers, antelope, elephants, water buffaloes and flamingos, among others—all in natural environments. An amiable guide will make awful jokes ("the difference between a male zebra and a female is that the male has white stripes on black and vice versa") and ceaseless commentary as to the imminent dangers from approaching beasts. The kids love it.

The aquarium, housing thousands of colorful fish, manta rays, giant turtles, dolphins, etc., is thrilling, as are the exotic birds. In the **Gentle Jungle,** you can cuddle up with baby lambs and fawns, later watch seals and sea lions cavorting at **Seal Cove.**

In addition, there are seven highly entertaining shows scheduled several times daily, and you can see them all in one visit. Don't be discouraged by the enormous crowds lined up waiting to see the shows; the stadiums are huge and everyone gets in.

At the **Dolphin Show** you'll see the sea mammals compete in the "Dolphin Olympics," complete with torch and electric scoreboard. (If you forget which team you're rooting for, remember they're the guys in gray.) One of the dolphins is a bit of a clown and keeps goofing up. They all do fancy flips, jump hurdles, laugh (dolphin style), catch hoops on their noses while blindfolded and jump through flaming hoops.

The **Lion Show** takes you inside a training session to view a trainer in a small cage with eight lions and a tiger.

Most popular is the **Killer Whale Show,** in which a trainer rides a killer whale, not to mention putting his head in its mouth or standing on a high-diving board with a fish clenched between his teeth—the whale jumps up and grabs it!

Other shows are the **Wild Bird Show, Ecology Theatre, Jungle Theatre** and **Water Ski and Boat Show.**

This is a full-day experience; come early and wear comfortable shoes and clothing. Bring your camera or borrow one on the premises for free. Picnic tables are available if you want to bring food, but there are plenty of inexpensive eateries to choose from.

The park is open daily from Memorial Day through Labor Day, 9:30 a.m. to 6:30 p.m.; Wednesday through Sunday during spring and fall; weekends and holidays in winter. Admission is $5.75 adults; $3.50 children five through 12, free for under-fours. The price covers all shows and the Jungle Raft Safari—as many times as you want to experience them during the day. We suggest you stop for a few minutes at the entrance and make up some itinerary of shows from the schedule you are given.

For further information dial D-O-L-P-H-I-N.

2. Marriott's Great America

A little further south along U.S. 101 (45 miles below San Francisco in Santa Clara—get off at the Great America exit) is a newly opened (1976), $50-million, 200-acre theme park with 27 major rides, 14 live shows and special attractions, games, arcades and plenty more for a full day's entertainment.

Attracting great hordes of daredevil San Franciscans, the ride-freak's favorite is the Turn of the Century, a corkscrew roller coaster that inches you up 95 feet, and turns you completely upside down in two terrifying corkscrew rolls in addition to the usual high-speed downward slopes and hairpin turns. You can get a great view of the entire proceedings from the top of the Sky Whirl, a triple-armed ferris wheel, or from the cable cars of the Delta Flyer skyride.

Also very popular are the Yankee Clipper and Logger's Run, two side-by-side flume water rides with 60-foot slides. Getting soaked is part of the fun.

In the Disneyland tradition, Great America has several themed areas: a 1920s rural American town; Yukon Territory—a replica of the legendary Klondike during 1890s Gold Rush days, the research for which took architects on a 6,000-mile trek across the Alaskan wilds; a 19th-century New England fishing village; a turn-of-the-century livestock exposition and county fair; and 1850s New Orleans.

There are 75 showtimes daily, with entertainment ranging from animal and dolphin shows to Bugs Bunny cartoons, a lively musical revue and a complete old-time circus with high-wire acts, clowns and a carnival side show. In addition to the regularly scheduled acts there are marching bands, barbershop quartets, parades, concerts, fireworks, puppet shows and magicians daily.

If all the activity doesn't unsettle your tummy, there are 28 low-priced eateries to choose from, serving everything from hamburgers (4,300 are wolfed down every day) to Swedish waffles and shrimp Creole.

Guests pay a one-price admission which includes everything except food and arcade games. Adults $7.95; children four to 11 $6.95; under three free. The park is open from 10 a.m. to 10 p.m. daily in summer; spring and fall weekends 10 a.m. to 6 p.m.

3. San Jose

This is the town that Burt Bacharach immortalized a few years back with the musical question: "Do you know the way to San Jose?" We can answer that one: just keep going south for 48 miles on 101, and you'll find yourself in a city that houses seven universities and colleges and an abundance of visitor attractions.

WINCHESTER HOUSE: Our favorite of all the local sights is the Winchester Mystery House, a 160-room Victorian mansion at 525 South Winchester Boulevard, built by Sarah L. Winchester, widow of the son of the famous rifle magnate. Convinced by a spiritualist that the lives of her husband and baby daughter had been taken by the spirits of those killed with Winchester repeaters, she was told that she too would share their fate . . . unless, that is, she began to build a mansion on which work could *never* stop. Whether the medium had a strange sense of humor or a husband in the contracting business, no one knows. Maybe she was right—Sarah Winchester followed her instructions and lived to be 85. Starting with an eight-room house, and with a fortune of $20-million and an income of $1000 a day, at her disposal, she proceeded to base her life on the medium's advice. At night passersby heard strange ghostly music wafting from the mansion, and a bell in the belfry tolled regularly at midnight to warn off evil spirits and summon good ones to protect her.

Her first move was to hire 22 carpenters and seven Japanese gardeners, the latter to keep a towering hedge thick enough to shut out all view of the premises from the road. None of them ever saw her, nor did the servants, except for the Chinese butler who served her meals on the Winchester $30,000 gold dinner service. All orders were issued by Miss Margaret Merriam, niece, secretary and finally heiress of the fortune. The work went on seven days a week, 365 days a year, even on Christmas. (And you thought Howard Hughes was peculiar.)

The rooms are palatially furnished, and beautiful to see: there are exquisite gold and silver chandeliers, doors inlaid with German silver and bronze, Tiffany stained-glass windows valued at $10,000 each, beautiful wood paneling, intricate parquet floors, windowpanes of French beveled plate glass, mantels of Japanese tile and hand-picked bamboo—we could fill pages describing the treasures within.

But equally, if not more, intriguing are Mrs. Winchester's bizzare constructions to foil the vengeful ghosts—particularly the ghosts of Indians, many of whom were dispatched to the Happy Hunting Grounds via Winchester repeaters. Doors lead to nowhere, staircases ascend to the ceiling only, and others contain steps just two inches high, and go up, down and up to climb to a height of about seven feet. Such schemes were supposed to confound spirits, particularly those of the "simple redskins" she feared the most. And the number 13 comes up often—13 bathrooms, 13 windows in a room, 13 palms lining the main driveway—and many multiples of 13, like 52 skylights.

Informative guided tours of this fascinating house take place daily between 9 a.m. and 6 p.m. in summer, till 5 p.m. in spring and fall, and till 4:30 p.m. in winter. Admission for the one-hour house tour is $3.50 for adults 13 and older, $2 for children; for a 2½-hour combination house and grounds tour, it's $4.25 adults, $2.75 children.

FRONTIER VILLAGE: Another San Jose draw is Frontier Village, 4885 Monterey Road (further south via Highway 82), an 1890s Old West themed amusement park of rides and attractions. Hourly gunfights and bank robberies take place on Main Street, the "Last National" enduring more holdups than any other bank in the world—but the marshal always gets the varmints. You can ride a burro through badlands (bandits might attack any time), navigate the waterways around Indian Island in a 32-foot war canoe, take a thrilling ride through the Lost Dutchman Mine, practice archery, or fish for trout and take home your dinner. If you're hungry, the Cantina Murieta has hot tacos, the Silver Dollar Saloon is always open, and there are four picnic areas.

The park is open daily in summer from 10 a.m. to 5 p.m. (till 10 p.m. Friday and Saturday nights). The rest of the year it's open 10 a.m. to 5 p.m. on Saturdays, Sundays and school holidays. One-price tickets for unlimited rides are $4.50 for both adults and children. Admission and ten rides will cost adults $4.25, children $4.

ROSICRUCIAN PARK & OTHER SIGHTS: Almost as strange (well not quite) as Winchester House is Rosicrucian Park and the various museums on its grounds. Inside the imposing **Administration Building,** which copies the design of the Great Temple of Rameses III, members of the ancient order, with titles like "Grand Master" and "Supreme Secretary," are doing the organization's work. In the **Egyptian Museum,** thousands of original and rare Egyptian, Assyrian and Babylonian antiquities are on display: statuary, textiles, jewelry and paintings; mummified high priests, animals and birds: toys entombed with a child 5,000 years ago; a full-size reproduction of an Egyptian limestone tomb, sarcophagi, etc.

The **Art Gallery** exhibits an eclectic variety of works of famous international artists.

The **Science Museum and Planetarium** deal with subjects ranging from seismography to space travel, demonstrating how fundamental laws of the physical sciences elucidate nature's mysteries. And if you should be interested in the Rosicrucian Order, there's much literature about, as well as people who can answer your questions.

The Planetarium is open October to May on Saturdays and Sundays from 1 to 5 p.m.; daily during summer for the same hours. Seven shows are presented yearly. Adults pay $1; those under 18 pay 50¢, and there's no charge to see the science exhibits.

There's no charge either for the Egyptian Museum or Art Gallery, both of which are open Saturday, Sunday and Monday from noon to 5 p.m., Tuesday through Friday from 9 a.m. to 5 p.m.

San Jose visitors can also take a stroll around the **Japanese Friendship Garden,** a serene symbol of the goodwill between San Jose and its sister city, Okayama, Japan. On the premises is the **San Jose Historical Museum,** 635 Phelan Avenue, which has exhibits on local history, including a replica of turn-of-the-century San Jose complete with blacksmith, doctor's office, printing shop, banks, fire house and residences. Open daily for a minimal admission fee.

DINING IN SAN JOSE: A convenient place for lunch following your exploration of Winchester House is **The Magic Pan,** 335 South Winchester Boulevard. Like the rest of the chain, this restaurant serves a ...ety of reasonably priced crêpe specialties in a French provincial sett...

For something a little more plush, there's H... ...'s at the Hyatt House, 1740 North First Street, open for lunch weekdays, dinner seven nights. Here you sit on handsome tufted blue leather banquettes, under dripping crystal, a fresh rose on every pink-clothed table. Evenings the luxe atmosphere is enhanced by candlelight, live harp music and a band for dancing. Among luncheon entrees are roast beef au jus ($3.95), eggs benedict ($3.50), fancy sandwiches and salads. At dinner, continental entrees like sole Veronique and duckling Montmorency begin at $6.75.

4. Santa Cruz

When San Franciscans feel like a day at the beach, they willingly drive the 74 miles south along State Highway 1 to Santa Cruz, one of the few northern coastal locations where the water is actually warm enough to swim in—at any rate Californians think it's warm. Whether you do or not, you'll find plenty of ways to amuse yourself at—

THE BOARDWALK: The hub of beach activities from May through mid-September and weekends the rest of the year is the old-fashioned Atlantic-City-style Boardwalk. You can spend the morning digging your toes into the warm sand, surfing, sunbathing and swimming; later take a walk on the Boardwalk, as the card says. There are over 20 rides, including a roller coaster, bumper cars, a hand-carved merry-go-round and, one of our favorites, the dizzying Super-Go-Round that turns at such high speed you stick to the wall by centrifugal force—which is just as well because the floor falls out. There's miniature golf and a big penny arcade, too. If you continue your ramble west along the Boardwalk you'll get to—

FISHERMAN'S WHARF: And a very nice wharf it is, with picturesque shops, fish markets and seafood restaurants. You can bring or rent fishing equipment, bait and tackle and fish off the wharf or in a rented boat. Deep-sea fishing expeditions depart daily from February 1 to November 15, with trips on weekends during December and January. Non-fisherfolk can take a 45-minute ocean excursion in a 65-foot cruiser Saturdays and Sundays at 3:30 p.m.

Among the seafood restaurants is **Malio's,** overlooking the water and serving seasonally fresh seafood lunches and dinners daily. It's a pretty place, with plank wood walls and ceilings, cream-colored walls, and red tablecloths adding a splash of color. A bit pricey, but the food is good.

Further along the wharf is **Miramar,** a little fancier than Malio's, with gold wallpaper, red leather chairs and large windows overlooking the water. Complete luncheons here are a good buy: priced according to entree they include soup or salad, chocolate mousse and coffee. With an entree of steamed clams or poached salmon, such a meal is $4.95; $3.95 for sole delmonico, shrimp curry, sand dabs or scallops. At dinner, similar meals are priced from $6.25 to $14.95 (for steak and lobster combination). Open daily 11 a.m. to 9:30 p.m.

No need for fancy dining, however. You can stop in any of numerous shops and snack bars and get shrimp cups and other tasty edibles—seating and view are free on the wharf. By the way, there's lots of parking at the wharf (four hours for $1).

SHOPPING AND BROWSING: Going north from the beach or wharf along Pacific Avenue, you'll come to the **Pacific Garden Mall** (a free shuttle operates from the beach to the mall and back on weekends every 15 minutes). Scene of frequent craft fairs and festivities, the mall has a wide variety of shops to explore, the biggest regular attractions being the **International Bazaar,** with imports from the world over, and the **Cooperage,** a restaurant-shopping complex that was formerly the County Courthouse. Short rambles up side streets from the mall will reveal Victorian and Edwardian mansions, as well as other architectural landmarks, including the **Mission Santa Cruz,** 126 High Street. A brochure detailing four historic walking tours will greatly enhance such an architecture stroll—pick one up at the **Chamber of Commerce,** corner of Church and Center Streets, a few blocks west of the mall.

DINING—THE VIEW FROM THE BRIDGE: A short distance from the mall, at 119 River Street South between Soquel and Water Street bridges, is **Castagnola's,** offering seafood with an Italian accent and a panoramic view. The handsome interior is plushly carpeted in orange, accented by pale sienna drapes and tablecloths and chocolate-brown napkins. Most seats look out over greenery, though a few, unfortunately, provide dynamite views of the parking lot. Lunch entrees include jumbo Louisiana prawns ($4.95), cannelloni a la Romana ($3.95) and veal scaloppine Marsala ($4.95)—all of which are served with soup, salad or cottage cheese and fruit, and coffee. A la carte items are also available. If you dine on the outdoor garden terrace amidst an abundance of hanging and potted plants, you get a different menu and classical music with your meal. Here you might choose avocado stuffed with shrimp ($3.60) or a half-pound chili burger ($3.25). Dinner entrees (indoors only) include a choice of two additional courses (shrimp cocktail, soup or salad) and coffee, along with entrees like halibut steak stuffed with avocado, mushrooms and tomato ($7.80). Castagnola's is open for dinner Tuesday through Sunday (live music for dancing from 9 p.m. Thursday through Saturday). Lunch is served 11:30 to 3:30 Tuesday to Friday. After lunch, a short drive will take you to our very favorite Santa Cruz attraction, the intriguing—

MYSTERY SPOT: Situated in a redwood forest, 2½ miles north of Santa Cruz on Branciforte Drive (just follow the signs; getting there is no mystery), the "spot" is a section of woodlands, 150 feet in diameter, where the laws of gravity seem to have gone haywire. Wildlife avoids the area and birds will not nest here; instruments on planes flying overhead go dead; even the trees grow aslant. It's all due to some mysterious, unexplainable, eerie "force."

There's some conjecture that a meteor, minerals or a magnet are buried deep underground, exerting a magnetic force or distorting the sun's rays. But such explanations don't satisfy scientists or sufficiently explain the phenomenon. The owners of the land have done a fine job in protecting the woodland setting and arranging excellent guided tours for visitors. A series of demonstrations allows you to experience the force for yourself: a ball set down on a slanted plank rolls uphill; (skeptics can place the ball themselves or try another object like a lipstick). As you climb the hillside, you'll find you're walking as straight-legged as you would on level ground. A tilted wooden house, used for demonstration purposes, makes the change in perspective most obvious. Ever walk up a wall? you can here, and it's easy. One of the most amazing demonstrations is when the guide places two people on either side of a level block (tested with a carpenter's level) and one seems to shrink while the other grows. It's not an optical illusion; it's been proven by snapshots. If it's all a hoax, it's a particularly good one. This is a definite not-to-be-missed attraction. The Mystery Spot is open daily from 9:30 a.m. to 5 p.m. Adults pay $1.50; kids five to 11 pay 75¢.

Youngsters adore the Mystery Spot. But an even bigger treat for the under-ten set is—

SANTA'S VILLAGE: Most refreshing in summertime (when it's open daily; weekdays and holidays the rest of the year), this Christmasy amusement park is located on Highway 17 between Santa Cruz and San Jose. There are 14 rides, most with holiday-related themes, like the Candy Cane Sleigh Ride, Snowman's Ride and the Christmas Tree Ride. In addition there are green-garbed elves and a plump, friendly, bearded Santa who gives each child a hug and a candy cane and patiently takes requests. A one-price ticket, including admission to all rides, is $3.75 for anyone over the age of four ($3.25 for those under four). We'd advise adults to buy the $1.75 admission ticket for themselves. A kid's ticket "à la carte" is 75¢, and with rides costing 40¢ to 50¢ it is unlikely to be a bargain.

RC&BTNGRR: No, the printer hasn't been drinking. That mess of letters stands for **Roaring Camp and Big Trees Narrow-Gauge Railroad,** a major Santa Cruz attraction located off Route 9 in Felton, north of Henry Cowell Redwoods State Park. America's last steam-powered passenger railroad, the RC&BTNGRR is a colorful reminder of Gold Rush days, operating authentic 1880 and 1890 equipment on a five-mile, one-hour round trip through magnificent redwood forests. Passengers board trains from the old-fashioned depot at Roaring Camp (sometimes greeted by a woman in pioneer dress and bonnet). The train chugs through forests of trees towering hundreds of feet overhead, past such quaint station points as Big Trees, Indian Creek, Grizzly Flats and Deer Valley en route to the summit of Bear Mountain. Passengers may detrain here for hiking or picnicking to return on a later train. On spring, summer and fall weekends there's live country music. You can take this delightful ride any day during summer; weekends and holidays the rest of the year. Departures on the hour from 11 a.m. to 4 p.m. Adults pay $4 round trip; ages three to 15 pay $2; under-threes free.

Chapter VI

HIGHLIGHTS OF NORTHERN CALIFORNIA

1. **Little River**
2. **Mendocino**
3. **Fort Bragg**
4. **Avenue of the Giants**
5. **Yosemite National Park**
6. **South Lake Tahoe**

THE PREVIOUS TWO CHAPTERS dealt with areas that could be easily explored in day trips from San Francisco. The following are a bit further along; you might still use San Francisco as a base, but plan to spend at least a night or two away. We'll begin by heading north to—

1. Little River

Take a leisurely drive up the coast, maybe stopping at historic Fort Ross along the way, where for 40 years Russians dominated Northern California (see Chapter IV). When you've traveled 123 miles north along State 1, you'll come to Little River, (in the vicinity of Mendocino) where charming and quaint old inns welcome north coast travelers.

Quaintest of the quaint is the **Little River Inn** (tel: 707/937-5942), a rambling Maine-style mansion built by pioneer Silas Coombs in 1853. Where Silas once ran lumber, shipbuilding and shipping operations, his great-granddaughter and her husband now maintain a quiet country retreat. Eucalyptus trees, planted as a windbreak for the Coombs' orchard, now shelter a nine-hole golf course. Homemade meals (including fresh-baked bread and desserts) are served daily in a dining room on the premises. All rooms offer sweeping sea views, and are equipped with baths. Three types of accommodations are offered at costs ranging from $20 double for Early California attic rooms at the old Inn (we like these, with their grandmother rockers and dome windows looking out to sea); $20 to $36 for cottage units; $28 for rooms in the contemporary Hilltop Annex.

Another vintage New England-style inn is the ivy-covered **Heritage House** (tel: 707/937-5885), on the sea side of the road. Its main building was also a farmhouse, this one built in 1877 by forebears of the present owners. Cottages, inspired by old-fashioned institutions and buildings, have names like Scott's Opera House, Country Store, Bonnet Shop and Ice Cream Parlor. Many antiques from old houses in the area have been used in furnishing rooms here. Heritage House operates on the modified American Plan (room with breakfast and dinner) and rates start at $45 for two with those meals included.

Advance reservations are advisable at either establishment.

2. Mendocino

Barely two miles further along is Mendocino, its mixture of 19th-century charm and beauty, weathered barns, old mansions, deep green forests, blue sea and white surf providing the backdrop for a major center for the arts on California's northern coast.

Originally known as Meiggsville, the town was so named for one Harry Meiggs, who came to Big River in search of a wrecked cargo of Chinese silk. He didn't find the silk, but he did find another treasure in giant redwoods. He built the area's first sawmill and began shipping cargoes of lumber back to fast-growing San Francisco. He later went to South America, where he built the first railroad across the Andes, but his legacy in California was a lumber boom that lasted over 50 years in Mendocino.

The New England woodsmen who followed him to California built a New-England-style town at Big River, thus accounting for the misplaced architecture still seen today. Steeply pitched roofs are slanted to shed snow—which, of course, never falls in Mendocino.

As the port grew in importance, coastal ships from Seattle and San Francisco made regular calls at Mendocino. Along Main Street a dozen hotels sprouted (along with about twice that number of brothels and saloons).

Lone survivor of these enterprising hostelries is the **Mendocino Hotel** (707/937-0511). Its renovated Victorian opulence evokes the day when prosperous lumbermen nicknamed $20 gold pieces "Big River bits." Today it has 24 rooms, most with bath, the rest served by spotless modern facilities just a few feet away. A bar and restaurant are also on the premises. A breakfast of fresh fruit, fresh-squeezed orange juice, and homemade nut and fruit breads is included in the double-room rate of $25 to $35 without bath; $40 to $55 with. Reserve in advance.

While a few years back Mendocino was a sleepy artist's community with seasonally oriented (May to September) tourism—a folksy town where residents knew everyone—today it is a year-round mecca for artists, tourists and vacationers of all sorts. You used to be able to sit in the **Seagull Cellar Bar** with a maximum of three or four other folks and talk and drink till they closed at 8 or 9 p.m. Today the Seagull (along with other Mendocino hangouts) is open till 2 a.m. and usually as packed as a San Francisco singles bar. But the town remains rich in picturesque natural beauty and vintage samplings of the past, and the community is still made up of a diverse and talented populace. Its integrity is further protected by the fact that it is preserved architecturally as a historical zone. A walk down Mendocino's wide streets takes you past weathered picket fences and houses once occupied by lumber barons. The **McCallum House** and the disused **Baptist Church** are among the better preserved.

Main Street and neighboring streets are lined with art galleries and craft shops showing a variety of works from landscape paintings to macrame, tie dyes, candles and ceramics. At **Zacha's Bay Window Gallery**, 560 Main, works by the faculty of the Art Center are shown. Other Main Street establishments include **Victorian Vignettes**, specializing in vintage sepia portraits in period costume; clothing boutiques; and **Kolor-Phorme**, featuring European toys. Pick up a guide to shops and galleries from any shop as soon as you arrive.

As for eateries, they abound, and suffice it to say that you will more likely come upon home-baked bran muffins, imported cheeses, organic grains and vegetables than Wonder Bread and Coca-Cola.

MENDOCINO ART CENTER: The hub of Mendocino activity, as well as the coast's artistic renaissance, is the **Mendocino Art Center** on Little Lake Street. Billing itself quite simply as a "place for learning art," the Center teaches everything from painting, photography, ceramics and sculpture to the art of boat-building. Textiles and weaving are also areas of study. Founded in 1959, it was the creation of William Zacha, a painter, and his wife Jenny, who had long dreamed of establishing a unique art school in an area of great beauty and creative energy.

In addition to classes, the Art Center offers a year-round program of activities: exhibitions, dance, drama, music, foreign and domestic film classics. And three art fairs yearly draw visitors from around the country and serve as a showcase for local and outside artists, musicians and craftspeople. And social events include dances, a wine-tasting and the annual Walpurgis Eve Rhododendron Ball.

BOTANICAL GARDENS: Five miles north on Highway 1, you'll come to the **Mendocino Coast Botanical Gardens**, a charming cliff-top park among the redwoods along the rugged coast. The Gardens were fashioned by a retired landscape nurseryman who spent years reclaiming wilderness and nurturing rhododendrons, fuchsias, azaleas, and a multitude of flowering shrubs. The area contains trails for easy walking, rustic bridges, streams, canyons, dells and picnic areas. From a cliff house overlooking the Pacific you can enjoy the play of the sea against the jagged rocks below. Open daily from 8:30 a.m. to 6 p.m., the Gardens charge $1.75 admission for adults, $1.25 for ages 13 to 18, 75¢ for children six to 12.

3. Fort Bragg

Continuing along the Mendocino coast another ten miles, you'll come to Fort Bragg, the largest coastal city between San Francisco and Eureka. Its southern gateway is the harbor town of **Noyo**, sport-fishing center of the county and locale of many gourmet seafood restaurants. From Fort Bragg you can foray into the ageless redwood groves in nearby parks, many of which have camping facilities.

One of the best ways to see the redwoods is to "ride the **Skunks**"— California Western Railroad's self-powered diesel trains which were at one time powered by gas. So potent were the gas fumes in those days that people used to say, "You can smell 'em before you can see 'em," and dubbed them, affectionately, "Skunks."

The trains, boarded at the foot of Laurel Avenue in Fort Bragg, travel along the Redwood Highway (U.S. 101) to **Willits,** 40 miles inland—a journey through the very heart of the towering redwood forest along a spectacular route inaccessible by auto. With windows front and side, they're wonderful for sightseeing.

Even more fun (especially for kids) is the **Super-Skunk,** tugged by an authentic steam engine and provided with old-time railroad cars, painted red and equipped with handsome leather seats.

The ride takes you across 31 bridges and trestles, and through two deep tunnels, its serpentine route encompassing changes of scenery from forest to sunlit fields of wildflowers, grazing cattle and apple orchards.

The Skunks run all year, leaving Fort Bragg at 9:50 a.m. daily. The trip takes about two hours, which allows ample time for lunch in Willits before returning on the 1:50 p.m. train. Super-Skunks operate only in summer from June 12 to September 11, with daily Fort Bragg departures at 10 a.m.. For either train the price of a round-trip ticket is $8.20; $5.45 one way. Children five to 11 pay $4.10 round trip, $2.75 one way; under-fives free. For further information phone (707) 964-3798.

Another Fort Bragg attraction is the **Georgia-Pacific Company** at the junction of Highway 1 and Walnut Street. You can stop in from May to November, 8 a.m. to 4:30 p.m., for a free look at some two-million trees and a guided tour of the extensive sawmill plant. There's a small logging museum on the premises, and occasionally films are shown. There are picnic areas, so bring lunch if you so desire.

If it proves convenient, hit Fort Bragg Labor Day Weekend, when crowds gather for **Paul Bunyan Days** activities: axe-throwing, pole-climbing, log-rolling and the like.

More redwoods? Hop in the car again and head north to **Sylvandale,** six miles above Garberville on Route 101 (Routes 1 and 101 converge at Leggett). Soon you'll come to a sign directing you to one of the most spectacular routes in the West, The—

4. Avenue of the Giants

Thirty-three miles long, this scenic avenue, roughly paralleling US 101 (240 miles north of San Francisco), was left intact for sightseers when the freeway was built. Its giants are majestic coast redwoods—*Sequoia sempervirens*—some 43,000 acres of them making up the most outstanding display in the redwood belt. Their rough-bark columns climb 100 feet or more without a branch and the arching forest roof creates an atmosphere of a huge outdoor temple.

Drive slowly, leaving your car occasionally for walks through the forest. En route you'll notice three public campgrounds: **Hidden Springs,** above Miranda; **Burlington,** two miles south of Weott; and **Albee Creek State Campground,** off to the left above Weott. You'll also come across picnic and swimming facilities, motels, resorts restaurants, and numerous resting and parking areas.

If you prefer to leave the driving to others, you can take a bus tour through the redwoods. A day-long ride on **"The Squirrel,"** an open sightseeing bus, leaves Garberville at 10 a.m. Mondays, Wednesdays, Fridays and Saturdays in summer.

You can have lunch a few miles past the end of the road in **Scotia**, where you can also take a tour of the **Pacific Lumber Company**, one of the world's largest mills. Here, for 50¢ or a dollar, those so inclined can drive their cars *through* a living redwood.

5. Yosemite National Park

This 1,200-square-mile park is a scenic wonderland of towering cliffs—sheer steel-blue domes of rock rising from the river, their peaks haloed in clouds; of waterfalls tumbling through misty rainbows to the valley below; of tranquil groves of giant sequoias, pine, fir and oak; of meadows of alpine wildflowers; and of hundreds of species of birds and animals.

It was barely a century ago that the first pioneers crested this canyon; they called the valley Yosemite after the tribe of Indians they found sheltered in the shadows of the cliffs.

Today it is a major recreational area and one of America's most spectacular national parks.

The center of activities is **Yosemite Valley.** Though occupying only seven square miles of the park, the Valley offers campgrounds, lodgings, and a complex of shops, restaurants and facilities known as **Yosemite Village.** We recommend that you begin explorations of Yosemite with a stop at the **Visitor Center** (tel: 209/372-4461) in the Village Mall to see audiovisual programs and other exhibits, obtain maps and information. Here you'll find out about the many daily activities, Ranger-guided walks, lectures and demonstrations; and those who are interested can learn about the geological sequence of Yosemite development, from its beginnings eons ago with the formation of granite beneath the earth's surface, to the glacial action which carved the valleys and formed the lakes. You'll also want to know how to reach the museums, the sequoia groves, the inspiring granite summits and the waterfall bases, and what to do if a begging bear approaches you for a handout (absolutely nothing).

While the Valley is the hub of everything that's happening, and contains many scenic features (Yosemite Falls, Bridal Veil Falls, Mirror Lake, Half Dome, Sentinel Rock, El Capitan. The Three Brothers, and Cathedral Rocks), you'll want to leave the Valley to explore the park's other natural bounties. There are 700 miles of trails you can cover, by horse, mule or foot only, many leading up north into the mountain meadowlands, blanketed in wildflowers, which are known as the **High Country** and are snowed-in nine months of the year. There are 216 miles of road which you can traverse by car (rangers will recommend tours). And many bus tours are offered by the Yosemite Transportation System. Things to see and do are suggested below, but first—

GETTING THERE: From San Francisco by car, take Interstate 580, then Interstate 5 to the Gustine off-ramp, and finally State Highway 140 to Yosemite Valley. You can make the trip by train via Amtrak; Greyhound or Continental Trailways buses, and a special weekend express bus from San Francisco; inquire at the San Francisco Chamber of Commerce.

ENTRANCE FEES: An entrance fee is charged to the Park to help defray the immense cost of maintenance. At each of the four entrances—**Route 120** on the northwest, **Route 140** toward the southwest, **Route 41** on the south and **Route 120** on the northeast (open in summer only)—rangers are stationed to check you in and out. The entrance permit costs $3 per car per day; if you plan to stay longer than three days it might be worth your while to purchase a season's pass at $10, which is good in national parks throughout the country for one year's time. Permits allow you to leave and enter the park at will. If you overstay or understay your limit, the difference will be made up when you leave.

THINGS TO SEE: As soon as you reach the Valley, stop at the **Visitor Center** and pick up the Yosemite Guide, a free newsletter describing the week's activities, and a map of the park. Beginning each morning as early as 8:30 a.m. (sometimes earlier, sometimes later) and going till about 9 p.m., well over a dozen daily activities are offered. They might include lectures on photography; a 30-minute Ranger-led fireside discussion on bears; a guided luncheon hike to a waterfall; a geological history tour or a puppet show with environmental theme. Activities are fewer off season.

Not to be missed are the following highlights:

Toulumne Meadows: Gateway to the High Country, at an elevation of 8,600 feet, this is the largest alpine meadow in the High Sierras. Closed in winter, it's 55 miles from the Valley by way of highly scenic Big Oak Flat and Tioga roads. A walk through this natural alpine garden makes a delightful day's excursion. In summer, the park operates a large campground and conducts a full-scale naturalist program here.

Happy Isles Trail Center: Another gateway to the High Country, Happy Isles is also a trailhead for the John Muir Trail, and Vernal and Nevada Falls (the Mist Trail). Accessible by shuttlebus, the Center is manned by Ranger naturalists who provide information about traveling in the wildlands. Nearby are the Indian Caves and natural Mirror Lake.

The Mariposa Grove: One of three groves of giant sequoias, this is the largest, with thousands of trees, over 200 of which measure ten feet or more in diameter; among them is the Grizzly Giant, largest and oldest tree in the park. (It takes 27 fifth-graders to reach around it; only 18 to reach around a school bus.) Private vehicles can drive to the entrance of the grove; beyond that you can hike or board the free shuttlebus. There are stops where you can get off to hear nature talks, stroll around, take photos or just absorb the peaceful atmosphere of the forest. Mariposa is 35 miles from the valley; other redwood areas are Toulumne and Merced groves near Crane Flat.

Glacier Point: Offering a sweeping 180° panorama of the High Sierras, and a breathtaking view from 3,200 feet of the Valley, Glacier Point looks out over Nevada and Vernal Falls, Merced River and the snowclad Sierra peaks of Yosemite's backcountry. The approach road from the Badger Pass intersection (closed in winter) winds through verdant red-fir and pine forest and meadow. Many fine trails lead back down to the Valley floor.

Pioneer Yosemite History Center: Reached via a covered bridge constructed in 1858, the Center, at Wawona, tells of man's history in the park. Exhibits include "living history" demonstrations, some of the early buildings and horse-drawn vehicles. In a similar category is the—

Yosemite Travel Museum: at the Arch Rock entrance, where exhibits— displays of old rail cars, a train station from Bagby, an antique snow plow, etc.—tell the story of early-day rail and auto transportation in the Yosemite region.

Yosemite Indian Garden: Behind the Visitor Center, during summer, you can watch Miwok Indians demonstrating ancient techniques of basket-weaving, making arrowheads and grinding acorns, among other things.

THINGS TO DO: A popular vacation destination in itself, Yosemite offers an exceptionally wide variety of visitor activities, from summer water sports and field trips to the more rugged snow-related pursuits.

Hiking

As we said before, over 700 miles of trails offer hiking possibilities to satisfy the hardy and the frail alike, as well as everyone in between. You can take anything from a leisurely stroll to a trip of a week or longer, on terrain ranging from plains to jagged mountains. If you wish to penetrate the less-traveled backcountry, a free wilderness permit is required. (Permits limit the traffic here, to help keep the wilderness wild.) This can be obtained at any of the ranger stations or by writing Box 577, Yosemite, California 95389. Fifty percent of the permits are granted by reservation; the other 50% on a first-come, first-served basis.

Horseback-Riding

Yosemite has excellent stable facilities, fully staffed with expert horsemen. There are 30 miles of bridle paths in the Valley, with all-day trips offered to the Valley's rim. Stables—at **Curry Village** and **Wawona**—are open in summer season only. Two-hour guided horseback-rides leave several times daily for tours of their areas; cost is $7. There are also half-day trips: from the Curry Stables, the ride goes to Clark's Point and Nevada Falls; from Wawona to the south fork of the Merced or to Chilualna Falls. Half-day tours cost $10 per person. There are also full-day guided mule trips from both stables going to such places as the base of Half Dome via Vernal and Nevada Falls, Glacier Point, the top of Yosemite Falls, or Mariposa Grove. Cost is $16.

Several days a week a six-day guided saddle trip leaves the Valley and tours the six High Sierra camps, stopping at a different one each night. About ten miles apart, each camp consists of dormitory tents and a central dining tent.

Anglers might enjoy the three-day saddle/fishing trip to Merced Lake from the Valley, escorted by an experienced fishing guide (California fishing license required).

Burros, especially popular with kids, are also rentable for $1.75 per hour. You might let the younger tots ride a burro while you hike along one of the scenic trails.

For information about saddle trips (or hiking trips, for that matter) write to the address mentioned above for wilderness permits, or call (209) 372-4611, ext. 248.

Swimming

Some accommodation facilities have swimming pools, but there are also the myriad sparkling streams, bracing rivers and waterfalls to bathe in or under. A favorite spot for swimmers is the Merced River.

Bicycling

Why not see the sights on two wheels? Many trails are specially geared to cyclists, and you can rent a standard or multi-speed bike from the Yosemite

Lodge bike stand or the Curry Village bike stand. Standard bikes rent for $1 per hour, $7.50 per day. Multi-speed vehicles are $1.25 an hour or $10 a day. Stands are open daily from 8 a.m. to 8 p.m.

Mountain-Climbing

With vertical granite walls surrounding two-thirds of the Valley, Yosemite is considered by experts to be one of the finest climbing areas in the western world. And **Yosemite Mountaineering School** has classes for beginning, intermediate and advanced climbers. Inquire at the Visitor Center.

Skiing and Other Winter Sports

The oldest ski area in California, **Badger Pass** (a 20-mile drive from the Valley) opened to skiers in 1935. Facilities include three double chair lifts, two T-bars (lift tickets $7.50), a child care center (for tots of three years and up) and snack bar. It's open through Easter, weather permitting, and the majority of the terrain is geared to the intermediate level, with about 30% for beginners and 10% for experts. An expert staff of instructors offers introductory and refresher courses, as well as children's ski lessons.

There are 90 miles of trails marked for cross-country skiing, with lessons scheduled daily; skiers can follow a trail across wooded Sierra slopes and stay overnight at **Ostrander Lake Ski Hut.**

Winter sports enthusiasts can also use an outdoor ice rink at Curry Village, open daily (weather permitting). Rental skates and lessons are available. In addition you can rent sleds, snow saucers, snowmobiles and cross-country ski equipment.

For information on Yosemite ski facilities, write to Badger Pass, Yosemite National Park, California 95389, or call (209) 372-4691.

Fishing

Fishing licenses (required for anyone over 16) are easily obtainable throughout the park. Beautiful High Country lakes, miles of rivers (the Merced and Tuolumne are especially popular), streams and tributaries provide anglers with not only excellent fishing but unsurpassed views. Various kinds of trout are the main catch here.

WHERE TO STAY: From luxury hotel to woodland cabin to simple tent, Yosemite offers a wide choice of accommodations. We'll begin with facilities for—

Camping

Yosemite has 337 campsites for year-round use, and 2,086 open in summer. They all charge a $3 entrance fee and a $1 to $4 daily camping fee. Campsites are scattered over 20 different campgrounds in three categories. Type A campgrounds are the most elaborate, with well-defined roads, parking, drinking water, flush toilets and, generally, a fireplace, table/bench combination and tent space. Type B areas may be accessible by road or trail, and conveniences are limited to basic sanitary facilities and a smattering of fireplaces and tables. Type C areas don't concern us, as they are limited to groups (e.g. Boy Scout troops).

All campsites are on a first-come, first-served basis, and from June 1 to September 15 camping is limited to seven days in the Valley and 14 days in the rest of the park. The rest of the year the limit is 30 days throughout the park. Backcountry campers need a wilderness permit.

For more details on campgrounds write to Box 577, Yosemite National Park, California 95389.

Other Accommodations

Reservations are advised at all times and especially in summer for all hotels, lodges and cabins in the park.

Within walking distance of the Valley, is **Yosemite Lodge**, with attractive deluxe units, hotel rooms with or without bath, and redwood cabins with or without bath. Rates are the same for one or two persons. Bathless hotel rooms are $12.50, bathless cabins $8.50, cabins with bath $15, standard hotel rooms $22 and deluxe rooms $27. A coffee shop, lounge, dining room and cafeteria are on the premises, as are several shops.

Rustic **Curry Village** also charges the same rates for singles and doubles. Hotel rooms are $19, cabins with bath $15, and cabins without bath $8.50.

There's less roughing-it at the **Wawona Hotel** which offers such gracious accoutrements as a swimming pool, tennis court and nine-hole golf course, as well as a dining room and nearby stables. Single or double hotel rooms are $21 to $24; bathless rooms $11.50.

The luxurious, and very centrally located, **Ahwahnee Hotel** has a nine-hole course, lovely dining facilities, a lounge and gift shop. Rooms with bath are $32 single, $40 double.

At any of the above, a deposit covering one night's lodging is required to confirm reservations, refundable if cancellation is received seven days before your arrival date. Write to the Reservation Department, Yosemite Park and Curry Co., Yosemite National Park, California 95389. In California reserve by calling toll-free (800) 692-5811; in other states dial (209) 372-4671.

6. South Lake Tahoe

"I ascended today the highest peak ... from which we had a beautiful view of a mountain lake at our feet, about 15 miles in length, and so nearly surrounded by mountains that we could not discover an outlet." These are the words of John C. Fremont, the early California pioneer who discovered the "Lake of the Sky," set at 6,225 feet above sea level in the heavily timbered Sierra Nevada mountains on the Nevada-California border.

Said by many to be the most beautiful lake in the world, Lake Tahoe is famous for its 99.1% pure water—objects at depths of 100 feet are clearly visible from the surface, and divers claim visibility at 200 feet under. The dimensions of the lake belie its immense capacity; the average depth is 989 feet, which is sufficient water to cover the entire state of California with 14½ inches of water! More important to the visitor, though, the play of light during the day causes the color of the lake to change from dazzling emerald to blues and rich purples. And due to atmospheric conditions in the area, some of the most beautiful sunsets in the world are seen here.

The 75-mile circle around the lake is filled with recreational, historical and scenic points of interest. In summer, you can enjoy the crystal waters of Lake Tahoe for swimming (if you're hearty enough for some pretty cold water), fishing, boating and water sports. Lakeside beaches, picnic areas and campgrounds are plentiful. In winter, Lake Tahoe becomes a popular ski resort. Year-round, there's glittering Vegas-style gambling and big-name entertainment on the Nevada border. And that's not the half of it.

SOUTH LAKE TAHOE

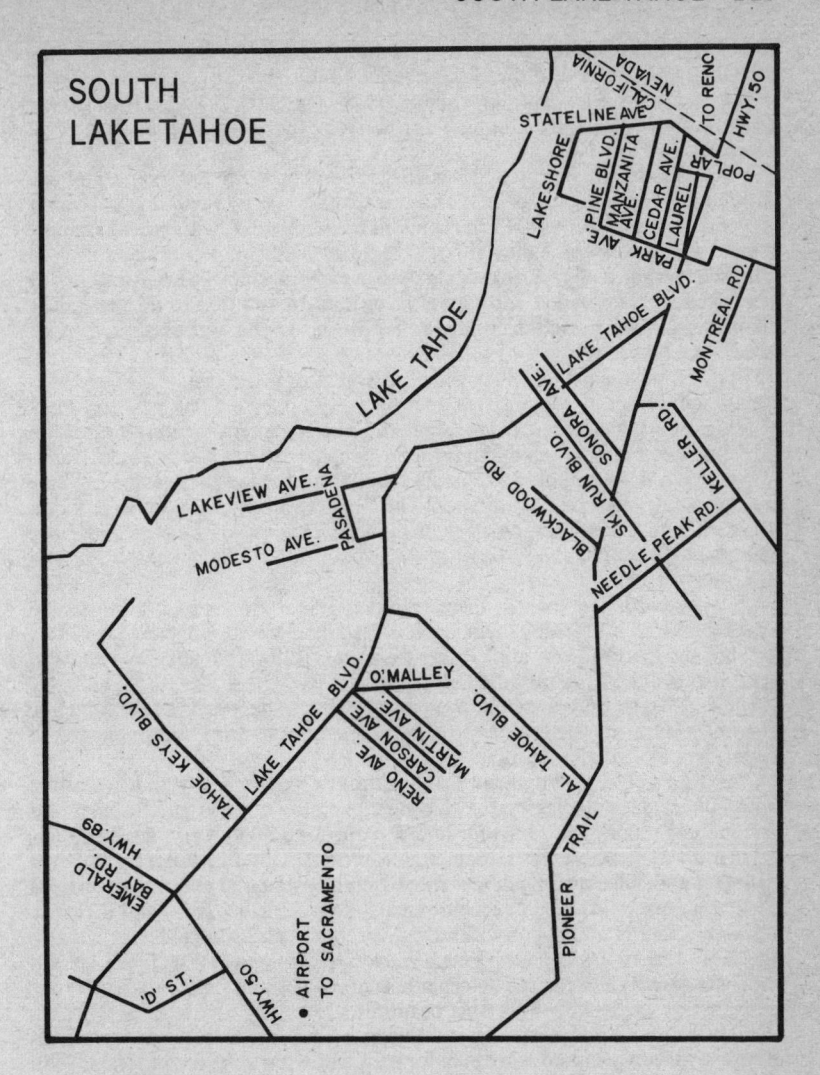

Lake Tahoe can be reached by Air California from San Francisco ($19). Pacific Southwest Airlines also flies to Tahoe from various California cities, not including San Francisco. Most cities offer Greyhound Bus connections. By car it's a fairly long drive—209 miles from San Francisco via Interstate 80 and Highway 50.

So popular is this multi-recreational area that hotel rooms tend to get booked heavily in advance. Don't arrive without reservations or you may find yourself a reluctant camper.

Make your first stop in Lake Tahoe the **Chamber of Commerce,** on Highway 50, three miles west of Stateline (tel: 541-5255), an excellent organization with a knowledgeable and friendly staff, and oodles of printed information about local activities.

WHERE TO STAY: All the gambling action is just across Stateline (AKA the state line) in Nevada, and the closer you are to it, the more expensive are your accommodations. The three top choices are the big hotel/casino extravaganzas actually in Nevada, just a stone's throw from the California border. Most renowned of these is—

Harrah's, right at Stateline (tel: 702/588-6611). With 250 rooms, and 240 more under construction as we go to press, this 18-story facility is a 24-hour hub of Lake Tahoe activity. Posh rooms all have color TV, with bedside remote control which also works the lights and radio; a small bar and refrigerator (you can order a choice of 14 drinks via a push-button mechanism); TV and phone in each of the two baths, and ice-water on tap. In addition to all these little luxuries, the rooms, each decorated to reflect one of the four seasons, happen to be gorgeous.

Of course, the principal attraction at Harrah's is the casino, a biggie with 50,000 square feet of gaming area offering everything from baccarat to Bingo. The kids are taken care of, too, with recreation centers—a nursery section ($1.25 an hour, four hours maximum) for youngsters ages two to six, a "varsity" section ($1.50 an hour, five hours maximum) for kids seven to 17. These are the only such facilities in town. The well-supervised nursery section has Playdough, toys, records, books, games and sleeping mats. The older kids have penny arcade games, Ping-Pong, bowling, pool, color TV, movies, a jukebox and lounge area.

In the South Shore Room there's big-name entertainment—headliners like Frank Sinatra, Bill Cosby, Olivia Newton-John, Merle Haggard, Anthony Newley and Barbra Streisand. Prices for dinner shows range from $12.50 to $15; $10 to $12.50 for the midnight show.

From 7 p.m. on you can also catch some pretty good acts at the Stateline Cabaret Lounge in the casino. No charge, just a one-drink minimum to see performers like B.B. King, Fabian and the Platters.

Harrah's chief dining facility is the Summit Restaurant, with a cascading waterfall inside and glass walls allowing panoramic views of the lake and surrounding mountains. Open for lunch, dinner and Sunday brunch, the Summit features live music for dancing nightly till 2 a.m. The brunch ($4.50) is elaborate and delicious; the dinner menu offers continental gourmet specialties like pheasant served with choucroute and champagne sauce ($14) and Etruscan chicken, baked in a clay pot with herbs, vegetables and wine ($17 for two). A bit on the expensive side, but perhaps you've been winning at the tables. If not, there are several less-costly choices and six bars if you'd prefer to drink your dinner.

We're not through yet. Harrah's has superb health-club facilities with massage, sauna, gym and whirlpool for men and women (men get steam, too). Elaborately equipped right down to the dressing rooms with shampoo, deodorant and cologne, there are even three-way mirrors and a scale to spur you on.

What does all this splendor cost? It depends on the season, but year-round the rates include free valet parking and transportation to and from the airport. Friday and Saturday all year, and Sunday through Thursday from May 30 to October 7, singles are $44 to $48, doubles $50 to $54. Sunday through Thursday, October 10 to November 24 and April 1 to May 27, singles are $37 to $41, doubles $41 to $45. The rest of the year singles are $30 to $33, doubles $33 to $36.

A similar Stateline operation is Del Webb's 525-room **Sahara Tahoe** (tel: 702/588-6211). Rooms are a mite less luxurious as far as extras go (rates are lower too), but they are attractively modern, with shag carpeting, vinyl wallpapers, full baths, Princess phones and color TV.

The main casino area is two city blocks in length and contains all the usual gaming action, including 1,000 slots.

Headliners appear in the High Sierra Theatre on the main floor in summer (off season there are big names only on weekends, and first-run movies during the week). Tom Jones, Helen Reddy, Engelbert Humperdinck, Elvis Presley and Liberace are among the superstars who have appeared here. The dinner show is about $15; minimum for the midnight show is $10. On the casino floor there's live rock music in the Pine Cone Lounge continuously from mid-afternoon till the wee hours.

The Sahara Tahoe's main restaurant is the House of Lords, a plush candle-lit establishment with deep-red banquettes, mirrored walls, crystal chandeliers and soft background music. Service is first-class, and the continental gourmet cuisine excellent. Entrees include a cold vegetable plate (a meal in itself), soup or salad, rice or potato, petits fours and coffee. Roast duckling à l'orange or with cherries is $8.50; filet mignon in Béarnaise sauce, $11.50. Flambée desserts are a specialty. The House of Lords is open nightly from 6 to 11 p.m.

Other dining choices here: the Bonanza Buffet, served from 5 to 11 p.m. nightly ($3.95 to $5.95); a 24-hour coffee shop called the Four Seasons, and a simple Snack Bar for hot dogs, hamburgers and sandwiches.

The Sahara has a big outdoor pool, massage and sauna available, shops and free valet parking for guests.

After April 1st rates are $42 double, $38 single. Generally these go down some (about $2) from November through March, and they're even lower Sundays through Thursdays in the winter season.

Beginning with a gas station and mom-and-pop restaurant, plus a handful of guest rooms upstairs and six slots, Harvey Gross has nurtured **Harvey's** (tel: 702/588-2411) from humble beginnings to one of Stateline's top luxury resort hotels. The original building has grown to 11 stories with 200 lake-view rooms, the six slots have become over 1,600, and craps, twenty-one, keno and Big Six have been added.

The rooms are standard luxury rooms with radio, color cable TV, and whatever else you'd expect.

You can dine at the Top of the Wheel enjoying the view 11 stories up in a South Seas setting of thatched roofing, rattan and bamboo. The decor reflects the cuisine—entrees like shrimp curry Singapore ($8.50) and Polynesian honey duck served with wild rice and a plum sauce ($10.25). Intoxicating rum concoctions are also a specialty here. Entertainment and dancing nightly.

Harvey's original eatery is now the Sage Room, specializing in steak and seafood offerings beginning at $8.50 for barbecued ribs. The ambience is Western. And buffet meals are served nightly in the El Dorado Room—all you can eat of seven entrees, 25 salads and 40 desserts costs $4.75 Monday through Thursday, $5.95 Friday through Sunday. A 24-hour coffee shop, a pancake parlor and three snack bars complete the culinary scene.

Singers and comedians entertain in the main bar (one of many) at the casino almost round the clock.

Rates for singles are $33 to $42; doubles and twins, $35 to $44.

Now moving over to the California side of town, within easy walking distance of all casino action (a shuttlebus is available in any case) is **Forest Inn**, 1110 Park Avenue (tel: 916/541-6655). So close is this luxury resort to Stateline that it adjoins the side entrance of Harrah's casino. Set in 6½ acres of garden and forest, it has 125 rooms housed in rustic buildings. There are three different types of accommodations. The first are regular motel units with all modern conveniences—color TV, dressing areas, tub/shower baths, phone, alarm clock, air conditioning and heating. Then there are one- and two-bedroom suites, which in addition to the above also have fully equipped modern kitchens with dishwashers, living rooms and dining areas. All the accommodations are well appointed and spacious, with attractive modern furnishings.

Parking is included in rates, and there are two large swimming pools with sunning areas, two whirlpools and sauna baths.

Motel units run from $31.50 to $36.50 single or double; one-bedroom units from $34.50 to $36.50 (add $3 for a third person in the room); two-bedroom suites $47.50 to $49.50 for up to three people. Off-season reductions are granted for stays of three nights and over. Highly recommended.

Well-located, but much cheaper accommodations at the **Stateline Lodge**, corner of Park Avenue and Pine Boulevard (tel: 916/544-3340). Cecil and Sue Bundesen operate this quiet and comfortable little motel, offering warmth and hospitality to guests. Nothing fancy, it has 15 units with black and white TV, bath, daily maid service and coffee-makers in your room. And though there's no restaurant on the premises, the Ramada Inn coffee shop is just across the street, and there are picnic and barbecue facilities. Phones are next to the lobby. The rates from June 15 to September 15 are $16 single, $18 queen, $20 twin; $2 less off season. The Stateline is a short walk from casino action.

If you're willing to stay a little further from the Stateline, you can get both good rates and luxury accommodations. And all you really sacrifice is a few minutes' time getting back and forth to the casino area, since free shuttlebuses run 24 hours a day. In this category, an ideal choice is the **Waystation**, U.S. 50 at Ski Run Boulevard (tel: 916/541-6220), just about a mile from Stateline and only blocks from one of Tahoe's largest ski areas, Heavenly Valley. Rooms are cheerful and rustic, with pine paneling, pretty, quilted bedspreads, bright, modern furnishings and baths with dressing rooms, color TV's and direct-dial phones.

The property has 400 feet of beach, as well as a heated pool, sauna and massage. Other facilities include ski and bicycle rental, vending and ice machines on all floors, a 24-hour coffee shop, a dining room, and beauty shop. And in addition to the casino shuttle, there's also free ski and airport shuttle service.

Double-occupancy rates are $26 to $38 from May 27 to September 30; $20 to $28 the rest of the year, except on major holidays. Less expensive yet, and still further away, is a **Motel 6** on Highway 50, 3½ miles west of the border, with 140 units and a small pool. See "California Hotels" in the Introduction for Motel 6 particulars.

Many accommodations hereabouts are, of course, especially geared to the ski crowd. One of the most popular, in the Heavenly Valley area, is the **Christiania Inn** at the top of Ski Run Boulevard (tel: 916/544-7337), a delightful 12-unit country inn with rooms opening onto sundecks facing the slopes or forest. You can ski right to the door. Each room is uniquely decorated, ranging from the Chamonix room with rustic barnwood walls, patchwork quilt spread, dried-flower arrangements and antique furnishings, to the luxurious Davos Chalet suite with plush fur throws and art nouveau pillows. There's no TV, but there are such extras as good artwork on the walls, flowers in your room, candles and a selection of books for late-night readers. All rooms have floor-to-ceiling windows, private tub/shower baths and individual heat control. There's a relaxing après-ski lounge and a fine fireside restaurant (see dining listings below). Singles pay $20, doubles $23. Open year round and you don't have to be a skier to stay here; if you have a car it's a five-minute drive to Stateline casinos.

SOUTH LAKE TAHOE

MORE CASINO ACTION: The biggest casinos are in the first three hotels described above, but Tahoe also has some independent casinos. They're all popular, since few gamblers are content to lose all their money in one place, under the theory that prosperity and a winning keno ticket are just around the corner. One of the biggest of these non-hotel casinos is **Barney's**, just adjacent to Harrah's. It's open 24 hours a day the year round, and most Tahoe hotels give out Barney's coupons for free games and discounts. Coupons are also distributed for the **South Tahoe Nugget**, under the same ownership and with the same hours, one of a cluster of motels and casinos about three quarters of a mile east on Highway 50.

The most important thing about Barney's and the Nugget is their year-round 24-hour free shuttlebus. Call the Barney's bus (588-2455) from any motel or hotel on Highway 50 up to and including the Waystation. It will come right to your door and drop you off in front of the Sahara Tahoe (across the street from Barney's). If you would like to go to the Nugget, hop the Nugget shuttle which plies the route back and forth between the Sahara Tahoe and the Nugget.

In the Nugget vicinity, the other main contender for your money is **Harvey's Inn**, a casino with a ski-lodge ambience, raw pine paneling, cork ceilings, and a seven-foot TV screen for airing sporting events. Between this and Harvey's Stateline casino, Harvey Gross claims to have more slots than anyone in Nevada.

Right next door is **Gary's**, a small and intimate operation with six 21 tables, a keno desk, about 100 slots and a poker room. Food in the coffee shop is very inexpensive, and there's a cozy fireplace lounge. These latter casinos, being a little further from Stateline, tend to be less hectic, which makes for a pleasant change.

WHERE TO DINE: Far and away the most romantic choice for dinner or Sunday brunch is the **Top of the Tram** (tel: 544-6263) at the end of Keller Road in Heavenly Valley. Unless you're a hearty hiker, this restaurant can only be reached by car, which is left in the parking lot while you ascend 8,300 feet to the top of the mountain via cable car. The ride up is part of the fun, and the view from the restaurant is breathtaking. It's particularly exquisite in the early evening, when the magnificent Sierra sunset over the lake and mountains is yours to behold. There's an outdoor cafe area; inside there are windows on three sides.

Brunch, served Sundays from 10 a.m. to 2 p.m., proffers fresh berries, melons and other fruits and juices, freshly baked breads and pastries, scrambled eggs, ham, bacon and sausage, beef stroganoff, creamed chicken and other delectable goodies, plus champagne. The price: $6.95 including the tram ride.

Dinner, served nightly from 5 to 11 p.m., is a $10.95 prix fixe (including tram ride). It begins with homemade soup or salad, followed by an entree choice of sirloin steak, stuffed Cornish game hen, stuffed trout or rack of lamb, potatoes, fresh vegetables, rolls and butter, ice cream or sherbert, and coffee. Reservations are suggested.

Top of the Tram is open for lunch, too, but then you have to pay for the ride, which is $3.50 round trip for adults, $1.50 for kids under 12.

Another restaurant catering mostly to the ski-resort crowd is **The Snow Goose**, 1444 Ski Run Boulevard (tel: 541-SNOW). Nestled in the mountains among towering pines and shimmering aspen, The Snow Goose offers truly fine cuisine. Everything is homemade, fresh and natural, prepared with love and skill in classical tradition with an innovative touch. No pre-cooked or frozen items here. Once again there's a lovely view of lake and mountains. The interior is intimate, dominated by a huge copper fireplace, with wood-beamed stucco walls and a color scheme of soft blues and greens. This is a place to order lavishly and savor every bite. You might begin with escargots bourguignons ($4.50) or a wilted spinach salad ($3 for two persons). All the entrees are terrific; one of the most interesting is a South African rijsttafel of curried lamb on a bed of rice with appropriate condiments and fruit ($20 for two). You might ask the waiter to help select the correct wine for your entree—the wine list here has been carefully and thoughtfully compiled.

The Snow Goose is open nightly from 6 p.m. to midnight (closed Tuesdays off season). There's live jazz the second Sunday of every month. Reservations suggested.

Also sheltered in the mountain pines near Heavenly Valley is the **Christiania Inn**, at the top of Ski Run Boulevard (tel: 544-7337). A charming candlelit restaurant with fresh flowers on butcher-block tables, blazing fireplaces in the dining room and lounge areas, and classical or mellow rock music in the background. The emphasis here is on creative and healthful cookery—lots of fresh vegetables and organic grains. Dinners at the Christiania include a salad of butter lettuce, romaine, fresh mushrooms and alfalfa sprouts with house dressing, freshly baked bread, coffee or tea and dessert. For an entree you might select mountain trout stuffed with cornbread dressing, shrimp, crabmeat and herbs, sauteed in butter sauce, served with mixed grains and fresh vegetables ($6.50). Open nightly for dinner. Reservations suggested.

One of the oldest and best-known restaurants in the area is the **Swiss Chalet**, on U.S. Highway 50 four miles west of Stateline (tel: 544-3304). Abounding in Swiss kitsch, the Swiss Chalet is filled with beer steins, cuckoo clocks, paintings of the Alps, hanging copper pots and large brass bells. And if the atmosphere wasn't quite corny enough there's even an accordion player. All in all it's a lot of fun, and the food is hearty and delicious. All entrees come with soup or salad, homemade rolls and butter. German sauerbraten with noodles and red cabbage is $6.50, beef stroganoff $7.50. Be sure to leave room for the scrumptious dessert cakes or pastries ($1 to $1.25). This is a good choice for family dining; complete children's dinners are $3.25 to $3.75. Open nightly from 5 to 11 p.m. Closed Mondays off season.

A New England seafood restaurant serving fresh Maine lobster (you can select your own from a tank) is the last thing you'd expect to find in the Tahoe mountains. But here it is. **The Dory's Oar**, 1041 Fremont Avenue off Highway 50 (tel: 541-6603), looking ever so much like a quaint Nantucket eatery, and serving all-fresh seafood flown in daily from the East Coast. The ambience is New England nautical, its pretty blue-and-white-papered and wood-paneled walls hung with bronze-plated plaques describing ships, ship lights and maps. There are white ruffled curtains on the windows; gaslight lamps and dried flowers grace every table. Dinners include bread, butter, salad-bar offerings, fisherman's fries or a baked potato. The above-mentioned lobster, served with drawn butter, is $11.95. Deep-fried soft-shell crabs are $7.50. The Dory's Oar is open nightly from 5 to 10 p.m. Closed Tuesdays off season.

No more would you expect a Japanese restaurant in this town, but it so happens there's a fine one on the California side of Highway 50 near Park Avenue. It's called **Tahoe Teriyaki,** and though it isn't heavy on ambience, it's simple and pleasant, offering friendly service and excellent Japanese food. A very good beef or chicken sukiyaki is $4.25, beef, chicken or salmon teriyaki is the same price. A bottle of sake with your meal is $1.50, and a tasty salad with a piquant house dressing 40¢—both recommended. Lunch items are in the $2-to-$3.25 range. Open daily in summer from 1 to 10 p.m.; the rest of the year Tuesday to Sunday from 3 to 10 p.m.

For Mexican fare in the casino area, there's **El Pavo**, 1097 Park Avenue (tel: 541-5005), a very friendly place where margaritas are poured by the pitcher ($4.50). Attractive and rustic, El Pavo has a six-foot video-beam projection TV up front on which sporting events and local skiing activities are aired. You can watch while you dine, but if you'd rather not, you can be free of noise in the back room. Here the ambience is cozy and intimate, with roomy booths, light provided by candles, wrought-iron chandeliers and cut-tin lamps, and with macrame hangings on the walls. Immense combination plates, including rice, beans, soup or salad and dessert, are $2.95 to $4.95, and you can create your own combinations. Open daily for dining from 11:30 a.m. to 11:30 p.m.; the bar is open till 2 a.m.

TAHOE SKIING: Sierra snow is unique. It falls quickly in great quantities (20 feet the average winter) about one day in four from late November to early April, and its crystalline structure retains a powdery perfection on the slopes. It's also unusually reflective, so skiers should beware of getting a bad sunburn.

About 22 ski resorts are clustered within 50 miles of the city, more than in any other area of the state, and including America's largest ski area—

Heavenly Valley

This vast two-state complex covers over 20 miles of High Sierra peaks. About 20% of the slopes are geared to beginners, 50% to intermediates, 30% to advanced and expert skiers, with directional and ability level carefully marked. An aerial tram and 18 other lifts convey over 16,000 skiers an hour to the slope of their choice.

Both the Main Lodge on the California side and the Nevada Base facilities offer half- and full-day passes. At the California entrance a full day is $11; $10 Nevada entrance. Half-day, either entrance is $7. Season passes at the Main Lodge begin at $90 for ten days.

A full line of ski equipment can be rented at both state sides. Ditto ski lessons, using Graduated Length Method and geared to various levels, under the auspices of Pepi Greimeister, an Austrian professional and racing coach who heads an expert staff of genial young American and European instructors. Private lessons are $15 an hour, $7.50 for each extra person. A full day of group instruction (morning and afternoon sessions) is $10; $7 for one session. First-time beginners do not need a lift ticket for obvious reasons. If you really want to make progress, take five consecutive full days of lessons, given Monday through Friday; price including lift tickets is $82.50. Heavenly Valley ski season is mid-November through May.

For further information about Heavenly Valley facilities, accommodations, package plans, etc., write to Heavenly Reservations, P.O. Box 822, South Lake Tahoe, California 95705. Or phone: in California (800) 822-5951; other states (800) 824-3852.

Squaw Valley

Site of the 1960 Winter Olympics, Squaw Valley is located on Highway 89 between Truckee and Tahoe City. Once an old mining camp, it is now an alpine resort offering winter sports from November to May. Twenty-five major ski lifts carry 26,000 skiers per hour to slopes offering a wide range of challenges to skiers at all levels of proficiency. Facilities include a day-care center for children ages two to six ($1.50 per hour from 9 a.m. to 4:30 p.m. midweek, 8:30 a.m. to 4:30 p.m. weekends); ski rental and equipment; a 10,000-seat ice-skating area (instruction and skate rental available); a ski school teaching Graduated Length Method; lodge accommodations, eating places and après-ski bars.

All-day lift tickets are $11, half-day $6.50; children under 12 go free when accompanied by a fully paid skiing parent. The price goes down for tickets purchased for two or more consecutive days.

The Ski School offers a half-day of lessons for $7, a full day for $10. Private lessons are $18, and a Monday through Friday intensive lesson package is $40.

For further information about facilities, accommodations and ski packages, write to Squaw Valley USA, Box 2007, Olympic Valley, California 95730; or phone (916) 583-4211.

Alpine Meadows

Five miles northeast of Tahoe City off Highway 89 is Alpine Meadows, its north-facing slopes and 7,000-foot base elevation assuring plenty of snow and good skiing conditions from November through May. Its 2,000 acres extend over two mountains of skiable terrain, the upper part mainly wide-open bowls left in a natural state for advanced and expert skiers, the lower mountain meadows groomed for the novice and intermediate.

Day care is available for children ages two to eight from 8:30 a.m. to 4:30 p.m. daily, and a ski-rental shop and excellent ski school are on the premises.

Lift fees are $11 for adults, $5 for ages 12 and under. A half-day for adults is $7; reductions for two or more full consecutive days. All-day instruction is $11; a half-day (two hours, beginners only) is $8; private lessons are $18 per hour; and five consecutive all-day lesson packages are $50.

For more information write Alpine Meadows, Box AM, Tahoe City, California 95730, or phone (916) 583-4232.

Ski Packages

The above are the major ski resorts in the area. Also popular are **Kirkwood,** 25 miles from South Lake Tahoe on Route 88, and **Northstar,** on Highway 267. Handling package tours, publicity and information for these five resorts, and also for **Incline Village,** is an organization called **Ski Lake Tahoe's High Sierra,** P.O. Box Z, Incline Village, Nevada 89450, tel: (702) 831-4222. One of their available packages provides lodging and interchangeable lift tickets at these six High Sierra resorts. Write to them for information on packages and the resort of your choice.

Packages can give you savings on airfare, ski schools, car rentals, tennis, golf or casino shows—there are lots of different ones.

Another worthy operation, very similar to the above, is **High Sierra Promotions,** in the Dart Building on Highway 50, just a short distance along the Nevada side of Stateline. They, too, offer a wide variety of package tours. Write for information to High Sierra Promotions, P.O. Box 4310, South Lake Tahoe, California 95729; phone (702) 588-3561 or toll-free (800) 648-3388.

You can also book tours through your local travel agent.

SUMMER RECREATION: Tahoe is more than just a little Las-Vegas-cum-ski-area. It's a year-round resort playground, probably offering more options to vacationers in one place than anywhere else in the world. There's enough to fill an entire book, but due to space limitations we can only skim the surface. In addition to what we've covered, there are countless historical sites around the lake and nearby. A tour around the lake, offered by major Stateline hotels is a must—not to mention spectator sports, biking trips, sailing, water skiing, antiquing, visits to ghost towns, backpacking and even panning for gold. So we'll reiterate what was suggested earlier in this chapter—make your first stop the Chamber of Commerce to discover the full range of activities available.

One such activity, very popular in this beautiful natural setting is—

Camping

Most of the campgrounds inside the Tahoe Basin are government operated (federal or state), and though a few operate sites on a first-come, first-served basis, reservations are highly recommended and often necessary in season. All California state campground reservations can be conveniently obtained through Ticketron. Privately owned campgrounds, however, usually provide more of the modern conveniences. We recommend the following:

Camp Richardson: A private campground two miles north of South Lake Tahoe on Highway 89, with 180 campsites for tent camping and trailers up to 30 feet, piped water, toilets and showers. Campers pay $3 a day; $4 to $4.50 for the Trailer Park. Phone: (916) 541-0801.

Fallen Leaf Lodge Campground: A private campground off Highway 89 at the south end of Fallen Leaf Lake, five miles from Stateline. There are 37 campsites for tent campers located in the woods or along a creek, with piped water, flush toilets and showers. Sites cost $3 per day for four persons or less. Phone (916) 541-3366.

Recommended government-administered campgrounds include **Emerald Bay State Park** on Highway 89; **Nevada Beach,** off Highway 50 just one mile north of Stateline; and **South Lake Tahoe–El Dorado County Recreation Area,** on Highway 50 one mile south of Stateline. For further information contact the U.S. Forest Service, Box 8465, South Lake Tahoe, California 95731, or call (916) 541-1130.

Horseback-Riding

Tahoe has many stables and miles of good riding trails. Most convenient to town are **Stateline Stables,** located at the end of Park Avenue behind the Crescent "V" Shopping Center (tel: 541-9896). Open all year from sunrise to sunset.

There's also a corral at the above-mentioned **Camp Richardson,** on Highway 89 on Emerald Bay Road (tel: 541-3113). Horses rent for $4 an hour. Open 8 a.m. to 5 p.m., May through October.

In addition to just renting horses, the former establishment offers trail and pony rides, moonlight rides, sleigh rides, hay rides and lessons. The latter features steak rides, breakfast rides, fishing trips and pack animals.

Fishing

Within the Lake Tahoe Basin exists a great variety of opportunities for fishing enthusiasts. A current California or Nevada license is required ($10 for ten days for non-residents). Headquarters for fishing information and licenses is **The Outdoorsman** on Highway 50 at the Truckee River (tel: 541-1660).

Boat Cruises

If Lake Tahoe is too cold to swim in, non-Polar Bears can at least take a boat cruise on its waters. An organization called **Lake Tahoe Cruises,** operating out of the Ski Run Marina at the end of Ski Run Boulevard (tel: 541-4652), offers three cruises daily to Emerald Bay from May 26th through October.

Cruises on 80-passenger boats leave at 11:15 a.m., 1 p.m. and 3 p.m. Adults pay $4; children ages two to 11 pay $3.

A romantic dinner cruise is offered aboard the *M.S. Dixie,* docked at the Timber Cove Marina, directly behind Timber Cove Lodge on Highway 50 (tel: 541-6617). Departing at 7:30 p.m., the cruise costs $15 per person, and includes steak and wine dinner, live music, dancing and cocktails. Call for reservations.

Golf and Tennis

Even the most dedicated crap-shooters might want to get out of the stuffy casinos once in a while to breathe the fresh mountain air and get a little more exercise than that involved in tossing dice. Gambler golfers needn't go far; one of the best courses in town is at the **Edgewood Tahoe Country Club,** (tel: 588-3566) located on the lake right next to the Sahara Tahoe Hotel at Stateline. Open May through November, this 18-hole championship course offers challenges to every golfer. The course has a fleet of 86 golf cars, a modern driving range, three practice greens, a fully equipped pro shop for men and women, and a lovely clubhouse with dining facilities.

As to tennis, the area has yet to develop facilities commensurate with this sport's popularity. You can, however, use the courts at Lyons Avenue just off Highway 50 daily during summer, from sunrise to 10 p.m., for no charge.

Hiking

A very big sport here, which is not surprising in a magnificent lake and woodland center. Both the Chamber of Commerce and the **Visitor Center** operated by the U.S. Forest Service (off Highway 89 just past Camp Richardson) can suggest guided and self-guided nature walks and trails for hikers of varying heartiness. One interesting trek is along the Rainbow Trail to the **Stream Profile Chamber,** for underground viewing of aquatic life beneath the surface of a flowing mountain stream.

Chapter VII

SOUTH ALONG THE SHORE

1. Monterey
2. Carmel
3. Big Sur
4. San Simeon
5. San Luis Obispo
6. Santa Barbara

THE TOURIST WHO SKIPS from San Francisco to Los Angeles, misses an awful lot. The stretch between Monterey and Santa Barbara, though not as celebrated as points north or south, is a delightful surprise. Throughout, the Pacific Coast scenery varies from picture-postcard-pretty to breathtaking (emphasis on the latter), with nary an eyesore along the way.

We begin in Steinbeck Country, Monterey; adjacent to it, the charmingly quaint village of Carmel. Here you'll notice that you've somehow left the 20th century behind. No one could be so jaded as not to find the rugged Big Sur coastline a thrill—and speaking of being jaded, there's Hearst Castle at San Simeon coming up. At the end of this stretch, you finally enter Southern California—though it seems more like Mexico—in the beautiful seaside resort of Santa Barbara. Santa Barbara's mission is the most idyllic of them all—set on a hillside, it looks like a little piece of heaven.

1. Monterey

Portuguese navigator Juan Rodriguez Cabrillo, was the first to sight Monterey, while sailing to Spain in 1542. In 1602, Sebastian Vizcaino followed in search of a suitable harbor for Manila galleons sailing back from the Philippines. He named the area Monterey in honor of the Count of Monterey, Viceroy of Spain.

But many years passed before the area was colonized. It was well over 200 years after Cabrillo's discovery that the place Richard Henry Dana called "the pleasantest and most civilized place in California" (we agree) was settled, when Father Serra established here the second of his now-famous chain of missions. His landing site is now a state historical monument, although the original mission has been moved to nearby Carmel.

Monterey was under Mexican rule from 1821 to 1846, and even today there are many architectural echoes—white-washed adobe houses and pueblos —of this period. About a dozen such buildings have been preserved as historical monuments, among them the **Custom House** where Commodore John Drake Sloat first officially raised the United States flag in 1846.

Monterey is also Steinbeck country. Mack and the boys lived down on **Cannery Row** in a place called the Palace Flophouse. In the '40s Steinbeck wrote: "Cannery Row in Monterey . . . is a poem, a stink, a grating noise, a quality of light, a tone, a habit, a nostalgia, a dream." Returning in the '60s to the street he had given fame, he had this to say: "The beaches are clean where they once festered with fish guts and flies. The canneries which once put up a sickening stench are gone, their places filled with restaurants, antique shops, and the like. They fish for tourists, now, not pilchards, and that species they are not likely to wipe out."

It's true that Cannery Row is touristy these days, but then, how many of you *really* want to see festering fish guts and flies?

Monterey is easily reachable from points north or south (it's 330 miles north of Los Angeles, 130 miles South of San Francisco) via Highway 101 and/or scenic Highway 1. By air, both Hughes Airwest and United Airlines serve the Monterey Peninsula.

WHAT'S DOING IN MONTEREY: There's so much to see and do in beautiful Monterey, and in the vicinity, that we suggest you make your first stop at the **Chamber of Commerce** at 350 Alvarado Street. Here you can pick up maps and pamphlets, including two excellent free newsletters, *Monterey Peninsula Review* and *Time Out,* both chock-full of information about local attractions.

In addition to exquisite natural beauty, the Peninsula area offers a cornucopia of visitor attractions. Accommodations range from luxurious resorts to the charmingly quaint Carmel inns we'll be discussing in the next section of this chapter.

The choice of fine restaurants is amazingly abundant—over 100 eateries include seven Japanese restaurants alone, as well as Indonesian, French, Filipino, Chinese, Hungarian or whatever else your palate craves.

The sports-minded will find every kind of facility from golf and tennis to skeet-shooting, horseshoe-throwing and fencing.

Concerts—both classical and jazz—are year-round events, and on our last visit the choice of local theatrical productions included *South Pacific, Fiddler on the Roof, Godspell,* and *Macbeth,* among others.

And that's not to mention about a dozen movie theaters, parks, exciting annual events like the **Indian Art Show, Sale and Powwow** and the Buddhist **Feast of Lanterns** (both in late July), flea markets, fish fries, kilt-clad bagpipers,

Sierra Club hikes, lectures, demonstrations and dozens of art galleries. Or the major Monterey sights detailed below, beginning with the—

PATH OF HISTORY: Marked by a red line painted on the pavement, the Path of History is a delightful walking tour which takes in 46 historical landmarks. Depending on the intensity of your historical fervor, you might want to take in all of them, or do an abbreviated tour of those grouped in the area called **Monterey State Historic Park**. Highlights of the latter tour include:

The Custom House (1 Custom Plaza)

As previously mentioned, this is the site where the U.S. flag was first raised in Monterey and another 600,000 square miles became part of our nation. It is the oldest government building in California. Until 1867, when the Custom House was abandoned, custom duties were collected here from foreign ships, and townspeople would gather to inspect the merchandise they brought—cloth, china, glassware, coffee, liquor, etc.

Restored by the Native Sons of the Golden West in 1901, the Custom House was purchased by the state in 1938 for historical preservation. Today a typical cargo is on display, and the interior has been restored. Open 9 a.m. to 5 p.m. daily.

Casa del Oro (corner of Scott and Oliver Streets)

This two-story adobe was built in 1845, when it was probably used as a barracks and hospital quarters for American seamen left at the port under consular care. In 1848 the building was leased to Joseph Boston and Company, a general store. The reason it's called Casa del Oro (house of gold) is that miners stored their treasures in an iron safe here in Gold R̶ ̶ ̶ ̶ ̶ys—or so rumor ha̶ it.

Today it is preserved as a general store (not in use), stocked wit̶ sacks full of coffee and beans, milk cans, ribbons, old tools, fabrics, dinnerware, and canisters of grains, noodles, etc., on display. Open daily from 9 a.m. to 5 p.m.

California's First Theater (corner of Scott and Pacific Streets)

California owes its first theater to Jack Swan, an English sailor of Scottish ancestry who settled in Monterey in 1843. In 1847 he gave the first stage performance here to entertain restless soldiers (who also served as actors); theatrical productions have been taking place ever since. For the first play, Swan furnished his lodging house with a barroom, a stage, rough benches, candles and lamps. Curtains were constructed of red and blue blankets. First-night receipts are said to have totaled $500; with seats at $5 each, the place was packed.

The building was given to the state for preservation in 1906, and it looks much the same today as in earlier times. It is open daily except Monday for viewing from 9 a.m. to 5 p.m. On weekends, the Troupers of the Gold Coast put on 19th-century dramas, and soft drinks and peanuts are sold.

Informal tours are free for children during the day; adults pay 25¢. For weekend theater performances children pay $1, teenagers $2 and adults $3. Box office phone number is 375-4916.

Casa Gutierrez (Calle Principal, near Madison)

In 1841 the municipality of Monterey granted a lot to Joaquin Gutierrez, who used the land to build a house for himself and his bride Josefa. It was an adobe typical of the homes of average Monterey citizens in that period, and the couple raised 15 children here. In 1956, the house was given to the State. It now houses a Mexican restaurant called **Sancho Panza**, which proprietor Leo Nieto has furnished with patio furniture fashioned from hatch covers and timbers salvaged from Cannery Row's old sardine boats.

The interior has low-beamed ceilings, plank wood floors, rough wood tables and wrought-iron chandeliers. There are three fireplaces, including a Franklin stove and an outdoor fireplace in the lovely brick patio garden.

So, if you'd like to dine in one of California's historical landmarks, Sancho Panza is open for lunch and dinner daily, with typical Mexican entrees priced in the $3-to-$4 range.

Larkin House (510 Calle Principal at Jefferson Street)

Built in 1834, this balconied two-story adobe was the home of Thomas Oliver Larkin, who served as U.S. Consul to Mexico from 1843 to 1846. The house also served as the consular office. Furnished in the style of the period with many original pieces, Larkin House is a museum of architecture and Monterey life. Next door is the house used by William Tecumseh Sherman; it now contains a museum depicting the roles of the two men in California history. Guided tours are offered throughout the day from 9:15 a.m. to 4 p.m., except Tuesday. Adults 25¢, children free.

Colton Hall (522 Pacific Street)

Named for the Rev. Walter Colton, U.S. Navy Chaplain who impaneled California's first jury, co-founded the state's first newspaper, and built its first public building, Colton Hall was planed as the town hall and public school. It was the scene of California's constitutional congress in 1849, when the constitution was written and the great seal of the state designed. There's a museum upstairs, and Old Monterey Jail adjoins, its grim cell walls still marked with prisoner's scribblings. Open daily from 10 a.m. to noon and 1 to 4:30 p.m.

Stevenson House (530 Houston Street)

The original portion of this two-story home dates to the late 1830s when it was the home of Don Rafael Gonzales, first administrator of customs of Alta California. In 1856 a French pioneer, Juan Giradin, and his wife became the owners; they made some additions and rented spare bedrooms to roomers, one of whom was Robert Louis Stevenson, who occupied a second-floor room during the autumn of 1879. He had come from Scotland to persuade Fanny Osbourne to marry him (she did). While here he wrote *The Old Pacific Capital*, an account of Monterey in the 1870s. Poor, unknown and in frail health, he was cared for by Jules Simoneau, in whose restaurant he had his one full meal of the day. The building has been restored to its period look, and several rooms are devoted to Stevensoniana. In an upstairs children's bedroom, it has been said that a ghostly spirit is sometimes seen, which makes for an additional point of interest. Open from 9 a.m. to 5 p.m. daily; tours every hour on the hour. Admission is free.

The Pacific House (Custom House Plaza)

Built in 1847, Pacific House was first used for army offices and to store military supplies. Army horses were corralled behind the building, and this was a popular spot for Sunday bull and bear fights. Later it housed small stores, served as a public tavern, a courtroom, county clerk's office, newspaper office, law offices, a church—even a ballroom, where a temperance society called the Dashaways held dances.

The Jacks family bought the property in 1880 and maintained the premises until 1954, when Miss Margaret Jacks made a gift of the historic building to the state. The first floor houses a museum of California history; the second floor an extensive collection of American Indian artifacts plus a few Mexican Indian and Eskimo pieces. Open 9 a.m. to 5 p.m. daily.

Serra Landing Site (just south of Monterey Presidio on Pacific Street)

This is the site where Sebastian Vizcaino landed in 1602, and where, in 1770, Father Serra and Don Gaspar de Portola founded Monterey, future capital and port of entry of California.

From here you're in a good position to proceed to—

CANNERY ROW: Entering Cannery Row, you still drive under the covered conveyor belts which once carried tinned fish from cannery to warehouse. But the corrugated steel warehouses, vacated by factories, have been renovated and now house restaurants, boutiques, art galleries, antique shops and other browsables. There's even a wine-tasting room from the **Bargetto Winery** at 10 Prescott Street.

The best way to explore the Cannery is simply to start at one end and meander along. There are a few complexes of shops, etc. One such is the **Runyon Trading Co.**, at 807 Cannery Row, with about six shops and a mall cafe serving sandwiches, burgers, wine and beer. The **Monterey Canning Company** at 711 Cannery Row houses about 20 shops, among them the above-mentioned winery. Yet a third complex, at #625, is called **Cannery Row Square** (four restaurants and about seven shops). And a new one is opening across the street from it as we go to press.

Cannery Row Dining

No need to eat out of tins here. Cannery Row boasts some of the finest restaurants in town, our favorite being the **Sardine Factory**, 701 Wave Avenue (tel: 373-3775). Excellent food, fine service and a poshly tasteful nautical decor make for a delightful dining experience here. We particularly like dining in the Victorian-style Captain's room, comfortably ensconced in gilt-framed plush velvet chairs by a blazing fire while the wine steward discusses our selection. Candlelight, tasseled velvet draperies, gilt-framed nautical portraits, and red globe chandeliers enhance the warmly intimate ambience.

At lunch a delicious fettuccine Alfredo is $2.95, and it comes with soup or salad and French sourdough bread. If you feel nostalgic about the area you might even order up a sardine sandwich ($2.75). Always a good selection is the fresh catch of the day for $3.50.

Dinner is a more elaborate affair. You might opt for a full dinner, priced by entree and including appetizer, soup, salad and hot cheese bread. With an entree of fettuccine con vongole (noodles with fresh cherrystone clams, seasoned with butter, garlic, parsley and freshly grated parmesan), the dinner is

$7.50. The same price obtains for sand dabs meunière or filet of sole sauteed in sherry. Save room for dessert, perhaps a homemade cannoli ($1.60), and be sure to cap your meal with a "flaming sardine"—coffee and galliano flamed at your table ($2.50).

Open Monday through Saturday for lunch from 11:30 a.m. to 3:30 p.m. and dinner from 5 to 11 p.m.; Sundays for dinner only from 2 to 11 p.m. Reservations essential.

Another good Cannery Row choice is Mark Thomas' **Outrigger,** 700 Cannery Row (tel: 372-8543). Lushly Polynesian, with rattan and peacock chairs and a central barbecue pit, the Outrigger even has an indoor waterfall and many tables looking out over the bay. A terrific luncheon buy is the $3.95 buffet (weekdays only) offering three hot entrees, a bountiful salad bar and dessert. A la carte entrees are also available at lunch; they include crab Louie ($4.75), as well as burgers ($2.25 to $2.65) and more elaborate fare like filet mignon and lobster tail ($7.45).

A sample complete dinner for $7.75 would include puu puus (Hawaiian appetizers), honey pork, fried shrimp, Islander soup, Polynesian steak, chicken Hawaiian, fried rice, tea and fortune cookies. More simply, you might just order chicken teriyaki ($5.95) or Mandarin duck ($7.50), both served with soup and tossed salad, saffron rice, and French-fried or baked potatoes.

There's an extensive wine list, not to mention intoxicating rum-and-fruit concoctions.

Open daily for lunch and dinner, with nightly entertainment (singers and comedians) beginning at 8:30 p.m. Reservations suggested.

FISHERMAN'S WHARF: Like San Francisco, Monterey has not only a Cannery, but also a Fisherman's Wharf. This one, near the old Custom House, is lined with craft shops, a commercial aquarium, boating and fishing operations and seafood restaurants.

If you want to do more than stroll, **Frank's Fishing,** at the end of the Wharf runs 30-minute bay pleasure cruises on fishing-party boats (no fishing on these trips). They depart at least once an hour year round. Adults pay $2; children six to 11, $1; under six free. In winter, Frank's also has 1½-hour whale-watching cruises: $3.50 for adults, $2 for kids under 12. *Benji's,* adjoining, offers similar outings.

If, on the other hand, you'd like to do some fishing, **Chris' and Sam's Fishing Fleet** has five fishing boats available, and they've been serving Monterey fisherfolk since 1914. Diesel-powered fishing boats, with deck lounges, depart at 7:30 a.m. daily. Adults pay $12; children under 12, $11; weekends and holidays it's $14 and $7, respectively. Rod rentals are $2, and bait is free. Bring lunch or order a box lunch at the shop when you make reservations. And dress warmly. To reserve call 372-0577.

There are quite a few shops selling candles, shells and suchlike to browse in on the Wharf, including a wine-tasting place at #2.

Wharf Dining

If you get hungry, the choice ranges from a paper cup of fresh shrimps to several excellent restaurant meals. To put together a picnic lunch (a bench on the Wharf offers a great view), head for the **Little Gourmet Shop,** #25C, specializing in sandwiches to go, stuffed with imported meats and cheeses, on fresh sourdough bread or pita. You can also get salads and small bottles of wine here, as well as Greek pastries. But you might want to pick up dessert elsewhere

2. Carmel

The serene beauty of Carmel, a forest village encircled by mountains and rolling hills, makes it a must on every California visitor's itinerary. White beaches, gnarled cypress trees, magnificent landscapes and seascapes are the background for a sleepy village of narrow streets, quaint storybook houses, charming hostelries and cozy restaurants. It's hard to imagine a more romantic setting—the perfect place for a first or second honeymoon.

Since the turn of the century, the town has been a haven for artists and writers (galleries abound), and aesthetic considerations carry so much weight in the community that you might have difficulty identifying gas stations under their wooden eaves. Most of the houses don't even have street numbers, and according to local regulations large, gaudy or illuminated retail signs in public places "shall not be suffered, permitted, allowed to be placed, erected or maintained." Nor can a tree be removed without specific permission from the police, which is often not granted: a gladdening sight are the old trees smack in the middle of roads and in other unlikely places.

This is also a village of shops—more than 150 of them, mostly little boutiques dispensing such wares as basketry, pottery, imported goods, etc.

And a yearly attraction is the annual **Bach Festival** in July which brings lovers of baroque music from far and wide. For ticket information (you must purchase in advance), write to the Bach Festival Office, Room 11, Sunset Center, San Carlos and 9th, Carmel, California 93921, or phone (408) 624-1521.

For more information on this and other Carmel happenings stop by the **Carmel Valley Chamber of Commerce,** at Forest and Central Avenues or the **Carmel Business Association** on San Carlos between Ocean and 7th; pick up maps, brochures, the two free publications mentioned in our Monterey chapter, and a copy of *The Carmel Pine Cone,* a 15¢ weekly newsletter that has been keeping Carmel residents informed about local events for well over half a century.

WHAT TO DO AND SEE: Carmel's principal village attractions are along Ocean Avenue and its side streets between Junipero and San Antonio Avenues. Begin your explorations on Ocean at Junipero at the multilevel mall complex of gourmet and cheese shops, craft stores, restaurants, etc., called **Carmel Plaza,** and continue meandering along Ocean, stopping at some of the many galleries and shops. Among the more interesting of these are the **China Art Center,** at Dolores and 7th, displaying jades, antiques and other fascinating chinoiserie; the **Gallery of Fine Comic Art,** at 5th and Dolores, displaying strips and cartoons from famous studios and artists; the **Boutique Antoinette,** in Carmel Plaza, filled with French and Italian top designer fashions; **The Mole Hole,** at San Carlos and 6th, where you can enjoy live harp music while browsing amidst decorator pillows, Brumm birds, wind chimes, nostalgia wreathes and other lovely items; and **Come Fly a Kite,** in Carmel Plaza, featuring a selection of exotic kites from 36 countries.

Biblical Garden

While you're in town take a stroll through the Biblical Garden of the Church of the Wayfarer on Lincoln and 7th Avenues. The garden contains plants and trees mentioned in the Bible and indigenous to the Holy Land. Stepping stones lead to various flora, all of which are labeled as to biblical context, beginning with the apple tree—the tree of knowledge of good and evil forbidden to Adam and Eve. An interesting note from the Garden Committee brochure: some Biblical authorities insist the forbidden fruit was actually the apricot!

Carmel Mission

Continuing on subjects spiritual, Carmel also houses the **Mission San Carlos Borromeo**, at Rio Road and Lasuen Drive. This mission is notable as the burial place of Father Junipero Serra, who founded it in 1770. The present stone church, with its gracefully curving walls, catenary arch and Moorish bell tower, was begun in 1793. Its walls are covered with a lime plaster made of burnt sea shells.

In the cemetery beside the church 3,000 Indians are buried, their graves decorated with seashells. Other interesting features include the old mission kitchen, the first library in California, the high altar, beautiful flower gardens, the sarcophagus depicting Father Serra recumbent in death, the cell where he died and the silver altar service he used.

This is one of the largest and most interesting of the California missions. It's open to visitors daily from 9:30 a.m. to 5 p.m., Sundays from 10:30 a.m.

WHERE TO STAY: Carmel boasts one of the highest-rated resort hotels in the country, **Quail Lodge,** 800 Valley Greens Drive, off Carmel Valley Road (tel: 624-1581). In a pastoral setting on 245 acres of sparkling lakes, woodlands and meadows, Quail Lodge offers all the facilities of the prestigious Carmel Valley Golf and Country Club to its guests. In addition to the golf course and clubhouse, amenities include four tennis courts, two swimming pools, bicycle rental and a sauna for men, as well as shops, a beauty salon, gas station and airport limo.

There are 96 rooms; we prefer the upstairs rooms and cottages with cathedral ceilings. All have color TV and suchlike, dressing rooms and balconies; some have fireplaces and wet bars. Furnishings are modern, with shag rugs, handsome hand-woven bedspreads, bamboo and rattan furnishings. There's complimentary champagne in every room and free newspapers are delivered daily.

The grounds are truly superb, with graceful bridges arching duck-filled lakes and ponds; on occasion you'll see wild water birds or catch a glimpse of a deer.

The posh Covey Restaurant on the premises serves continental fare nightly except Sunday in warmly elegant surroundings (complimentary continental breakfast, and lunch that you pay for are served daily in the clubhouse). The interior is done in rich brown tones with chocolate suede and barnwood walls. Tables are beautifully appointed in Belgian linen, set with pewterware, and adorned with fresh flowers and gaslamps. A delightful fireplace bar/lounge adjoins.

An appetizer of a half-dozen escargots will cost $3.50. Entrees, served with potato and a fresh garden vegetable, include poulet à l'orange ($6.50), fresh trout amandine ($7.50) and a sizzling steak au poivre flambé in brandy ($11). For dessert, we like the crêpes flambé au Grand Marnier ($6 for two persons). Jackets are required for men, and reservations are essential.

The cost of luxury living at Quail Lodge is $52 to $58 single, $58 to $64 double, including continental breakfast.

Our next three selections are all right in the heart of Carmel activity, and each has its own unique charm.

Normandy Inn, Ocean Avenue between Monte Verde and Casanova Avenues (tel: 624-3825), is a delightful provincial hostelry housed in a shingled Tudor building. The terrace poolside patio (the pool is heated) is lined with trees and hundreds of potted plants.

Rooms are just lovely, though each is somewhat different: about a quarter of them have fireplaces and/or kitchen areas, 70% have TV (black and white), and most baths have tub and shower combinations. All have switchboard phones and are charmingly decorated in country motif, with ruffled bedspreads, maple furnishings, shuttered multi-paned windows, and old-fashioned print wallpapers. Complimentary breakfast is served in a quaint country kitchen-style room adorned with antique Quimper plates and fresh flower arrangements.

Rates for single accommodations are $25 to $28; doubles $28 to $38. Cottages for two to nine persons cost $51 to $76. Be sure to reserve far in advance, especially in summer, or it's unlikely you'll find a room at the inn.

The same warning obtains at the nearby **Lamp Lighters Inn,** Ocean Avenue and Camino Real (tel: 624-7372). This storybook establishment consists of five adorable old-fashioned cottages grouped around a fairytale garden. Any moment one expects Little Red Riding Hood to round the corner; surely grandma lives in one of these. And speaking of storybooks, one *is* called the Hansel and Gretel Cottage. It accommodates two to five persons in a living room and bedroom, both carpeted in hand-loomed rag rugs. A log fire is built in the fireplace for you every day. There's a complete kitchen where you can whip up your morning porridge, and a bath with tub and shower. Price: $45 per day.

The Blue Bird Room, sleeping two to four, is similar, but has no kitchen facilities and a shower only. A large picture window overlooks the oak tree, potted ferns and flowering plants of the garden court. Price: $40. The other three rooms are much like the latter but a bit smaller: the Katydid Room sleeps up to three and costs $27; the Early Bird Room sleeps up to four and costs $35; and the Tree-Top Room (it's upstairs) accommodates just two persons and costs $28.

Owners Bill and Penny Baylor give very personal service to guests (who include a fair sprinkling of celebs, like Goldie Hawn), making dinner reservations, advising on sightseeing and keeping records of guest preferences in various matters.

More quaint rooms (these are Victorian in style) at the **Pine Inn,** Ocean Avenue and Monte Verde (tel: 624-3851). At the risk of being repetitious, we'll once again advise early reservations. The Pine Inn has an opulent lobby/lounge complete with red-flocked wallpaper, a blazing fireplace, plush furnishings, lots of stained glass and a big grandfather clock. Each room is individually designed, but all are in turn-of-the-century motif—shuttered windows, lovely wallpapers and antique furnishings, including brass beds in some rooms. Every room has a TV (most have color sets), direct-dial phone and tub/shower bath.

The Crystal Room restaurant is on the premises, also a masterpiece of Victoriana, with large globe chandeliers, stained-glass panels and the rest. A beautiful indoor garden room, The Gazebo, adjoins. Here, diners sit under a skylight dome that rolls back on sunny days and warm starlit nights. Both the Sunday champagne brunch and the Friday night seafood buffet at the Pine Inn are popular. Dinner in the Crystal Room features continental gourmet specialties like beef Wellington ($10.50) and veal Oskar—sauteed in butter, topped with crabmeat, and served with asparagus and Béarnaise sauce ($8).

Single rooms at the Pine Inn cost $21 to $38; doubles and twins $21 to $48.

WHERE TO DINE: We've already made a couple of suggestions in the hotel listings above, and you can also check out our restaurant selections in nearby Monterey. A few more choices follow.

Right out of a fairy tale is the **Tuck Box English Tea Room,** Dolores and 7th, a brick and shingle-roofed stucco cottage that serves only breakfast, lunch and afternoon tea. The wee dining room has red-and-white-checked cafe curtains, a beamed ceiling and stone fireplace, and there's a small patio outside. At breakfast you can have freshly squeezed orange juice (75¢), bacon and eggs with a muffin or scone, homemade preserves, coffee and tea for $2.45.

The lunch menu is the most extensive; there's usually a choice of two or three daily entrees for $2.85, such as shepherd's pie, salad, vegetable, muffin or scone, and coffee or tea. Excellent sandwiches, omelets, salads and cold plates are also served. Leave room for a dessert of homemade pie or cake with whipped cream (85¢). The latter is also available at afternoon tea, but more traditional would be an order of homemade scones with homemade preserves, and a special blend of black tea ($1.25).

Closed Monday and Tuesday; otherwise open 8 a.m. to 4 p.m.

The French answer to the Tuck Box is an equally charming little tea room, the **Patisserie Boissière,** on Mission between Ocean and 7th (tel: 624-5008). Also housed in a shingle-roofed stucco cottage, it boasts an entrance heralded by a real Parisian street sign reading Rue Boissière. The decor is provincial, with white stucco walls and a low beamed ceiling, antique maple sideboard, tiled fireplace, pretty curtains and Louis XV chairs. You can also dine in a skylight cafe with garden furnishings. The food is exquisite, beginning with the homemade pâté ($2.50). It's the perfect place for a light meal—perhaps a ham or camembert sandwich on French bread ($1.30) or a quiche Lorraine ($1.40) with a glass of wine (80¢), topped off by a delicious homemade patisserie (like a chocolate eclair, or chocolate butter cream with crisp meringue) and coffee.

For a heartier meal, specialties include coquilles Saint Jacques—scallops, shrimps and fresh mushrooms in a cream and sherry sauce ($3.50); and a provincial chicken dish with white wine sauce, tomatoes and olives, served with rice ($4). The Patisserie Boissière is open from 10 a.m. to 9 p.m. every day except Wednesday.

More French charm at **Le Coq d'Or,** Mission and 5th (tel: 624-4613), a pretty little establishment with pale-yellow tablecloths on tables set with fresh flowers, red-and-white-striped cafe curtains and a mural of a French town on one wall. Dinners include soup du jour, salad, a fresh vegetable, rice in butter and potato soufflé. Such a dinner with an entree of chicken in a rich cream and Madeira sauce, with fresh mushrooms, is $6.25; $4.15 for filet of sole in wine sauce.

The wine list offers a good selection of domestic and imported labels, and luscious desserts come from the Patisserie Boissière. Open nightly except Tuesday for dinner from 5:30 to 9 p.m. Reservations advised.

If you like to read while you eat, or just like to be around books, head for the **Thunderbird Bookshop,** at the intersection of Carmel Valley Road and Highway 1 (tel: 624-1803). Over 50,000 books are for sale (it actually is a bookstore), and you can browse through any of them while you're eating—just be careful with the gravy. The ambience is attractive; works of local artists are displayed on white wood walls, there are lots of potted ferns, tables are covered with bright red cloths, and classical music is played in the background. In good weather you can also dine outdoors under Cinzano umbrellas.

At lunch, sandwiches and soups are all under $2. Dinners are a terrific bargain: fresh poached salmon or roast beef au jus, served with tossed salad, relish dish, hot popovers, coffee and a homemade dessert for just $4.75. A children's dinner containing smaller portions of the same items is $3.

The Thunderbird is open daily for lunch from 11:30 a.m. to 4 p.m., and for dinner Tuesday through Saturday from 6 to 10 p.m. Make reservations for dinner.

The **General Store Western Union Restaurant**, 5th and Junipero (tel: 624-2233), has just the kind of relaxed funky-rustic atmosphere its name evokes —brick floors, low beamed ceiling, bentwood chairs and marble-topped tables, lots of hanging plants and ships' lanterns overhead. The bar is a limb of white oak the owner found. Many diners prefer to sit outside on the garden patio (very delightful) in orange director's chairs under Cinzano umbrellas; two large brick fireplaces keep everyone warm and cozy.

The food is great; only fresh fish and vegetables are served, and desserts are homemade. At lunch a wide variety of sandwiches, burgers and omelets range in price from $1.85 for an avocado, alfalfa sprouts and Monterey jack cheese sandwich, to $4.50 for a smoked salmon omelet. Or you might opt for quiche and salad ($2.75) or a bucket of steamed clams ($4.15).

Dinner entrees include burgers and tasty salads (Greek, Niçoise, spinach or Caesar—$3 to $4.25) for those who want a light meal. Among the heartier entrees are fettuccine Alfredo with prosciutto ($4.85), and spiced marinated chicken with hot sauce and cucumber salad ($4.50). In addition to menu listings, ten specials are always posted on the blackboard—perhaps sweet and sour duck ($7.50) or salmon Béarnaise ($7.25).

Be sure to leave room for one of those aforementioned homemade desserts, like rum and chocolate cheesecake ($1.50) or apple pie à la mode with delicious McConell's ice cream.

The General Store also does a big Sunday brunch business, from 10 a.m. to 2:30 p.m., offering a wide selection of omelets, eggs rancheros, benedict or florentine, as well as salads, burgers, and quiche—most of it in the $2 to $4 range.

Open seven days for lunch and dinner.

Shabu-Shabu, in the Carmel Plaza Mall (tel: 625-2828), invites you to take off your shoes, refresh yourself with an oshibori (warm towel), and let the kimono-clad waitress serve you. It's easy to relax over your sake in this lovely country-inn-style candlelit Japanese restaurant. You can sit the Japanese way on cushions at low tables, or in rattan chairs at highly polished redwood tables. Redwood-paneled walls are adorned with colorful Japanese kites, lights are filtered through rattan shades, and Japanese music is played in the background.

The specialty is, of course, shabu-shabu ($7.95); the name means "swish-swish," which is the sound the meat makes when cooking. It consists of thin ribbons of beef, soybean cake, mushrooms and fresh seasonal vegetables cooked at your table in a copper pot and served with dipping sauces. A seafood version, made with fresh clams, scallops, shrimps, lobster tails, rock cod and vegetables, is also available ($21 for two). Other items include prawn (enormous ones) and vegetable tempura ($6.50), teriyaki steak, ten ounces of it ($8.50), and sukiyaki ($6.50). All dinners come with soup, salad, tsukemono (Japanese pickle) and a pot of delicious genmai tea which is steeped in toasted rice. Shabu-Shabu has a knockout dessert—the Japanese answer to the banana split and far superior: bananas deep-fried in tempura butter and topped with green tea ice cream ($1.50).

Open nightly from 6 to 10 p.m. Reservations essential.

3. Big Sur

Not a town, but rather a loose description of the famous 90-mile stretch of rugged coastline between Carmel and San Simeon, the dramatic Big Sur region is probably the only place in the world described by its own Chamber of Commerce as a place "to slow down . . . to meditate . . . to catch up with your soul." Flanked on one side by the majestic Santa Lucia Mountain Range, and on the other by the rocky Pacific coast, it is traveled via breathtakingly scenic Highway 1. Drive through slowly, making frequent stops at viewing turnouts, and taking in the sea and cliffs.

Though the area attracts many tourists, its highly individualistic residents make few concessions to them, and in no way is Big Sur touristy or in danger of becoming so. There are few recreational distractions—no town, or shops, no cute boutiques and art galleries, no tennis, golf, horseback-riding, boating or even movie theaters. Just the tranquility of unparalleled natural beauty where you can hike through redwood forests along miles of trails, picnic, go camping, fish or enjoy the beach at several points along the coast: **Pfeiffer Beach, Kirk Creek, Plaskett Creek, Jade Beach** and **Willow Creek Beach.** (The only beach accessible by car is Pfieffer, via Sycamore Canyon Road.)

The River Inn, 29 miles south of Monterey on Highway 1, is generally considered the starting point of Big Sur, with most of the area's accommodations, restaurants and other facilities between it and Deetjen's Big Sur Inn about six miles south. You can visit Big Sur on a day trip from Monterey or Carmel, perhaps stopping for lunch at Nepenthe, the area's most widely touted "in" restaurant. (Mention Big Sur, and nine out of ten Californians will respond with "Did you eat at Nepenthe? Isn't it great?") If you'd like to stay awhile, the following is a pretty complete rundown on the accommodations situation.

WHERE TO STAY: Accommodations are many and varied, but few attempt the luxury-hotel trappings you'd find on any other major highway going through an area with such a high tourism rate—room service, even phones and TVs (the latter considered a Philistine in these parts) are rare. Nevertheless, they all run at close to full occupancy, especially in summer, so reserve early. To write to any of the places below, just address inquiries to the name of the establishment, Big Sur, California 93920. The same goes for the Chamber of Commerce.

Our absolute favorite is the least typical of Big Sur hostelries, the **Ventana Inn,** on Highway 1, 4.3 miles south of Big River Inn (tel: 667-2331), a luxurious wilderness resort on a 1,000-acre oceanfront ranch, high in the mountains overlooking the Pacific. It's the realized dream of hip entrepreneur Larry Spector, a man of many successes, whose previous credits include managing rock groups like The Byrds and Buffalo Springfield, and producing the movie *Easy Rider.* Opened in 1975, it fulfills a long-standing need for accommodations worthy of the wild and magical Big Sur countryside. Among the notables who have already flocked to pamper themselves at Ventana are Steve McQueen and Ali MacGraw, Norman Lear, Jack Nicholson, Art Garfunkel, Robert De Niro and Francis Ford Coppola, not to mention the Prime Minister of Finland.

The resort's 24 guest rooms are housed in contemporary natural-wood buildings with slanted roofs that blend with the landscape. The interiors are exquisite, in blue or yellow color schemes, each with wall-to-wall carpeting color-coordinated to patchwork-quilt bedspreads handmade in Nova Scotia. Walls are a combination of white stucco and cedar paneling, furnishings are wicker, and some rooms have wood-burning Franklin stoves, others very high ceilings. All have dressing rooms, private terraces or balconies overlooking the ocean or forest, Princess phones, color cable TV, heating, air conditioning, and baths with tub and shower.

There's a 90-foot heated outdoor swimming pool, as well as three outdoor Japanese hot baths with multiple jets where you can soak *au naturel,* one for men, one for women, and one for the uninhibited mixed crowd.

Moving along now to culinary luxuries, complimentary breakfast (fresh-baked croissants, Danish pastries and tea or coffee) is served in your room or in the guest lobby each morning. The restaurant on the premises is, like everything else, first-rate. This will be considered sacrilege by many, but we prefer it muchly to Nepenthe. The airy raw cedar interior, with heavy redwood beams, a large stone fireplace and cedar tile floor, is furnished with redwood tables, cane and bentwood chairs, and rattan-shaded globe lamps overhead. Baskets of ferns, potted plants and baskets of fruit are placed here and there.

You can dine on either of two levels, with vista-revealing windows everywhere, or on a large outdoor patio terrace overlooking a dramatic expanse of ocean with the Sur coast in view for 50 miles.

Lunch and brunch fare ranges from shrimp Louie ($5.50) to a Monte Cristo sandwich—ham, cheese and chicken in a sandwich dipped in egg batter and grilled ($4), to steak tartare ($6).

For dinner we suggest prime rib with Yorkshire pudding ($8.50), pepper steak sauteed in brandy ($10.50) or, for the less meaty, fresh trout Veronique sauteed with toasted almonds and grapes ($7.75). All entrees are served with fresh steamed vegetables, Hollandaise sauce and homemade bread. The dessert of choice is Swiss chocolate fondue with cake tidbits and fruit to dip into a creamy chocolate, honey and nuts mixture ($3).

The Ventana's restaurant is open daily from 11 a.m. to 10 or 11 p.m., and after you dine you can browse through the adjoining general store, which carries everything from imported buttons and bows to garden tools. Call for reservations.

If you'd rather create your own meals, splendid picnic makings can be found at Ventana's gourmet **Market and International Delicatessen,** at the resort entrance on Highway 1; imported meats, cheeses, delicious breads, homemade desserts, wine and health-food items can be enjoyed on the umbrellaed terrace outside or prepared to go. A gas station is also conveniently situated here.

Do you believe it, there's more. From June to October, free film classics like *The Bank Dick* and *Guns of Navarone* are shown on the restaurant terrace. Drinks and hot buttered popcorn are available.

Rates for doubles begin at $50 and go up to $140 (the latter for a townhouse). If you can't afford to stay here, at least splurge at the restaurant, and take a look around. If you do want to stay here, try to reserve at least eight weeks in advance.

Less glamorous, and decidedly less expensive, is a cabin in the woods at **Ripplewood Resort,** on Highway 1 about six tenths of a mile from River Inn (tel: 667-2242). The young owners have done a good job of providing accommodations and services here. They have 14 cabins set in a tranquil redwood forest, all rustic and charming with wood-paneled and stone-wall interiors and sunlight streaming in through lots of windows. All have terraces, hot-water showers and heaters. We prefer the nine that are right on the Big Sur River, all of which also have kitchens, and two of which have fireplaces. You can swim, sunbathe and fish in the river, and there are horseshoe and shuffleboard courts available. In addition, there's a small comfy wood-paneled restaurant on the premises with highly polished pine and redwood tables and a blazing stone fireplace, plus a grocery store, wine room, gift shop and gas station.

If you're driving by, you can use Ripplewood's picnic and swimming facilities free. Summer rates for cabins are $18 to $35 for two people; $12 to $27 in winter. Year round an additional person in a cabin pays $2.

Traveling with the family? Best bet (unless you're camping, about which more shortly) is the **Big Sur Lodge**, located in Pfeiffer Big Sur Park, a little over two miles south of River Inn on Highway 1 (tel: 667-2171). Operated in conjunction with the state, the Lodge has 61 units beautifully situated on 810 parkland acres of towering redwoods, sycamores, big-leaf maples and other sheltering trees. The cabins are quite large, with high peaked cedar and redwood beamed ceilings and walnut-paneled walls; all that wood makes them rather attractive in spite of indifferent furnishings. However, if they lack flair, they are certainly clean and most presentable. All are heated and equipped with private bath and parking spaces; most have porches, some have dressing rooms, and about a dozen even have fireplaces.

A great advantage in staying here is that you can use all the facilities of the park: a large outdoor heated swimming pool, with an adjoining sauna ($1 for use) and snack bar; a recreation hall with Ping-Pong and the like; a gift shop, two grocery stores, coin-operated laundromat; and, of course, fishing, hiking, camping, barbecue and picnic facilities.

The Big Sur Lodge dining room is open from April to September. At lunch you can get sandwiches, salads and burgers (all under $2.50), as well as hot items like sauteed fresh rainbow trout with soup or salad and potato ($3.95). Dinner, served with the same accompaniments plus a vegetable, offers a wider choice of entrees—broiled chicken ($4.95), French-fried shrimp ($4.95) and brochette of beef ($6.25) among them. At either meal, try the homemade pies, baked fresh daily (65¢).

The dining room is very pretty, by the way, with big windows all around providing glorious woodland views; if you want to be in the forest rather than looking at it through glass, there's lots of patio seating under umbrellaed tables overlooking the river.

Cottage rate for two persons is $21, $25 for three, $30 for four, ascending to $39 for six (maximum occupancy). Fireplace units are $25 to $45, and housekeeping cottages begin at $22 for one room and $25 for two rooms, double occupancy.

An actual motel, and quite a nice one, is the **Glen Oaks**, on Highway 1 right next door to Ripplewood. The 15 rooms here, housed in shingle-roofed, post-adobe structures, are pleasantly furnished with pretty maple pieces, wall-to-wall carpeting, pictures on the walls, frilly lamps and reading lights over the bed—snug and homey. All have tile baths, most with showers and some with tubs. There's a restaurant on the premises, which is in a transitional state at this writing—check it out; otherwise you can use the Ripplewood facilities. There's swimming nearby, and they even have Ping-Pong. Double rooms are $19 to $22 for two persons, $3 for each additional.

Finally we come to **Deetjen's Big Sur Inn**, nestled in the mouth of the Castro Canyon, 5.7 miles from River Inn (tel: 667-2377), as much a haven for the soulful elite as an actual hostelry. Its Norwegian-style cottages and cabins are usually booked up a year in advance, and not only does the publicity-shy owner not advertise, he even disdains and discourages those who don't seem sufficiently hip, spiritual or whatever in outlook. The cottages and cabins are quaint, funky and very delightful, and with rates beginning at $14 for a double, they're also the least expensive in Big Sur. If you're interested, you might try writing a soulful letter in advance, or dropping in to see if you can create a properly righteous impression. Even if you do, there's unlikely to be a vacancy, but one never knows. Whatever you do, don't mention you read about Deetjen's in a guidebook—just driving by and thinking it looked exactly your kind of place is more the ticket. Such oddities probably exist only in Big Sur, and we include it for those who enjoy being judged. Evidently, many do.

Less difficult to enter, and well worth the while, is the Inn's restaurant, very charming with painted wooden chairs and lots of ye olde inn ambience. There are two seatings nightly, at 7 and 8:30 p.m., and you can choose from a few entrees like red snapper or beef stroganoff ($5.75 for either) with soup or salad. A vegetable plate is always offered as well, and so are homemade pies for dessert. Classical music in the background combined with the high quality of the food make this a pleasant dining experience.

Camping

Once again, best bet is the 1,000-acre campsite belonging to **Ventana** (667-2331), off Highway 1 just before the resort. Ninety-eight campsites, in a gorgeous redwood setting, are spaced well apart for privacy. Each has a picnic table and fireplace, and bathrooms with hot showers are conveniently located. You can swim in the creek (or at Pfeiffer State Beach, a mile away), and the Market and International Delicatessen (see resort write-up), and adjoining gas station are a short walk. Campsites are $5.50 a night, $1 extra for electrical hook-up.

Another good choice for camping is the **Big Sur Campground,** two tenths of a mile below the River Inn (tel: 667-2322). Open year round, it has 85 campsites, bath houses with hot-water showers, laundry facilities, fresh-water faucets within 25 feet of each site, a lovely large swimming area surrounded by towering redwoods, play area with swings, etc., and a volleyball/basketball court. Each campsite has its own wood-burning stove and picnic table.

From May to September, rates are $5 for two persons in a car, 50¢ for each additional adult and 25¢ for each additional child. Trailer hook-ups are 50¢ extra. The rest of the year it's $5 no matter how many people.

More well-equipped camping facilities in **Pfeiffer State Park**—with three areas of campsites open from May 30 to October 1. There's a ten-day limit on stays; for information write to the Department of Parks and Recreation, 1416 Ninth Street, P.O. Box 2390, Sacramento, California 95811.

WHERE TO DINE: In addition to the dining facilities at the above-mentioned accommodations, be sure to experience Big Sur's most acclaimed restaurant, **Nepenthe,** five miles south of River Inn. It stands on the site of The Log House, which was built in 1925, 808 feet above sea level. Housed in a redwood and stucco structure, the dining room is ski-lodgy, with director's chairs at heavy wood tables, redwood and pine ceilings, and lots of windows. But unless the weather is really bad, everyone sits outside on the oceanview terrace enjoying one of the most awesomely magnificent vistas anywhere. It's a magical place to while away a lazy and delightful afternoon; stay long enough to catch the sunset. Usually there are a few musicians hanging out here, playing to a background of scores of gaily chirping birds, and, in general, it's a lively, unpredictable, idyllic and fun place to be. Service is a little ho-hum, in keeping with the casual style of the place, but no one really cares. Two people might easily share the continental cheese board served with fresh fruit and bread ($3.75), and a liter of wine ($4.50); follow up with a pot of English tea (60¢) and dessert—perhaps homemade pumpkin spice cake or cheese pie (both $1.50). You can also get hamburgers, salads and sandwiches at lunch. Dinner fare includes steak dishes, broiled or roast chicken, or salmon steak ($5.25 to $10). Open daily from 11:30 a.m. to midnight.

We've mentioned the **River Inn** countless times already, and though the accommodations, right on the road, are not to our taste, it does have a good restaurant. Pleasantly rustic, it's housed in a redwood log cabin, with lots of leafy plants suspended from a skylight roof, and one wall of window overlooking the river and woods. There's a huge fire blazing in the stone fireplace nightly (a hideous boar's head is mounted above it), and the furnishings are heavy redwood tables and chairs of the "Three Bears" variety. (More tables are outside for patio dining.) Friday, Saturday and Sunday nights there's live music—folk or country and western; other times you can amuse yourself at the enormous chess boards with oversize pieces. It's the kind of place where people hang out, rather than eat and run. In typical easygoing Big Sur fashion, it's open from 7:30 a.m. to 10 p.m. daily from March to December, and the rest of the year when the spirit moves.

A ham and eggs breakfast with hash browns ($2.95) comes with a big platter of homemade biscuits, jelly and coffee. At lunch a 1/3-pound charcoal-broiled burger on French roll, with French fries and salad, is $2.60; same price for a French dip roast beef sandwich accompanied by the salad only.

Dinner entrees are all served with soup or salad, biscuits, a fresh vegetable and coffee. Char-broiled fresh salmon is $5.95, lobster tail in drawn butter $8.50, and country meat loaf with mashed potatoes $4.50. Only prime aged meat, fresh vegetables and fresh fish are used, which makes for good fixin's. Dinner reservations advised.

ESALEN INSTITUTE: The original avant-garde California center for the human potential movement, Esalen, 16 miles south of River Inn, pre-dates EST, primal, T.A., T.M. and all the rest. Experimental and ever-changing, it offers a wide variety of programs, seminars and activities. Write for information to Esalen Institute, Big Sur, California 93920 or call (408) 667-2335.

THE COAST GALLERY: This beautifully situated gallery, eight miles south of River Inn, is Big Sur's original, and practically its only, art gallery. Uniquely rebuilt from watertanks after a flood in 1972, it shows works of local artists and craftspeople—pottery, woodcarving, macrame, paintings, sculpture, jewelry, etc. In addition, candles are made on the premises. A bit commercial, but the folks who run it are awfully nice, and it makes for good browsing. Open daily from 9:30 to sunset.

4. San Simeon

Ever wonder what you'd do if you had the really big bucks? Not just a million, but hundreds of millions—money-is-no-object millions.

In the verdant Santa Lucia Mountains of San Simeon, on a hill he called **La Cuesta Encantada** (The Enchanted Hill), William Randolph Hearst has left an astounding monument to wealth, a veritable shrine worthy of kings and maharajahs, the ego trip par excellence—**Hearst Castle.**

The history of Hearst Castle dates back to 1865, when 43-year-old George Hearst purchased a 40,000-acre ranch adjacent to San Simeon Bay. He built a comfortable ranch house on the property, ran large herds of cattle over its ranges and foothills, and also trained thoroughbred race horses on the premises. He often entertained at the ranch (it still stands today, incidentally), and his only son, William Randolph, developed a great liking for the informal life at

SAN SIMEON

"Camp Hill." As a young man, busy launching his newspaper career, W.R. would often steal off to the San Simeon property for a quiet retreat. In 1919, when George Hearst's widow, Phoebe Apperson Hearst, died and William Randolph came into possession of the ranch, the present Castle was underway.

Located on Highway 1 about 94 miles south of Monterey, Hearst Castle was given to the state as a memorial to the late publisher after his death in 1958.

The focal point of the estate is the incredible **Casa Grande,** with over 100 rooms all filled with priceless art treasures. Items collected by Hearst, which can be seen by visitors to the grounds, are valued at $50 million! There are Tiffany lamps, Flemish tapestries, 15th-century Gothic fireplaces, 16th-century Spanish and intricately carved 18th-century Italian ceilings, a 16th-century Florentine bedstead, Renaissance paintings, and here and there such items as a third-century Etruscan jar, or an ancient Egyptian statue created over 3,500 years ago. That barely skims the surface. The Celestial Suite of the house was reserved for the most important guests, among them Winston Churchill and President Calvin Coolidge and his wife. In the library, 5,000 volumes of rare books are housed, along with one of the world's greatest collections of ancient classical pottery dating from the eighth to the second centuries B.C.

There are three opulent mini-castle guest houses on the premises, also furnished with magnificent art treasures—one contains the black walnut bedstead that belonged to Cardinal Richelieu.

A lavish private theater was used to show first-run films twice nightly—once for employees and again for the guests and host. Guests could also play pool and billiards in a room that would make one feel as if he were shooting pool in the middle of the Louvre.

And there are two amazing swimming pools—the Byzantine-inspired indoor pool with intricate mosaic work surrounded by the most famous statues of antiquity copied in Carrara marble (at night, light filtering through alabaster globes created the illusion of moonlight) and the Greco-Roman Neptune pool, flanked by Etruscan marble colonnades and surrounded by more Carrara statuary.

Which is not to even mention the magnificently landscaped grounds, where in Hearst's time a zoo's worth of animals roamed in a 2,000-acre enclosure—monkeys, cheetahs, giraffes, camels, elephants, bears, bison, llamas, zebras, deer, eagles and other birds. For riding, he had over 30 Arabian horses. Today only a few elk, deer and zebras roam with the goats and cattle.

If you can fit San Simeon into your itinerary, it will make for a very interesting and enjoyable day's outing—a glimpse into a lifestyle that barely exists today, and that few, if any, of us have come near experiencing.

Two-hour tours are conducted daily, except Thanksgiving and Christmas, between the hours of 8:30 a.m. and 3:30 p.m. Two to five tours leave every hour, depending on the number of reservations. Don't just arrive; make reservations for your tour at any local Ticketron, or by writing to the Reservations Office, Department of Parks and Recreation, P.O. Box 2390, Sacramento, California 95811. Arrive without reservations and you're guaranteed a long wait; you may not get in at all.

There are three possible tours. Tour 1 is recommended for first-time visitors. It includes the gardens, pools, guest houses, main house and the movie theater—where you'll see Hearst "home" movies. Adults pay $4; children over six, $2; under-six free. If you purchase your tickets through Ticketron, add a 35¢ service charge per ticket.

Visitors park their cars at the Visitors Center parking lot and are transported by bus to the Castle. If you bring lunch, there are picnic tables. Wear comfortable shoes—you'll be walking about a half-mile and climbing over 300 steps.

5. San Luis Obispo

What a pretty and delightful place is San Luis Obispo. Nestled in the Los Padres mountains midway between L.A. and San Francisco, it's an easygoing, postcard-picturesque little college town that grew up around an 18th-century mission. Among its many tourist attractions are over 15 historical landmarks, shops, restaurants and sporting facilities. This is the beginning of Southern California beach country—the first point south where you don't have to be a member of the Polar Bear Club to dare stick your big toe in the water.

Other attractions? Concerts—an annual Mozart festival (August 2 to 8), jazz and bands, etc.—often outdoors and under the stars, are frequent events, interspersed with dance performances, poetry readings, theater productions and diverse activities ranging from wine-tasting dinners to tug-o-war competitions.

It's an easy town to walk around—most places of interest can be reached on foot—but the best thing about San Luis Obispo is the friendly townspeople, who always seem to have time to help a tourist, converse and pass the time of day. A local cop once even gave us a ride when we asked for directions.

Forty-two miles south of San Simeon on Highway 1, San Luis Obispo is a good base for visits to Hearst Castle.

Make your first stop in town the **Chamber of Commerce,** on Chorro Street between Monterey and Higuera, to pick up maps, a Path of History guide, calendar of events and other interesting literature. Get a bus schedule, too—taxis, costing $1 at the drop and 10¢ every tenth of a mile thereafter, eat up your coins faster than a Las Vegas slot machine.

THE PATH OF HISTORY: Like Monterey, San Luis Obispo has an easy-to-follow path, here linking 19 historical landmarks. Get a map and follow the green line on the street. Highlights include—

Mission San Luis Obispo de Tolosa

The focal point of Mission Plaza, the old mission, constructed of adobe bricks by the Chumash Indians in 1772, is one of the most beautiful and interesting of the Franciscan chain. A 1793 statue of Saint Louis (San Luis) is above the altar, and the 14 Stations of the Cross in the main church date from 1812. The belfry houses three large bells that were cast in Peru in 1818.

Most interesting is the Mission Museum, which contains a wealth of mission artifacts, among them vestments, books, handmade knives, a wedding dress brought over from Spain in 1831, portraits and photos of mission workers, bisque dolls, samplers, a wine press, tallow-making pot, and corn sheller. Many Indian relics are also displayed here: flints, arrowheads, wampum beads, dolls, baskets, clothing, cooking pots, drums, grinding stones for making flour, and office furniture hand-carved by the Cherokees in 1880.

Particularly lovely is the mission's garden setting, with winding brick paths and benches by a creek, a small hill blanketed in morning glories as a backdrop. All is peaceful here.

San Luis Obispo County Historical Museum

A wonderful cluttery place to browse, the museum contains a fascinating collection of local lore: architect Julia Morgan's original working model for Hearst Castle (yes, the architect of Hearst Castle was a woman); intricate hair wreaths, handmade mission nails, old trunks, a turn-of-the-century mail cart, antique clothes, nursery books and children's high-button shoes; and an invaluable tome from 1853 called *The Matchmaker,* which purports to tell "how to woo, to win, and to wed," and while you're at it, "how to procure pleasant dreams." Ask one of the curators to show you around; they love to do it, and can provide very interesting commentary.

The museum is open daily except Monday from 10 a.m. to noon and from 1 to 4 p.m.

St. Stephen's Episcopal Church

Dating back to 1867, this pine and redwood structure is one of the first Episcopal churches in the state. The original pipe organ was donated by Phoebe Apperson Hearst (Patty's great-grandmother).

Romona Depot

An official depot of the Southern Pacific Railroad Company, built in 1889, it's the only vestige of the luxurious Romona Hotel, an elegant Victorian hostelry that once hosted Presidents McKinley and Theodore Roosevelt.

The Ah Louis Store

Practically unchanged since it was opened in 1874, this century-old establishment is still in the hands of the original Cantonese family. Ah Louis was lured to California by gold fever in 1856. Unsuccessful in this venture, he came to San Luis and took a job as a cook, but soon began a lucrative trade as a labor contractor, hiring and organizing Chinese crews to build the railroad. In addition to the store, he also started the first brickyard in the county, created county roads, had a vegetable and flower seed business, bred race horses and was the overseer of eight farms.

Today you can chat with his son, Howard, who runs the store, while you browse about a clutter of Oriental merchandise. Hours are irregular, since every once in a while Howard just closes up and goes fishing.

Sinsheimer Bros. Store

Founded in 1876 by the pioneer brothers Bernard and Henry Sinsheimer, and built mainly of bricks from the Ah Louis brickyard, the building remains a living example of 19th-century mercantile architecture. The cast-iron colonnaded facade was cast in San Francisco and shipped here. Originally a general store catering to early ranchers, the place still has an old-fashioned country-store atmosphere, and it is still run by the Sinsheimer family. An interesting exhibit of silkscreen prints inside depicts the town at the turn of the century.

Bull and Bear Pit

This Court Street landmark is the site of a cruel sport indulged in by early Californians, when a bull and bear were pitted against each other in deadly combat.

MISSION PLAZA: In addition to the historical attractions in Mission Plaza, it houses several restaurants, shops and boutiques that sell sandals, kites from various countries, hand-crafted gifts and jewelry, leather goods, pottery, glass sculpture and other such quaint-little-town-artsy-craftsy paraphernalia. While you're meandering about, you might drop in at the **Art Center,** a sort of co-op for local amateur and professional artists, which sometimes has interesting exhibits of Indian art. The work displayed tends to be mediocre (the less you know about art, the more you'll enjoy it), but it's free, so what the heck.

THE CREAMERY: Californians just can't resist turning their old factories and whatnot into tourist attractions. The Creamery, located on 570 Higuera Street, was originally the Golden State Creamery, built in 1906, and for the next 40-or-so years one of the most important milk-producing centers in the state. After that, it's importance began to decline, and in 1974 it was turned into a shopping and restaurant mall, centered around the old cooling tower. Old freezer doors, workhouse lights overhead and milk-can lamps attest to the Creamery's original function. There's an old Nickelodeon (costs a dime) showing scenes of devastation from the 1906 quake. Among the interesting shops are the **Executive Playpen** featuring games for adults, and a natural-foods supermarket called **Foods for the Family.**

CALIFORNIA POLYTECHNIC STATE UNIVERSITY: It's not quite Berkeley, but it does have a beautiful 5,169-acre campus, much of it devoted to agricultural studies. Kids especially like to visit the feed mill, meat-processing plant, dairy operation, ornamental horticulture greenhouse, barns and chicken coops. As well, there's some interesting experimental architecture to see, and the student recreation center has everything from pinball to bowling.

Get a map outlining a self-conducted tour from the information desk in the administration building. You might also stop in at the Relations with Schools Office in room 217; they handle prospective students and can tell you the high points on campus.

A bus from City Hall goes right to the administration building.

BEACHES: The two main beaches in the area are **Pismo Beach,** about a 15-minute drive south, and **Morro Bay,** about the same distance north on Highway 1.

Pismo offers a 23-mile stretch of beautiful sandy beach. Clam-digging (this is one of the best spots in the world for it) is a year-round favorite sport, as is exploring isolated dunes, cliff-sheltered tide pools, caves and old pirate coves. There's fishing from the Pismo Beach Pier (other pier amusements include arcade games, bowling, billiards, etc.). It should be good, since the Spanish word *pismo* means "a place to fish." (On the other hand, this resort town may be named for the Chumash Indian word *pismu,* which means "the place where blobs of tar wash up on the beach.")

You'll also find a wide variety of restaurants and shops in the area, and it's a good place for antique-hunting.

Nearby **Avila Beach,** a quaint seacoast village, offers chartered deep-sea and scenic pleasure cruises from the Port St. Luis Marina.

Stop by the **Pismo Chamber of Commerce,** 581 Dolliver, and pick up a free copy of the area *Visitor's Guide;* it gives detailed information about local attractions, and also clamming instructions for the novice.

SAN LUIS OBISPO 149

Equally beautiful is **Morro Bay,** site of Morro Rock, the last of a chain of long-extinct volcanoes, and a winter and fall sanctuary for thousands of birds—cormorants, pelicans, sandpipers, even the rare peregrine falcon. It's wonderful to watch them from the beach or a window table at one of the bay-view restaurants.

The hub of the community is the **Embarcadero,** with its numerous seafood-with-a-view eateries; commercial fishing boats often unload their catch right at the restaurants. There are also seafood markets, boat and pier fishing facilities, shops and art galleries to explore, as well as a nearby aquarium.

Morro Bay has many, many visitor attractions, including a state park, golf course, natural history museum, hiking trails and, of course, miles of beach.

Once again, head for the **Chamber of Commerce,** 213 Beach Street, for a handy, free *Visitor's Guide.*

BICYCLING: A pleasant and healthy way to see the area is on a bike. A shop called **The Mountain Air,** 858 Higuera Street, has bikes for rent and maps of good bike routes.

WHERE TO STAY: The **Madonna Inn,** at 100 Madonna Road (tel: 543-3000), the bizarre, Disneyesque creation of Alex and Phyllis Madonna, is the most famous (or infamous) of the coast's hostelries. Nestled on the hillside, up a road lined with bubble-gum pink streetlight posts, is a fairyland stone and white wood castle with outdoor winding staircases, and a shingled roof topped with turrets and a weathervane. This imposing structure is the Madonna Inn's main building, one of five on the 1,500-acre site. The pink of the streetlights, by the way, is everywhere—even sandwiches in the restaurant are served on pink bread!

Each of the 109 rooms here is a unique and slightly eccentric thematic fantasy environment. They're all far out: you can choose Spanish, Italian, Irish, Alps, Currier and Ives, super-romantic, American Indian, Swiss or hunting decor. A "Canary Cottage" room is all yellow, with birdcage light fixtures; several are posh rock-walled caves; and there's even one for height-mismatched mates, with a bed five feet long on one side and six feet on the other.

When you enter the registration area, you can select the decor and theme of your room from a collection of hundreds of post cards. This doesn't mean you can just drop in and get a room—reserve as far in advance as possible; the place is always filled. Our favorite rooms—the results of careful perusal—are described below, and we suggest you ask for one that sounds appealing to you (maybe even give a few alternatives) when you make reservations. When you arrive, if something you prefer is vacant, you can always change.

One of the most romantic is "Love Nest," an incredible honeymoon suite with a pink-carpeted winding stairway (all romantic-themed rooms lean very heavily to pink) leading to a cupola hideaway. In the same category is "Morning Star," a two-room suite with a high beamed cathedral ceiling, gold bed, gold tables and gold and crystal chandelier. "Carin," named for a Swiss word of endearment, is also a honeymoon favorite, with gold cherub chandeliers over the bed, a peaked slanted ceiling, love birds adorning the bath and lots of guess what color. A little less of said color—here only the carpet, drapes, bathroom walls and phone are pink—in the delicate "Anniversary Room," with flowery rose light fixtures and floral print wallpaper.

The rock rooms are plush stone-walled caves, many of which have working fireplaces and/or rock-walled waterfall showers. "Old World" is one that has both of these features, and a predominantly red decor. Fireplaces but no cascading showers in "Yosemite Rock" and "Kona Rock," both furnished in lush green tones. On the other hand, "Cave Man" with leopard-skin bedspread and upholstery, has the waterfall but not the fireplace. This room connects to make a suite, if you so desire, with "Daisy Mae," which has the most elaborate waterfall shower in the entire inn, and several stained-glass windows depicting Daisy Mae herself. Another favorite rock room is "Cabin Still" (there's a still in the bath), and of course there's one called "Flintstone" in classic abba-dabba-doo decor.

Additional choices, these for fairy-tale prettiness more than weirdness, (not that they're conventional rooms by a long shot) are: "Old Fashioned Honeymoon" (ornately Victorian), "Victorian Gardens" (ditto), "Harvard Square" (absolutely gorgeous, and sleeps eight people); "Swiss Bell," "Wilhelm Tell," "Edelweiss" and "Matterhorn" (all with very charming Swiss decor); and finally the "Safari Room" (wild game theme) and "Buffalo Room," this latter of special significance to the Madonnas, since the buffalo head mounted on the wall was once attached to their own buffalo, killed in an accident.

Each room has a TV (most are color), direct-dial phone, and bath; you won't need a clock, since every hour is heralded by bells, Swiss yodels and a musical passage on the Swiss alphorn.

Additional facilities in the main building include an enormous coffee shop, a dining room (rather pricey), and two cocktail lounges, all as outlandishly ornate and plushly pink as the rest.

The rate schedule is as follows: singles $20 to $26; doubles and twins $32 to $46; three persons $38 to $46; four persons $42 to $48; suites with fireplace $39 to $55.

More conventional accommodations are available at any of three conveniently located, excellent little motels, all at the junction of U.S. 101 and Highway 1, within walking distance of each other and of town.

The **Coachman Inn**, 1001 Olive Street (tel: 544-0400), is housed in a two-story shingle-roofed stucco building, with pots of geraniums enhancing the exterior. Rooms are large, attractively and comfortably furnished, with dressing areas, bath/shower combinations, switchboard phones, radios and color cable TVs. There's a swimming pool on the premises, and a restaurant 100 feet away. The staff is most friendly and helpful.

Singles at the Coachman Inn cost $16 to $18, doubles $18 to $22; two-room suites accommodating six to eight persons are $40 to $48. Lower rates from October to May 14.

Just across the street at 1000 Olive is the **Olive Tree** (tel: 544-2800), offering very similar accommodations. The main differences are that the Olive Tree has a restaurant on the premises, The Stuffed Olive, which offers a very good service and tasty, reasonably priced coffee-shop-style food; there's also a sauna here, along with the pool, and room phones are direct-dial instead of switchboard.

The unique feature of the Olive Tree is its eight apartment suites, housed in four attractive shingled buildings, all with large terraces and big, fully equipped modern kitchens. These cost $38 to $40 for four to six persons. Regular singles are $20 to $24, doubles $24 to $30. Once again, off-season rates are a few dollars less.

Completing this motel triangle is the **Homestead**, 485 Osos Street (tel: 543-7700), with facilities—swimming pool, color TV, etc.—almost identical to those at the above-mentioned establishments. By way of differentiation, the Homestead has slightly prettier rooms than the other two, with quaint little paintings and prints on the walls and ruffled lampshades. Singles pay $15 to $20, doubles $18 to $24, and off-season rates are slightly lower.

Budget-minded travelers might want to stay at **Motel 6,** 1433 Calle Joaquin (tel: 544-8400), with 87 units and a swimming pool. Best if you have a car, since otherwise it's just a mite out of the way (Motel 6 details in the Introduction).

Camping

Facilities for camping abound in the San Luis area. For information about Pismo Beach and Morro Bay campsites, write to their respective chambers of commerce (addresses above). Morro Bay has two "luxury" campgrounds: **Tratel Morro Bay,** 1680 N. Main Street (tel: 772-8581), and **Morro Dunes,** 1700 Embarcadero (tel: 772-2722). Both are right on the beach, and have laundry facilities, rest rooms, hot showers and even TV rental available. If you'd like to write to either directly for information, the zip code in Morro Bay, California is 93442.

WHERE TO EAT: Expect the unexpected at **The Moor,** 967 Osos Street, between Palm and Monterey (tel: 543-6798). Owners Steve and Vicki believe that change is part of being alive and creative, so they change the menu frequently, and even alter the tasteful decor from time to time. The no-rut formula seems to work: their food is great and original, and the ambience delightful.

Housed in what was previously a beer hall and pool room, the Moor has high ceilings, off-white stucco walls hung with Indian tapestries and carpets, potted plants and ferns about, and soft lighting from wall sconces—the effect is funky-elegant. At least that's the way it looked when we were last there.

The changing menu ranges around exotic cuisines: Indonesian, Middle Eastern, Indian, etc. At our last visit there were several curry entrees—vegetable, lamb, shrimp and chicken ($3.85 to $5.85), as well as shrimp pilaf ($5.25) and Philippine lumpia (sort of a crêpe) filled with vegetables ($3.25), or chicken and shrimp ($4). All of the above are served with salad, vegetable, homemade bread and butter, and after-dinner coffee. Wine and beer are available, and the coffee menu runs to 150 choices (combined with liqueurs, etc.). Of these, 120 are "owners choice/diners chance." Tell Steve your preferred tastes and leave it to him. If you don't like his creation, he'll make you another one. Ours was heavenly, first try. Homemade desserts include cheesecake ($1), baklava (60¢) and a kind of Philippine ice cream sundae, halo halo ($1.25). Every morsel we ate here was just outrageously good.

The Moor is open nightly for dinner from 6 p.m. on; closed from December to mid-January.

A cheerful and homey place for a light meal is **Chocolate Soup,** 980 Morro at the corner of Monterey. Service is cafeteria-style, and the people behind the counter are young, friendly college kids. Walls and tables are rich chocolate brown (the former with white barnwood wainscoting), seating is in director's chairs, white enamel lamps are suspended from chains overhead, and there are white shutters on the windows. Coffee brews atop a white antique coal stove (secretly converted to electricity), and, in a similarly deceptive vein, taped music of the swing era emanates from an antique wood radio. It's all very cozy.

Soup (homemade and hearty) is the specialty, served with homemade bread (90¢). A fruit salad or spinach salad is 60¢; pocket sandwiches (in a pita) are filled with egg and olive ($1.35), avocado ($1.05) or taco ingredients ($1.45).

For dessert, there *is* chocolate soup—chocolate cake floating in rich hot pudding, topped with whipped cream and nuts (75¢). Cheesecake, delicious cookies and fruit pies are also available.

Breakers (tel: 544-6060), 1772 Calle Joaquin (take the Los Osos Valley Road turnoff from Highway 101), is San Luis Obispo's hilltop restaurant-with-a-view. From the picture windows you can see miles of beautiful rolling countryside, mountains, fields of grazing cattle and even the town in the distance. The interior is elegant, entered via a fireplace lounge. Diners sit on comfortable leather-upholstered oak chairs and plush couches, at candlelit tables decked out in gold cloths and napkins. Elaborate wagon-wheel chandeliers are suspended from high beamed ceilings.

Monday through Friday there's a $3.75 buffet luncheon ($1.95 for kids under 12)—a sumptuous feast of hot beef, chicken and fish entrees, salads, cold cuts, vegetables, potatoes and coffee. An equally hearty Sunday buffet brunch in $4.50, $2.95 for kids.

There's also a regular lunch menu Monday through Saturday, with items like shrimp Louie ($3.95), cioppino ($4.95) and several sandwich and burger listings. The dinner menu offers predominantly steak and seafood entrees. Seafood brochette with rice and fresh vegetables is $6.50, prime rib au jus with creamed horseradish $8.

Reservations are a good idea, and while you're at it, request a window seat.

Housed in a complex of restaurants and shops called the Network, **Wine Street Inn**, 774 Higuera Street (tel: 543-4488), is a low-ceilinged, long rectangular room, bordered by planters and dimly lit, even at lunch, by candles. The furnishings are bentwood chairs and oak tables, some covered by red cloths, all arranged haphazardly on a brick floor. An old-fashioned bar spans one wall and a wine shop adjoins. Lots of "atmosphere" here, to be sure.

At lunch, very good sandwiches are served on fresh-baked egg bread or dark bread—a Reuben ($2.25); cold beef, butter, blue cheese, tomatoes and chives ($2.65); or perhaps guacamole and bacon ($2.35). For 85¢ additional you can partake of the salad bar. Swiss or cheddar cheese fondue, served with chunks of sourdough bread, is $2.50, and a fondue for one is easily enough for two people. A glass of wine with your meal is 65¢.

Dinners are more elaborate. You might begin with an appetizer of pears and apples served with smoked cheese dip ($1.50). The selection of fondues is increased to include beef bourguignon ($5.75) and shrimp fondue ($5.95), both served with baked potato, salad and sourdough bread. Other items served with same are prime rib au jus ($7.95), teriyaki chicken ($5.50) and fresh baked sea bass ($5.50). For dessert, we simply cannot resist the creamy chocolate fondue ($1.75).

The Wine Street Inn is open for lunch from 11:30 a.m. to 2 p.m. Monday through Saturday, dinner nightly from 5:30 p.m.

While you're following the Path of History, you can take a break and dine at one of its landmarks, **The Cigar Factory**, 726 Higuera Street (tel: 543-6900), behind the foot bridge on Mission Plaza. Beginning in 1897, German immigrant George Kluver and his family made cigars in this brick building from Cuban and Sumatran tobacco. George Kluver's son, Fred, operated a retail cigar and tobacco business here until his death in 1962.

The upstairs portion has been transformed into a plush Victorian-style restaurant with deep red carpeting, walls of exposed brick or papered in red flocked wallpaper, overhead fans, Tiffany-style lamps and lace cafe curtains. Original wood signs from the cigar factory, framed cigar labels and letters from businessmen in San Francisco lamenting losses from the 1906 earthquake are displayed on the walls. The basement, where the Kluvers once stored 400-

pound packing boxes of tobacco leaves, has been fashioned into an attractive brick and shingle-walled cocktail lounge. There's also a brick garden patio with wrought-iron chairs for outdoor luncheons.

The lunch menu features such tasty items as a tortilla stuffed with fresh vegetables, cheese, salsa, sour cream and guacamole ($2.25), a meat loaf, cheese, avocado and onion sandwich on warm sourdough bread ($2.45), and a platter of barbecued ribs ($2.50), all served with a small green salad. The dinner menu (shown in a cigar box) emphasizes steak and seafood: a chicken and beef teriyaki combination is $5.75, steak and lobster $9.95, filet mignon $7.95, barbecued ribs or chicken $5.75. Entrees come with all the soup and salad-bar offerings you want. A baked potato, ear of corn or a glass of wine is an additional 75¢.

Lunch is served Monday to Friday from 11:30 a.m. to 2 p.m., dinner nightly from 6 p.m., and cocktails daily from 11:30 to 2 a.m.

6. Santa Barbara

The best thing that ever happened to Santa Barbara was an earthquake! On June 29, 1925, a quake with a Richter magnitude of 6.3 virtually destroyed the entire business district, leaving the uninspired architecture of the town in shambles. An Architectural Board of Review was formed soon after, to guide the rebuilding of the city, and a brilliant decision was made, which has been in effect ever since. All new buildings had to be in a similar Mediterranean style—basically the California adobe characterized by light-colored, sparkling stucco walls, low sloping terra-cotta tile roofs, a glimpse here and there of lacy wrought-iron grillwork, and above all, a comfortable human scale.

Though the buildings which sprang up have many influences—Mediterranean, Spanish Colonial Revival, Mexican, early California, Monterey, and even Moorish and Islamic—all are unified by the above standard, and all are in styles of architecture from areas with warm climates similar to Santa Barbara.

Already blessed with the Santa Ynez Mountains as a magnificent backdrop, and a gorgeous coastline, Santa Barbara has, with careful planning, become one of California's most beautiful and exotic cities.

As you drive along State Street (a plaza boulevard, and the town's main drag) from U.S. 101, you'll first pass through the old section of town which is slated for renovation. But once you get into the heart of the city you can easily forget that you're not south of the border. The sidewalks are wide and landscaped, enhanced by flowering trees and planting beds, store signs are limited in size, mailboxes and newsstands built into stucco walls, and at every pedestrian crossing is a living Christmas tree, which serves as just a regular tree the rest of the year. Even billboards have been banned in this delightful, no-eyesore city.

Just 92 miles north of L.A., and 332 south of San Francisco, Santa Barbara is reached by car via Highway 1 or U.S. 101. Both United Air Lines and Hughes Air West link both major cities with Santa Barbara, as do Greyhound bus lines and Amtrak.

Once again, there's so much to do and see in this lovely beach resort city that we advise you to visit the local **Chamber of Commerce,** 1301 Santa Barbara Street, for maps, literature, and a calendar of the many and varied events taking place at all times. Among other things, they've planned out a scenic drive that takes in 15 major points of interest, and a suggested walking tour of Santa Barbara's historical landmarks.

THINGS TO DO AND SEE: It would be a pleasure to while away an entire summer here, sunning oneself on the beach, taking long walks, visiting museums, dining in lovely restaurants, playing golf and tennis, horseback-riding, bike-riding, fishing, going to concerts and luxuriating in the amazingly beautiful surroundings. A rundown of Santa Barbara highlights follows.

El Paseo—The Street in Spain (814 State Street)

A picturesque shopping arcade with stone walkways, El Paseo is reminiscent of an old street in Spain. Built around the 1827 original adobe home of Spanish-born Presidio Commandante Jose De la Guerra, El Paseo is lined with charming shops and art galleries. This is the hub of the city, itself centered around the famous El Paseo restaurant, about which more later. Across the street is the **Plaza de la Guerra**, where the first City Council met in 1850, and where the first City Hall was erected in 1875.

County Courthouse (1100 block, Anacapa Street)

Occupying a full city block, and set in a lush tropical garden, the County Courthouse is a supreme and exquisite example of Santa Barbara nouveau-Spanish architecture—a tribute to bygone days when style and elegance outweighed more practical considerations. Few would guess that it was built as late as 1929. The architect, William Mooser, was aided by his son, who, having spent 17 years in Spain, was well-versed in Spanish-Moorish design.

Turrets and towers, graceful arches, unexpected windows, brilliant Tunisian tilework, winding staircases, intricately carved and stenciled ceilings, palacio tile floors, lacy iron grillwork, heavy carved wood doors and Spanish lanterns of hammered iron are among the impressive interior features. Magnificent historic murals by Dan Sayre Groesbeck, depicting memorable episodes in Santa Barbara history, are worth a visit in themselves. An elevator whisks visitors up to El Mirador—the 70-foot-high observation and clock tower, wherein sweeping views of the ocean, mountains and terra-cotta tiled rooftops of the city.

The Courthouse is amazingly impressive and inspiring—don't miss it. You can take a free guided tour at 10:30 a.m. daily.

Santa Barbara Mission (Laguna and Mission Streets)

Called the "Queen of the Missions" for its graceful beauty, this awe-inspiring hilltop paradise overlooks the town—its gleaming white buildings surrounded by an expanse of lush green lawn, flowering trees and shrubs, a Moorish fountain under a weeping willow, and a misty backdrop of cloud-enshrouded mountains.

Established in 1786, the present mission is still used today by the parish of Santa Barbara. On display within are a typical missionary bedroom, tools, crafts and artifacts of the Chumash Indians, 18th- and 19th-century mission furnishings, paintings and statues from Mexico and period kitchen utensils—grinding stones, baskets, and copper kettles. You can take a self-guided tour any day from 9 a.m. to 5 p.m., Sundays from 1 to 5 p.m. Adults pay 50¢, children under 16 free.

Museums

Three privately maintained Santa Barbara museums are open to the public and charge no admission.

The **Museum of Natural History,** beyond Old Mission Road at 2559 Puesta del Sol Road (tel: 963-7821), is devoted to the display, study and interpretation of Pacific Coast natural history—flora, fauna and prehistoric life. Museum architecture, in typical Santa Barbara style, reflects early Spanish and Mexican influence, with ivy-covered stucco walls, graceful arches, arcades, a central patio and lovely grounds. Exhibits range from diagrams and photographs of the life cycle of worms, to Indian basketry, textiles, and a full-size replica of a Chumash canoe; from Peruvian art to fossil ferns to the complete skeleton of a gray whale.

In addition to six halls dealing with Indians, birds, mammals, the Paleolithic age, minerals and marine life, a planetarium offers daily shows.

Open 9 a.m. to 5 p.m. Monday through Saturday, 1 to 5 p.m. Sundays and holidays.

The **Museum of Art,** 1130 State Street (tel: 963-4364), houses an eclectic collection encompassing Indian, Chinese, Greco-Roman and Egyptian antiquities; works of the Italian Renaissance and Flemish schools; the American school—Eakins, John Singer Sargent, Edward Hopper, George Grosz; abstract expressionists like Tworkov and Hans Hoffmann, and a sampling of other artists including Monet, Pissaro, Chagall, Kandinsky and Raoul Dufy. There's even a Claes Oldenburg litho called "Pizza."

Some unique and very enjoyable exhibits are Edward Borein's ink drawings and watercolors of the early American West; the extensive and enchanting Alice F. Schott doll collection, ranging from 18th-century French to first-century B.C. Egyptian dolls; and a collection of Oriental musical instruments.

There are occasional concerts, and during the summer a program of classic films is presented on weekends (donation 80¢); call for schedule.

The museum is open Tuesday through Saturday from 11 a.m. to 5 p.m., Sundays noon to 5 p.m. Free guided tours are given on Wednesdays at 12:30 p.m.

The **Historical Society Museum,** 136 E. De la Guerra Street, at the corner of Santa Barbara Street, deals with local lore. It's most interesting to take the free guided tour, given by a knowledgeable guide Wednesdays at 1:30 p.m. Exhibits include paintings of California missions by Edwin Deakin done between 1875 and 1890; a 16th-century carved Spanish coffer that belonged to Padre Serra; Peruvian silver stirrups and a Spanish cape, both of the 17th century; oil portraits and artifacts of the De la Guerra family and other early notables of Santa Barbara history; many interesting pieces of correspondence; the costumes and accoutrements of Abel Maldanado, a famous magician who lived in Santa Barbara in the '20s and '30s; antique dolls, teddy bears, doll houses and a wonderful horseless carriage with three doll occupants; lots of period clothing and many other relics and memorabilia that make early California history come alive.

Open Tuesday through Friday from noon to 5 p.m., Saturday and Sunday from 1 to 5 p.m.

Botanic Gardens (1212 Mission Canyon Road)

About 1½ miles north of the mission, the Botanic Gardens, 60 acres of native trees, shrubs, cacti and wildflowers, also are the site of a dam built by the Indians in 1806. There are three miles of nature trails to follow. Open daily from 8 a.m. to sunset, with free guided tours offered Thursdays at 10:30 a.m. Free admission.

Moreton Bay Fig Tree (Chapala and Montecito Streets)

We're not grasping for sightseeing attractions—this tree is really something. Native to Moreton Bay in Eastern Australia, the *figus macrophylla* is related to both the fig and rubber tree, though it produces neither figs nor rubber. This massive century-old example would fill half a football field, well over 10,000 persons could stand in its shade at noon, and over an acre of ground covers its woody roots! It's among the largest of its kind in the world.

Once in danger of being leveled—for a proposed gas station, of all things—and later threatened by excavation for nearby Highway 101, the revered tree has been fervently protected each time by Santa Barbara fans, who will no doubt go on protecting the fig tree's territorial rights for another century.

Stearn's Wharf (foot of State Street)

Pacific Ocean wharves with seafood restaurants, fishing facilities and novelty shops are a delightful California tradition in every coastal city. This one extends for three blocks, and is in the heart of the Cabrillo Blvd. beach-resort area. Take a stroll, buy a cup of fresh shrimps and enjoy the view—it's free.

A Child's Estate (East Cabrillo Blvd. near Milpas Street)

This small zoo is especially geared to kids. At the entrance are farmyard animals (you can feed and pet them), donkeys, goats, ducks and chickens, and of course kids, ducklings and baby chicks. Further along are otters, exotic birds (the peacock is always the biggest hit), llamas, lions, pumas, tigers, bears, seals, elephants and the rest of the usual zoo crowd.

There's also a park and playground. Adults pay $1.25, teenagers 75¢, kids two to 12 and senior citizens a meager quarter. Those under 14 must be accompanied by an adult.

Andree Clark Bird Refuge (1400 East Cabrillo Blvd.)

Adjoining A Child's Estate, the refuge is a lovely lagoon in a garden setting, where many varieties of fresh-water fowl can be seen and fed. A foot and bike path skirt the lagoon, and it's so beautiful it doesn't even matter if you don't see birds. Serious bird-watchers can pick up a 25¢ eight-page pamphlet about local birds at the Museum of Natural History

Antiquing, Gallery-Browsing and Shopping

There are close to 80 antique shops in Santa Barbara. **Brinkerhoff Avenue,** off Haley between Chapala and De La Vina Streets is where you'll find the greatest concentration, selling early American furnishings, quilts, antique china, jewelry, Orientalia, memorabilia, not to mention bric-a-brac and interesting junk. The free *Santa Barbara Visitor Press* (pick it up at the Chamber of Commerce), lists them all, along with the town's many art galleries, boutiques, leather and handicraft shops, etc. In Santa Barbara you can buy everything from out-of-print books to mounted butterflies.

At 813 State Street, a cluster of such shops (45 in all) is located in an arcade called **Picadilly Square;** it's in process of expansion at this writing.

Boating and Fishing

Motorboats, sailboats and rowboats are available for rent at the **Santa Barbara Breakwater** (tel: 962-2826). From the same location, you can also go out on sport-fishing boats, the *Seasport* and *Corsair,* the former offering half-day outings Saturdays, Sundays, Tuesdays and Thursdays from 7 a.m. to noon or 12:30 to 5:30 p.m. (fare $8, children half-fare); the latter, totally equipped with stocked galley (food and drink served on board), rental rods and tackle available, leaves at 6 a.m. daily for a full day (fare $18, including bait). Fishing licenses can be obtained at all sporting-goods stores ($5 for a special ten-day non-resident license).

Scenic cruises (no fishing) also leave from the Breakwater. In summer, *Shirley Ann,* a 48-foot tour boat, leaves for two-hour excursions daily at 10 a.m. (fare $5) and one-hour excursions hourly from noon to 4 p.m. (fare $3). Same rates and schedule in winter, but on weekends only.

Bicycling

This scenic and relatively flat area is marvelous for biking, along the four mile palm-lined coastal bikeway, through town, on miles of country roads or to nearby Montecito. **Open-Air Bicycles** at 8 West Cabrillo Boulevard, right at the beach, has carefully maintained three-speed, ten-speed and motorized (European-style) bikes for rent, and they'll suggest bicycle tours, too. Open 9 a.m. to 9 p.m. daily. Bring I.D. and a $10 deposit.

Horseback-Riding

Several stables in the area rent horses, and offer escorted trail rides along the many local trails. **Gene's San Ysidro Stables,** 900 San Ysidro Lane (tel: 969-2079), charges $5 for one hour; **University of California Santa Barbara,** out in Goleta, offers beach rides for $3.25 an hour (tel: 961-3738).

Hiking

The **Sierra Club** (tel: 962-2210) is active in Santa Barbara, and it welcomes guests on all of its outings, which include day hikes, knapsack trips, bike trips even occasional picnics. They can also tell you about the many scenic trails in the Los Padres National Forest and other locations.

Golf

Many courses to choose from: The 18-hole **Sandpiper Golf Course** at 7925 Hollister Avenue in Goleta (tel: 968-1541), charges a daily fee of $6, $9 on weekends; less expensive is the **Santa Barbara Community Course,** also 18 holes, at Las Positas Road and McCaw Avenue (tel: 687-7087), charging $3.50, $4.50 on weekends.

Nine-hole courses include the **University Village Golf Course,** Storke Road south of Highway 101, west of Goleta (tel: 968-6814), $2 daily, weekends and holidays $2.50; and **Fairview Community Golf Center,** 6034 Hollister Avenue, Goleta (tel: 964-1414), daily fee $1.40, $1.65 nights and weekends.

Most of the above have equipment shops, and some offer instruction.

Tennis

Public facilities include the **Municipal Courts** near Salinas Street and Highway 101 (access off Old Coast Highway); **Las Positas Municipal Courts,** 1002 Las Positas Road; and **Pershing Park** courts at Castillo Street and West Cabrillo Boulevard. In addition there are several private tennis clubs and country club courts, some of which allow guests. Check with the Chamber of Commerce.

Fiesta

The most exciting time to visit Santa Barbara is in early August during the **Old Spanish Days Fiesta,** since 1924 a yearly homage to the city's Spanish past, patterned after the community harvest festivals of Andalusia and Castile in Old Spain.

This is no piddling little festival—it's a big five-day bash with an official theme song, colorful costumes, an opening ceremony of pageantry and traditional blessings on the steps of the Old Mission, equestrian events, rodeo, famous flamenco guitarists and dancers, variety shows, barbecues, big-name entertainers (last year Helen Reddy and Crosby and Nash), a Spanish marketplace, a dazzling parade down palm-lined Cabrillo Boulevard with dozens of fancy floats, art shows, carnivals, outdoor dancing on the beach, symphony concerts, folk dancing and much, much more. Many events are free.

Plan to arrive a little before Fiesta (make reservations as far in advance as possible—the town gets booked up 100%), and to stay till it's over. Even if you could get a room, you wouldn't be able to get to it during Fiesta; you'd have to lug your suitcases through the crowded streets, many of which are blocked to traffic. The same problem pertains to getting out. Another reason to arrive early is to have time to pore over the schedules of events, get tickets when required, and enjoy the quiet of the beach and town before all the excitement begins.

Nightlife

The **Lobero Theatre,** 33 East Canon Perdido Street (tel: 966-7181), dates back to 1872, when it was built by Guiseppi Lobero, an Italian who changed his name to José Lobero in deference to the Spanish traditions of Santa Barbara. When the theater went bankrupt in 1892, Lobero, faced with financial ruin and the failure of his dream, put a bullet through his head. By 1922 the building was closed and condemned.

The present Lobero Theatre stands on the same site, then a honky-tonk slum area, today a respectable part of downtown Santa Barbara. Among those who have played here are Lionel Barrymore, Edward G. Robinson, Clark Gable, Robert Young, Boris Karloff, Betty Grable and Anna May Wong. The Martha Graham troupe has also graced the stage, and concert luminaries have included Lotte Lehman, Igor Stravinsky, and Leopold Stokowski.

A wide variety of productions are offered throughout the year—concerts, dance programs, recitals, operas and plays. Call the theater to find out what's on during your stay.

The **Arlington Center for the Performing Arts,** 1317 State Street (tel: 963-3686), derived its name from a hotel which occupied the same site from 1875 to 1909. It opened in 1931 in grand style, at the birth of the talking picture era, presenting movies, vaudeville and stage shows. The luxe Arlington became Hollywood's testing ground for unreleased movies; big stars flocked to Santa Barbara to check audience reaction at Arlington sneak previews.

After World War II, when vaudeville had died, road shows began to book into the Arlington to supplement the movie fare. Mae West appeared here in "Diamond Lil," and was panned!

Recently the old theater has been given a total facelift, reupholstered seats, new furnishings, facilities, and even exterior landscaping. And although film festival classic movies will be shown occasionally, the theater will feature primarily big-name entertainers like Lily Tomlin, Wayne Newton and Ray Charles; world-famous symphony orchestras like the Los Angeles Philharmonic with Zubin Mehta conducting; and jazz greats from Benny Goodman to Herbie Mann.

More superstar entertainment (from the Average White Band and Leon Russell to Van Cliburn) at the **Santa Barbara County Bowl** (tel: 962-8101).

The Earl Warren Showgrounds

Indian art shows, antique shows, barbecues, flea markets, horse shows, dances, cat shows, Bible rallies, the circus, a rodeo or even a big-name entertainer is likely to be at the Earl Warren Showgrounds, Las Positas Road and Highway 101 (tel: 687-0766). Check it out.

WHERE TO STAY: So popular is Santa Barbara in summer that you simply must book in advance.

The most elegant digs in town happen to be at one of the most prestigious and glamorous hotels in California—**The Biltmore,** 1260 Channel Drive, (tel: 969-2261; 800/228-9290), located on 21 acres of beautiful gardens and private ocean beach in the exclusive Montecito community. A refined resort hotel of the old school, when it opened in 1927 a concert orchestra played twice daily in the dining room and separate quarters were available for personal servants accompanying guests. Though few people travel with servants these days, the Biltmore is still heavy on service; cards on every guest list such minute preferences as a request for an extra pillow.

The award-winning Spanish architecture (what else in Santa Barbara?) was the work of Reginald Johnson. He utilized Portuguese, Basque, Iberian and Moorish design elements in a graceful combination of arcades, winding staircases, ramadas, patios and artistic walkways, with exquisite hand-painted Mexican tile and grillwork throughout. The beauty of the estate is further enhanced by imposing views of the blue Pacific, the Santa Ynez mountains and the hotel's own palm-studded formal gardens.

The 180 guest rooms are housed in terra-cotta-tile-roofed low stucco buildings and cottages. Many have an ocean or garden view, and all are extremely cheerful and lovely, decorated in sunny resort colors. There's an extra phone in every bath, handmade tiles in the shower, and extra-thick towels; your color TV has remote control, and there's a refrigerator and bar.

Cottages are particularly lovely, and some have kitchens. Some rooms also have fireplaces.

Extra services include the maids turning down your bed each evening, not a surprising detail in a hotel where they draw designs in the ashtray sand each morning!

Adjacent to the hotel is the posh Coral Casino Beach and Cabana Club; guests can use its Olympic-size swimming pool and other facilities. There's another pool right on the property, as well as an 18-hole putting green, croquet, shuffleboard, badminton, and complimentary bicycles. Golf, tennis and riding facilities are nearby.

Breakfast, lunch and dinner are served in the elegant La Marina dining room, with white stucco walls, carved oak doors, heavy wrought-iron chandeliers suspended from vaulted ceilings and lovely panoramic views of the ocean. The Patio Room, for al fresco dining under a white tent top, adjoins. Dinner entrees, prepared under the careful supervision of gourmet French chef, Jacques Le Borgne, include seafood crêpes Mornay ($5.95), roast rack of lamb in Madeira sauce ($24.50 for two), and a prawn casserole with mushrooms and shallots in white wine sauce ($7.95). A very good buy is the Sunday night $10 buffet, a hearty gourmet feast served from 6 to 9 p.m.

A single room at the Biltmore is $40 to $70; doubles and twins are $45 to $75. In the cottages, singles are $55 and $65, doubles $60 and $70, with one- to five-bedroom suites beginning at $120.

Good news for the not-so-well-heeled: Biltmore's Anacapa wing, which few people know about, offers much lower rates: $30 to $35 for a single, $35 to $40 for a double. You get all the luxury, service and facilities of the Biltmore, but the rooms are decidedly less glamorous—the old servant quarters, perhaps.

Meanwhile, back at the ranch . . . back at the **San Ysidro Ranch** that is, 900 San Ysidro Lane off Highway 101 (tel: 969-5046), we have another famous Montecito hostelry nestled in the Santa Ynez mountains. Originally part of a Spanish land grant, on which the padres raised cattle, and later a citrus orchard (there are still orange groves on the property, the produce of which is used for fresh-squeezed juice each morning), San Ysidro opened as a guest ranch in 1893. Over the years Winston Churchill, Sinclair Lewis, Rex Harrison, Groucho Marx and Sidney Poitier have signed the register, and Jack and Jacqueline Kennedy spent their honeymoon here.

A quiet, beautifully landscaped 500-acre retreat, San Ysidro offers its guests tennis, a swimming pool, riding stables, a private beach, badminton, croquet, miles of hiking and riding trails, and nearby golf. All facilities on the premises are free, except horse rental.

Gourmet French cuisine is served at the Plow and Angel dining room, under the watchful eye of chef Camille Schwartz, the talented and charming man who launched Ireland's and helped establish their fine reputation (see restaurant listings). The restaurant, housed in the old citrus packing house, is a charming candlelit establishment with a beamed ceiling, shuttered windows, antique furnishings and paintings of local landmarks on the white sandstone walls.

A delightful and airy glass-enclosed cafe area adjoins, the view of the grounds enhanced by many hanging plants inside. We love to come here for a leisurely lunch—perhaps salad Niçoise ($3.95) or a ham, cheese and mushroom omelet ($3.45).

Dinners are more elaborate—and expensive: filet au poivre—steak sauteed in peppercorns and flamed in cognac (our favorite) is $9.95; also very good is the sauteed chicken in white wine sauce with grapes and mandarin oranges ($5.95). Either meal, save room for a sumptuous dessert.

Accommodations consist of 37 quaint cottages with exquisite country-inn antique furnishings. Every evening the maid turns down your bed; during the day a woodman makes the rounds with wood and kindling for your fireplace, and fresh flowers from the garden are left in your cottage. The cottages are all secluded in a random pattern among lush foliage and flowers, and each has a porch so you can sit outside and enjoy the view. All have phones and modern baths, but no TV to interrupt the sounds of rustling leaves, gentle wind and babbling brook. For diehards (alas, we too hate to miss the doings of Tom, Mary, Charlie and Loretta), there is a TV in the lounge, wherein also an honor-system bar.

There are 17 doubles priced at $37; other cottage rooms, studios and suites for two are $56 and $78. Additional persons in a room pay $8 each.

At the Beach

You can't get closer to the beach than **El Patio**, 336 West Cabrillo Boulevard (tel: 965-6556), which is also right across the street from Pershing

Park. The hotel is already quite nice, but we expect it will get even better under the new ownership of Mr. Alex Mahler, a man of taste and experience, who really cares about the quality of his lodgings.

There are 60 large and immaculate rooms, all with color cable TV, direct-dial phones and tub/shower baths. Most have dressing rooms and balconies or patios; furnishings are modern Mediterranean with shag carpeting, and colorful paisley bedspreads. Ocean and park views are an added bonus.

Facilities on the premises include a large swimming pool, a coffee shop open daily from 6:30 a.m. to 9 p.m., and a wood-paneled dining room open for dinner nightly.

The rate structure here is a bit complicated: July 1 to September 30, singles are $22 to $28, doubles and twins (two double beds) $26 to $30. October 1 to March 15, singles are $18 to $22, doubles and twins $22 to $26. March 16 to June 30, singles are $20 to $24, doubles and twins $24 to $28. Cheaper rooms are in the older wing, where there are also some two-bedroom suites that sleep four people (ideal for families) and cost $28 to $34.

Another good choice is the pink stucco **Tropicana Motel**, 223 Castillo Street (tel: 996-2219), a 29-unit accommodation just a short walk from the beach. Rooms are homey and attractive, furnished in maple pieces, with blue-green shag carpeting, and white chenille bedspreads. All are equipped with color TV, phone, bath with shower, electric alarm clock and coffee-maker.

There are also suites available—an excellent buy if you would like to do your own cooking. These have large eat-in kitchens, fully equipped right down to eggbeaters and potholders, not to mention a good oven, stove and toaster. The suites sleep up to four persons, and must be rented for a minimum of three days.

Other facilities include a nice-sized pool and Jacuzzi, both away from the street and very private, with lots of room for sunning.

Singles, which are hard to come by in summer, rent for $20, doubles are $20 to $26, twins (two double beds) $26, and three-room suites (bedroom, living room and kitchen) are $29 for two persons; add $3 for each extra person.

Even closer to the beach is the **Royal Inn**, 128 Castillo Street (tel: 963-4471), with 44 immaculate rooms in tip-top condition, a secluded swimming pool with lots of sunning area, whirlpool and sauna bath.

The rooms, furnished in Italian motif, with white silk drapes and bedspreads, come in two color schemes: gold rooms have rugs the color of a slightly gold teddy bear, gold upholstery and pale yellow walls; blue rooms have royal blue rugs and upholstery and pale sky-blue walls. All the rooms have color cable TV, phones, air conditioning, tub/shower baths and dressing rooms with big mirrors, and they're all quite lovely. Second- and third-floor rooms have balconies.

In summer, singles are $20 to $26, doubles and twins $22 to $30, one-bedroom suites $35 to $45. An additional person in your room is $4. Rates are slightly lower off season (October to mid-May).

Adequate but less fancy beach accommodations at **Del-Mar-Y-Sol**, 18 Bath Street (tel: 965-7600). There are 22 units here, 14 of which have kitchens; plus a small pool and Jacuzzi. If you want kitchen use, you'll have to rent the unit by the week; but you can rent one on a daily basis, use only the refrigerator, and enjoy some extra space. Rooms vary in attractiveness—we prefer the upstairs ones; if you don't like the first one you see, ask to see another. All have bath and most have TV; phones are outside. In summer, doubles are $19 to $24; off-season, $14 to $20.

Right on the beach, too, with a swimming pool and everything, is one of those ubiquitous **Motel 6** branches, 443 Corona Del Mar (take the Milpas off-ramp from 101); tel: 965-0300. Once again, refer to the Introduction for particulars.

In Town

Most people prefer to stay at the beach, but if you have a car you might consider the **Encina Lodge**, 2220 Bath Street, at Los Olivos Street (tel: 965-1021). Set in a quiet residential area, a short walk from the Mission and other attractions, it's a mere five-minute drive from the beach. All rooms are very high quality, immaculate and tastefully decorated—furnishings, bedspreads, rugs, etc., all look spanking new and expensive. We especially like the rooms on the second floor of the oldest building, with beamed raw pine ceilings. All rooms have color TV, air conditioning, private patios or balconies, direct-dial phones and clocks. Old-wing rooms have shower only; the rest have tub/shower combinations and dressing rooms.

Facilities include a fairly large pool, a whirlpool, sundeck, lobby shop and a very fine restaurant, which you should try even if you don't stay here. Owner-chef Ron Ousey is a teacher of culinary arts, and his meals are prepared with loving care and the finest ingredients. His ever-changing lunch menu might feature sweet and sour chicken ($3.25) or barbecued ribs ($2.95), both with soup or salad. We particularly recommend dinner here (5 to 9 p.m.), when you can try Ousey's award-winning crab Mornay ($6.50), served with soup or salad, saffron rice or au gratin potatoes, fresh vegetables, homemade bread and butter. Don't miss the homemade pastries for dessert. The ambience, by the way is quite nice: candlelight, hanging ferns, flocked wallpaper, oak paneling, beamed stucco ceiling—somewhere between French provincial and fancy coffee shop.

In summer, single rates are $23 to $29, doubles $25 to $31. Suites for four persons are $37. Winter rates are about $5 less.

WHERE TO DINE: Santa Barbara's most unique restaurant, and a great favorite of ours, is the **Tea House**, 301 E. Canon Perdido Street, at Garden Street (tel: 963-9612). A gourmet natural-foods vegetarian and seafood restaurant, the Tea House has a particularly delightful atmosphere, always enhanced by good music—recorded classical selections at lunch, live guitar, sitar or flute at dinner, and live chamber music for Sunday brunch.

The decor is Oriental—big fluffy pillows (the only seating) are strewn about on Oriental rugs at low tables, and an alcove under a red tent roof is separated from the main dining area by a moss-green velvet curtain. There's also outdoor seating on a patio lush with foliage and an enormous bougainvillea vine. It's all very lovely, the creation of owner Bill White, an architect with many other areas of expertise. Bill spent a whole year researching wines, to prepare a carefully selected list that features the best dinner wines at reasonable prices, along with sake, mead, fruit wines (apricot, pomegranate, etc.) and hot spiced wine.

As the name of the place suggests, a wide selection of imported teas is available, by the pot, as is heartily satisfying fresh roasted imported coffee.

The menu is pretty much the same lunch or dinner. We like the $4.90 curry dinner that includes carrot raita (spiced yogurt with shredded carrots and assorted condiments), a rich curry made of squash, potatoes, fruit, raisins, nuts and coconuts, served over brown rice, and Kashmiri chutney. Also very good is the cheese fondue, made of Swiss Emmenthal cheese, kirsch and wine, served with a large platter of fresh vegetables and pieces of whole-grain toast ($2.50

per person). At dinner only, bouillabaisse is an added option, served with tossed salad and homemade bread ($5.95). Our Sunday brunch preference is cheese blintzes with sour cream and fruit sauce ($4.25). Homemade desserts are superb, especially the luxuriantly creamy cheesecake ($1.10).

The Tea House is a very special experience, a treat for all the senses—don't miss it. Open 11 a.m. to 11 p.m. every day except Monday.

While we're on the subject of natural foods and fine teas, the nutrition-conscious crowd often lunches at the **Earthling Books and Tea Room**, 22 East Victoria Street. At this read-while-you-feed eatery, diners can cozy up on a plush couch by the fireplace with any of the many books, bask outside on the sunny patio, or even sit at a regular table. There's always taped music, usually classical and occasionally country. Service is cafeteria-style, and all breads and desserts are fresh-baked on the premises. The fare is simple, healthy and good. A typical lunch would be a sandwich, perhaps avocado, cheese, sprouts and tomato ($1.55), or cream cheese, olives, walnuts and raisins ($1.40), followed by scrumptious carrot cake or peach pie (60¢), and a pot of one of the wide selection of herbal and gourmet teas. All very comfy and relaxing.

Open Monday through Saturday from 10 a.m. to 4 p.m.

More organic-natural-veggie-snacking at **Nature's Prophet**, 800 De la Vina Street, a tiny hole in the wall attached to a health-food store. A blackboard menu lists two items nightly—all vegetarian, like a buckwheat casserole ($2.25). You can also get sandwiches, salads, and a variety of smoothies—strawberry, pineapple, etc.—made with a frozen banana base. They're healthfully refreshing on hot days. Open daily for lunch and dinner.

Needless to say, in Spanish-style Santa Barbara, Mexican eateries abound. Most famous is the **El Paseo Restaurant** (tel: 965-5106), housed in part of the De la Guerra house, right in the Street in Spain. Since 1926, Santa Barbara residents have been flocking to this extraordinarily lovely and festive courtyard restaurant. Its balconied stucco walls reach skyward to an orange tent top, which is rolled back in good weather. The furnishings are carved Spanish wooden chairs and tables, the latter adorned with fresh flowers; leafy vines climb the columns towards the balcony, and through the high archway is an intimate bar and cocktail area dominated by a Mexican mural.

At lunch Mexican combination plates are $2.95 to $4.95, and there are many other items on the menu, ranging from Welsh rarebit over poached eggs with bacon ($3.25) to a deluxe chili burger ($1.95). At dinner you might try the marinated Mexican-style stuffed shrimps, wrapped in bacon and served with rice ($6.75), or a simple hacienda-style arroz con pollo (chicken with rice) for $5.95.

If you want to order everything in sight, come on Sunday when an immense buffet (help yourself to all the guacamole and enchiladas you can eat) is $4.50 for adults, $2.85 for kids under 12.

Open daily, Monday through Friday from noon to 10 p.m., Saturday (with music for dancing beginning at 8 p.m.) from noon to 11 p.m., and Sunday (buffet only) from noon to 8 p.m.

Restaurants come no prettier, romantic evenings no cheaper, than at **Casa Linda**, 1235 Coast Village Road in Montecito (tel: 969-2404), a low wood and stucco building (previously an inn) painted forest green with white trim, its entire roof blanketed in flowering trumpet vines. If that's not charming enough, there are even pots of geraniums suspended from a white picket fence out front. The quaintly homey interior has raspberry pink walls adorned with Mexican paintings, festive red lanterns hanging from a sloping beamed ceiling, red-and-white-checked tablecloths, and little red curtains on the windows. In good weather you can sit outside on a brick patio. South-of-the-border ambience is further enhanced by waitresses in Mexican garb, and a flamenco dancer and guitarist Friday, Saturday and Sunday nights from 7 p.m. on.

Luncheon specials, served Monday through Saturday, are wonderfully inexpensive—all the beans, rice, enchilada, taco, burrito combinations for just 90¢ to $1.95.

Dinner entrees include two chicken enchiladas topped with guacamole and sour cream ($3.25), a cheese and a beef enchilada ($2.75), sauteed steak ranchero in special sauce ($2.75); a deluxe combo of one enchilada, a beef taco, chile relleno and guacamole at $3.90 is the most expensive item on the menu. All of the above are served with tostaditas, hot sauce, salad, Spanish rice and refried beans.

Open daily 11 a.m. to midnight. Reservations are necessary at dinner.

Many Santa Barbarans maintain that the best Mexican eateries are the unpretentious Chicano haunts along State Street. They usually have blaring Spanish music, insipid paintings of Mexican scenes on the walls, artificial flowers on the tables, and a warm, friendly, relaxed atmosphere.

In this category, our favorite (which meets all the above standards) is **Azteca**, 623½ State Street—especially dear to us because they only charge $1.25 for a big portion of guacamole ($1.75 and up everywhere else). Daily luncheon specials, served from 11 a.m. to 3 p.m., are just $1.35, and immense combination plates are in the $3 range. The food is great. Open daily 11 a.m. to 11 p.m.

A close runner-up is **Casa Blanca**, 509 State Street.

If Santa Barbara has a lot of Mexican restaurants, it has even more bastions of haute cuisine. The one with the most ambitious menu is **Casa Madrid**, at the El Encanto Hotel, 1900 La Suen Road (tel: 965-5231). This once luxurious resort hotel, on seven woodland acres, has now settled into a faded elegance, but the restaurant is still first-rate and lovely. Light and airy, it has many windows offering expansive views of the city and ocean. Red linen tablecloths are smartly draped over floor-length pale pink ones, with pink napkins, deep-red water glasses and fresh flowers enhancing the effect. There are lots of plants, gold-framed mirrors adorn the walls, and the draperies are a gold and rose brocade print. Chandeliers overhead cast a rosy glow.

We said the dinner menu was ambitious—it's 24 pages long (not including desserts), and even has a table of contents! Hors d'oeuvres and appetizers include escargots bourguignon ($4.25), creamed herring ($3.25) and Beluga caviar ($10.50 for two). To us, the most irresistible appetizer is fettuccine Alfredo—noodles tossed in cream, melted butter, parmesan cheese and chopped parsley ($4.25); the most interesting is broiled prunes, marinated in port wine, stuffed with spiced mangos and wrapped in bacon ($6.50).

If that all sounds too pricey, don't give up. Just skip the openers and turn to the entrees, all of which are served with soup, salad, vegetables, potatoes, bread and butter and a complimentary glass of wine.

House specialties include a paella Valenciana ($8.95); flambé chicken sauteed with guava, mushrooms and rum ($7.50); and sauteed lobster stuffed with wild rice, garnished with scampi asparagus, pimento and olives, topped with clam sauce ($12.95). You're sure to find something you crave; after all, there's a choice of over 70 entrees, not including the 20 or so items that require two days' advance notice—like roasted pheasant basted with butter and cognac ($46 for two).

Of course, there's a fine wine list available (not part of the menu book). And on some nights, after guests are served, chef Armando plays "music of the masters" on the grand piano.

The lunch menu is confined to six items on a little card, so to get the full effect, go for dinner. Sunday—from 11 a.m. to 2 p.m.—is also a good time to visit Casa Madrid, a $5.50 prix-fixe brunch includes champagne, fruit juice, compote, crêpes de jour, choice of omelet or eggs de jour, fresh-baked muffins and coffee.

Open for lunch and dinner daily. Reservations suggested.

Owned by actor John Ireland, because he really loves food, is (you guessed it) **Ireland's,** 1279 Coast Village Road in Montecito (tel: 969-5969). Is Ireland's prestigious? Well, their advertisements show none other than Prince Charles of England grinning happily over his victuals, if that's any indication.

The gourmet French cuisine, exquisite provincial decor and service are all fittingly *haute*. Banquettes and chairs are upholstered in moss-green velvet, tablecloths and curtains are of a cheerful Indonesian batik, which is also used to create a tentlike ceiling. Walls are barnwood and stucco, their rusticity enhanced by tasteful arrangements of dried flowers and a blazing fireplace. There's another fireplace outdoors, where, on the awninged patio, you can dine al fresco. In short, everything is perfectly lovely.

And that, of course, includes the food. At lunch you might begin with a chilled avocado soup ($1.50), follow it up with filet of sole meunière ($4.25) or a cheese soufflé ($4), and conclude with coffee and a gateau au fromage ($1.75) —that's cheesecake, folks.

Dinner entrees include flamed duckling served with peaches ($9.50), fresh salmon with fine herbs ($8) and veal piccata ($9.50). Domestic and French wines, stored in a wine cellar on the premises, are available to complement your meal. For dessert, forget the fromage cake and order the Grand Marnier or chocolate soufflé ($3.50).

Ireland's is open daily for lunch and dinner. Reservations are essential.

The glamorous in crowd goes to Ireland's, but if you want to mingle with old wealth, the D.A.R. ladies and suchlike, head for **Talk of the Town,** 123 West Gutierrez (tel: 966-4910). So proper is this gracious old bastion of the establishment that not only are men required to wear jackets and ties, women in slacks are not admitted.

The New England decor is, as you might expect, substantial. The cocktail area is a handsome wood-paneled room with hunting prints on the walls, red leather couches and settees, and a hunting trophy (a moosehead) over the blazing fireplace. The dining area is similar, with the addition of old-fashioned print wallpaper, big bouquets of fresh flowers here and there, and a scalloped ledge where ceramic plates are displayed. There are gaslamp candle-holders on every table, and brass chandeliers overhead. In all, it's a return to a gracious, almost Victorian, style of life that has all but disappeared in the modern world, and we think it's lots of fun. Moreover, prices are very reasonable.

Complete dinners are served with soup, salad, potato, vegetable, dessert and coffee. Entrees include such fancy items as roast royal squab, under glass no less, with wild rice dressing and sauce financière (that's not a money sauce, it's a terrific brown sauce made with livers, white wine, chopped peppers, mushrooms and shallots) for $9. Simpler folk might opt for broiled fresh salmon with lemon butter ($9.25).

All of the goodies are served to you by pretty young waitresses in Tyrolean peasant dresses. It's quite an experience. Talk of the Town is open for dinner Tuesday through Saturday from 6 to 10:45 p.m., Sunday 5 to 10 p.m. Reservations are essential.

In another category completely, practically another universe, is **Mom's Italian Village,** 421 East Cota Street (tel: 965-5588), probably the most authentic-looking Italian restaurant in the United States. Mrs. Brima Signor (AKA

Mom) came over from Northern Italy in 1921 and, along with Mr. Signor (Pop), opened a small cafe in front of their home with seating for 11 people. The food was good and over the years the place grew to accommodate loyal customers; today there's seating for 400, and Mom, 82 years old, is still supervising her son and daughter in the kitchen.

The well-patinaed gold walls are adorned with murals of Venice and Rome, seating is in brown leather booths, and Mom's old dolls, antique furniture and other memorabilia from Italy are displayed, museum-like, on a little altar.

At dinner small pizzas are $2.50 to $3.50 (this for the works), spaghetti with sauteed chicken livers is $3.75, with oil and garlic or meatballs $3.25; a small salad on the side costs 75¢. There are eight items on a children's menu, making this an ideal choice for families.

A lunch of salad, veal scaloppine and spaghetti is $3.50.

Wine is available and advisable. Open Tuesday through Friday for lunch from 11:30 a.m. to 1:30 p.m., Tuesday through Sunday for dinner from 5 to 10 p.m.

The back of the menu at **Suishin Sukiyaki,** 511 State Street (tel: 962-1495), explains why Japanese families dine out when interviewing prospective new family members (a possible bride or groom): because people are more at ease in a restaurant. When the candidate is engrossed in eating, he is probably natural in his conduct, giving the family an opportunity to judge his behavior more accurately. The blurb continues with the hope that you will feel natural and relaxed in this Japanese tradition.

Though we can think of few less relaxing occupations than being given the once-over by future in-laws, we do find Suishin a relaxing and delightful dining experience. We particularly like sitting on the cushions in the intimate tatami rooms, separated from the main dining area by shoji screens, and decorated with murals of Japan. There are also leather booths for less agile diners, Japanese music is played in the background, and kimono-clad waitresses provide deft and pleasant service.

Moreover, the food is excellent. A terrific sukiyaki dinner ($6.25) comes with soup, a delicious salad with piquant sauce, tempura shrimp, rice, tea and the perfect dessert, green tea ice cream. A la carte you can order sukiyaki for just $2.95. Full beef teriyaki dinners are $6.25 ($4.25 à la carte), and an order of sashimi, accompanied by rice and soup, is $3.85.

Open from noon to 11 p.m. Wednesday through Monday.

Maggie McFly's Saloon and Maggie's Kitchen, 534-536 State Street (tel: 965-1444), looks like a San Francisco singles bar. It does, in fact, attract a crowd of affluent-looking hip types, and it does offer laid back singles action. The decor is Victorian, in classical singles bar tradition: plush velvet couches, lots of potted and hanging plants, overhead fans, oak paneling, gorgeous beveled and stained-glass doors and windows, pressed-tin ceiling and an exquisite old solid mahogany bar. (Rumor has it that the bar's marble columns were originally ordered by the White House and destined for Nixon's San Clemente house.)

Pub fare consists largely of burgers in sourdough buns, with salad or French fries ($2.50).

In the adjoining restaurant section, however, luncheon fare encompasses a wide choice of sandwiches and salads, as well as heartier fare like baked lasagne ($2.50). At dinner, you might begin with an appetizer of mushrooms à la Marsala ($1.65), continue with an entree of Hungarian goulash ($4.50), Sicilian calamari ($5.95) or roast prime rib au jus ($6.50), all served with soup or salad, potato or vegetable, and a bread basket. A glass of wine is 65¢; a dessert of mint parfait with whipped cream, $1.25.

Maggie's is also popular for Sunday brunch, for items like eggs benedict ($3.95) and seafood crêpes ($4.25) served with juice, homemade muffins, homefries and coffee.

The saloon is open seven days from 11 to 2 a.m.; the restaurant, Sunday through Thursday from 11 a.m. to 10 p.m., Friday and Saturday nights to 11 p.m.

The most *simpatico* of our restaurant choices is **Head of the Wolf**, 633 State Street (tel: 963-2907), a congenial and rustic eatery run by an attractive (very) and friendly young staff. The tasteful decor consists of exposed brick and raw cedar-paneled walls hung with old photographs and good paintings by local artists, raw pine floors, an abundance of plants, candlelit tables clothed in burnt orange linen, and stained-glass lamps overhead.

Seafood is the specialty, though at lunch the fare consists largely of omelets, sandwiches on sourdough bread and burgers, the latter served with corn on the cob ($1.65 for a plain quarter-pounder to $3.50 for your own culinary masterpiece combining any available toppings).

Dinner fare is enhanced Tuesday through Thursday evenings by live guitar music. Posted-on-a-blackboard entrees might include fresh red snapper ($5.25), char-broiled steak ($7.95), and eggplant parmigiana ($4.25), as well as an omelet or hamburger. All entrees include soup or salad and baked rice garnished with fresh fruit. A particular favorite of ours here is the spinach salad with hot bacon dressing ($2.25); two people might share one as an appetizer. For dessert there's a delicious homemade cheesecake with fresh strawberries ($1.25) and very good coffee.

Open for lunch Tuesday through Friday from 11 a.m. to 3 p.m.; dinner Tuesday through Sunday from 5 to 11 p.m. Dinner reservations suggested.

Chapter VIII

LOS ANGELES

1. Getting Around
2. Hotels
3. Restaurants
4. Sights
5. Nightlife

HOW CAN WE DEFINE the enigma that is Los Angeles? It's an unrelated string of suburbs in search of a city; a megalopolis sprawl connected by 1,500 or so miles of freeway; a promised land of sea, sand and year-round sunshine; decadent playground of the rich; stomping grounds of the stars; the most status-conscious city in the U.S.; a second home to sophisticated New Yorkers who dismiss the rest of the country as "the flyovers"; headquarters for every kind of kook, cultist and spiritual movement, a haven for the eccentric and yet a bastion of political conservatism. And finally, Los Angeles is about not caring what it's all about.

The variety of lifestyles, of activities and places to see and experience is mind-boggling. Don't waste time trying to understand this pleasure-oriented paradox. Forget your preconceptions, relax, enjoy. Let L.A. work its magic on you, and soon you'll be right at home in fantasyland.

There's so much to do, your only problem might be having time to do it all.

You'll want to tour the studios—thrill to the feigned attack of the shark from *Jaws* . . . watch Johnny tape a "Tonight Show" . . . show off your new bikini (or perfect unclothed body) on the beach . . . go shopping in chic Beverly

Hills . . . gape at the homes of the stars . . . bring the kids to or be a kid at Disneyland, Busch Gardens, Lion Country Safari, etc., etc., etc. . . . eat homemade fudge, Belgian waffles, tacos or shrimp Louie at the international stalls at the Farmer's Market . . . have a drink and a celebrity gawk at the Polo Lounge . . . match your footprints with those of over 200 stars at Mann's Chinese Theatre . . . don your tightest sweater and order a Coke at Schwab's drugstore . . . see hit shows at the Music Center, or big-name entertainment at the Hollywood Bowl.

That doesn't begin to skim the surface of visitor attractions which you'll be reading about in this chapter. They're seemingly endless, and they're scattered all over the place. First item on the agenda is to get a good map, orient yourself, and plan out your sightseeing priorities.

GETTING YOUR BEARINGS: A glance at the map will show you that the center of Los Angeles lies east of the Pacific Ocean (about 12 miles), on a direct line with the coastal town of Santa Monica. This is the **downtown** business and shopping center of the city. Greater Los Angeles radiates out from the downtown area in an ever-increasing number of suburbs. A vast network of freeways links the separate districts to each other, and to downtown, and the city as a whole to the state.

Hollywood, which is on every tourist's itinerary, is just northwest of the downtown Civic Center via the Hollywood Freeway (Route 101). **Beverly Hills** adjoins Hollywood on the southwest. You can reach Beverly Hills by taking the Hollywood Freeway from the Civic Center and turning off on Santa Monica Boulevard.

Connecting the downtown area and Beverly Hills, then continuing on through **Westwood** en route to the **Santa Monica** shoreline beaches, is **Wilshire Boulevard.** L.A.'s main drag. As Wilshire enters Beverly Hills, it intersects **La Cienega Boulevard.** The portion of La Cienega that stretches north from Wilshire to Santa Monica Boulevard is known (for obvious reasons) as **Restaurant Row.**

The next boulevard to the north of Santa Monica is **Sunset Boulevard** in Hollywood. The section on Sunset between Laurel Canyon Boulevard and La Brea Avenue is the famed **Sunset Strip** nightclub district. Above that is equally famous **Hollywood Boulevard.**

Further north via the Hollywood Freeway is **Universal City;** a right turn on the Ventura Freeway takes you to Beautiful Downtown **Burbank.**

Venice, Marina del Rey's yacht-filled harbors, and the **Los Angeles International Airport** are all south along the shore from Santa Monica.

TOURIST INFORMATION: As we've suggested in other chapters of this book, make use of the local Chamber of Commerce. In Los Angeles, it's the **Southern California Visitors Council,** 705 West 7th Street, downtown (tel: 628-3101). A courteous and informed staff has put together exceptionally comprehensive information for visitors. You can get maps, brochures on hotels, resorts, climate, self-guided tours, sightseeing attractions, calendars of events and advice on transportation problems.

The Bureau is open Monday through Friday from 9 a.m. to 5 p.m.

1. Getting Around

It's a theory of ours that one of the reasons behind the great interest in things spiritual and mystical in L.A. is that if residents could only achieve astral

GREATER LOS ANGELES

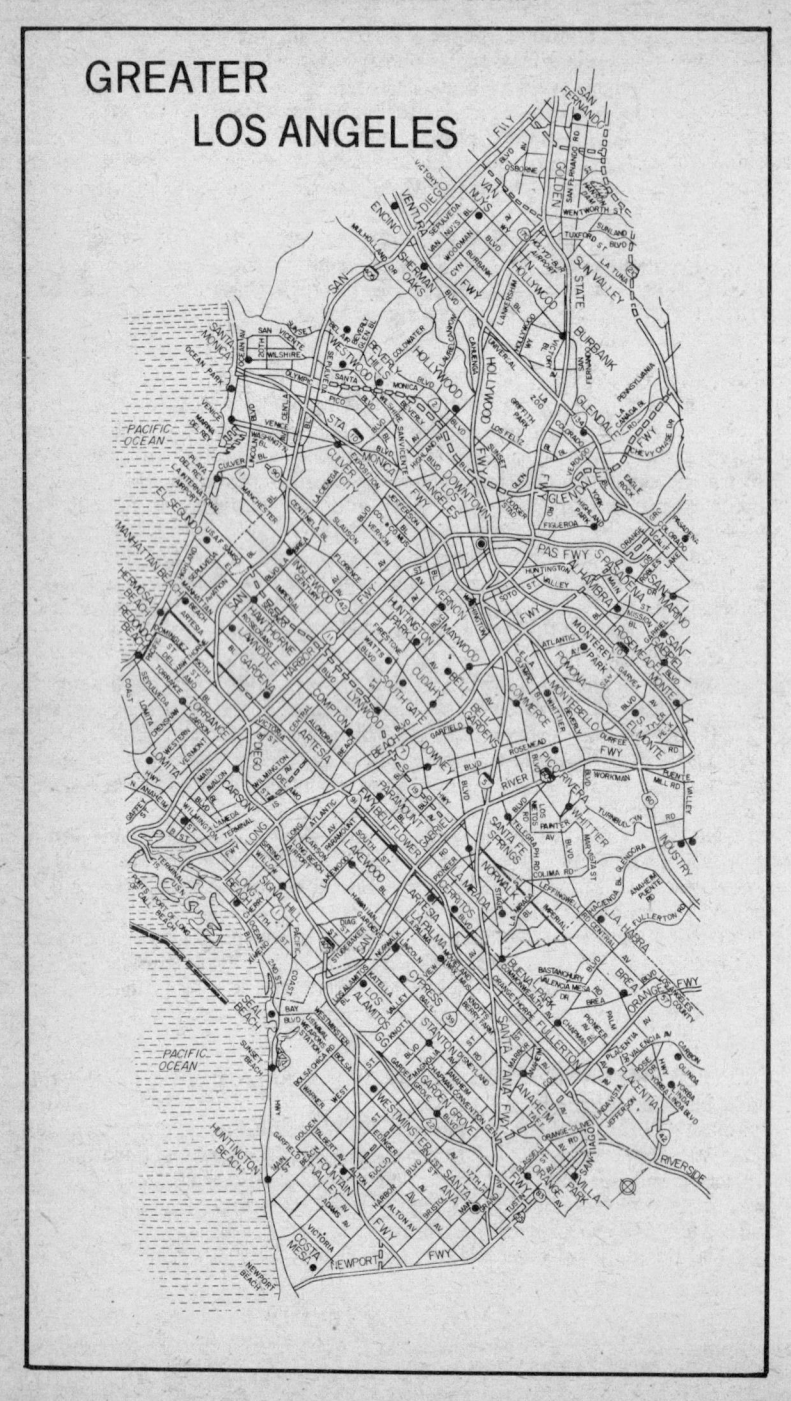

projection, they could finally get somewhere without a car. Los Angeles is car city. Where else can you find drive-in churches where the traditional response of "Amen," has been replaced by "honk, honk?" (We're not kidding.)

Although there is bus service, everything is so spread out you usually have to make three transfers to get where you're going, and wait at least half an hour at each change. Whereas the elaborate network of freeways that connects this incredible urban sprawl will whisk you to your destination in no time at all—unless, of course, it's rush hour. Do your homework with a good map, and you'll find getting around easy, if not always pleasant—the freeways are not what you'd call scenic routes. The most interesting things to look at are all the Rolls-Royces, Cadillacs and Porsches driving along with you.

CAR RENTALS: The sights and restaurants are so far apart here, you'll probably do best to seek an unlimited mileage arrangement, or at least one with sufficient free mileage to make your trip economical. On the freeways, those few "cents per mile" tend to mount rapidly into dollars.

Hertz has depots throughout Southern California, and, of course, at the airport. They have all kinds of rental combinations, but we recommend unlimited mileage. A Pinto costs $97.65 for seven days, a Gran Torino $139.65. Basic insurance is included, and you pay for the gas. Full coverage for either car is $28 a week. Telephone 646-2851 or toll-free (800) 654-3131.

No. 2, **Avis,** is also well represented in Southern California, having a desk and car space at Los Angeles International Airport, plus locations throughout the city. Call 646-5600 or the toll-free number, 800/331-1212.

Do check, too, with **Econo-Car** (tel: 776-6184; 800/228-1000), and **Budget Rent a Car** (tel: 646-7160; 800/228-2800); both firms offer good service and competitive prices.

BUSES: If you don't have a car, you can reach most of the sightseeing centers in Greater Los Angeles by bus (take a good book along to while away ride time, something like *War and Peace*).

The network of local and express buses is operated by the Southern California Rapid Transit District (RTD). Their **Information Office** is at 425 South Main Street, where you can obtain maps and schedules on request, either by writing, stopping by or calling 972-6455. You can also call them for detailed information on a given trip from point to point (e.g. "I'm in Burbank and I want to get to Wilshire and Santa Monica Boulevards").

The office provides a pamphlet—prepared in conjunction with the Southern California Visitors Council—outlining "20 Vest Pocket Tours," including visits to Busch Gardens, Beverly Hills and Disneyland.

The general bus fare is 35¢ for the first two zones in Los Angeles County (transfers for another 10¢). Senior citizens pay only 10¢. Students with a valid ID can enjoy the same arrangement at 25¢.

RTD covers four counties—Los Angeles, San Bernardino, Orange and Riverside. Exact fare is required, as no change is given on the bus. For $25 you can buy a pass for unlimited riding for an entire month ($4 for senior citizens).

A mini-bus runs every four to six minutes in the downtown area of Los Angeles, covering such places as Olvera Street, the Civic Center, Chinatown, Pershing Square, the Plaza arcade and City Hall. It charges only 25¢ per ride (once again, exact fare required) and operates from 7 a.m. to 6 p.m. Monday through Saturday (holidays excepted). It's easy to spot with its wide orange-and-white-canopied roof. Hop on, get off whenever you want to visit or shop, then catch another bus later, paying only another quarter. There are marked bus stops along the route. Its longest runs are Hill Street, Broadway and First Street.

TAXIS: You don't hop cabs as blithely in L.A. as you do in other cities—it seems the fare for any given ride is always at least $10.

Yellow Cab Company (tel: 481-2345) uses rates set by the city of Los Angeles: 90¢ drop and 20¢ per quarter-mile after that. No charge for extra passengers, luggage or groceries. They will drop off passengers in Beverly Hills, but not pick up there, since Beverly Hills has its own taxis, the **Beverly Hills Cab Co.** (tel: 273-6611). This company charges a 65¢ drop and 70¢ a mile in Beverly Hills, 80¢ a mile outside Beverly Hills. They can pick up passengers only in Beverly Hills, but drop passengers anywhere.

2. Hotels

Generally, when you look for a hotel you try to choose one with a convenient location. In sprawling Los Angeles, however, a convenient location is a very limited concept. Nothing is convenient to everything, and wherever you stay you can count on doing a lot of driving to somewhere else.

The most elegant digs are, for the most part, in Beverly Hills and Bel Air. Hollywood is probably the most central place to stay; downtown is good for business people, and offers proximity to many cultural attractions; Santa Monica and Marina del Rey are right on the beach. And families with kids might want to head straight to Anaheim or Buena Park.

We've listed more upper-bracket hostelries here than in other chapters—there are simply more of them in star-studded L.A. than in other cities.

Hotel listings are broken down by area, since L.A. communities are so far-flung, then further divided into the following categories: deluxe, upper bracket, moderately priced and budget. All listings have been measured by the strict yardstick of value—the most for your money.

Keep in mind that there's a 6% tax on all hotel bills in Los Angeles, which must be added to the prices quoted here.

We'll lead off our hotel survey with glamorous—

BEVERLY HILLS—DELUXE: The Beverly Hills Hotel, 9641 Sunset Boulevard at Beverly Drive (tel: 276-2551), is the stomping grounds of millionaires and maharajahs, jet setters and movie stars. There are hundreds of anecdotes about this famous hotel and the world's most glamorous bar on its premises, the Polo Lounge.

For years, Howard Hughes maintained a complex of bungalows, suites and rooms here, using some of the facilities for an elaborate electronic-communications security system, and keeping a food-taster housed in one room! Perhaps this is the only hotel in the world that would provide him with such services as 23 kadota figs (24 would be angrily returned) in the middle of the night. No problem for a hotel that imports bear steaks from Alaska every time a certain Texas oil millionaire who favors them makes a reservation.

Several years ago Katharine Hepburn did a flawless dive into the pool—fully clad in her tennis outfit, shoes and all; Dean Martin and Frank Sinatra once got into a big fistfight with other Polo Lounge residents. And in 1969 John Lennon and Yoko Ono checked into the most secluded bungalow under assumed names, then stationed so many armed guards around their little hideaway that discovery was inevitable. So it goes. The stories are endless, and concern everyone from Chaplin to Madame Chiang Kai-shek.

What attracts them all? For one thing, each other. And of course you can't beat the service—not just the catering to such eccentricities as a preference for bear steak, but little things like being greeted by your name every time you pick up the phone. There are nearly 400 employees here to serve 275 guests.

And the Beverly Hills Hotel is a beauty, its green and pink stucco buildings set on 16 carefully landscaped and lushly planted acres. Paths lined with giant palm trees wind throughout, and the privacy of verandas and lanais is protected by flowering and leafy foliage.

Each of the 325 rooms is custom-designed in the best Hollywood tradition, with tropical overtones—they're gorgeous. And of course you can count on every amenity in your room.

In addition to the world-famous Polo Lounge, rendezvous headquarters of international society for almost 40 years, the Beverly Hills also has the Loggia and Patio (which adjoin the Polo Lounge) for breakfast and luncheon in a delightful garden ambience. We particularly enjoy morning croissants and coffee al fresco on the brick-floored Patio, where tables are clustered under the shade of a large Brazilian pepper tree.

Then there's the Lanai Room for gourmet luncheons and dinners, papered in the banana-palm wallpaper that is a famous trademark of the hotel. With its forest-green carpeting, green upholstered Louis XV chairs, and pink tablecloths it looks like an exquisite Faberge item.

Dinner here might begin with an hors d'oeuvres of Iranian Beluga caviar ($10.50), or less extravagantly with Holland herring in sour cream ($2.75). House specialties include veal sauteed with apples in Calvados, served with rice pilaff ($10.50), and poached boned trout stuffed with salmon mousse in wine sauce ($9.95). For dessert there are fresh-baked French pastries, cakes and pies ($1.65), but we usually pass them up in favor of the sumptuous chocolate soufflé Grand Marnier ($6.95 for two).

The Pool and Cabana Club is centered around an Olympic-size turquoise pool, where hardly anyone ever swims, but from which it is imperative, if one is *anyone,* to be paged to the telephone. The Club is surrounded by colorful tent-top cabanas, and also has two tennis courts. If you order lunch by the pool, it's not a hamburger on a paper plate—it's served up on fine china and your little table is adorned with fresh-cut flowers.

An unusual facility is the Cinema Room, an intimate private screening room with the latest audio-visual equipment, and beverage service available.

Now for the rates, which are determined by the size and location of your room: singles range from $37 to $82, doubles from $59 to $82, suites from $96 to $578. If you can't afford to stay here for your entire L.A. trip, you might want to splurge for just a few nights to experience authentic Hollywood glamor at its best. If even that is out of the question, at least come by and have lunch or a drink in the Polo Lounge.

Closest Beverly Hills competitor for prestigious guests is hotelier Hernando Courtright's **Beverly Wilshire,** 9500 Wilshire Bouelvard, one block from Beverly Drive (tel: 275-4282), with more duplex townhouses than any other hotel in the world. In the palatial style of European grand hotels, the Wilshire's private cobblestone entranceway, heralded by Louis XV bronze and iron gates, is lined with pear trees, flowering plants and gaslights from Edinburgh Castle. Among the hotel's notable features are a winding, red-carpeted marble staircase, gigantic Italian mission arches of gleaming white Carrara marble, an imposing glass-domed *porte cochère,* a marble and inlaid mosaic tile mural of early California, monumental mirrors, and bronze doré Louis XVI chandeliers.

The Paris-influenced new wing has curved balconies framed by wrought-iron railings and floor-to-ceiling bay windows.

Most famous of the rooms is the Wilshire's $500-a-night Christian Dior suite, a two-bedroom, four-bath duplex containing original Dior fashion-design sketches and antiques and furnishings worth $100,000! The suite has been occupied by King Hussein of Jordan, Emperor Hirohito of Japan and Norway's King Olaf, among others.

In addition to royalty, frequent guests at the Wilshire include superstars Warren Beatty, Steve McQueen, Paul McCartney and Elton John.

Though accommodations in the new Beverly wing are the most lavish, all the rooms are elegantly furnished, offering every convenience and luxury. All have Carrara marble baths, with embroidered monogrammed towels, extra-large beds and the finest furnishings, fabrics, carpets and wall coverings.

Facilities include a gorgeous swimming pool (modeled after Sophia Loren's), and a Spanish-tiled sundeck patio decorated with murals, ceramics, and fragrant lemon and orange trees.

There are a dozen stores on the premises, including a branch of Tiffany's. A health spa offering massage, sauna, gym and whirlpool is open from 10 a.m. to 6 p.m. daily, and there's every kind of ticket, sightseeing, airline and car rental desk—even one where you can get chauffeur-driven limousines.

Not to mention five restaurants and bars, of which the most famous is the award-winning La Bella Fontana. A bubbling three-tiered fountain, topped with a cherub, is the room's centerpiece; other features are Pompeian fluted columns, hand-carved gilded Mexican chandeliers and wall sconces, walls covered in French velvet, and Belgian lace curtains. Gourmet entrees range from brochette of chicken liver on wild rice ($7.95) to a superb grilled rack of lamb ($26 for two). Bella Fontana is open for lunch weekdays noon to 3 p.m., and dinner Monday through Saturday from 6 to 11 p.m. Jackets and ties are required for men.

A little less formal (and less expensive) is El Padrino (the Godfather), a rotisserie/bar with a Western theme, open daily for lunch, dinner, cocktails and late supper. We also like Don Hernando's, a Mexican-themed restaurant with leather chairs, walls adorned with Mexican folk arts and bullfighting pictures, and colorful piñatas overhead. At lunch you can choose from an à la carte menu that runs the gamut from cheese blintzes to chiles rellenos, or partake of the sumptuous luncheon buffet priced according to your entree—poached salmon is $5.95, baked chicken $4.55, etc. At dinner, Wednesday through Saturday, a Mexican mariachi band entertains while you dine.

For cocktails there's the exotic East-Indian-style Zindabad Pub, its plush love seats heaped with Indian mirror-work pillows. For snacks and sandwiches, the Pink Turtle Coffee Shop fills the bill.

The least expensive rooms are in the Wilshire wing: singles are $51 to $85, doubles $63 to $97. In the newer Beverly wing, singles are $61 to $89, doubles $73 to $101. Suites throughout begin at $147 for two persons.

BEVERLY HILLS—UPPER BRACKET: The **Beverly Hilton,** 9876 Wilshire Boulevard at Santa Monica Boulevard (tel: 274-7777), is one of the poshest of the Hilton chain. Room decor is suitably luxurious, with velvet bedspreads, provincial furnishings and flocked wallpaper, plus such amenities as in-room first-run movies, and refrigerators. Most of the 634 rooms have balconies and some open onto a swimming pool terrace.

A miniature city (like most Hiltons), this one has every kind of shop and service desk, not to mention two heated swimming pools, one Olympic-size.

LOS ANGELES: HOTELS 175

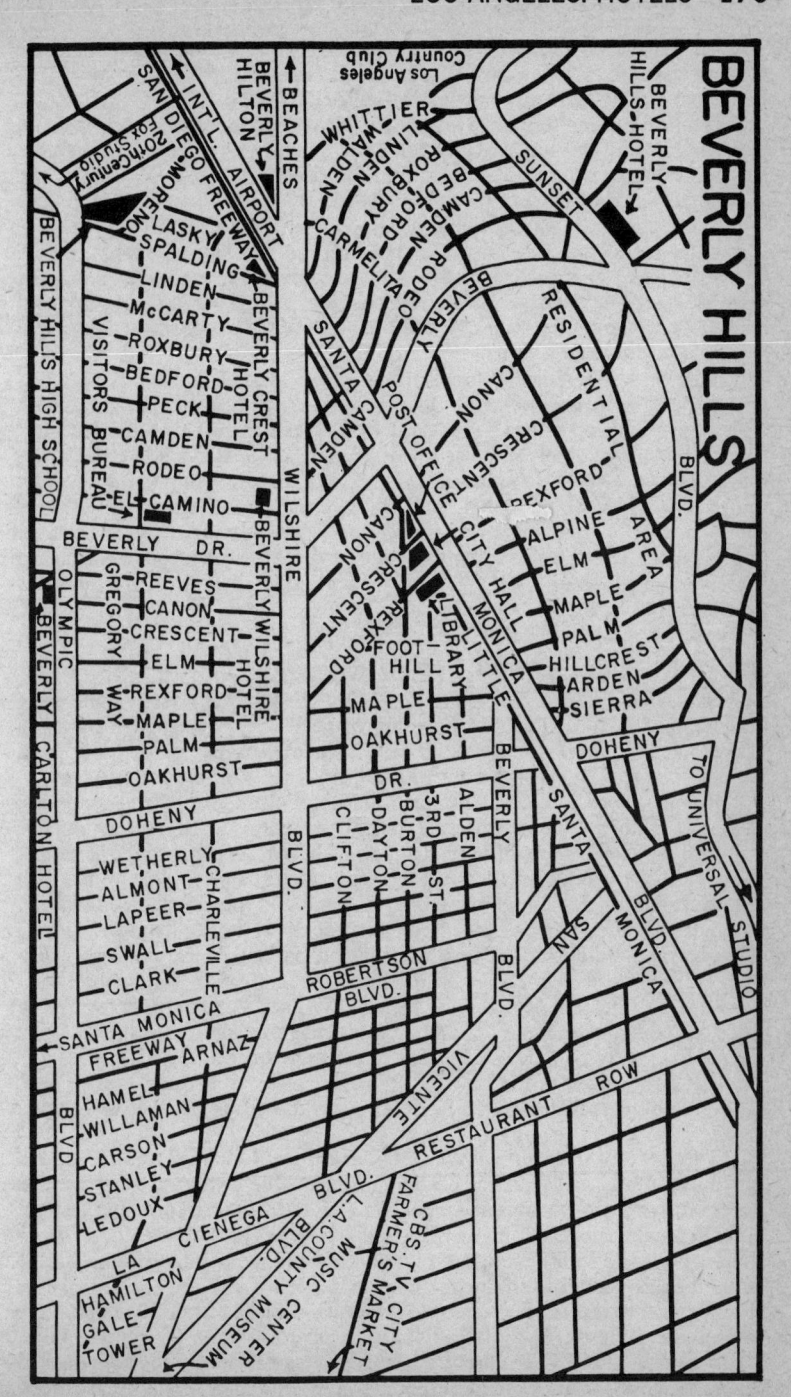

The Hilton's penthouse restaurant, L'Escoffier, combines gourmet cuisine with a panoramic view of the city. The plush decor utilizes such finery as lace tablecloths, filmy gold drapes, gold crushed-velvet Louis XVI-style chairs, black leather banquettes, and a handsome brass candelabra on every table. A full dinner is $17 per person. Open for dinner nightly from 6 p.m., L'Escoffier also has music for dancing and a delightful parlor lounge for cocktails.

Sunday champagne brunch ($7.50) and $9 prime rib buffets served nightly from 6 to 10 p.m. are most popular at Mr. H.—another elegant Hilton eatery, this with paneled damask walls, crystal chandeliers and Jacobean chairs. In the intimate Library, you can have a snack or cocktails while browsing among the many books. Equally cozy, with an immense fireplace, is the Red Lion pub and chop house, offering fish and chips ($3.50) and other traditional English fare at lunch, cocktails until 2 a.m.

There's a coffee shop for informal snacking, and last but certainly not least, an especially attractive branch of Trader Vic's, facing a small Oriental garden with a red-lacquered bridge. Open daily from 4:30 p.m. to 1 a.m., Trader Vic's menu offers tempting possibilities ranging from sauteed chicken breast in peanut butter sauce ($7.50) to pressed almond duck served with plum sauce ($5).

Room rates at the Hilton depend on size and location, with stiffer tabs for rooms overlooking the pool or on higher floors. Singles range from $38 to $52, doubles from $50 to $64, the upper range for poolside lanai rooms. A plus is that there is no charge for children (even teenagers) in the same room as parents.

BEVERLY HILLS—MODERATE: **Beverly Rodeo,** 360 North Rodeo Drive, a block north of Wilshire Boulevard (tel: 273-0300; 800/421-0545), has recently been completely redecorated in French provincial style. Owner Max Baril has packed a lot of luxury into this intimate, 100-room, European-style hotel, from the liveried attendant at the door to the posh Chez Voltaire restaurant.

Rooms are very pretty with matching floral-print spreads and draperies, and baths with marble-topped sinks and extra phones. All have color TV, AM/FM radio and air conditioning, and some have balconies and refrigerators.

The above-mentioned restaurant, Chez Voltaire, is plushly furnished with red velvet booths, fine pink linen tablecloths and glittering crystal chandeliers. A handsome wood-paneled piano bar and cocktail lounge adjoins, as does a very charming outdoor courtyard where breakfast and lunch are served. Entrees include steak Diane ($10.50) and chicken sauteed in wine with cream sauce ($6.95). Flamed desserts are a specialty. The twilight dinner, served to those seated between 5 and 7:30 p.m., is considerably cheaper. Chez Voltaire is also deservedly popular for Sunday champagne brunch ($3.95).

Rates for singles at the Beverly Rodeo are $30 to $36; doubles are $36 to $42; and opulent suites, $70 to $110. The one drawback here: no swimming pool.

The **Beverly Hillcrest,** Beverwil Drive at Pico Boulevard (tel: 277-2800), is a multi-million-dollar luxury hostelry at the southern edge of Beverly Hills. Rooms are notably spacious and elegantly appointed in restrained and tasteful French provincial decor, many with half-canopied beds. Each room has a refrigerator (with ice), remote-control color TV and radio, plus genuine marble (and an extra phone) in the bath.

A gleaming steel and glass outdoor elevator whisks you up 12 floors to the Top of the Hillcrest, a rooftop restaurant offering views of Beverly Hills, Hollywood and the Pacific Ocean. Its lavish interior is done up in gold flocked draperies, gold leather upholstered chairs and glittering crystal chandeliers.

Most luncheon entrees are in the $3-to-$5 range; dinners including an appetizer and salad range from $5.95 for coq au vin to $10.95 for Australian lobster tail.

Breakfast, lunch and dinner are also served daily on the lower level Portofino, a candlelit Old World Italian eatery with tufted red leather booths, exposed brick and wood-paneled walls. Dinner entrees here include a salad, Italian bread, a cheese wedge and a basket of fresh fruit. Scampi with rice Valencia is $8.25, chicken cacciatore served with eggplant parmigiana $6.50, and an order of fettuccine Alfredo $3.50. Cheesecake with warm cherries ($1.25) is a delicious dessert.

Other facilities: a swimming pool with a palm-fringed terrace for sunning and refreshments, and free garage parking.

Single rooms at the Beverly Hillcrest are $34 to $41, doubles $40 to $49.

Not to be confused with the above is the 54-room **Beverly Crest Hotel**, 125 South Spalding Drive, just south of Wilshire Boulevard (tel: 274-6801). Many of the rooms encircle a tropical courtyard wherein a large swimming pool surrounded by towering banana and palm trees.

Rooms are harmoniously furnished in modern pieces, the beds with rather elaborate headboards and quilted spreads. All have plenty of closet space, full-length mirrors, direct-dial phones, color TV, air conditioning and heating, and tub/shower baths.

Overlooking the pool is the Venetian Room Restaurant, serving breakfast, lunch and dinner daily. And you can park your car in a spacious covered garage at no extra charge.

Single rooms are $24 to $27, doubles $30 to $33.

BEVERLY HILLS—A BUDGET CHOICE: Beverly Vista, 120 South Reeves, a block from Wilshire Boulevard and Beverly Drive (tel: 276-1031), is a conveniently located modest three-floor hotel situated on a lovely Beverly Hills street. The hotel has a large European clientele, probably because Europeans are quite used to rooms containing only hot and cold running water. Much effort has been made to refurbish this little hostelry; the work of painters, upholsterers and carpet layers is clearly visible. Rooms are not fancy, but they are clean and adequate—all with switchboard phones and daily maid service provided. There's a TV in the lobby.

Bathless rooms are just $5 a day, $25 a week! Singles with full bath are $8 nightly, $45 weekly. Doubles with bath or shower are $10-$12 nightly, $50-$60 weekly.

HOLLYWOOD—UPPER BRACKET: Continental Hyatt House, 8401 Sunset Boulevard, two blocks east of La Cienega Boulevard (tel: 656-4101; 800/228-9000), is popular with celebs and rock stars (who have been known to fling their color TVs out the windows in the wee hours) who play the nearby Palladium. It's a lively place, close to Restaurant Row and Sunset Strip nightlife. The 300 spacious bedrooms, housed on 14 floors, overlook the Los Angeles skyline and the mountains. Rooms, decorated in autumnal tones—brown, orange and gold color schemes—have modern furnishings, shag carpeting and dressing areas, plus all conveniences from color TV to modern tub/shower bath. Most have private balconies.

Facilities include a heated rooftop swimming pool/sundeck and valet parking. There's a coffee shop open from 7 a.m. to midnight, dispensing good food at reasonable prices, including such unlikely coffee-shop fare as avocado, cheese and sprout sandwiches on whole wheat bread. In addition, there's the

Red Roulette room for cocktails and entertainment (a singer and combo for dancing) Monday through Saturday nights till 2 a.m. The plus here is that many of the resident celebs get up and entertain just for the fun of it—people like Redd Foxx, Stevie Wonder and Gordon Lightfoot, to name a few.

Singles cost from $28 to $33, doubles from $33 to $41, and suites run from $50 to $150.

There isn't enough space to list all of the famous people who have resided at the **Chateau Marmont**, 8221 Sunset Boulevard at Havenhurst Drive (tel: 656-1010), a chateau-style apartment hotel lodged on a cliff just above Sunset Strip. Carol Linley was in residence when we visited; Humphrey Bogart, Jeanne Moreau, Boris Karloff, Dustin Hoffman, Marilyn Monroe, John and Yoko, Al Capone and Valentino have all been guests. Carol Channing met her husband here; Greta Garbo has checked in under the name Harriet Brown, and even Howard Hughes once maintained a suite.

Guests often gather in the great baronial living room, furnished with grandiose Hollywood antiques. Otherwise you'll find them lounging around the oval swimming pool, edged with semi-tropical trees and shrubbery.

The entire place was completely remodeled recently and is looking better than ever. At this writing nine townhouse bungalows are being added. All accommodations are furnished in tasteful English style, and all have color TV, direct-dial phone and daily maid service.

Regular rooms cost $25 single, $30 double. All the others have fully equipped kitchens and dens. Double rate in a studio with living room and bedroom is $40 a day; one-bedroom suites are $50, two-bedroom suites $60; a two-bedroom bungalow or three-bedroom penthouse is $80. Free valet parking is included in the rates.

HOLLYWOOD—MODERATE: Highest recommendation to the **Hollywood Roosevelt**, 7000 Hollywood Boulevard (tel: 469-2442; 800/421-0767), just across the street from Mann's (formerly Grauman's) Chinese Theatre. The original portion of the hotel was built in the '30s; since then a group of two-story buildings with lanai rooms has been erected in the rear garden. These latter accommodations are centered around an Olympic-size swimming pool set against a lush tropical background of flowering shrubs and lofty date palms. The whole place has a resort feel—even the lobby is done up in garden decor with green carpeting, green-and-white-flowered wallpaper, trellises, potted ferns and white wrought-iron garden furnishings.

Rooms are spacious and very attractively decorated, also in cheerful garden decor; we particularly like those on the seventh floor of the Main Building and the lanai rooms overlooking the garden. Throughout, all rooms have small foyers, built-in wardrobes, gleaming tub/shower tile baths, color TVs, and direct-dial phones. Some of the lanai rooms also have refrigerators.

Facilities include valet service, hairdresser, barber, theater agency, shops and a covered garage. This is also the major air terminal limousine stop for Hollywood. In the Cinegrill (its walls lined with photos of Hollywood stars) there's dancing nightly from 9 p.m. to 2 a.m.; breakfast, lunch and dinner are served in the delightful Garden Room dining room/coffee shop.

The least expensive rooms—a terrific buy—are in the Main Building, with doubles and twin-bedded rooms in the $23-to-$27 range. More modern and elaborate lanai doubles go for $30 to $35.

Reliable standard accommodations can be found at the good old **Holiday Inn**, 1755 North Highland Avenue at Hollywood Boulevard (tel: 462-7181), a 22-story (they claim 23, but there's no 13th floor), 460-room hostelry in the heart of Old Hollywood. Rooms are done in two color schemes, orange or blue/green (on alternating floors), all with shag carpeting and mural wallpaper depicting ancient Greek or Roman ruins. Every room is equipped with a color TV, air conditioning, direct-dial phone and modern tub/shower bath. For your convenience there are three laundry rooms, ice machines on every floor and Coke machines every other floor.

A revolving circular rooftop restaurant, Oscar's, features dancing and dining with a view nightly except Monday from 9 p.m. Down on the second floor guests can lounge around a swimming pool/sundeck. Papagayos, the hotel's rather plush coffee shop, serves breakfast, lunch and dinner, and a garage on the premises offers free parking.

Single rooms are $26 to $30, doubles $35; an extra bed in the room is $4.

HOLLYWOOD—BUDGET: Convenient to many L.A. attractions, the **Saharan Motor Hotel,** 7212 Sunset Boulevard, two blocks west of La Brea (tel: 874-6700), provides comfortable accommodations at low prices. All rooms are centered around and overlook a flagstone courtyard which contains the swimming pool and sundeck.

Rooms are quite nice, decorated in contemporary style, all with phones, TV, music and air conditioning. Extras include dry cleaning and laundry service, free parking, complimentary morning coffee and free TV tickets; families with small children will welcome the baby-sitting service.

Double-bedded rooms for one or two persons are $16 with black and white TV, $17 with color. Twin-bedded rooms with black and white TV go for $18; $22 for two double beds and a color set. Suites with kitchenettes begin at $26 for two people.

HOLLYWOOD—SUPER-BUDGET: **El Centro & La Mirada Weekly Apartments,** 1225 North El Centro, on the corner of La Mirada (tel: 464-0948), is an amazing bargain hideaway of stylish apartments, just off famed Vine Street. While about half of them are used permanently by TV and film employees, the rest are available to in-the-know travelers at startlingly low rates.

The genius behind this operation is Gordon R. Howard, a colorful L.A. personage who owns 25 antique motor vehicles (he's a friend of famous fellow collector Bill Harrah), including a Stutz Bearcat (1920) which was used in the movie *Compulsion*. He stops by the apartments frequently to see that everything is shipshape, sometimes tooling up in a flashy 1910 model. If you're interested in cars, he'll likely chat with you about them; he might even show you his collection or tell you about the time back in 1932 when he fell into the La Brea Tar Pits.

But we digress. In addition to being a fascinating conversationalist, Mr. Howard has managed to work things out so that his apartments can cut your living costs. Rental charges begin at a low of $29.95 per week in the older building on La Mirada. These apartments are small, but very ample for one person. They have private baths, a refrigerator and a counter-top bar. The apartments in the newer building at El Centro rent for $39.95 weekly for a single, accommodating an additional person for a fee of $10 weekly. Phones are conveniently located in the hall. Rooms are simply furnished in contemporary style—nothing fancy, but they are adequately attractive and immaculate.

Guests who stay for a few weeks are preferred. When available, weekly parking for your car is $2.50, $5 in a covered carport and $10 in a locked garage. A $25 deposit is required to confirm mail reservations.

Gordon Howard has another incredible budget apartment complex, **Cine Lodge** (also known as **Howard's Weekly Apartments**), at 1738 North Whitley Street, off Hollywood Boulevard (tel: 466-6943). Here you can rent a tastefully decorated bachelor apartment with a counter bar, refrigerator, private bath and convertible sofa bed. Yet the cost is only $44.95 weekly. If you take a double, with two studio beds, it's only $54.95, averaging out to less than $3.95 per person per day. Again, $25 deposit is required to confirm reservations.

This one—a high-rise building with a two-story glass-paneled lobby—was Mr. Howard's pilot venture. He has since taken over a number of buildings with hundreds of apartments, operating them on a do-it-yourself basis, with a minimum of staff—and passing the savings on to guests. The short-cut service means you make your own bed, although fresh, clean linens are provided with the regular weekly cleaning service. There is no telephone in your room, though there is a message service with a hook-up on every landing (for that all-important call from your agent). In addition, there's a laundromat on the premises, and a basement garage where you can park your car for $5 weekly. Another asset is the convenient location: half a block from Hollywood Boulevard, and about four blocks from the Hollywood Freeway.

Apartments are rented for a minimum of seven days; if you give a week's notice that you're leaving, any portion of the second or third week will be computed on a daily basis—whichever arrangement is cheaper for you.

Mr. Howard has recently begun offering a Mini-Week Special—a three-night package, subject to availability. Call on arrival or up to 24 hours in advance. Three-day mini-rates range from $30 (for one person in an efficiency apartment) to $45 (for two persons in a new kitchenette apartment).

If the Lodge has no space, the manager may offer to secure you an apartment at associated establishments, such as the above-mentioned El Centro apartments, or at an exceptionally fine accommodation near NBC and Warner's in Burbank (about which more later).

DOWNTOWN LOS ANGELES—DELUXE: One of the largest hotels in Los Angeles, the 1,250-room **Hilton**, 930 Wilshire Boulevard at Figueroa (tel: 629-4321), is centrally located near downtown attractions and offers easy access to major freeway entrances. Many rooms overlook the oval swimming pool, set in a semi-tropical garden of palm and banana trees and surrounded by umbrellaed tables for outdoor dining.

Rooms are decorated in the usual Hilton mode, elegantly furnished in 18th-century English styles like Queen Anne, Chippendale and Hepplewhite. They're completely geared to luxury living, with first-run at-home movies on your color TV, dressing rooms, full-length mirrors, 24-hour room service and convenient laundry doors—leave your laundry in them in the morning and it comes back clean at night.

There are several restaurants to choose from. The Beef Barron features a Gay '90s Western ambience and entrees like barbecued ribs ($7.75). A complete dinner of black bean soup with sack sherry, salad, a full pound of tenderloin filet, a carafe of red wine, cheese enchiladas, fresh vegetables, pecan ice cream and coffee is $19.75 for two; all entrees are half-price for the little cowpokes. Beef Barron is open for lunch Monday through Friday, and dinner Sunday through Friday; there's a lively piano bar weeknights.

The Veranda Room converts from a poolside garden-style luncheon cafe to a romantic candlelit restaurant for dinner and dancing. Roast prime rib of beef from the open hearth ($5.95) is featured at dinner; at lunch, diners get a fashion show along with hearty sandwiches. Buffet dinners are served nightly in the main dining room, and the Lobby Bar is especially popular at cocktail hour when hors d'oeuvres are free, plentiful and delicious.

We're particularly partial to Kiku of Tokyo, an authentic gourmet Japanese restaurant. Luncheon fare features entrees like beef teriyaki ($5.75) and sashimi ($5.75), served with rice and soup. At dinner teriyaki, tempura and sashimi entrees are in the $7.95-to-$11.35 range, and include soup, salad, fresh vegetables and rice.

Room rates at the Hilton depend on placement and size. Singles are $35 to $44; double and twin-bedded rooms, $45 to $54.

Not quite as big, but even more dazzlingly ultra-modern, is the 500-room, 24-story **Hyatt Regency Los Angeles**, 711 South Hope Street at 7th Street (tel: 683-1234; 800/228-9000). It's part of the **Broadway Plaza**, a 21st-century-style complex of shops, restaurants, offices and galleries that includes a huge parking garage. The avant-garde tone is set by the two-story skylight-covered entrance lobby with a garden plaza, lounges, a sidewalk cafe and boutiques. Wide escalators glide down to the lobby/reception area and gardens. Everything is a melange of rich browns, reds, rusts and golds, adorned with super-graphics and warmly enhanced by exposed brick, potted plants, trees, old-fashioned gaslight street lamps and overstuffed furniture. Informal banjo, organ, mariachi and steel band concerts are presented here during the day.

We're most impressed with the innovative and attractive rooms at the Hyatt. Each has a full window wall offering surprisingly nice views for a downtown hotel, deep pile carpeting, oversized beds, dressing rooms, small sofa, color TV, etc. Strikingly futuristic in design and furnishings, they utilize the same bold textures and russet-gold color scheme prevalent throughout the building.

There's a revolving rooftop restaurant called Angel's Flight, offering a full-circle panoramic window tour of the city every hour. Open Monday through Saturday, the restaurant features gourmet luncheon items like coq au vin ($4.95) and beef stroganoff ($4.75). The dinner menu is a sumptuous one-choice prix-fixe for $14.50; it includes a delicious lettuce salad topped with bay shrimp and fresh mushrooms, prime rib of beef au jus, creamed spinach, quiche, stuffed baked potato, chocolate fondue with fresh seasonal fruits and coffee.

On the garden level is Joint Venture, where gleaming silver mirrors and shining plexiglas reflect a million prismatic images. Entertainment and dancing nightly. The opulent Hugo's V (open for lunch weekdays and dinner nightly) is the Hyatt's gourmet restaurant, offering exotic dinner fare like Indonesian rack of lamb bouquetière, spiced with exotic herbs and honey ($20 for two).

Also on the premises are the Nook' N Cranny for cocktails, and the Sun Porch, a sidewalk cafe coffee shop.

Rates are $46 to $58 single, $56 to $68 for doubles and twins; suites are $75 to $160. Note: Like most downtown hotels, the Hyatt has no swimming pool.

Under new ownership as of March 1976, **The Biltmore**, 515 South Olive Street, between 5th and 6th Streets (tel: 624-1011), for half a century the grande dame of L.A. deluxe hotels, is getting a $13-million face-lift. The new owners are showing a proper respect for the aesthetic and architectural beauty of the hotel, while updating each of its 1,072 spacious and attractive rooms. There are new bursts of color in the hallways, where wall friezes have been specifically created for The Biltmore by artist Jim Dine, and even the staff is in spiffy new uniforms.

Each room has been decorated in warm colors, but they still have big walk-in closets along with modern amenities like color TV, air conditioning, direct-dial phones, radios and circulating ice water. In the tradition of the old Biltmore, however, messages are all hand-delivered.

The seemingly endless miles of corridors and public rooms are a virtual museum: the three-story Renaissance lobby with vaulted ceilings; the Castilian Lounge, a reproduction of the royal hall in which Columbus told Queen Isabella about America; and the Galeria, decorated by artist Giovanni B. Smeraldi.

As we go to press, the Biltmore's restaurants are in a state of flux, except for the Ranchero, probably the world's largest coffee shop, with booths and counter space for 550.

Single rooms at the Biltmore are $36 to $46; doubles, $46 to $56. Suites begin at $80. A convenient underground garage on Pershing Square holds 2,000 cars.

At this writing, two new luxury hostelries—the Bonaventure and the New Otani—are about to open in downtown Los Angeles, which augurs well for the development of this part of town.

You can't miss the gleaming gold cylindrical towers of the **Bonaventure**, 350 South Figueroa Street, between 4th and 5th Streets (tel: 624-1000; 800/228-3000), certainly the most spectacular hotel in town—the most recent and most outstanding creation of world-famous architect John Portman (he also did San Francisco's innovative Hyatt Regency). The exquisite six-story skylight lobby, a Portman trademark, contains a one-acre lake surrounded by towering trees. A cocktail lounge is at the center of things; there's also an entertainment lounge, a gourmet restaurant and a sidewalk cafe on this level.

Above the lobby is the Shopping Gallery with five levels of diversified shops and boutiques. You can take a break from shopping and have a drink on one of the circular "cocktail pods," seemingly suspended in space, overlooking the lake and bustling lobby activity. Crowning the Bonaventure is an elegant rooftop (35th floor) revolving restaurant and cocktail lounge serving lunch and dinner.

A huge game deck offers all the attractions of a posh country club: men's and women's health spas, landscaped garden terraces, an Olympic-size outdoor pool, a putting green and a poolside restaurant; tennis courts are located just across one of the pedestrian bridges at the Los Angeles Racquet Club.

Twelve outdoor glass bubble elevators whisk you to your room (getting there is half the fun). Each of the 1,500 rooms are ultra-modern in decor, with one wall of windows, thick carpeting, color TV, radio, etc., plus luxurious extras like huge soft towels and electric blankets (to see you through those freezing L.A. nights?).

There's 24-hour room service, and beneath everything is ample parking space for 10,000 cars. In short, there's nothing wanting at this exciting new establishment—if you don't stay here come by for a look around.

Single rooms range from $39 to $54, doubles and twins from $49 to $64, and suites are $110 and up.

The other deluxe newcomer (still under construction as we go to press) is the **New Otani**, 120 South Los Angeles Street, adjacent to the Music Center (tel: 629-1200), perhaps not as spectacular, but certainly as unique as the Bonaventure. For one thing, it's the city's only Japanese hotel, complete with a classical 16,000-square-foot Japanese garden for the exclusive use of guests. There's also a Japanese health club called the Golden Spa, offering sauna, Japanese baths and shiatsu massage in a garden setting.

The 450 rooms are housed in a 21-story triangular tower. Facilities include four underground parking levels, a shopping arcade, car-rental desk, etc., airport limousine service, and a wide choice of restaurants.

The Canary Garden serves breakfast, lunch and dinner (fresh-baked breads and pastries are a specialty) in garden setting with rare live birds and lots of greenery. Pacific overtures and gourmet French specialties are the respective theme and fare at The Black Ship, named for Commodore Perry's famous ship that forced Japan to open trade with the West (most apt, since Perry is belatedly responsible for hotels like the New Otani in California). And A Thousand Cranes is the evocative name of the Otani's Japanese restaurant, serving traditional lunches and dinners in an authentic setting overlooking the garden.

A classical pianist entertains in the Rendezvous Lounge off the lobby. It's open from morn till the wee hours for drinks, fresh-ground coffees and delicious fresh-baked pastries. Lunch, hors d'oeuvres and cocktails are also served in the Genji Bar, designed in the style of Japan's feudal-age country villas—few of which offered live jazz music!

The luxurious rooms are mostly Western in style: each has a refrigerator, oversized beds, showers and extra-deep tubs, bathroom extension phone and radio, button-selector radio with city and hotel information channels in Japanese and English, direct-dial phones with message-alert lights, alarm clocks, color TV, air conditioning and heating.

Rates for single rooms are $48 to $56; doubles are $58 to $66. We particularly like the Japanese suites with tatami-mat bedrooms, deep whirlpool baths and balconies overlooking the garden—$120 a night. Other suites range from $75 to a whopping $500.

The New Otani is scheduled to open in September 1977.

DOWNTOWN—MODERATE: Old-fashioned and substantial, the **Mayflower Hotel,** 535 South Grand Avenue, between 5th and 6th Streets (tel: 624-1331), has been welcoming Los Angeles visitors to its traditional precincts since the '20s. The cheerful yellow lobby boldly states the hotel's theme with murals of Pilgrims and Indians at Plymouth Rock.

The 350 rooms are homey, comfortable and immaculate; each is uniquely decorated, but most have cream-colored textured wallpaper, shag carpeting, tufted leather chairs and brightly colored bedspreads, and about half look out over Library Park. Every accommodation is equipped with color TV, direct-dial phone, air conditioning and radio.

The Mayflower's coffee shop and room service operate around the clock. The same menu, but fancier surroundings, prevail in the Chart House, a nautical nook decorated with navigational charts and maritime mementoes, open for lunch, cocktails and dinner.

Single rooms range from $22 to $32, doubles and twins from $26 to $38 (minimum-rated rooms have showers instead of tubs and are less spacious).

In its heydey, the 70-year-old **Alexandria,** Spring Street at 5th Street (tel: 626-7484), was the chosen hostelry of presidents and movie stars. Taft, Theodore Roosevelt and Wilson all stayed here, Tom Mix once rode in on his horse, and Chaplin did improvisations in the lobby. The hotel's restaurant was the rendezvous of the rich and famous—equivalent to The Polo Lounge today.

Throughout the years, the Alexandria has had many ups and downs; by the 1950s it was known as a cheap transient hotel, generally filled with boxing fans booked here by fight promoter George Parnassus. Today the Alexandria is in a new incarnation, its 500 rooms, hallways and public areas fully restored to Victorian elegance—particularly the plush lobby.

There are four eating places: Guvnor's Grille, serving steaks, chops and seafood, is done up like an old English tavern. Charley O's, for lunch and dinner buffets daily, is a cheerful 1890s-style Irish pub. Most elegant is the Palm Court with its stained-glass ceiling, and the hotel's coffee shop is also quite nicely done in turn-of-the-century decor.

The Alexandria has two kinds of rooms, Mediterranean and Victorian. The former are rather drab, but the latter are attractive and a good buy. They have beds with tufted-leather headboards and quilted silk spreads, flocked wallpaper, marble-topped tables and marble shower stalls, and of course phones and color TVs. The rooms are named for stars who once frequented the Alexandria—Valentino, Mae West, Gloria Swanson, Mary Pickford, etc.—and their photographs adorn the walls.

Victorian singles go for $26 a night, doubles and twins for $29 to $32.

EAST WILSHIRE—UPPER BRACKET: The **Ambassador**, 3400 Wilshire Boulevard, two blocks east of Normandie Avenue (tel: 387-7011; 800/421-0182), is another venerable California hotel with an impressive history. Opened in 1921, at an unheard-of (in those days) cost of $5-million, it was the raison d'être for Wilshire Boulevard's development as L.A.'s main artery. Countless numbers of the wealthy and famous—Hollywood stars, financiers, world leaders and high society—have rubbed elbows at the Ambassador. When Madame Chiang Kai-shek stayed here, Oriental furnishings were brought in specially for her room and the lobby was decorated with rows of cherry trees. From 1930 to 1943 the hotel hosted the Academy Awards shindigs. Presidents F.D.R., Truman, Eisenhower, Kennedy and Johnson all stayed here, as did Nikita Khrushchev, Nehru and everyone else from Charlie Chaplin to Haile Selassie. And many will remember a tragic footnote in the annals of the Ambassador's history—the hotel was the scene of the assassination of Senator Robert F. Kennedy.

Today this gracious and luxurious resort, set on 23 acres of lush lawn and garden with splashing fountains and towering palms, is undergoing a total renovation and refurbishment. It still preserves the plush '20s atmosphere, but with a modern accent.

Spacious, air-conditioned rooms, with tub/shower baths and wide-screen TV sets, are being redone in a tasteful mixture of French provincial and modern furnishings in bold blue and red color schemes.

Eateries include the posh Restaurant Lautrec, for dinner and dancing; the Cafe Ambassador, a coffee shop; and the Palm Bar and Casino Bar, mainly for cocktails, the latter also offering nightly entertainment. At this writing all dining facilities are in a state of flux, so we'll skip details.

The hotel is very proud of its spanking-new Tennis and Health Club with ten outdoor lighted tennis courts, saunas, whirlpool, steam rooms, an Olympic-size pool, running track for joggers and modern gym equipment (massage and facials available). There's also a putting green and tennis pro shop; fitness buffs can refuel at the health-food snack bar.

And like any big luxury establishment, the Ambassador houses the requisite number of shops—beauty salon/barber shop, boutiques, art galleries, airline and car rental desks—plus free parking facilities for 1,200 cars.

Single rooms range from $29 to $41, twins from $35 to $47. Suites are in the $50-to-$200 bracket.

Not far from the Ambassador is the **Wilshire Hyatt House**, 3515 Wilshire Boulevard, corner of Normandie Avenue (tel: 381-7411), a luxury hotel popular with business people for its push-button comfort and convenient location. Its 400 rooms are housed on 12 floors; each is furnished in attractive modern style with one all-glass wall and, of course, all amenities. Facilities are those street), and Jacuzzi, free parking, and a putting green; golf and tennis can be arranged nearby.

A bonus is free limousine and Mercedes bus service to and from the airport; a free Sunday harbor champagne cruise through Marina del Rey and out into the Pacific is another.

Rates vary according to room location. Singles are $34 to $48; doubles, $44 to $58.

Under the same ownership is the **Marina del Rey Hotel,** 13534 Bali Way, at Admiralty Way (tel: 822-1010). When we were last here a complete renovation and spiffing-up of facilities was in progress. Particularly lovely are the rooms with balconies looking out over the boat-filled harbor, a view which all guests can enjoy from the beautifully landscaped swimming pool and sundeck area.

Rooms are done in strikingly bold color schemes, and fitted out with all modern conveniences, including clock radios. The baths have large adjoining dressing areas.

As at the International, tennis and golf can be arranged, the beach is a stone's throw away, and guests can utilize free limousine airport service and are invited to join the Sunday champagne cruise.

Don the Beachcomber is on the premises, serving up Polynesian specialties and potent rum concoctions with names like "Missionary's Downfall" in an exotic South Seas atmosphere.

Single rooms cost from $34 to $38, doubles from $44 to $48, and suites are $150 a day.

BURBANK—BUDGET: Remember the old "Laugh-In" show and all those jokes about "beautiful downtown Burbank"? Well, Burbank certainly isn't the most exciting place in the world, but **Howard's Weekly Apartments,** 322 North Pass Avenue near Alameda Street (tel: 843-9283), do provide an exciting money-saving bargain. Once again, remarkably low rates are provided because of the efficient planning of owner Gordon Howard. The charge is just $49.50 to $55 weekly for one person in an efficiency apartment; $69.50 weekly for two in a one-bedroom garden apartment. A bonus is the charge of only $9.50 a week for each additional person.

The garden apartments—in a pretty landscaped setting—come complete with a fully equipped kitchen and dining area. And even the regular rooms have a full bath and refrigerator. Costs are cut on maid service, which is provided once weekly along with clean linens. Phones are in the hall (a switchboard takes messages), and the building manager can advise you about TV rental.

All the rooms are air-conditioned, nicely furnished, roomy and immaculate.

And getting back to the Burbank location, all joking aside, it's quiet and safe, and two major freeways nearby (Hollywood and Ventura) allow for zippy 20-minute rides to downtown L.A. Howard's is also very convenient to Toluca Lake's Restaurant Row, the Burbank Studios, Warner Bros., the Columbia Movie Ranch, NBC Studios, Universal Studios, Hollywood and Forest Lawn, should you drop dead of Burbank boredom. A large shopping center is across the street and Verdugo Park tennis courts and swimming pool are within walking distance. Besides, living in Burbank is a conversation piece.

Generally it's wise to reserve these apartments far in advance, securing your reservations with a $25 deposit. If you have arrived without reservations, you can try to get a three-day mini-week package, subject to availability.

One such is the **Roman Inn**, a 189-room hotel just a few blocks from Santa Monica Bay at 530 Pico Boulevard and 6th Avenue (tel: 399-9344). Facilities include ample free parking and an Olympic-size swimming pool, sundeck and Jacuzzi for those days you're too lazy to walk to the beach. And when you've had enough sun you can play the pinball machines in the game room off the lobby, or have a snack in the cheerful coffee shop.

Rooms are furnished in attractive standard modern hotel style—shag rugs, matching floral-pattern drapes and bedspreads. Unique aspects include sailboat murals on the walls, mattress-ticking wall covering and marble sinks in the bath. Each room is equipped with air conditioning, color TV, direct-dial phone, special security lock, oversized beds, tub/shower bath and a dressing room. Many have balconies.

Singles pay $30 a night; doubles and twins are $36.

In the lower range of moderately priced hotels is the **Royal Inn**, 1819 Ocean Avenue at Pico Boulevard (tel: 451-8711; 800/255-4141), a 167-room beachfront hotel that offers a great deal at a low price. The entire hotel has a relaxing resort feel, and the rooms are pleasantly decorated. They have white walls enhanced by one wall covered in striped paper or a mural, bright red, blue or gold carpeting, white wood furnishings upholstered in the room's main color and white quilt bedspreads. Each is equipped with a color TV, direct-dial phone and tub/shower bath; all offer views of the city or beach.

The hotel's facilities include a Sambo's coffee shop, heated swimming pool, whirlpool and cocktail lounge. An outdoor glass elevator gives you an ocean view en route to your room.

Singles are $24 to $32; doubles, $28 to $38. Suites are decidedly more expensive at $80 and up.

And once again there's a **Holiday Inn** in town, this one offering a top-notch location at 120 Colorado Street and Ocean Boulevard, right at the Santa Monica Pier and one of the area's most popular beaches (tel: 451-0676). Facilities include a swimming pool, free parking, laundry room, ice and soda machines on every floor, and a coffee shop off the lobby misleadingly named Top of the Pier.

Rooms are fitted out with all modern appointments and facilities.

Rates are seasonal: May 28 to September 6, singles are $28 to $39, doubles $34 to $40; the rest of the year rates are about $3 less. Kids under 18 can stay free in a room with their parents.

MARINA DEL REY—UPPER BRACKET: Sandwiched between Santa Monica and the Los Angeles International Airport, Marina Del Rey is a popular waterfront resort, just two minutes from major freeways that connect with most L.A. attractions.

One of the most luxurious Marina del Rey hotels is the **Marina International**, 4200 Admiralty Way, at Palawan Way (tel: 822-1010). Twenty-three new suites and villas—each featuring the decor of a different country—are presently being added, which bring the International's room capacity to 134. And very lovely rooms they are, with heavy oak furnishings, earth-tone color schemes, ship lamps and nautical-theme paintings on the walls. Of course, each room is fitted out with color TV (with remote control from your bed), direct-dial phone, tub/shower bath and the like.

The hotel's Flagship Restaurant, also nautical in theme, offers continental cuisine and flambé specialties; dancing and entertainment are featured in the lounge. Other facilities include a swimming pool (the beach is right across the

Three-day mini-rates range from $34.50 (one person, efficiency apartment) to $49.50 (two persons, kitchen garden apartments).

Howard's has more apartments at an annex down the street at 115 North Pass Avenue.

UNIVERSAL CITY—UPPER BRACKET: Want to stay right on a movie set? The **Sheraton-Universal**, 30 Universal City Plaza, at Lankershim Boulevard and Hollywood Freeway (tel: 980-1212; 800/325-3535), is right smack on Universal Studios' lot. Special free trams run daily from the entrance to the hotel to the studio's tour center (where you can enjoy such thrills as being attacked by the shark from *Jaws*). And in season you're on the spot for concerts at the Universal Amphitheater, a 5,000-seat open-air theater where people like Helen Reddy, John Denver and Tom Jones perform.

The 20-story hilltop structure—almost a skyscraper in these parts—allows an unblocked vista from every room. And speaking of the rooms, they're just lovely, with extremely cheerful bamboo furnishings, pretty print bedspreads and draperies, very nice art reproductions on the walls, at least one wall of window, and every modern convenience.

There are shops, airline counters, etc., plenty of free parking, and a huge swimming pool and flagstone sundeck planted with tropical trees and vines. Transportation is provided to and from the airport, and tours to major L.A. and Buena Park attractions originate at the door.

The most original of the restaurants here is the Four Stages, a simulated movie set complete with cat walks and kleig lights. You can dine on any of four sets: the Captain's Deck, fashioned after a clipper ship; the Grenadier Stage, a medieval castle; an ornately exotic Oriental palace called the Marco Polo Stage; and the Gold Rush Stage, with Western frontier saloon decor. The production schedule includes lunch weekdays, dinner nightly and Sunday brunch. Steak and seafood entrees are featured.

A delightful place to dine is the Cafe Universal, overlooking the pool and fountain in a garden courtyard setting. Equally pretty is the hotel's coffee shop, with terra-cotta tile floors and ceramic tile walls. Both are open daily from 6:30 to 1 a.m.

Adjacent to the pool-patio is the exquisite Portuguese Lounge, glass-enclosed on three sides and decorated in a restful sea blue. There's blue carpeting, a blue-and-white-striped awning over the bar, and a blue-and-white-tile mural of Lisbon on the wall. This room has been used in many TV films. It's open for drinks from 10 to 2 a.m. daily (we'd be hard-pressed to find more congenial surroundings), and there's a piano bar nightly except Sunday.

One more plus about the Sheraton—you're likely to see a lot of movie stars about.

Rates for one person range from $25 to $36; doubles, from $31 to $42. Suites begin at $60.

STUDIO CITY—MODERATE: A little further west from our previous listing is the **Sportsmen's Lodge**, 12825 Ventura Boulevard at Coldwater Canyon Avenue (tel: 769-4700). Because of its proximity to so many studios, movie actors and actresses are always in residence—you might see Jack Palance, Dick Van Dyke or even Marlon Brando strolling about the grounds.

The hotel is nestled among redwood trees, with rustic wooden foot bridges crossing fresh-water ponds (the hotel's name derives from the fact that guests used to fish for trout in these ponds), waterfalls, rock gardens and lush tropical greenery. There's an Olympic-size swimming pool, with lots of sundeck area, a variety of shops and service desks, bowling and golf adjacent, and airport limousine service.

A major asset is the adjoining restaurant, one of the finest in San Fernando Valley. It's very attractive, the glass-enclosed main dining room overlooking a swan-filled pond and small waterfall. You might begin a meal here with an order of baked clams ($3), then order an entree of veal piccata ($6.75), duckling à l'orange with wild rice ($7) or fresh trout stuffed with crabmeat ($7.50). An early-dinner menu (served from 5:30 to 6:30 p.m.) is cheaper. Cakes and rolls are fresh-baked daily. There's an extensive wine list, and an adjoining piano bar lounge serves late suppers from 10 p.m. Open nightly and for delicious Sunday brunches. Reservations are a good idea.

There's also a coffee shop on the premises serving breakfast, lunch and dinner.

Rooms are large, but not luxurious in any way; they do have color TV, direct-dial phones, AM-FM radio etc., and refrigerators are available. Many have balconies and some have dressing rooms with lighted make-up mirrors. The executive studios ($29 single, $34 double) are the most attractive accommodations. Regular rooms are $23 to $25 single, $26 to $30 double.

PASADENA—UPPER BRACKET: The only reason to st y in Pasadena, 11 miles northwest of the downtown district and not particul ly convenient to anything, is, of course, the annual Rose Bowl football game and Tournament of Roses Parade. If you're coming to Pasadena for these events, make reservations far in advance.

The grand dame of Pasadena hotels is the posh **Huntington-Sheraton**, 1401 South Oak Knoll at Huntington Drive (tel: 792-0266; 800/325-3535), a gracious turn-of-the-century resort set on 23 exquisitely landscaped garden acres. Its ivy-covered facade gives it a bit of prestige-university look (perfect ambience if you're in town for the football game). The grounds are famous, particularly the Japanese garden, with its little wooden foot bridge, and the wisteria-covered Picture Bridge adorned with Frank Moore's very charming paintings of early California scenes and the accompanying verses of Don Blanding—a touchingly beautiful work of art.

Facilities include badminton, Ping-Pong, a nine-hole putting green, Olympic size swimming pool, tennis courts, airport limo service, free parking, and a variety of service desks and shops.

There's dining in the nautical-themed Ship Room, where glass cases filled with valuable antiques line the walls; in the aptly named Crystal Terrace (note the chandeliers) overlooking the pool and gardens; or al fresco at the romantic Deck and Quarter Deck, where you can dance under the stars.

Accommodations are attractively modern, light and airy, with color TV, air conditioning, direct-dial phone and other such appurtenances. Rates are based on location, view and room size. Singles are $23 to $41, doubles $30 to $48. Suites begin at $50 a night.

PASADENA—BUDGET: Right on the path of the annual Rose Parade is the **Pasadena Motor Hotel**, 2131 East Colorado at Craig Street (tel: 796-3121). Here you get standard motel accommodations at a convenient location and low cost. All units are equipped with switchboard phones, air conditioning, TV (half have color sets) and bath. And there's even a swimming pool. Single rooms range from $9.50 to $12.50, doubles from $10.50 to $14.50.

AIRPORT—UPPER BRACKET: If you're just passing through and want to stay at the airport, the **Los Angeles Marriott,** Century and Airport Boulevards (tel: 641-5700; 800/228-9290), is the plushest choice. It offers 1,000 cheerfully decorated bedrooms with all luxury extras including bedside remote control of the color TV, alarm clocks and even ironing boards, irons and hair driers if you like. There's also a guest laundry room—everything, in short, geared to the weary in-transit traveler.

There's a gigantic pool and garden sundeck, with a swim-up bar (the barstools are actually in the pool) and a cabana for refreshments. It's just one of seven eating and drinking facilities here serving specialties ranging from Italian to Mexican.

Singles go for $37 to $45, doubles for $45 to $53.

3. Restaurants

Los Angeles probably has a greater number and diversity of restaurants than any other American city except, maybe, New York. When *Los Angeles* magazine recently published an annual report on *noteworthy* restaurants in and around the city, they came up with an astounding 500 recommendables running the gamut from Arabic to organic eateries.

And not only are there a lot of restaurants—there are a lot of restaurants competing for the glittering movie-star trade. Every other coffee shop boasts of a celebrity clientele, often as not backing up the claim with scores of intimately signed photos plastered over the walls.

The first section of our restaurant recommendations is devoted to the most glamorous, fashionable—and usually expensive—gathering places of the rich and famous. We've chosen them for culinary excellence as well as chic popularity. The remainder of our selections are broken down into expensive, moderately priced and budget categories, then further subdivided as to nationality or type of cuisine. This being L.A., many of the following are "in" places, too. Many of the restaurants we recommended in our hotel section above are equally fashionable—be sure to consider them, too. Reservations are advised at all Los Angeles restaurants, except Pink's Hot Dog Stand and suchlike. Reservations are imperative at—

THE TOP RESTAURANTS: Perhaps the most acclaimed is **Scandia,** 9040 Sunset Boulevard at Doheny Drive, Beverly Hills (tel: 278-3555). An appropriately impressive and posh haute-cuisine rendezvous, Scandia is divided into several dining areas. Our favorite, especially at lunch when the sun streams in, is the Belle Terrace, its garden ambience enhanced by hanging ferns, lots of white latticework, and fresh flowers on tables cheerfully decked out in pink cloths. The oak-paneled Danish Room is charmingly provincial, with beamed ceilings and hanging copper pots. In the cozy Skaal Room tables and oversized black leather armchairs face a blazing fireplace. And a popular nook is Hansen's Vin Stue, inspired by Copenhagen wine shops and named for owner Ken Hansen.

At lunch and late supper—both served Tuesday through Saturday—Danish smorrebrod (open-face sandwiches) are featured with fillings like coral pink shrimps ($3), camembert cheese ($1.50) or perhaps sliced chicken breast with curry salad ($3.50). Heartier fare, ranging from omelets ($3.50) to wiener schnitzel with cucumber salad ($5.75), is also available.

Dinner (Tuesday to Sunday) needn't be exorbitant if you stick to the less pricey entrees, like duckling roasted on a spit, served with apples, prunes, red cabbage, cucumber salad and lingon pear ($6.50); or spring chicken sauteed in butter with shallots and mushrooms in cream and sherry sauce ($5.50).

A lovely time to experience Scandia is at Sunday brunch, a sumptuous eight-entree affair served from 11 a.m. to 3 p.m. and costing $6.25.

Housed in an early-California-style cocoa-colored stucco building, **Le Restaurant,** 8475 Melrose Place, corner of La Cienega, West Hollywood (tel: 651-5553), not only has a star clientele (Yul Brynner and Kirk Douglas among them) but celebrity ownership—singer Patti Page.

It's also one of the most beautiful restaurants we've ever seen, with an ambience as fresh as country air. The front room has pale mauve silk wall coverings, pink tablecloths, green velvet booths and upholstered cane-backed chairs. There's lots of oak paneling throughout, and tables are separated by etched glass di/iders. Here and there are bouquets of roses, asters and cornflowers in cut-glass vases. The treillage and patio rooms adjoin, both adorned with lots of latticework, the latter with a live tree, a brick floor and a skylight roof from which many plants are suspended. A few intimate dining nooks are equally exquisite, and lovely watercolors by C. Terechkovitch further brighten the scene.

The menu is as classically French as the decor. Dinner should begin with an appetizer, of which there is a wide selection ranging from escargots de Bourgogne ($5) to foie gras de Strasbourg ($9). Entrees are simply described— sole grilled in butter ($12), homard (lobster) au whiskey ($14), steak tartare ($11)—belying their subtly superb preparation by culinary artist Jean Bonnardot. For dessert we prefer the patisseries du chef ($2.50).

Luncheon at Le Restaurant is about half the price, with entrees in the $4.50-to-$5.50 range. It's served weekdays 11:30 a.m. to 2 p.m.; dinner is served from 6 to 10:45 p.m. Monday through Saturday.

Perino's, 4101 Wilshire Boulevard near Crenshaw Boulevard, Hollywood (tel: 383-1221), is an award-winning bastion of haute cuisine, patronized by old families, presidents (the Kennedys, Johnsons and Nixons among them) and other notables. It's suitably impressive from the colonnaded entrance and stained-glass doors to the Empire setting of the oval dining salon with its faded peach damask walls, tufted dusty-rose banquettes, wall mirrors and glittering crystal chandeliers.

So established is Perino's that they don't even bother with the icy hauteur so common in posh eating places—service is actually friendly.

An immense dinner menu runs the continental gamut from boned royal squab stuffed with wild rice ($13.75) to broiled lobster tails with French-fried potatoes ($14.50). Once again, descriptions of food are unadorned—that's class. There's a wide selection of appetizers to preface your meal, as well as accompaniments like a salad Italienne ($3.25) or fettuccine Alfredo ($7.50), which could suffice for a light meal. Desserts range from a refreshingly simple raspberry sherbert ($1.50) to lush chocolate, vanilla, Mandarin or Grand Marnier soufflés ($10 for two).

The lunch menu is equally varied and extensive, but entrees start in a much lower price range; a mushroom omelet is $3.75, stuffed avocado with shrimp or roast half-chicken with fruit compote $6.50.

Open noon to midnight weekdays and from 6 p.m. to midnight on Saturday. Closed Sunday.

One clue to the high quality of **The Windsor,** 3198½ West 7th Street, corner of Catalina Street, Hollywood (tel: 382-1261), is that the Los Angeles Gourmet Society throws its parties here. Not only is the cuisine excellent, the ambience—very English clubby—provides a genuine feeling of well-being. The walls, paneled in rich mahogany or papered in flocked wall covering, are hung with coats of arms and $50,000 worth of original oil paintings. Lamp bases are statues of old English aristocrats, windows are leaded glass, seating is in substantial red-leather horseshoe banquettes, and fresh flowers adorn every table.

But it's not only the decor that's reassuring. The Windsor is the kind of place where a dedicated staff of fifty have been employed an average of 12 years.

The menu offers a formidable number of choices: there are over 20 seafood entrees, including a terrific scampi at $7.95. Or perhaps you'll opt for breast of turkey à l'Indienne with wild rice and condiments ($8.25), breast of pheasant ($11.50) or a succulent rack of lamb bouquetière ($21 for two). Careful preparation takes time, so you might order a Caesar salad ($3.25) to ward off hunger while waiting for your entree and perusing the lengthy wine list. For dessert we favor the zabaglione ($2.50) or, in a lighter vein, fresh strawberries ($2.25).

There's no notable reduction in prices at lunchtime, but there are many additional listings—sandwiches, salads and omelets in the $2.50-to-$6 bracket.

Open daily from 11:30 a.m., Saturday and Sunday from 4:30 p.m.

Chasen's, 9030 Beverly Boulevard at Doheny Drive, Beverly Hills (tel: 271-2168), is a long-enduring favorite. The original Chasen's, a chili parlor, was financed by none other than *New Yorker* editor Harold Ross, and early patrons at this "Algonquin West" included Jimmy Durante and James Cagney. (There's still a New Yorker Room, used for private parties.) Once James Thurber spent hours drawing murals on the men's room wall—they were immediately removed by an unimpressed and overly industrious cleaning lady who was fired posthaste. Dave Chasen originated the idea of serving food on airplanes, and was the first supplier of food to TWA.

Run these days by his widow, Maude Chasen, the restaurant has always been one of L.A.'s most famous spots for star-gazing. We recently saw a hilarious old Lucille Ball skit, in which Lucy gawks without reserve at William Holden in the next booth at Chasen's.

You can dine in the richly wood-paneled and softly lit Chestnut Room, with beamed ceilings, brass reading lamps and plush tufted red leather booths; or al fresco on a trellised brick patio with umbrellaed tables and white wrought-iron garden furnishings.

The menu has come a long way since chili (Elizabeth Taylor's favorite, still served), but the continental fare retains an American simplicity that we're sure Harold Ross would have approved. Specialties include deviled beef bones with baked potato ($8.25), chicken livers with rice pilaff ($8.50) and veal scaloppine with French peas ($9.75). You can top off your meal with strawberry shortcake ($1.75), or go exotic and order baba au rhum flambé ($2.25).

Chasen's is open for dinner only (by the way, they honor no credit cards) till 1 a.m. Closed Mondays.

One of the chicest "in" places for the movie set and other socially prominent citizens is **The Bistro,** 246 North Canon Drive at Dayton Way, Beverly Hills (tel: 273-5633). The decor is authentically and elegantly Parisian, with mirrored walls, tables smartly clothed in white linen and set with gleaming silver, cane and bentwood chairs, fresh roses on every table and perfectly arranged in big baskets and pots here and there. There's more seating up a stairway lined with art posters.

Both service and cuisine are top-notch. Menus are posted on a blackboard that is brought to your table. At lunch excellent rich soups are $2; entrees like medallion of salmon and cucumber salad are $5.25. Typical dinner entrees (generally in the $8-to-$12 range) are rack of lamb ($26 for two) and duck à l'orange ($9.50). The chocolate soufflé ($3) is a dessert worth blowing your diet for.

Lunch is served from noon to 3 p.m. weekdays; dinner nightly till 11. Closed Sundays.

For over half a century, **The Palm** has been a favorite New York tradition, and Walter Ganzi's new Beverly Hills branch, at 9001 Santa Monica Boulevard (tel: 550-8811), is already drawing an S.R.O. crowd of celebrities, onlookers and homesick Gothamites. The casual saloon-like ambience is refreshingly unstuffy—sawdust on the floor, green-and-white-checkered tablecloths, roomy wooden booths and irrepressibly spirited Italian waiters. The walls are plastered with original comic-strip art by the world's most famous cartoonists, and caricatures, many of them signed, of everyone from Groucho Marx and Johnny Carson to Elsie the Cow. Mixed in with the above are rave reviews of the restaurant.

The menu raises no-frills listings almost to an art form—entrees are described as chicken ($7), duck ($8), steak ($12) and, the most elaborately evocative item, veal cutlet ($9). It's all terrific, though, and you can get plenty fancy when ordering wines—like a bottle of Chateau Lafite-Rothschild for $65. For dessert the New York cheesecake ($2.50) is a Palm specialty.

The Palm is as popular for leisurely lunches (weekdays only) as it is for dinner (nightly). Lunch entrees are in the $3.50 (for a hamburger) to $5.50 (for veal piccata) range, and are served with hash browns or cottage fries.

One of the finest and most delightful French restaurants in Southern California is **La Chaumière,** 207 South Beverly Drive, just south of Wilshire Boulevard, Beverly Hills (tel: 276-0239). The word *chaumière* means a thatched cottage, which accurately evokes the warm and cozy ambience—a combination of Tudor beamed walls, a stone fireplace, old-fashioned maple chairs with calico cushions, hanging copper and brass pots, ruffled curtains on the windows and fresh flowers on tables covered with pretty red cloths. It's hard to remember that you're in Beverly Hills and not some quaint Normandy inn.

Entrees are all served with a delicious homemade soup—it could be avocado, crab bisque or pumpkin. There's a daily fresh fish special ($8.25 to $8.75), along with such items as grenadin de veau Normande—veal sauteed with apples and cream sauce ($11.25). All are skillfully prepared by chef Georges E. Peyre, who is also a skilled pâtissier; try his tarte tatin—an upside-down apple tart with caramel ($1.75).

La Chaumière is open for dinner only, from 6 p.m. Monday through Saturday.

Jean Leon's La Scala, 9455 Santa Monica Boulevard, Beverly Hills (tel: 275-0579), is the liveliest, most glamorous, intoxicating and intimidating of celebrity-packed see-and-be-seen L.A. restaurants. Gene Kelly, Dean Martin, Warren Beatty, Candice Bergen, Natalie Wood, Jacqueline Bisset and Michael Caine are just a few of those who patronize La Scala (and the adjoining Boutique) on a regular basis, and anyone you can't identify looks gorgeous or well-heeled.

Owner Jean Leon, the darling of the movie set, arrived here from Basque country in 1950, and began his American career bussing tables at the Cafe de Paris. By 1956 he had launched the now-renowned La Scala and was teaching President Kennedy how to distinguish superior from run-of-the-mill caviar! (If you want to the sample the former it comes at $15 per superior ounce.)

Take your eyes off the beautiful people for a minute or two, and you'll see that the main dining room is a comfortable, softly lit salon, with big bunches of flowers in brandy snifters and wine bottles everywhere. Leon is a connoisseur of fine wines who owns over 450 vineyard acres in Northern Spain; his wine list is reputed to be one of the best in town.

The Italian cuisine is expertly prepared by chef Emilio. At dinner, the spaghetti carbonara ($7.95) is exquisite, made with minced bacon and raw egg; the cannelloni La Scala, a delicate crêpe stuffed with chunks of lobster, shrimp and crab, smothered in white cream sauce with grapes ($7.95), is also rave-worthy. The calorie-conscious will do well to order a perfectly prepared filet mignon ($13.50), and then perhaps cheat just a little with a dessert of zabaglione ($5 for two) or soufflé au Grand Marnier ($7 for two).

Lunch also features many pasta items, along with a mushroom omelet ($5.45), poached salmon ($6.95) and grilled scampi with just the right wine and herb seasoning ($7.45). And if the fashionably slim clientele is making you painfully aware of midriff bulge, opt for fresh fruit salad with cottage cheese ($4.95).

La Scala is open for lunch weekdays from 11:30 a.m. to 2:30 p.m.; dinner Monday through Saturday from 5:30 p.m. to midnight.

The adjoining **La Scala Boutique** (tel: 550-8288), opened in 1962, also entices a perennial flow of celebs and notables who don't seem to mind standing on long lines until one of the few red leather booths or handful of tables becomes vacant. It's probably the most chic luncheon spot in L.A. Large windows look out on the Beverly Hills scene; inside there are shelves overflowing with gourmet fare—canned cassoulet, imported pâtés, etc., wine racks and a delicatessen showcase brimming with imported meats and cheeses. The walls are lined with Gerald Price caricatures of famous Hollywood faces; and Chianti bottles overhead add to the bistro ambience.

Overstuffed delicatessen sandwiches on rye or French roll—corned beef ($3.45), deviled eggs ($2.95), pâté de foie maison ($2.95), etc.—served with potato salad and cole slaw are the most popular lunchtime fare, along with salads, cold plates and Emilio's hot pasta dishes.

You can dine here in the evening until 9 p.m. Closed Sundays.

EXPENSIVE RESTAURANTS: We must admit that there's a fine line differentiating the following restaurants from the preceding ones. The upcoming selections are an iota less celebrated and chic, possibly a trifle less expensive. And at lunch many are moderately priced. Blurry classifications notwithstanding, we can guarantee you a fine dining experience at any of our listings.

American Continental

The (original) Brown Derby, 3377 Wilshire Boulevard, corner of Alexandria Avenue, East Wilshire (tel: 384-4147). You'll spot the brown dome from the street; you see, part of the restaurant's exterior is actually shaped like a brown derby. It's a landmark that has been here since 1926 when H.K. Somborne and Wilson Mizner first planned their "beanery."

A very elegant and famous beanery it became, the menu (continental with an Italian accent) expanding considerably since the day when Wallace Beery used to pour ketchup over his hash and sponge cake. Today you might dine on beef stroganoff ($5.95), shrimp scampi sauteed in sherry and garlic butter ($6.95) or perhaps veal Oscar garnished with asparagus, crab legs and sauce béarnaise ($6.50). Entrees include soup or salad and rice pilaff, baked potato or spaghetti.

At lunch, Italian entrees like veal scaloppine Marsala or parmigiana with spaghetti are just $3.50, sandwiches and omelets are in the $2-to-$3 range, and a terrific buy is cold poached salmon with cucumbers in sour cream ($2.95).

The decor is early California style, intimate and traditional, with red leather booths, soft lighting (mostly candlelight), hacienda archways, landscapes and hunting prints on the walls, and marvelous derby-motif carpeting.

Lunch is served from 11:30 a.m. to 4 p.m., dinner from 4 to 10:30 p.m. Weeknights there's a piano bar.

The **Musso & Frank Grill**, 6667 Hollywood Boulevard, a few blocks west of Cahuenga Boulevard (tel: 467-7788), bills itself as Hollywood's oldest restaurant (est. 1919). It's the kind of place we return to again and again for the comfortably substantial ambience, superb service and consistently excellent food that chef Jean Rue has been turning out for over half a century.

Musso & Frank Grill is a favorite of Jonathan Winters, Merv Griffin and Raymond Burr, among countless others.

The setting is richly traditional—beamed oak ceilings, deep-red leather booths and banquettes, oak furnishings, and soft lighting emanating from wall sconces and chandeliers with tiny shades.

The menu is extensive. We like to order the delicious seafood salads like shrimp Louie ($6), perhaps along with some camembert ($1.10) that comes with crusty bread and butter. Diners wishing heartier fare might consider the veal scaloppine with peas ($7.75), roast spring lamb with mint jelly and baked potatoes ($8.75) or broiled lobster ($8.75). A variety of omelets is quite inexpensive ($3 to $4), and many entrees are moderately priced, e.g. ravioli for $3.75. The back of the menu lists an extensive liquor and wine selection.

Open 11 a.m. to 11 p.m. daily except Sunday.

With its entranceway obscured under an illuminated Pepsi-Cola sign, you might think the **Studio Grill**, 7321 Santa Monica Boulevard, Hollywood (tel: 874-9202), was a taco stand. As it happens, it's a warm and intimate little restaurant, with plum-colored walls, plants suspended from a high skylight ceiling, comfy brown leather booths and bentwood chairs, an old copper boiler filled with fresh-cut flowers atop the bar, and vases of same on every table. The paintings and a geometric mural by talented owner Ardison Phillips grace the walls, and recorded jazz or classical music further enhances the tasteful atmosphere.

The eclectic and rather original menu lists 11 entrees in addition to the nightly special, ranging from an Eastern-influenced beef and black mushrooms in oyster sauce ($6.95) to shrimp Portuguese ($7.95) and game hen with cherry-plum sauce ($6.95). You might precede your entree with an appetizer of pâté maison ($2.25) or a mushroom salad ($2.50). For dessert we like the orange chocolate mousse ($1.80). The wine list is well chosen and reasonably priced.

At lunch (weekdays only) the Studio Grill offers seafood items like red snapper ($4.95), along with tasty salads, omelets, burgers, steaks and chops, the latter priced from $4.75 (for pork chops) to $11 (for a big porterhouse).

Dinner is served nightly except Sunday.

Appropriately set on one of L.A.'s most scenic canyon roads, the **Cafe Four Oaks**, 2181 North Beverly Glen, two miles north of Sunset Boulevard, Bel Air (tel: 474-9317), has a deservedly enthusiastic following. It's the creation of former actor/writer Jack Allen, who turned a greasy-spoon joint (in the early 1900s it was a brothel) into a rustic New-England-style restaurant. The original four oaks are no longer extant, but you can dine al fresco under the shade of spreading sycamores. Inside, the ambience is innlike, with a fireplace, brick patio floor, Indiana cedar walls and old-fashioned wallpaper. There's a second fireplace and more seating upstairs.

Waiters and waitresses are attractive and amiable out-of-work actors and actresses; for that matter, the clientele tends to be attractive, too. No two menus are alike, since the chef creates according to whim and the morning's shopping, but the food is always artfully prepared, the relaxed and casual atmosphere a delight.

Especially popular (the place is almost full at opening time) is the sumptuous Saturday and Sunday brunch served from 11 a.m. to 2 p.m. (3 p.m. on Sunday). It's a $6.95 prix-fixe affair, and the combination of good food, live music (perhaps a harpist, guitar player or pianist) and fresh air is unbeatable.

At dinner the menu might feature an appetizer of escargots with mushrooms ($3.75) and entrees like stuffed chicken breast with sauce Béarnaise ($8.75), salmon with parsley butter ($9) or imperial beef with water chestnuts and mushrooms ($10). Delectable desserts are also listed, and appropriate wines are suggested. Dinner is served Tuesday through Saturday from 6 to 9:30 p.m.

Music Center Restaurants are, of course, downtown at the Los Angeles Music Center (Dorothy Chandler Pavilion), 135 North Grand Avenue, between 1st and Temple Streets (tel: 972-7333). You certainly can't find a more convenient spot for pre-theater/concert dining or late supper after the show. There are two restaurants here, the elegant fifth-floor **Pavilion,** and the more informal **Curtain Call,** as well as a partly enclosed sidewalk eatery called the **Patio Cafe.**

Most posh is the Pavilion, with a deluxe European ambience made up of swagged gold draperies, crystal chandeliers, Louis XV-style chairs, and a European staff headed up by German chef Hugo Fressler. The lavish buffets here are a good buy. The $3.95 luncheon spread offers French gourmet items, along with Scandinavian dishes and California salads—everything from marinated herring and apricot mousse to guacamole. Seconds are encouraged. Alcoholic beverages and coffee are extra. At night the cost rises to $8.95; the fare is more elaborate, and there's a carver slicing off choice roasts. You can also dine à la carte at either meal. Lunch is served from 11:30 a.m. to 2:30 p.m.; dinner from 5:30 to 9:30 p.m. The restaurant is open on Sundays only when there's a performance at the center.

The Curtain Call, on the Grand Avenue level, has a theatrical bistro-like atmosphere, its bentwood chairs set on a recreated stage with stylized scenery, bits of theater boxes and photo blow-ups of old L.A. theaters on the wall. It's very inexpensive at lunch, with entrees like beef enchiladas, chef salad, and eggs Florentine all under $3. Dinner entrees are a more serious business; they include veal piccata ($6.50), roast prime rib of beef with baked potato, vegetable and creamed horseradish ($7.95) and big salads like a shrimp Louie ($4.95). The carrot cake (85¢) is our favorite dessert, and a demi-carafe of house wine with your meal is $1.95. Open for lunch from 11:30 a.m. to 2 p.m., dinner from 5 to 9 p.m., and late supper from 9 p.m. to 1 a.m.

The adjoining Patio Cafe has a garden decor—latticework, lots of greenery and white wrought-iron furnishings—and features the same menu as Curtain Call.

John Oldrate's Cyrano, 13535 Mindanao Way, Marina Del Rey (tel: 823-5305), is the kind of place where you might see Marlon Barlon at the bar or Jerry Lewis tying up his boat. Fine views of the Marina, comfortable leather booths, mini-skirted waitresses, good continental fare and an attractive yachting ambience make for a winning combination. Late at night, it's a popular rendezvous for movie and TV personalities.

House specialties—all served with salad, rice, vegetable, hot rolls and butter—include a number of veal preparations: scaloppine, piccata or à la maison (in heavy cream sauce with shallots and mushrooms), all priced at $7.25. Alternatives range from London broil stroganoff ($6.95) to frog legs meunière ($7.25), as well as many seafood and salad offerings. The wine list is adequate and unpretentious. Good desserts—try the French pastries ($1.25).

The moderately priced luncheon menu is equally extensive, and contains several items for calorie-counters.

There's nightly entertainment at the piano bar. Cyrano's is a delightful place for Saturday or Sunday brunch, the former offered from 11 a.m. to 4 p.m. and costing $3.25, the latter from 10:30 a.m. to 3 p.m. and costing $3.95. By the way, they also have a special late-supper menu served after 10 p.m., after 11 p.m. Friday and Saturday nights. Cyrano's is open daily.

Gourmet Organic/Natural Foods

Housed in John Barrymore's former guest home and garden (Errol Flynn once lived here), **Butterfield's**, 8426 Sunset Boulevard at Kings Road, West Hollywood (tel: 656-3055), offers gourmet natural foods in a natural environment. Set back from the busy street and down two flights of steps lined with greenery and small fountains, it has tables out under the trees on a brick patio amidst banks of ivy and flowering shrubbery. On busy days a tree-shaded upstairs deck is also used for seating; it adjoins the wood-paneled wine-tasting room. And in the evenings meals are served in the old Victorian living room. There's always good recorded music, usually classical, in the background, and the atmosphere is casual and chic.

Only organic produce, fresh fish, fertile eggs and natural cheeses are served. At dinner we especially like the fresh trout in lemon, butter and macadamia nuts ($7.75) and the chicken cooked in apricot brandy, topped with cheddar cheese ($7.25). All entrees include French-fried parsley, fresh vegetables, soup or salad. A dessert worth eating is the homemade chestnut mousse ($1.25).

Luncheon entrees, such as lamb chops with fresh mint and honey glaze ($5.50) and quiche Lorraine ($3.50), are served with the same accompaniments. And then there's the "anything" sandwich, which starts out at $1.75 with cream cheese and wheat berry bread plus three-bean salad on the side. For 30¢ per you can add any of about 20 garnishments ranging from alfalfa sprouts to strawberry jam. Go to it! A large selection of wines and beers is available.

Just across from the Continental Hyatt House, Butterfield's is open daily from 11:30 a.m. to 3 p.m. for lunch; for dinner from 6 to 10:30 p.m. Monday through Saturday.

The very first person to cross the threshold of the **Aware Inn**, 8828 Sunset Boulevard at Larrabee Street, West Hollywood (tel: 652-2555), when it opened its doors in 1958 was Greta Garbo. From this auspicious beginning, the first of L.A.'s organic eateries has continued to attract scores of health-conscious luminaries—Igor Stravinsky, Dr. Spock, Gloria Swanson, Julie Christie and Jon Voight among them. Proprietress Elaine Baker was serving organically grown fruits and vegetables, whole-grain products, raw sugar and sea salt long before such nutritional fare became a fad. And she continues to do so in a charming candlelit restaurant, decorated in turn-of-the-century motif with art-nouveau wallpaper, globe chandeliers, hanging ferns, bentwood chairs and etched-glass panels dividing tables into intimate dining areas.

There's more seating in a patio garden amidst abundant foliage, or upstairs in a room that offers a picture-window view of L.A.; the art-nouveau booth up here is the most romantic seat in the house.

Service is very friendly, and one is more aware that the food is delicious than that it is healthy; of course, it's both. There are big and tasty salads, our favorites being the wilted spinach with hot bacon dressing ($2.95) and the

Aware salad, made with seven vegetables, tomatoes, romaine, avocado, sunflower seeds and pignola nuts ($3.95). Organically grown fresh-squeezed fruit and vegetable juices are $1.35 to $1.75. If you'd rather have wine or beer, however, there's a fairly wide selection.

Heartier entrees include shrimp curry over brown rice with coconut, roasted peanuts and homemade chutney ($8.25); chicken in peach brandy sauce with whole mushroom caps ($8.50); and vegetable casseroles like the one of sauteed eggplant with herb tomato sauce, chopped mushrooms and melted jack cheese, served with brown rice, salad, vegetable and whole wheat rolls ($5.95). At this writing a new category of low-calorie gourmet entrees is being added. Moderately priced omelets and burgers are available every night except Friday and Saturday, when you can't order them before 10 p.m. Desserts made with honey and raw sugar include homemade ice cream ($1.15), a rich, creamy cheesecake ($1.75) and even butterscotch pie with whipped cream ($1.75).

Open for dinner only, from 6 p.m. to midnight. Closed Mondays.

The Inn of the Seventh Ray, 128 Old Topanga Canyon Road, Topanga Canyon (tel: 455-1311) offers creekside dining under the shade of ancient trees in a tranquil mountain setting. The most orthodox, and we think the most beautiful, of L.A.'s natural-food restaurants, the Inn was opened a little over a year ago by Ralph and Lucille Yaney as a place to practice and share their ideas about the relationship of food to energy. For this reason, entrees are listed in order of their "esoteric vibrational value"; the lightest and least dense (more purifying items) are listed first and are also less expensive.

The good vibes you get from lovingly prepared food are further enhanced by the natural setting (most seating is outdoors) and carefully selected music. And to make sure their own vibes are peaceful, the entire staff meditates before preparing and serving dinner.

There's indoor seating, too, in a slope-roofed shingled and stucco building with one glass wall overlooking the verdant mountain scene. The interior reminds us of a country church, with a peaked raw-wood ceiling from which many flourishing plants are suspended, stained-glass windows, simple wood furnishings, a central fireplace, Persian carpeting, flickering candles and fresh flowers on every table.

All foods and baked goods are prepared on the premises, all soups are homemade, and the greatest care is taken to see that everything is fresh, natural, without chemicals or preservatives. Even the fish is caught in deep water far offshore and served the same day. And everything is as delectable as it is healthy. The menu contains eight entrees, all served with soup or salad, complimentary hors d'oeuvres, steamed vegetables, herbed brown rice and homemade bread. The lightest item is called Five Secret Rays: lightly steamed vegetables served with herb butter and tamari nut sauce ($4.25); the densest, vibrationally speaking, is a ten-ounce New York steak cut from beef fed on natural grasses, served in a wine and mushroom sauce. A glass of delicious fruit wine ($1) is suggested as an aperitif, and delicious desserts are also available.

Open daily for lunch and dinner. If you're at all into natural foods, this is a not-to-be-missed experience.

A funkier approach to healthy eating is taken at another Topanga natural foods eatery, **Discovery Inn,** 156 South Topanga Canyon Boulevard (tel: 455-9079). Now under new ownership, it was begun 15 years ago by composer Richard Dehr ("Maryann," "Memories are Made of This," etc.) and his wife Marjorie.

Housed in a rustic mountain bungalow, the Inn is cozy inside, with a pot-belly stove in every room, lace cafe curtains on the windows and recorded classical music in the background. Many patrons prefer to dine outdoors, though, in a lovely flagstone patio garden with an outdoor brick fireplace and a grape arbor overhead (reach up and pick a bunch if you like).

Once again only farm-fresh organic vegetables and fine prime meats are used; processed or pre-prepared ingredients are avoided. All entrees are served with soup, salad, homemade rolls, fresh vegetables and baked potato or brown rice. They range from a tasty vegetarian cheese walnut loaf ($6.75), to curried lamb with brown rice and chutney ($7.50), to what must be the ultimate hamburger-type item—a 14-ounce grilled "swinger" made with choice ground sirloin, black and white mushrooms, sweet green peppers, olives, onions, pimentos, cheddar cheese, wheat germ, fresh tomato and spices from Samarkand, no less. For dessert the cheesecake (90¢) is recommended. Open for dinner nightly except Tuesday.

Steak and Seafood

Not to be confused with the original (see above) this **Brown Derby**, 1628 North Vine Street, a block south of Hollywood Boulevard (tel: 469-5151), is steeped in Hollywood tradition. Once it drew movie stars in great numbers—you can still get a plug-in phone at your table—but today the clientele leans more to affluent business people than show folk. You might recognize the interior from old movies about Hollywood. It's an extremely comfortable place to dine—high-ceilinged, with amber lighting, roomy semicircular black leather booths and cream-colored flocked wallpaper. But no one notices all that—the mainstay of the decor consists of wall panels plastered with 400 autographed caricatures of the stars and more chandeliers overhead than we've ever seen anywhere.

The smart-looking dinner menu features various cuts of prime rib ($7.85 to $8.85) and steaks ($7.25 to $12.50), served with French fries or baked potato, salad, and French bread and butter. In the seafood category, broiled lobster tail in drawn butter is $12, $16.50 combined with filet mignon; broiled red snapper is $6.50, sand dabs almondine $6.85. For dessert you might select a pastry from the cart ($1.50) or try the Derby's famous grapefruit cake ($2.).

The luncheon menu is more extensive, with sandwiches and omelets added, plus a terrific $5.85 Cobb salad (it originated here and was named for former maitre d' Bob Cobb).

Open daily except Sunday from 11 a.m. to 11 p.m. Piano music nightly.

A family enterprise started in 1938, **Lawry's**, 55 N. La Cienega Boulevard, West Hollywood (tel: 652-2827), enjoys an excellent Restaurant Row location. It is the unique creation of Lawrence Frank, along with his brother-in-law Walter Van de Kamp. Frank set out to offer "the greatest meal in America," serving one entree—the hearty roast beef he had enjoyed every Sunday for dinner as a boy (his father was in the meat business)—and serving it gloriously with flair and elegance. In order to showcase his famous beef, Frank originally purchased three gleaming silver carts (each cost as much as a Cadillac!) and hired experts to carve tableside. He also invented his now famous Seasoned Salt as the perfect seasoning for roast beef. When appreciative diners began swiping it off the tables, he turned an expensive trend into a very profitable operation; today Lawry's Seasoned Salt is marketed the world over.

The ambience at Lawry's is like an English country estate or posh private club. You might start out in the homey cocktail lounge, where drinks are served from a pewter-topped wood-paneled bar. The dining room is richly decorated with valuable original oil paintings (including one of the Duke of Windsor at age seven), Persian-carpeted oak floors, plush burnt-orange leather booths and high-backed chairs at tables decked out in orange-sherbert cloths, and graceful brass chandeliers overhead.

As we noted before, there's only one entree—award-winning prime ribs of beef—a choice of three cuts, priced at $8.95 and $10.75. With it you get Yorkshire pudding, salad with sherry dressing, mashed potatoes and creamed horseradish. A side order of creamed spinach or buttered peas is 40¢. A liter of house wine $3.50, and a good wine list is available. Children under 12 get a complete dinner for $5.95.

There are delicious desserts to end the "perfect meal". Always drawn by some mysterious force to the rich and creamy, we immediately gravitate to the chocolate pecan pie ($1), though the English trifle ($1.25) is also scrumptious.

When you're in the mood for a traditional roast-beef dinner, you just can't beat Lawry's. Open Monday through Saturday from 5 p.m. to midnight, Sunday from 3 to 11 p.m.

One of the most famous eateries along Palisades Park in the Santa Monica beach area is **Chez Jay**, 1657 Ocean Avenue (tel: 395-1741), a family-run establishment (Jay is Jay Fiondella) that has the look of a bar that incidentally serves food. During the day, it is, complete with a television blaring in the corner. But at night Jay's is magically transformed into a rather charming bistro serving gourmet fare to an enthusiastic and devoted clientele. The decor is vaguely nautical, with porthole windows, and candlelit tables covered with checkered cloths; a red-and-white-striped awning covers the bar and booths, and the floors are covered with sawdust and peanut shells (there are bowls of peanuts on the bar and tables).

The house specialty is steak au poivre comme chez Maxims ($8.75); regrettably, we haven't grounds to make a comparison, but this one was excellent. Also very good were the scampi en brochette with saffron rice ($6.50) and the combination filet mignon and lobster tail ($10.25). All entrees come with soup or salad, vegetable, potato and crunchy garlic toast. A reasonably comprehensive wine list is on the back of the menu. For dessert dig into a slice of Jay's homemade cheesecake (90¢).

At lunch (weekdays only) Jay's offers much plainer—and cheaper—fare: a seafood salad is $2.85, steamed clams $2.50, cheese omelet $2, and a cheeseburger is $1.75. But to get the really good meals, come any night, Sunday through Thursday from 6 to 11 p.m., Friday and Saturday from 6:30 to 11:30 p.m.

Though it opened well after Prohibition days (1964) **Sneeky Pete's**, 8907 Sunset Boulevard at San Vincente (tel: 657-5070), looks exactly like a speakeasy, or, more accurately, like the Hollywood version of a speakeasy. Pretty waitresses in fringed '20s garb serve up gigantic portions of steaks and chops. The decor: dimly lit, of course, by small table lamps and globe wall sconces, red tablecloths, tufted red leather booths, and walnut-paneled walls covered with hundreds of photos from the '20s era; the light being what it was, we could make out only Orson Welles, Babe Ruth, Shirley Temple, Aunt Jemima and a very early photo of J.F.K. There are also newspaper headlines announcing noteworthy events of the period, like "Lindbergh in Paris."

Only prime meats are served. All entrees come with potatoes or pasta and—surprise—a complimentary dish of fresh fruit. New York cut, filet mignon, or tournedos Béarnaise are all $10.95; steak Sinatra (sauteed with green peppers and marinara sauce) is $9.95, B-B-Q ribs $8.95, and stuffed shrimp with rice pilaff $8.95.

There's music, a piano bar trio, nightly. Dinner is served from 6 p.m. to 2 a.m.

Irish

There's only one place to go on March 17th, and that's **Tom Bergin's Tavern**, 840 South Fairfax Avenue just south of Wilshire Boulevard, Hollywood (tel: 936-7151)—headquarters for L.A.'s Irish community and, like many an Irish bar, a famous gathering place for sports writers, athletes and rabid fans.

This was the first L.A. restaurant to charter buses to pro football games—they still do, and hold 104 seats to the games reserved five years in advance. We always thought this kind of place existed only in New York and Dublin, but Bergin's has been going strong since 1936. Actors Bing Crosby and Pat O'Brien were early friends of the house. And drinkers who also happen to be actors and sports figures are still coming—you might see Cary Grant or even Marlon Brando (the only person who would dare come here in a ponytail) cached in a booth.

The pub ambience consists of photos and paintings of Bergin's friends plastered all over richly wood-paneled walls, not to mention some 1,000 cardboard shamrocks attached to the beamed ceiling above the bar. Jack Ohlsen, general manager emeritus, dreamed up the idea of hanging shamrocks to please Saint Patrick—each one bears the name of a favorite customer.

Irish coffee is a house specialty—about 5,000 are served up on Saint Patrick's Day. But you can also sit down to a hearty dinner in a rather charming fireplace dining room—perhaps a 12-ounce New York steak with onion rings, garlic cheese toast, salad, vegetable and baked potato ($8.25). More traditional Irish fare, served with soup or salad and garlic cheese toast, is Dublin corned beef and cabbage with a steamed potato ($5.50); or chicken Erin, simmered in cream and cider sauce, with bacon, leeks, mushrooms and rice pilaff ($6). Burgers and salads are also listed, and for dessert you can sample the pieman's wares—fresh fruit pies (95¢).

Lunch is less expensive, with entrees like Irish pot roast served with soup or salad, potato and garden vegetables ($3.75).

For the record, Bergin sold the Tavern in 1973 to two trusted regulars, Mike Mandekic and T. K. Vodrey, both of whom he knew would stick to traditions. They're expanding, opening a **Bergin's West** at 11600 San Vicente Boulevard, Brentwood, as we go to press.

Bergin's serves lunch from 11 a.m. weekdays, dinner from 5 p.m. nightly, and late supper until 12:30 a.m.

Italian

Emilio's, 6602 Melrose Avenue at Highland, Hollywood (tel: 935-4922). Save this one for a special—preferably romantic—occasion, but if you don't have one, make one. Not only is the food out of this world, but the atmosphere is authentic and romantically mellow from the traditional Italian music in the background to the gregarious Italian waiters. We don't wonder that Emilio's attracts a big celebrity clientele, people like Sinatra and Telly Savalas among them. It's a superb dining experience.

The downstairs dining room centers around the "Fountain de Trevi," bathed in colored lights. The decor is unrestrainedly ornate, with marble columns from floor to lofty ceiling, brick archways, stained-glass windows, lots of oil paintings and roses on every red-clothed table. You can also dine in the wine room, but our favorite spot for tender evenings is the cedar-paneled balcony, intimate and softly lit by red-bulbed papier-mâché lamps.

As for the award-winning Northern Italian cuisine, forget your budget and your diet; plan to order lavishly and savor every bite. You might begin with an Italian salad ($4 for two). The cioppino ($9) is a heartily recommended entree; another delectable choice is scampi in white wine ($8). There's a house specialty named for a famous Emilio's patron, chicken Don Rickles ($7), the preparation and ingredients of which we prefer to leave to the imagination—perhaps the waiter is required to insult you when serving it. Along with the entree, we like a small order of green fettuccine ($2.75)—what's an Italian meal without pasta? Ditto wine; if you're not sure what to order, ask the waiter to suggest an appropriate wine for your entree.

The other five desserts here are probably wonderful, but we've never been able to resist the creamy rich zabaglione ($3 for two) to find out.

Emilio's is open nightly from 5 p.m. to midnight, to 12:30 a.m. Friday and Saturday nights.

Chianti, 7383 Melrose Avenue, at Martel Avenue, Hollywood (tel: 653-8323). Opened in 1936 by the famous New York restaurateur Romeo Salta, this charming Northern Italian ristorante has a long history in Hollywood, going back to the days when the cast party for *Gone with the Wind* was held here. It's still the prestigious winner of many awards, and it's certainly one of the most popular restaurants in town. The decor successfully combines turn-of-the-century and art-nouveau elements with traditional Italiana; walls adorned with patinaed murals of Italy and gilt-framed oil paintings, romantic Italian background music, candlelight, and fresh flowers on every table.

The fare is the authentic *alta cucina* of Northern Italy, and the menu is completely in Italian; your waiter will be happy to help you out of linguistic dilemmas. The Caesar salad ($2.75) makes a good beginning. From there you might proceed to pasta, preferably the fettuccine alla Alfredo ($5)—one order is enough for two people if this isn't the main course. Veal dishes are the specialty, and we suggest you choose one for your entree—maybe scaloppine al Marsala, or piccata with lemon and butter. Both are priced at $7.75. For dessert why not linger over assorted fruits and cheeses ($2.75) with a pot of espresso?

Chianti is open for dinner Monday through Saturday from 5:30 to 11:30 p.m.

If you'd like an aria along with your Italian fare, head for **Christiani's**, 7066 Santa Monica Boulevard at La Brea, Hollywood (tel: 464-8635). Owner John Christiani, a tenor, entertains with Neopolitan ballads at dinnertime, and guests and friends—some of whom are professional opera-singers—get up and perform arias, light opera and show tunes. The festive atmosphere attracts many movie people from nearby studios. It's a warm and cozy place, with seating (in leather-upholstered captain's chairs) under a green awning, candlelight and framed art reproductions on light wood-paneled walls. The bar is under an awning, too—a red-and-white-striped one.

Traditional Italian entrees are served with a relish tray, homemade soup, salad and garlic toast. You might order a delicately sauteed veal piccata with lemon sauce and butter ($6.95), or an antipasto ($2.50) followed by one of the pasta dishes, like spaghetti Caruso ($3.75) with tomato sauce and chicken livers.

Christiani's is open for lunch weekdays from 11 a.m. to 2:30 p.m. (no music) and dinner from 6 p.m. Tuesday through Saturday.

Moroccan

Pass through the immense carved brass doors and you're in another world, the exotic Arab world of **Dar Maghred**, 7651 Sunset Boulevard at Stanley, Hollywood (tel: 876-7651). You enter into a Coranic patio, at the center of which is an exquisite fountain under an open skylight. The floor is marble, and the carved wood and plaster walls are decorated with handmade tiles in geometric designs. A kaftaned hostess greets you and leads you to either the Rabat or Berber room. The former, named for the palatial decor typical of wealthy Rabat homes, features high ceilings, intricately hand-painted and gold-leafed in geometric pattern. There are rich Rabat carpets on the floor, marquetry tables, silk cushions with spun-gold-thread designs, and velvet-covered straw bread baskets from Fez strewn about. The Berber rooms are more rustic, reflecting the homes of the cold mountain country of the High Atlas. Warm earth tones—orange, brown and gold—are used, the rugs are from the mountain areas, brass tables and trays from Marrakech replace the marquetry ones, and the wood-beamed ceilings are painted in a traditional design.

In both rooms, diners sit on low sofas against the wall and on goatskin poufs (cushions). Berber and Andalousian music is played in the background.

The meal is a multicourse feast, eaten with your hands and hunks of bread, and shared, from the same dish, with other members of your party. It begins when the tea girl in traditional costume comes around and washes everyone's hands. There are five possible dinners, priced at $11.50 or $12.50 per person. We suggest the Fassi Feast (from Fez). It begins with a Moroccan salad of cold raw and cooked vegetables, including tomatoes and green peppers with eggplant, carrots and oranges, and cucumbers. You scoop it up with hunks of fresh-baked bread. Eat sparingly and slowly—there's a lot more to come. Next is bstilla, an appetizer of shredded chicken, eggs, almonds and spices wrapped in a flaky pastry shell and topped with powdered sugar and cinnamon.

Now comes a tajine (bell-shaped pottery dish) of chicken cooked with pickled lemons, onions and fresh coriander. By this time you're well into enjoying eating with your hands, and hopefully you've ordered some wine to drink each course down with. We still dream about the next course—lahm Mrhosia—lamb slowly cooked in honey, almonds, onions, raisins and spices. It's followed by couscous with vegetables—squash, carrots, garbanzo beans, turnips, onions, eggplants, raisins and a very hot sauce on the side.

Dessert is a bowl of several kinds of fresh fruit, and sometimes a cookie or pastry. Now it's time for another hand-washing, with hot towels perfumed with orange-blossom water, followed by the tea-pouring ceremony—a veritable performance, the mint tea poured with expertise from a height of several feet.

The emphasis is on relaxed and leisurely dining; you'll enjoy it most if you eat just a little of everything, and eat very slowly. Don't miss Dar Maghred; it's a memorable experience. Dinner is served nightly from 6 p.m.

French

L.A. restaurant critics and *Gourmet* Magazine has heaped lavish praise on **Le Cellier**, 2628 Wilshire Boulevard in Santa Monica (tel: 828-1585). The food, prepared under the careful and demanding scrutiny of award-winning chef Jean Bellordre, is divine, and the decor is cozily French provincial.

To begin, the authentic onion soup gratinee ($1.75) will evoke memories of late-night Les Halles (assuming you were ever in Les Halles, of course). Favorite dinner entrees include the veal forestière (served with wild mushrooms) for $8; a terrific steak au poivre blanc—entrecôte sauteed with white cracked pepper and flamed in brandy ($8.95); and whole baby rack of lamb bouquetière (surrounded by fresh vegetables), $7.95. All entrees include soup, salad and assorted vegetables. The sous-chef is an expert pâtissier, so be sure and sample one of his homemade desserts ($1.75).

Our idea of a perfect lunch is the salad Niçoise ($3.60) or a cheese soufflé served with a mixed green salad ($3.25). A good wine list is, of course, available.

Open for lunch Tuesday through Friday from 11:30 a.m. to 2:30 p.m.; dinner is served nightly except Monday from 5:30 p.m.

Another notable French restaurant, this one in the heart of downtown, is **François,** in the Atlantic Richfield Plaza on Flower Street between 5th and 6th Streets (tel: 680-2727). (The Plaza, by the way, is a meandering world of shops, boutiques, restaurants, bookstores, galleries, etc., beneath the Atlantic Richfield/Bank of America Twin Towers—a worthwhile place to browse.) François, one of several Plaza eateries, is ornately Old World, offering a sumptuously appointed European decor and an equally sumptuous menu of French specialties. It's kind of a formal place; gentlemen are required to wear jacket and tie even at lunch.

The menu lists a wide selection of hot and cold hors d'oeuvres; we're partial to the mousse of fresh salmon with Nantua sauce (that's a sauce made up of crayfish, butter, vegetables, cognac, white wine and spices, among other things) for $3. If we're ordering a soup course as well, it's the avocado cream ($1.50) every time. The most impressive specialty of the house is roasted pheasant prepared in a sealed earthenware casserole with foie gras and truffles ($22 for two). Simpler palates and smaller budgets might content themselves with the red snapper ($5.95) or sand dabs Grenobloise—with diced lemon and capers ($5.85).

Desserts are listed (in rough translation), as the devil's temptations on a cart; sell your soul for $1.50.

Lunch can be managed for less if you order carefully, and from 6 to 7:30 p.m. a full pre-theater dinner is just $8.95. Lunch is served weekdays from 11:30 a.m. to 2 p.m.; dinner Monday through Saturday from 6 to 11 p.m.

Japanese

We've already made mention of **Yamato,** Century Plaza Hotel, Century City (tel: 277-1840) in our hotel listings, but just to make sure you get there, we're repeating it here, too. We think it's L.A.'s most beautiful Japanese restaurant, adorned with valuable antiques from all parts of Japan. Two massive Buddhist temple dogs—at least four centuries old—stand as guardians against evil in the foyer. The elaborately carved overhead beams, 350 years old, are from Kyoto, and the fusumas—made into decorative panels—are 250 years old.

You can dine Occidental style at tables with bamboo chairs, but we much prefer the privacy of the shoji-screened tatami rooms, where you sit on cushions. These latter rooms are simply adorned with a Japanese painting or scroll, and a flower arrangement. Shoes are checked, and your meal is served by a waitress in classic kimono. There's no problem sitting, as there's a well under the table—actually you can change positions with much more freedom than at a regular table. And we love lingering over relaxed conversation and sake in our own private dining compartment. If you want a tatami room, it's a good idea to so specify when making a reservation.

The fare is authentic and artfully prepared, and where concessions are made to the Western palate they're so innovative that they enhance rather than diminish the traditional cuisine. Our favorite meal at Yamato begins with the ordering of sake, served warm in a porcelain bottle ($2.35). The sashimi appetizer is a must, priced according to the kind of fish and the amount ordered. Next—here comes the West—half an avocado stuffed with shrimps, in a perfectly delicate and tangy dressing only the Japanese could create ($3.50). If we have a willing dining companion, we can think of nothing better than sharing orders of lobster tail seasoned in sake, butter and miso sauce ($11.50) and top sirloin teriyaki ($8.75). The entrees are served with soup, rice, vegetables and green tea; somewhere along the way, another bottle of sake is indicated. Green tea ice cream ($1) makes a very refreshing dessert.

That's rather an expensive meal, and we think it's well worth the price, but you can choose carefully and dine for considerably less. Catering to the ABC Entertainment Center crowds from across the street, Yamato also offers very reasonable pre-theater and late supper (from 10:30 p.m.) specials. Meals are also moderately priced at lunch, served weekdays only. Dinners are served nightly from 5 p.m. to midnight.

Scandinavian

Right in the heart of chic Beverly Hills shopping turf (about half the lunchtime patrons are loaded down with shopping bags), **Konditori**, 362 North Camden Drive at Brighton Way (tel: 550-9950), looks like an especially attractive coffee shop with a few provincial touches—old-fashioned wallpaper, beamed ceilings and wood-paneled walls. It's light and airy, the red and blue booths are most comfortable, and the food is very good indeed.

At dinner you can sample Swedish delicacies from a groaning smorgasbord: for a prix-fixe $7.50 you get three kinds of homemade herring, egg with shrimps, cured and poached salmon, cold cuts, liver pâté, cheeses and salads, plus a hot entree of Swedish meatballs or biff Lindstrom, the latter not Willy Loman's Swedish nephew but ground sirloin with chopped onions, beets and capers.

If smorgasbord eating doesn't appeal to you, entrees are also available à la carte, served with soup or salad. You might consider the poached filet of sole Walewska, served with chablis and cheese sauce, lobster and truffles ($6.50). And it's folly not to order the homemade desserts, be they the temptingly showcased cakes ($1.50) or Swedish pancakes with lingonberries ($2.75). At lunch, cold open-faced sandwiches are mostly in the $2.35-to-$3 range, and there are marvelous cold plates like boiled salmon with cucumber salad and dill sauce ($4.25).

Lunch and dinner are served Monday through Saturday.

A Mixed Bag

The Warehouse, 4499 Admiralty Way, Marina Del Rey (tel: 823-5451), is the creation of photographer Burt Hixson, who traveled 23,000 miles in a quest to find the perfect decor for his dream restaurant. Remembering the exotic wharves he had seen, he erected a two-level dockside structure, where one now dines on casks and barrels, or inside wooden packing crates. Burlap coffee bags line the walls; there's netting, rope and peacock chairs. The place is entered via a tropical walkway of bamboo and palm that extends over a large fish pond. Hixson's photos line the walls, and customers line up to get into this unusual restaurant, which is not only colorful, but surprisingly unfunky and elegant. Most of the tables have a view of the marina, and many are outside right on the water.

The most lavish buffet we've ever seen, and one of the best we've ever eaten, is served at lunch weekdays for $3.95. Dinner is à la carte, with entrees from the world over: Brazilian-style chicken and beef brochette ($6.95), Bangalore chicken curry ($6.50), steak teriyaki ($7.75), etc. You can even get a steak, American style, with a baked potato and corn on the cob ($9.50). Drink it down with beer from whatever nation you wish, or an exotic rum concoction.

A talented harpist entertains nightly. Is the Warehouse touristy? Certainly, but with a free concert, excellent food and all that atmosphere, who cares?

Open from 11 a.m. to 2 a.m. weekdays, from 2 p.m. Saturday and Sunday.

MODERATELY PRICED RESTAURANTS: The following kinder-to-your-wallet selections are in the price range most of us choose when dining out if there's no special occasion. But take note that many of the aforementioned expensive places are very affordable at lunch.

American/Continental

One of L.A.'s oldest and most cherished restaurants is the **Pacific Dining Car,** 1310 West 6th Street, corner of Witmer, East Wilshire (tel: 483-6000). The Idol family has been running a tight ship (or should we say train—it's actually housed in a wood-paneled Pacific Railroad luxury dining car with a few rooms added on) since 1921. The winning combination of large portions of terrific food and a relaxed ambience makes this one of the few "in" diners in America; you might see Glenn Ford, Richard Thomas or Liza Minnelli—big P.D.C. fans all—at the next table. It's also one of the few diners with an extensive list of imported and California wines.

Open-grill, charcoal-broiled items are the house specialties; only prime meats and fresh vegetables are used, and all desserts are homemade. At lunch a steak sandwich is $4.95, an eight-ounce cheeseburger with cole slaw $3.25. Broiled half chicken ($6.50) is a favorite dinner entree. For dessert dig into some homemade apple pie ($1.15).

Pacific Dining Car is open weekdays from 7 a.m. to 11 p.m., Saturday 5 to 11 p.m. and Sunday 4 to 10 p.m.

Cafe Figaro, 9010 Melrose Avenue at Santa Monica Boulevard (tel: 274-7664). The original Figaro was a Greenwich Village institution, New York headquarters of the beat generation. But rent drove this renowned cafe out of town (it was replaced by a Blimpie Base much to the horror of old patrons) and where should it resurface but in West Hollywood. Those of you who hung out at the New York Figaro will experience a definite feeling of déjà vu—it's almost identical to the old place with a meandering series of rooms, Tiffany lamps overhead, an eclectic assortment of chairs and oak pedestal tables, walls covered with shellacked copies of the French newspaper *Le Figaro,* classical music, hip-looking waitresses, even a real Macdougal Street sign at the cash register. And like its New York prototype (which, for the record, has recently re-replaced the Blimpie Base at its old location) it's the perfect funky hangout. People sit for hours sipping espresso, playing chess, chatting, reading, discussing the art scene, and doodling on the napkins.

The menu lists a lot more than espresso, however; you might order shrimp curry ($5); ground sirloin with fresh mushrooms and ragoût sauce, served with fresh vegetables and potatoes ($3.75); omelets filled with anything from strawberries and sour cream ($3.50); to diced chicken and mushrooms in white wine sauce ($2.25). All the above items are served with fresh-baked bread and fresh fruit. A goblet of house wine is 80¢, and there's a wide selection of teas and fancy coffees. Best yet, this may be the only place in California (maybe in the world) where you can dine on escargots ($6.50) and have a hot fudge sundae ($1.50) for dessert.

Open weekdays 11:30 to 2 a.m., Friday and Saturday till 3 a.m., and Sunday 4 p.m. to 2 a.m.

The **Great American Food and Beverage Co.**, 8500 Santa Monica Boulevard at La Cienega, West Hollywood (tel: 652-9594), is a friendly, funky and fun-loving place, where regular patrons include Cher, J.J. Walker and many of Kotter's Sweathogs. The decor is vaguely Victorian, with Tiffany-style lamps and slow-turning fans overhead, lots of plants, bentwood chairs, 19th-century inn and shop signs, old photographs, even an oil portrait of Queen Victoria. There's also seating on the patio under the shade of an awning.

Waitresses in long dresses and waiters in knickers and suspenders not only serve food, but also entertain. One by one, throughout the day, they put down menus, pick up guitars and sing; occasionally there's a mime, juggler or comedian. They're all quite good.

The specialty here is the hi-pocket, a sandwich in pita bread served with the unusual accompaniments of corn on the cob, fresh fruit and the unprecedented choice of BBQ ribs or yogurt. Prices range from $2.95 to $3.95, pita fillings from Italian sausage with onions, peppers, mushrooms and mozzarella cheese to sauteed mixed Chinese vegetables, egg and melted cheese. The same variety of fillings can be had in an omelet. You might finish up with a fancy coffee creation like the cafe Gauguin—chocolate ice cream, cinnamon, espresso and real whipped cream ($1.50), a Ghirardelli hot chocolate drink (95¢) or a super banana split ($2.95).

About 15 items are listed at $1 less than usual on a special luncheon menu served from 11:30 a.m. to 4:30 p.m. Open 11:30 to midnight Sunday through Thursday, till 2 a.m. Friday and Saturday.

Organic/Natural Foods

The Source, 8301 Sunset Boulevard at Sweetzer Avenue, West Hollywood (tel: 656-6388), is a vegetarian organic restaurant that doesn't serve anything that, when alive, could have walked, swum or flown away. The place attracts a young and indeed healthy-looking crowd. Inside it's quite pleasant with dark wood-paneled walls, brown carpeting, maple chairs and round pedestal tables. Those who want fresh air with their health food shouldn't be in L.A., but they can gasp for what's available while dining outside at one of the umbrellaed tables.

A typical dinner is the cheese walnut loaf ($4.25), served with soup or salad, a basket of whole wheat rolls and butter. Homemade soups, salads and sandwiches are also available. For dessert there's a so-good-it's-hard-to-believe-it's-healthy homemade date nut cheesecake ($1.25).

Open weekdays for lunch and dinner. On Saturday and Sunday it's open from 9 a.m. to 1 p.m. for breakfast and lunch. For breakfast, how about hot cereal ($2.65) made from ground oats and wheat, topped with sunflower seeds, raisins, bananas, apples and nuts?

Old World, 1019 Westwood Boulevard at Weyburn, Westwood (tel: 477-2033), is our favorite kind of health-oriented eatery. They serve wine and beer along with the organically grown veggies and grainy breads, and you can keep your junk-food-laden system from going into sudden health shock with a rich, sugary dessert. As the name suggests, the interior is a rambling series of rooms with a country-inn ambience—plank wood floors, stained-glass windows, a lovely antique fireplace filled with plants, lots of ceramic tiling, Tudor walls and beamed stucco ceilings.

Omelets made with organic eggs, and served with whole wheat toast and German fries, are priced according to the filling—$3.60 for chopped sirloin, spinach and onions, $3.25 for avocado and cheese, etc. A turkey sandwich (turkeys are also organically grown) with melted cheddar, alfalfa sprouts and tomato on whole wheat, served with fresh vegetables, is $2.75. Vegetable casseroles and salads are also listed. Those with heartier appetites can dig into a "swinger steak," 12 ounces of ground beef mixed with chopped onions, olives, green peppers and cheddar cheese ($4.95); or baked organic chicken with mashed potatoes and gravy ($5.25). Serious health-food enthusiasts might put together a meal of fresh vegetables (50¢), brown rice (75¢), yogurt (75¢) and fresh fruit ($1.25).

Popular for breakfast, dessert or any time throughout the day are the Belgian waffles made with soya and wheat flour and topped with maple syrup or wild honey ($1.65), strawberries and whipped cream ($2.10), or homemade (with only natural ingredients) ice cream with hot fudge, whipped cream and nuts ($2.75).

Open weekdays from 11 a.m. to midnight, Saturday from 10 to 1 a.m., Sunday from 9:30 to 12:30 a.m.

Crêpes and Omelets

The Egg and The Eye, 5814 Wilshire Boulevard, right across from the La Brea Tar Pits, is one of the most popular restaurants in town (tel: 933-5596). As the name vaguely implies, the Egg stands for the 54 varieties of omelets featured upstairs in a pleasant and airy restaurant furnished with butcher-block tables and bentwood chairs; the Eye symbolizes the visual arts and crafts found in the galleries on the first and third floors—contemporary works ranging from Moroccan handmade rugs to Byzantine painted eggs and Eskimo sculpture. You can enjoy the exhibits before or after dining; if there's a long line waiting for the 150 seats (a more than likely occurrence), give your name to the maitre d' and you can browse around until your table is ready.

The reason for the lines is that the omelets are truly excellent, artfully prepared the French way and filled with all kinds of good things: caviar and sour cream ($5.25), capers, anchovies, parsley and shallots ($4.20), potatoes, sour cream and chives ($3.80), pâté de foie gras, truffles and asparagus spears ($5) and even, for those folks who like it on everything, peanut butter ($3.85). If we're dining with a friend, we like to share an omelet (they're big) and a salad Niçoise ($3.50). A basket of black raisin bread and butter comes with all meals, and though there are dessert omelets (shaved chocolate, powdered sugar with rum flambée), we prefer a more traditional strawberry shortcake ($1.75).

Open Tuesday through Friday from 11 a.m. to 3:30 p.m. and again from 5 to 10 p.m.; Saturday 10 a.m. to 11 p.m.; Sunday 11 a.m. to 6 p.m.

Moving from omelets to crêpes, there is a branch of **The Magic Pan** in Beverly Hills at 9601 Brighton Way at Camden (tel: 274-5222). This member of the deservedly famous chain turns out, like all the others, luscious French crêpes and delicate Hungarian palacsintas prepared on the special Magic Pan crêpe wheel. As always, the ambience is charmingly French provincial.

An order of two crêpes filled with spinach soufflé is $3.30, $4.85 with king crab in bechamel sauce and sherry, $1.65 for cheese blintz filling with sour cream and strawberries. An avocado salad on the side is $1.20, a glass of wine 95¢. The dessert crêpes are irresistible with fillings like vanilla ice cream smothered in melted bittersweet chocolate and topped with pecan cream ($1.75).

Open weekdays 11 a.m. to midnight, Friday and Saturday till 1 a.m., and Sunday from 10 a.m.

A wide selection of light and delectable crêpes is featured at **Chez Puce,** 708 Pico Boulevard at Lincoln, Santa Monica (tel: 399-5162). The charming, slightly eccentric owners, Brittany-born Jeanne Caradec (everyone calls her

"Puce") and Parisian Robert Duc (everyone calls *them* "Puce Deux") have been running this unpretentious and thoroughly delightful place for five years. The white walls are decorated with photos of dogs, leopards and lions—les Puce Deux love animals "because they are so sincere." There are also signed photos of celebrity customers like Diahann Caroll.

Over 30 tasty crêpe selections are listed: garlic butter, cheese, clams and shrimp is $4, ratatouille and cheese $3, garlic butter, egg, mushroom and pepperoni $3.25. In addition you can create your own combinations. Only fresh vegetables are used. They also serve pizza, which Puce tells us is popular in the south of France; prices begin at $2 for an unadorned small pie (not really so small) and ascend to $4 with the works—bell pepper, mushrooms, onions, olives, anchovies, salami, pepperoni and sausage. A mixed salad on the side is 70¢, and there's quite a nice selection of wines for so simple an establishment; a quarter liter of the house wine is 80¢. For dessert how about a crêpe with almond custard, ice cream and chocolate fudge ($2.75)?

Open Sunday through Thursday from 5 p.m. to midnight, Friday and Saturday till 2 a.m.; closed Tuesday.

Mexican

Macho's, 939 Broxton Avenue, just west of Westwood Boulevard, Westwood (tel: 478-1241), offers an unusually subtle Mexican cuisine, all made with prime-grade beef and other fine ingredients. Though indoors, the dining area has the look of a colorful Mexican courtyard, with tables and booths separated from each other by macrame hangings, old-fashioned globe street lamps, terracotta tile floors, leather-upholstered bamboo chairs, and baskets of dried flowers hanging from narrow pillars. There's more seating in the balcony under lovely Indonesian batik-fringed lamp umbrellas.

A Mexican paella is $6.50 at dinner. Arroz con pollo (chunks of chicken breast in a rich sauce of green peppers, onions, tomatoes and spices) is $4.15, served with two hot tortillas rolled in butter, rice, beans and fresh fruit; the same meal substituting large shrimp for chicken is $5.25. It's all incredibly good, and the deserta quesadilla—a deep-fried flour tortilla coated with honey and cinnamon, topped with a scoop of sherbert ($1.50)—is spectacular. Be sure to try one of Macho's famous frozen margaritas with your meal.

At lunch there's a choice of six $2.95 combination plates, all served with rice, beans and fresh fruit, and that heavenly dessert is only 95¢.

There's live Mexican entertainment Friday and Saturday nights, when Macho's stays open till 1 a.m.; Monday through Thursday the hours are 11 a.m. to midnight; Sunday, 4 to 11 p.m.

Lucy's El Adobe, 5536 Melrose Avenue at Plymouth Boulevard, Hollywood (tel: 462-9421), was a base for Jerry Brown's presidential campaign, and has long been a great favorite of his. In the early days he used to help out owners Lucy and Frank Casado in the kitchen, and there's even a Jerry Brown special, arroz con pollo ($4). The Governor's not the only famous patron—you might see Hubert Humphrey downing the enchiladas here, not to mention Orson Welles, Louise Lasser or Richard Thomas.

There are two dining rooms, neither of which is particularly fancy, with cream-colored brick or stucco walls, gaslight-style lamps, and seating in bentwood chairs or comfortable leather booths.

But if the decor is unpretentious, the food is great and the service very friendly. Best bet is the chef's special combination—taco, enchilada, chile relleno, soup, salad, rice, beans and hot buttered tortilla ($3.75). A smaller combination dinner for the "leetle people" is $2.25.

Open Monday through Saturday from 11:30 a.m. to 11:30 p.m.

Antonio's, 7472 Melrose Avenue at Stanley, Hollywood (tel: 655-0480), has received rave reviews in *Gourmet* and many other magazines. One writer called it "one of the most outstanding dining bargains in the city." We think it lives up to its reputation. The decor is simple but attractive—there are three rooms with terra-cotta tile floors, leather booths divided by grillwork partitions, Mexican murals and lots of oil paintings on the stucco walls and big baskets of paper flowers hanging from the ceiling.

But the artfully prepared food is where Antonio's really comes into its own. Especially good is the chicken mole ($4.25), which subtly combines about 20 ingredients, including chocolate, chopped blanched almonds and a variety of finely chopped chilies, to produce a fantastic taste and texture. We like to precede this treat with an order of guacamole and corn chips ($1.50). Other highly recommended entrees are shrimp in garlic sauce ($5.95) and Antonio's Special, enchilada, taco and New York steak with guacamole ($5.95). All entrees are served with rice and refried beans. Fried bananas ($1) make a delicious dessert, but if you've put away a lot of food you might prefer the lighter Mexican flan (95¢).

On the luncheon menu, all items but one are under $2.50.

Lunch is served weekdays only, dinner nightly from 5 to 11 p.m. (till midnight Friday and Saturday).

The Red Onion, 6424 Conoga Avenue, Woodland Hills (tel: 340-5653), is an excellent and delightful reproduction of an old Mexican village—a big stucco and brick building with a terra-cotta tile roof, a rambling outdoor patio, and room after room connected by stucco archways. The attention to architectural detail is astounding; even the steps are well worn, belying the fact that the Red Onion is only a year old. There's lush tropical foliage everywhere, and the rooms have old beamed ceilings and barnwood or stucco walls, adorned with authentic ceramic crockery, photos of old Mexico and antiques.

It's a particularly pleasant place to while away an afternoon—have a cocktail in the Cantina Bar, maybe even enjoy a game of backgammon in a peacock chair before you dine or over after-dinner drinks.

We like to begin by ordering a pitcher of margaritas ($1.25 to $5, depending on how tipsy you want to get). For an appetizer we suggest guacamole salad ($1.75) or a bowl of gazpacho served with sour cream, croutons and a slice of lemon (85¢). Dinner specialties, served with soup or salad, include a casserole of arroz con pollo—big chunks of chicken breast on a bed of Spanish rice with tortillas ($4.75). And scrumptious combination plates are $2.10 to $4.95, the latter for the all-inclusive deluxe which could feed an entire Mexican family for two weeks. There's even a section of the menu for the weight-conscious gringo, and hearty Mexican breakfasts—like an avocado omelet with Spanish rice ($2.95)—are served all day.

There's live music (easy listening) for dancing in the Cantina Bar Monday through Saturday, and live rock music in the Sonora Saloon downstairs several nights a week.

Open daily from 11 a.m. to 2 a.m.; Sunday brunch, served from 10 a.m., is extremely popular.

Chinese

The **Cafe de Chine,** 1066 South Fairfax Avenue, between Olympic and Pico Boulevards, midtown (tel: 935-4713), is a lone Chinese restaurant in the midst of Jewish-deli land. The decor is your basic Chinese restaurant hodgepodge, with red leather booths, linoleum tile floors, red-and-white-checked tablecloths adorned with plastic flowers, and a Chinese seascape mural along one wall.

But the food, basically Mandarin with some Szechuan items, is excellent. This is one of the few restaurants where in addition to moo shu pork ($3.75), there's also moo shu chicken ($3.50) or beef ($3.75). Also recommended are the sizzling rice chicken ($3.75) and garlic shrimps ($3.75). A half bottle of Christian Brothers wine with your meal is $2.50. At lunch, weekdays, in addition to the regular menu you can choose from any of ten complete meals priced from $1.60 to $2.

Open daily from 11:30 a.m. to 10 p.m.

Twin Dragon, 8597 West Pico Boulevard at Holt Avenue, just south of Beverly Hills (tel: 657-7355), is the domain of owner/chef Mr. Chang Yuk Sun, a master of Shanghai culinary arts. A little fancier than our previous listing, Twin Dragon is a large and comfortable restaurant with Chinese instruments decorating the walls and a medallion of a dragon complete with red electric eyes.

Highly recommended are the spicy diced chicken with peanuts ($4.50), braised shrimp spiced with chili peppers ($4.75), and the sauteed shredded beef ($4.60). If you're in the mood for noodles, there's a wide variety—with shrimp, ham and chicken, beef, etc. ($2.50). Special weekday luncheons are just $1.45; unfortunately they're in the chop-suey-wonton-eggroll category.

Open daily 11:30 a.m. to 10 p.m. (till 11:30 p.m. Friday and Saturday nights).

Madame Wu's Garden, 2201 Wilshire Boulevard, Santa Monica (tel: 828-5656), is entering its 16th year as an L.A. institution. John Canaday gave it one last rave in his swansong restaurant column before retiring, and the banquet-room walls are lined with photos of famous clients—Bob Hope, Mae West, Johnny Carson, Carol Burnett, Jack Lemmon, et al. The decor in the main dining area is suitably posh, with Madame Wu's extensive jade collection displayed in glass cases lining the walls, a gently splashing fountain at the courtyard entrance, a tree growing through the roof inside and live birds in cages enhancing the nature motif.

The famous specialty is Wu's beef ($5.50), a delicious concoction smothered in crunchy rice noodles.

Open for lunch weekdays, dinner nightly till 10 p.m.

A landmark in the downtown garment district, the **New Moon,** 912 South San Pedro Street (tel: 622-1091), is a local favorite for top-notch gourmet Cantonese fare. The decor is undistinguished but quite pleasant, with a few little niceties like fresh flowers on every table. Most notable is the New Moon's size—it's huge.

The menu is more wide-ranging than at most Cantonese restaurants. You might begin your meal with an appetizer of rumaki—chicken livers stuffed with water chestnuts and wrapped in bacon ($1.75 for an order of six); or out-of-this-world bacon pressed butterfly shrimp ($3.10 for an order of four). Some of the unique entrees you can try here include steamed cubes of chicken with mushrooms and Chinese sausage ($3.55), shredded chicken salad mixed with shredded lettuce and crisp fried wonton in a soy and sesame dressing ($3.30), and, continuing in a "fowl mood," chicken walnut ($3.55). Also very good are the steamed fish ($4.50), ginger beef ($3.35) and crusty almond duck in cherry sweet and sour sauce ($3.40). Ginger ice cream is the perfect dessert (55¢). Prices are slightly reduced at lunch.

Open daily for lunch from 11 a.m. to 3 p.m. and dinner from 3 to 10 p.m.

Japanese

One of the top-rated Japanese restaurants in L.A. is **Tokyo Kaikan,** 225 South San Pedro Street between 2nd and 3rd, downtwon (tel: 489-1333). It's designed to look like a traditional Japanese country inn with brightly colored globe lights overhead, barnwood, bamboo and rattan covered walls adorned with straw baskets and other provincial artifacts. In addition to the regular seating, there are four food bars—tempura, steak, shabu-shabu and sushi.

A la Carte entrees served with soup, vegetables and rice include beef sukiyaki ($5.50), chicken teriyaki ($4.50), and salmon butter-yaki ($4.50). A bottle of hot sake with your meal is $1.50. At lunch we like to order the tekka-maki sushi—raw tunafish rolled with seaweed ($3.50), though shabu-shabu is also tempting at $4.50. The lunch menu also offers some great combination meals, like chicken teriyaki, umani beef and vegetables, fried shrimp, sweet potato and vegetables ($3.20). Either meal, green tea or ginger ice cream (50¢) is the perfect dessert.

Tokyo Kaikan is open for lunch from 11:30 a.m. to 2 p.m., for dinner from 6 to 10:30 p.m. Closed Sundays. There's another branch nearby at 337 East 1st Street, off San Pedro. The menu and the hours are the same, except that this one is closed on Mondays.

A little-known but very fine restaurant, **Mikasa,** 12468 Washington Boulevard near Centinela, Venice (tel: 391-8381), caters to a small but devoted crowd of Japanese-food aficionados. The decor is pleasant; there are about nine leather booths, a few shoji-screen dividers, paper lanterns overhead and colorful little umbrellas on the walls.

Best buys are the combination dinners, such as the one that includes sashimi, beef or chicken teriyaki, soup, salad, sunomono (marinated cucumbers), rice and green tea ($4.35). If raw fish is not your thing you can substitute shrimp and vegetable tempura for the sashimi. Full donburi meals—large bowls of rice covered with sukiyaki, shrimp, chicken or pork—are $2.35 to $2.50. Interesting side orders are the cold spinach in sesame and soy dressing (95¢) and the cold bean curd ($1), both of which are infinitely more appetizing than their descriptions sound. And, of course, a decanter of sake ($1.50) is *de rigueur.*

Open nightly for dinner, except Tuesday, from 4:30 p.m.

Another good choice, if you happen to be in Pasadena, is **Miyako,** 139 South Los Robles, just south of Colorado Boulevard (tel: 795-7005). The surroundings are a little more elegant than the above-mentioned, and there's a choice of tatami-room or armchair service. Those who choose the latter will enjoy a view of a small Japanese garden.

All full dinners include soup, salad, rice, tea and cookies. With a combination entree of top sirloin teriyaki, shrimp tempura and skewered chicken teriyaki, such a dinner would run $6.95; $5.50 for salmon teriyaki; $5.75 for chicken teriyaki and shrimp tempura combination.

Complete children's dinners are offered for $2.75 to $3.25, which makes Miyako an excellent place to introduce the kids to Japanese cuisine. And at lunch, full meals are much reduced in price: $2.20 to $3.75.

Miyako offers some exotic drinks like the Madame Butterfly—a coconut-flavored vodka creation ($1.40)—and a gin and sake martini ($1.25), in addition to sake and Japanese beer.

Lunch is served weekdays from 11:30 a.m. to 2 p.m., dinner nightly from 5:30 to 10 p.m.

Genji, 310 Washington Street, Washington Square (tel: 822-5152) is a relative newcomer to the Marina del Rey restaurant scene, and a most welcome addition it is. It's named for a charming and talented prince of ancient Japan, who was always a favorite historical personage of owner George Matsuda. The prince was married to a girl called Murasaki, which means purple and accounts for the generous use of purple and plum shades in the attractive decor, e.g. the carpeting. Furnishings consist of butcher-block tables and modern design teak chairs, Japanese prints adorn the walls, and there's taped Japanese music in the background.

We like the kamemeshi—beef, chicken or shrimp on seasoned rice served in a special cooker ($4.95). Also recommended are the mixed shrimp, fish and vegetable tempura ($5.95) and the mixed sushi dinners ($5.75). All of the above are served with soup, salad, rice, dessert and Japanese genmai cha (a delicious green tea steeped in popped rice).

Open for lunch Monday through Saturday, for dinner nightly from 5 to 11 p.m.

Polynesian

Don the Beachcomber, 1727 North McCadden Place, just north of Hollywood Boulevard, Hollywood (tel: 469-3968), has been delighting locals with South Seas fare since 1934. (There actually is a Don the Beachcomber, now suitably retired in Honolulu.) The famous "Zombie," an intoxicating blend of light and dark rums, triple sec, creme de almond and fruit juices, was created here, and early patrons included Charlie Chaplin and many other Hollywood greats. Of course the island decor is lush and exotic—lots of tropical foliage, indoor waterfalls, peacock chairs, an abundance of bamboo and rattan, and hula music in the background.

Lunch, served Monday through Friday, is buffet only—an enticing $3.50 spread. There's also a bountiful dinner buffet priced at $4.95—lots of hot dishes like sweet and sour pork, barbecued chicken and ribs, turbot in cream, fried rice, several salads and dessert. If you're watching your budget, the buffets are the best buy; à la carte ordering can get expensive here.

A la carte, dinner might begin with an order of fried shrimp ($3.65) or eggrolls ($2.75). For an entree perhaps chicken sauteed with thinly sliced pineapple, green pepper and mushrooms ($5.50). Desserts vary from three simple but tasty almond cookies (50¢) to coconut and macadamia nut ice cream served in a pineapple shell with flaming liqueurs ($1.95).

Open for dinner nightly.

English

The **Cock 'n Bull,** 9170 Sunset Boulevard at Doheny Road, West Hollywood (tel: 273-0081), is "dedicated to serve those multitudinous wayfarers who wish to whet their appetites and titillate their sensitive palates in an atmosphere of tranquil charm and serene antiquity." Well, "those multitudinous wayfarers" who hang out at Sunset Strip's official pub include Richard Burton (previously with Liz), Jack Lemmon, Paul Newman and Joanne Woodward, among many, many others. This pleasantly atmospheric bar, with heavy oak tables, copper lanterns, beamed ceilings, a large brick fireplace, hunting prints and mounted trophies on the walls, is a Hollywood tradition that has been going strong since 1937. A leaded-glass case displays mementoes of original owner John Morgan (his son now runs the place), including a letter from Buckingham Palace.

Though many come here for serious drinking and schmoozing, many also come to partake of the hearty buffet meals. An $8.50 dinner from "the board" might contain rare roast beef, roast turkey, duckling, lamb, steak and kidney pie and perhaps a curry dish, not to mention appetizer, salad, dessert and coffee. The $3.75 luncheon is reduced, but still more than ample; ditto the famous $5 Sunday brunch that adds the likes of kippered herring and finnan haddie to traditional American fare. All desserts are homemade on the premises, and fresh-baked crumpets are served with lunch and dinner.

Open daily.

Hungarian

Old-world atmosphere and food like mamma used to make are the homey offerings at **Budapest,** 432 North Fairfax Avenue between Oakwood and Rosewood, West Los Angeles (tel: 655-0111). This is where nostalgic Eastern Europeans come for cooking from the "old country," and many authorities consider it the most genuine Hungarian restaurant in the West. The dining room is large and well lit, surely but elusively European in feel with a sea of white linen tablecloths, big green leather booths, gold and brown print wallpaper and imposing chandeliers overhead.

The cost of your entree includes relishes, soup, appetizer, dessert and coffee—a very filling meal indeed. And everything is homemade right on the premises. Eat darling, it's good for you! The soup is usually borscht, the appetizer perhaps stuffed cabbage, the dessert a flaky strudel. With an entree of chicken paprikash or Hungarian goulash, the entirety would cost $5.75; $6.95 for roast young goose, and just $4.95 for blintzes. Children under 12 can have a complete dinner for $3.95.

Open from 4 to 10 p.m. (Sundays from 1 p.m.). Closed Mondays.

Jewish Deli

So where do you get a good pastrami on rye in this town? **Nate & Al's,** 414 North Beverly Drive, off Brighton Way, Beverly Hills (tel: 274-0101), has been slapping pastrami on fresh-baked rye for over 30 years, not to mention chopped liver and schmaltz, kosher franks and hot corned beef. It has the requisite Jewish-deli decor—tiled floors, leather booths and overly bright lights; a big counter up front handles take-out orders and there's always a big line waiting to get in.

This is our favorite kind of Jewish deli—rather than strictly kosher, it is kosher style, which means that the incredibly extensive menu can range around both meat and dairy items. The above-mentioned pastrami and corned beef sandwiches are $2.35, chopped liver $1.95; other traditional favorites include cream cheese and Nova Scotia salmon on a bagel ($3.15) and the famous Reuben ($2.85). An appetizer of gefilte fish with horseradish is $1.75, chicken soup with matzo ball or kreplach is 80¢. And then there's potato pancakes ($2.75) and cheese, cherry or blueberry blintzes with sour cream and apple sauce ($2.75). A difficult decision, to be sure. Leave room for a homemade dessert, perhaps apple strudel (80¢) or chocolate cream pie (75¢). Wine and beer are available.

Open daily from 7:30 a.m. to 9 p.m.

Similar menu, decor and price structure prevail at **Zucky's,** 431 Wilshire Boulevard at 5th Street, Santa Monica (tel: 393-0551). Zucky's is open 24 hours a day.

Danish

Carl Andersen's, 10930 Weybourn Avenue, Westwood Village (tel: 479-1776), is a homey, old-world restaurant that specializes in Scandinavian haute cuisine. Owner-chef Carl Andersen, who established the place in 1939, once cooked for the king of Denmark, and he recently catered a private dinner for Queen Margrethe when she visited L.A. The ambience is rather charming, with many dining nooks and crannies, Tudor walls covered in grasspaper and hung with paintings and copperware. High book cases filled with books for your perusal enhance the *gemütlich* atmosphere.

At lunch you can get those famous open-face Danish sandwiches, like steak tartare ($3.50) and roast duck with apple sauce and red-pepper jam ($3.40), as well as a large variety of closed sandwiches, cold buffet plates ($2.10 and up) and salads. Hot specials are also offered, served with soup or salad: Danish meatballs with cranberry sauce is $2.95, veal paprika with linguine Alfredo $3.25. Dinner entrees are served with soup, salad, dessert and coffee. They include roast rack of lamb paysanne ($6.75), Danish goulash ($6) and breast of chicken fricassee with egg dumplings ($5). It's all scrumptious, but the rich homemade desserts swimming in fresh whipped cream are particularly unforgettable.

Open for lunch and dinner Monday through Saturday.

Indian

Owners Paul and Joyce Bhalla have designed a suitably exotic setting for **Bhalla's** 10853 Lindbrook Drive, just north of Wilshire, Westwood Village (tel: 478-8535). The smell of incense and the strains of Indian raga music greet you at the door. A tiger skin graces one wall, cut-brass chandeliers are suspended from chains overhead, and carved sandalwood screens create intimate dining areas. The festive decor is furthered by candlelit tables with gold cloths and bright red napkins, and menus adorned with Moghul miniatures.

The specialty here is tandoori cooking, with the tandoori chef tending a special clay oven in an open area. A tandoori beef or chicken dinner costs $7.50, and includes soup, salad, dal (curried lentil sauce), raita (yogurt with fresh vegetables and herbs), rice pilaf, naan roti (Indian bread) and an array of chutneys and condiments. Beef or lamb biryani dinners (deliciously spiced rice and meat casseroles) are $6.95. Some of the other entrees are rather unique, like the kofta paneeri—meatballs stuffed with cheese, cooked in spices with yogurt, tomatoes and onions ($5.95). All entrees are also available à la carte for 20% off the dinner price. For dessert we suggest the gulab jaman—milk balls in sweet syrup ($1). The wine list includes good French and California selections.

Bhalla's serves dinner only, Tuesday through Sunday from 5:30 p.m.

We also like **Gypsy's,** 1215 4th Street, off Wilshire, Santa Monica (tel: 451-2841), the funky-exotic creation of dynamic owner Tina Todd. Your surroundings are an eclectic collection of Eastern paraphernalia, artifacts, fabrics, etc., along with many plants. Tables are candlelit, and the combined effect is pleasantly intimate. Only complete dinners are offered; they include an appetizer, salad, poories (Indian bread), dal, vegetable bhaji (deep-fried vegetable balls) and rice. Vegetable curry is $4.50, beef curry with a subtle coconut flavor $4.95, the same price for Hyderabad murg—chicken marinated in yogurt and spices for 12 hours, then oven-baked with roasted almonds and raisins and saffron seasoning.

Gypsy's is open for dinner only, from 6 to 10 p.m.; closed Mondays.

BUDGET RESTAURANTS: With all the struggling young actors and actresses in this town, you'd better believe there are quite a few places where you can eat cheap. The surprising thing is that some of the places below are actually quite chic, and you'll see the famous lining up to get in with the would-be famous. Our very first listing is a venerable L.A. institution.

American/Continental

The Original Pantry Cafe, 877 South Figueroa at 9th Street (tel: 972-9279), has been open 24 hours a day for 52 years. Never closed, and never without a customer, they don't even have a key to the front door. Delightfully and unfakedly funky, its well-worn decor consists of shiny cream-colored walls graced with old patinaed oil paintings, tile floors, hanging globe lamps overhead, and big stainless-steel water pitchers and bowls of celery, carrots, and radishes on every Formica table. In addition to that bowl of raw veggies, you also get a whopping big portion of homemade creamy cole slaw and all the homemade sourdough bread and butter you want—a meal in itself before you've even ordered. When you do order, you'll be amazed at the bountiful portions of delicious food set before you by waiters in long flowing aprons (or are they really character actors sent over from Central Casting?).

Terrific Pantry breakfasts served at any hour consist of two eggs any way you like them, big slabs of sweet cured ham, home fries, plenty of fried sourdough bread and cup after cup of freshly made coffee. The tab: $2.35. A huge T-bone steak is $5.40, home-fried pork chops $4.15.

The Pantry is an original—don't miss it.

Schwab's, 8024 Sunset Boulevard at the corner of Laurel Canyon Boulevard (tel: 656-1212), is of course the famous Hollywood drugstore, where, according to legend, Lana Turner was discovered sitting on a soda fountain stool (Mervyn Leroy, who cast the sweater queen in her first role, denied the story on a television interview in 1969). However, Sidney Skolsky made Schwab's his Hollywood headquarters, and movie mags over the years set so many stories here that we bet any number of pretty young hopefuls who have just hit town from Dubuque, or New York, are still being picked up daily with variations of the old line "I can get you in pictures."

At any rate, Schwab's underwent an expensive face-lift several years ago, becoming super modern and slick looking, fully conscious of its position as a Hollywood legend. It's extremely popular for breakfast—eggs benedict with grilled Danish ham on an English muffin is $3.50. You can get fresh-squeezed orange juice here, too, and homemade desserts. Triple-decker club sandwiches are $2.75 to $3, cheese blintzes $2.50, and, naturally, there are diet specialties available.

Open daily from 8 a.m. to 10 p.m.

Clifton's Cafeteria, 10250 Santa Monica Boulevard, Century City Shopping Center, is the newest of the Clifton chain of economy cafeterias, once famous for its 5¢ meals. This one is right at the threshold of swank Beverly Hills and can be just the thing when you've spent a few dollars too many at I. Magnin's or splurged on third-row-center seats at the theater across the street.

The ambience is cheerful, with orange leather booths and orange and brown carpeting. And the food is really quite good. An economical meal might consist of old-fashioned navy bean soup (50¢), a beef enchilada ($1.03) or tender roast pork with dressing ($1.55). A small spinach salad on the side is 39¢, a broccoli and cauliflower salad 41¢, and a loaf of home-baked cornbread is 16¢. Desserts include generous pieces of homemade German chocolate cake

(55¢) and carrot cake (60¢), as well as fresh strawberries with real whipped cream.

Open daily from 11 a.m. to 8 p.m.

Hot Dogs and Hamburgers

Celebrities line up along with the rest of L.A. cognoscenti for **Pink's Hot Dogs**, on the northeast corner of La Brea and Melrose near the heart of old Hollywood. The walls are lined with photos of famous hot dog fans, all signed affectionately to Paul Pink. The big treat is the 60¢ chili dog, loaded with beans and onions and served with infinite skill by the "Great Johnny" for the past 20 years. Some 4,000 of these delicious dogs are sold daily between the hours of 8 a.m. and 3 a.m. Outdoor tables are placed at the corner, but most people eat standing up.

The search for the perfect hamburger has ended. Just head on over to **Cassell's Patio Hamburgers**, 3300 West 6th Street at Berendo, East Wilshire, where Alvin Cassel has dedicated his life for the last 30 years to perfecting a gastronomic triumph—the compleat burger.

He begins each exquisite creation with over a third of a pound of freshly ground USDA prime Colorado beef, grinding it personally each day after trimming off every bit of suet. Your burger is cooked to exact specification on a uniquely slanted range that griddles the bottom and broils the top. Then it's served on a five-inch bun—the most natural kind obtainable and always fresh. It costs $2.35 ($2.60 with imported Swiss cheese), and you can top it with what amounts almost to a buffet of all-you-can-eat fixin's: two kinds of lettuce, homemade mayonnaise, homemade Roquefort dressing, freshly sliced tomatoes, chopped onions, pickles, peaches, cottage cheese and homemade potato salad. Even the produce is all carefully selected, and more beautiful vegetables we've not seen since the country fair. The perfect drink with your perfect burger is homemade lemonade (60¢). There are tables inside and on the umbrella-shaped terrace. Keep your eyes open and you might see Cassell habitué Mel Brooks piling on the relish at the next table.

Open Monday through Friday from 11 a.m. to 3 p.m.

Italian

When you're traveling with the kids, restaurants like the **Old Venice Noodle Company**, 2654 Main Street, Santa Monica (tel: 399-9211), can save you a pretty penny. It's almost as cheap as feeding them at home. Moreover, they'll love the eclectically furnished turn-of-the-century-extravaganza decor: tables made out of old Singer sewing machines, opulent chandeliers, a converted trolley car with tables, barbershop chairs, brick fireplaces, an antique Wurlitzer jukebox (with up-to-date rock selections) and more stained glass than in any other L.A. restaurant.

Spaghetti dinners are featured, and all are served with a salad, sourdough bread, coffee or tea and spumoni ice cream. It comes with meatballs ($3.25), with meat sauce ($2.80) and even with chicken cacciatore ($3.95), but most under-12s will be happiest with no-frills spaghetti and tomato sauce ($1.85).

At lunch you can also order the sandwich offerings—like a meatball sandwich ($1.95) or Italian sausage ($2.10), either of which will be topped with melted cheese if you so desire. The salad comes gratis. Grown-ups will find that the house wine at 65¢ a glass helps soothe kid-ruffled nerves. Turn to the back of the menu, which offers educational tidbits of spaghetti lore, such as: "Spaghetti was originally brought to America to be used as telegraph wire or dental floss, but. . . ."

Open for lunch weekdays, dinner nightly.

A Mixed Bag

The **Farmer's Market,** at Fairfax and 3rd Avenue in West Hollywood, dates from 1934 when farmers, hard-pressed by the Depression, set up stalls in a large vacant lot to eke out a living selling their produce. It's still there, no longer a smattering of crude stalls, but a colorful and unique outdoor market with over 160 individually owned businesses and numerous outdoor tree-and umbrella-shaded tables. You can range around the stalls and stands snacking as you browse, or carefully select several items, assemble a proper meal and find a table. A rundown of some of the major food stalls follows:

Boris' Juice and Salad Bar has Waldorf salads for $1.65 and luscious Hawaiian fruit salads for $2.85. As for the juices—45¢ to 60¢ a glass—there's pomegranate, cherry, papaya, strawberry, coconut, passion fruit and a specialty called "green drink," a unique combination of pineapple, celery, watercress, spinach and parsley.

Magee's Kitchen has been dispensing big platters of corned beef, cabbage and parsley potatoes ($3) since the end of World War II. At the **Fish & Oyster Bar** you can select crab Louie ($3.60) or bay shrimp Louie ($2.45). **Michael's** is famous for blintzes, an order of two with sour cream and preserves costing $1.60; scrumptious pastries here, too. **Castillo's Spanish Kitchen** specializes in early California fare—delicious tacos (beef or bean) for 75¢. Real Texas chili is 94¢ a bowl at **Bryan's Pit Barbecue,** where you can also get a barbecued beef, ham and pork dinner for $3.55 or a tasty Texas salad for $1.74.

For dessert the choices are legion. You'll soon nose out **Carson's Candy Kitchen,** where rich chocolate fudge is being made and sold at $3 a pound. Then there's **Belgian Waffles,** serving guess what topped with whipped cream and fruit for $1.35; a cappucino with your waffle is 50¢. The pie's the thing at **Le Mart,** and the house special is "black-bottom" cream pie ($3.95 for a whole one).

There are a few inexpensive indoor eateries, too, like **Du-Par's Restaurant,** specializing in homemade baked goods and open from 6:30 a.m. to 1:30 a.m.

That's not the half of it. And should you overdo, relief is just a stall away at **Chudacoff's Pharmacy.**

Chinese

Man Fook Low, 962 San Pedro Street, between 9th and 10th, downtown (tel: 972-9467), has been delighting knowledgeable L.A. residents for over half a century with low-cost Cantonese specialties. It's a tiny place, with the emphasis on food rather than atmosphere—the kitchen is right out in the open. It's especially popular for "dim sum" lunches served between 10 a.m. and 2 p.m. daily. If you've never had the Chinese tea lunch, it consists of a wide choice of tidbits, little plates of scrumptious Chinese hors d'oeuvres and tea cakes at 25¢ to 40¢ a plate. Don't take every plate that's offered, only those that appeal to you—more choices are on the way. Two people can dine sumptuously at dim sum for about $2 each.

The regular menu also offers many excellent and inexpensive dishes, like the steamed sea bass ($2.50), cashew nut chicken ($2.75) and ginger beef ($2.25).

Open 10 a.m. to 11 p.m. daily, Saturday till midnight.

4. Sights of Los Angeles

By now you're settled into your hotel room and ready to explore the town. After all, there's more to do in L.A. than just laze around those sun-drenched beaches. Hollywood's movie studios long ago opened their doors to visitors, revealing their fascinating "special effects" to one and all. Needless to say, these people can put on quite a show—it's their business. And in Hollywood-influenced L.A., even non-show-biz attractions take on a dramatic quality. The natural history of the La Brea Tar Pits takes on the aura of a sci-fi horror movie with life-sized replicas of ancient beasts struggling for their lives in a bubbling death pit right in the center of town. Even death is more dramatic here, as you'll see at Forest Lawn, where funerals are "staged."

All of which makes sightseeing in Los Angeles very special fun. We'll begin in—

DOWNTOWN LOS ANGELES: This ever-expanding sprawl of a city did have a germination point, in and around the Old Plaza and Olvera Street. Later growth pushed the heart of the city about seven blocks west to **Pershing Square.** Opening onto the square (now tunneled with parking garages), the deluxe **Biltmore Hotel** was constructed, and elegant residences lined **Bunker Hill** in the late 19th century, the mansions on the hill connected to the flatlands by a cable car poetically named Angels' Flight.

Then came the earthquake scare, and buildings over 150 feet high were prohibited by city-planning authorities. This limitation drove many companies out to Wilshire Boulevard and the outlying areas, and Los Angeles proper fell into relative disrepair, with beautiful townhouses giving way to slums.

It wasn't until 1957 that the ban on tall structures was removed (ostensibly because new building techniques have lessened earthquake disaster potential—seeing is believing, say we). At any rate, the removal of the ban marked the beginning of a renaissance in the downtown area. The **Civic Center,** which had been expanding since the mid-'20s, culminated in the 28-story **City Hall.** You can take an elevator to the observation deck Monday to Thursday from 10 a.m. to 4 p.m. (Fridays 10 to 10, weekends 10 to 5).

The shimmering, $36-million **Music Center** went up in the '60s, making downtown a cultural center. New office buildings were erected in great numbers; the **Los Angeles Convention & Exhibition Center,** occupying a 38-acre site at 1201 South Figueroa Street, was erected, and, more recently, the **United California Bank** on the corner of Hope and Wilshire—at 54 stories the tallest building west of Chicago.

Though much of downtown is still run-down and undeveloped, that state of affairs is rapidly changing. There's much here to draw the visitor. We'll begin with—

A Walking Tour of Old Los Angeles

This is one of the few areas of L.A. that you can see without your wheels. It's the district around the **Pueblo de Los Angeles,** the birthplace of the city in 1781, now restored along with 42 surrounding acres as a state historical park. Organized walking tours are offered by the **Visitors' Center,** 100 Paseo de la Plaza (tel: 628-1274); there's no charge, and they leave Tuesdays through Saturdays at 10 and 11 a.m., noon and 1 p.m.

The tour begins at **Old Plaza,** the site where Spanish governor Felipe de Neve purportedly founded the pueblo. The founding was part of Spain's plan to colonize California by establishing presidios, missions and pueblos. Planting lands were given to the first 11 families who settled here, and five years later each settler received his own registered branding iron, by which his cattle could be distinguished from his neighbors'. In the old days bullfights were often held in the Plaza; nowadays concerts and religious festivities take place here.

Opening directly on the square is the **Plaza Church,** on which construction was started in 1818 and continued till 1869. Though much of the original structure is gone or restored, it is filled with paintings and ecclesiastical relics, and open daily to visitors.

Many of the area's attractions are along colorful, traffic-free **Olvera Street,** one of the oldest streets in Los Angeles. It was originally called Vine Street because of the vineyards growing along it. In 1930 it was established as a typical Mexican marketplace, paved with bricks and Spanish tile. It contains 88 shops and stalls, open from about 10 a.m. to 11 p.m. daily, selling pottery, jewelry, leather goods, piñatas, Mexican pastries and, of course, tacos, enchiladas and so on. There's even a blacksmith. Make sure you drop in at the **Trade Mart** (no admission) to see the south-of-the-border crafts exhibits.

Also on Olvera Street is the **Avila Adobe,** the oldest existing residence in the city, dating from 1818. It has been restored, and is open free of charge to visitors every day of the year.

Across the street is **Pelanconi House,** the finest of the early Los Angeles brick structures built mid-19th century. It first served as living quarters and wine cellar for the original owner; Pelanconi did not purchase the place until 1865. Subsequently it became a warehouse for Chinese merchants, and today it houses a Mexican restaurant, **Casa La Golondrina.** The Victorian **Sepulveda House** is also of interest.

Pico House, completed in June, 1870, was designed to be the finest hotel in the city at a then-astronomical cost of $82,000. Lighted with gas, and housing several bathtubs, it was considered the last word in luxury.

Just south of Pico House is the first wooden-frame building erected in Los Angeles—the **Merced Theatre.** It opened in 1870, with seating for about 400, and performances were advertised in Spanish. In later years it was used as a saloon, a Methodist church and an armory. If projected plans materialize, it will once more stage plays in the near future.

The Music Center

This $35-million gleaming glass complex of buildings, dedicated in the spring of 1967, is located at 135 North Grand Avenue at 1st Street. It houses three theaters: the 3,250-seat **Dorothy Chandler Pavilion** for opera, recitals, musicals and dance performances—home of the Los Angeles Civic Light Opera and the Los Angeles Philharmonic; the **Mark Taper Forum,** seating 750, for intimate drama and forums; and the 2,100-seat **Ahmanson Theatre** for plays, musical dramas and, sometimes, dance attractions.

The latter two are usually taken up with rehearsals during the day, but the public is invited to tour the Dorothy Chandler Pavilion. Free tours are conducted on Monday, Tuesday, Thursday and Friday from May to October. The rest of the year the tours are Monday through Thursday. Parking in the garage below is 35¢ for a half-hour.

Natural History Museum

Located in **Exposition Park,** this exciting museum, the largest of its kind in the West, houses seemingly endless exhibits of fossils, minerals, birds, mammals and suchlike. It is, at this writing, undergoing a major transformation, with the construction of a new Exposition Boulevard entrance and esplanade, as well as indoor and patio dining facilities, new quarters for the Bookshop and Ethnic Arts Shop, and most important, many new galleries.

Exhibits and displays chronicle the history of human beings and their environment, going back some 400 million years before we appeared on the scene and up to present day. They range from Maya, Aztec, Inca and pre-Inca arts and crafts from the period 2500 B.C. to 1500 A.D., to complete depiction of insect families, their life cycles, habitats and relationships to other life forms.

Informative free films, such as *The Great Barrier Reef* and *The Insect War*, are shown Saturdays at 2 p.m. from June to September in the Museum's Jean Delacour Auditorium.

Until recently the Natural History Museum housed the fossil birds, mammals and plants excavated from the Rancho La Brea Tar Pits. Most of these, including the imperial mammoth (largest of the Ice Age elephants of North America), have now been moved to the Hancock Park Page Museum at the 23-acre Rancho La Brea site (see below) on Wilshire Boulevard. Sorry to say there are no fossilized dinosaurs, as they were already extinct by the time the tar pits began to trap their unsuspecting victims.

Both the museum in Exposition Park (900 Exposition Boulevard) and the Hancock Park Page Museum (5801 Wilshire Boulevard in the "Miracle Mile") are open Tuesday to Sunday from 10 a.m. to 5 p.m. Admission and parking are free at both.

Lawry's California Center

Just a few minutes from downtown, at 586 San Fernando Road, is Lawry's California Center, a brand-new early-California-style complex of restaurants, plazas, shops and exquisitely landscaped gardens. Entered from Avenue 26 (where the parking area is), the wide driveway leading to the Fiesta Gates is flanked by shade trees, lush foliage and flowering plants. A splashing fountain and serenading mariachi music provide an appropriately south-of-the-border backdrop.

You can take a free 45-minute tour of the Center Monday through Friday at 11:30 a.m., 1:30 or 2:30 p.m. Plan to have a relaxing meal at one of the Center's delightful restaurants. They're indoors and out, under whitewashed Mexican archways and umbrellaed tables, and feature food ranging from steak to tacos.

HOLLYWOOD: The legendary city where actresses once pranced with leashed leopards, and Louella Parsons daily chronicled everyone's most intimate doings, is certainly on everyone's must-see list. Unfortunately the glamor—what's left of it—is tarnished, and Hollywood Boulevard has been labeled "the Times Square of the West," for all its porno shops, massage parlors and X-rated movie theaters.

Still, if you look down, you'll be thrilled to see the bronze medallions along the Boulevard's **Walk of Fame**, bearing the names of over 1,500 stars who have trod these sidewalks from nickelodeon days to the present. And everyone heads for **Hollywood and Vine**, that star-crossed intersection where the old **Hollywood Palace Theater** stands, now the setting for the "Merv Griffin Show." For tickets, write to the Merv Griffin Show, 1735 North Vine Street, Hollywood 90028. It's also possible to get tickets at the box office.

Near the corner of Hollywood and Vine is the disc-shaped **Capitol Records Building**, the first circular office building in the world.

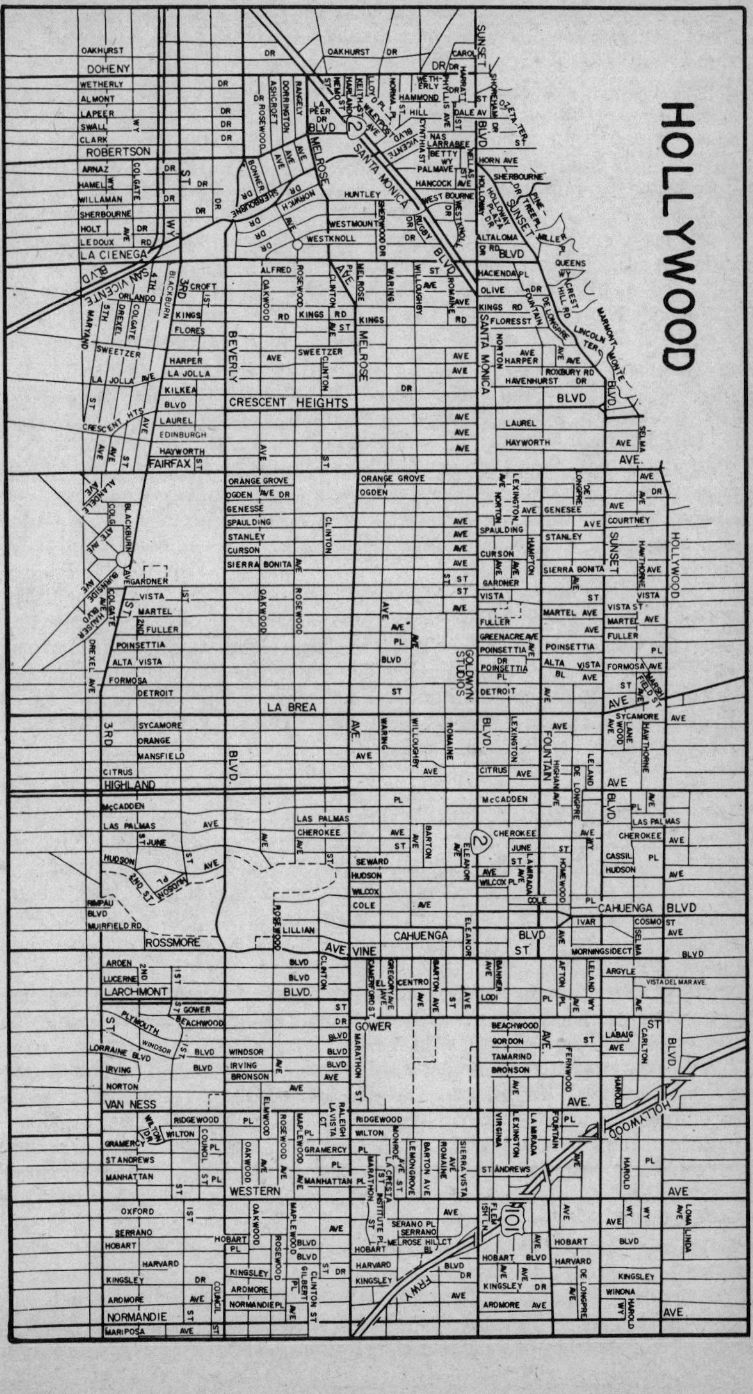
HOLLYWOOD
OAKHURST DR
DOHENY
WETHERLY DR
ALMONT
LAPEER DR
SWALL DR
CLARK DR
ROBERTSON
ARNAZ
HAMEL
WILLAMAN
SHERBOURNE
HOLT
LE DOUX RD
LA CIENEGA
SAN VICENTE BLVD
MELROSE
SANTA MONICA
BEVERLY BLVD
CRESCENT HEIGHTS
FAIRFAX
3RD ST
SUNSET BLVD
HOLLOWAY
FOUNTAIN
LA BREA
HIGHLAND
ROSSMORE
LARCHMONT BLVD
VAN NESS
WESTERN
NORMANDIE
CAHUENGA BLVD
VINE ST
GOWER
HOLLYWOOD FRWY
GOLDWYN STUDIOS
ORANGE GROVE
OGDEN
GENESSE
SPAULDING
STANLEY
CURSON
SIERRA BONITA
GARDNER
VISTA
MARTEL
FULLER
POINSETTIA
ALTA VISTA
FORMOSA
DETROIT
SYCAMORE
ORANGE
MANSFIELD
CITRUS
McCADDEN
LAS PALMAS
CHEROKEE
JUNE
HUDSON
WILCOX
COLE
LILLIAN
ARDEN
LUCERNE
GOWER
BEACHWOOD
PLYMOUTH
WINDSOR
IRVING
BRONSON
NORTON
RIDGEWOOD PL
WILTON
GRAMERCY
ST ANDREWS
MANHATTAN
OXFORD
SERRANO
HOBART
HARVARD
KINGSLEY
ARDMORE
MARIPOSA
ELEANOR
SEWARD
CENTRO
LODI
IVAR
MORNINGSIDE CT
ARGYLE
VISTA DEL MAR AVE
CARLTON
TAMARIND
FERNWOOD
LEXINGTON
VIRGINIA
LA MIRADA
DE LONGPRE
HAROLD WY
LOMA LINDA
WINONA
MARATHON
LEMON GROVE
BARTON AVE
ROMAINE
WILLOUGHBY
WARING
ROSEWOOD
OAKWOOD
CLINTON
KINGS RD
SWEETZER
HARPER
LA JOLLA
KILKEA
LAUREL
EDINBURGH
HAYWORTH
HAVENHURST DR
ROXBURY RD
LAUREL
SELMA
COURTNEY
HAWTHORNE
CASSIL
COSMO ST
LABAIG
GORDON
SERANO PL
MELROSE HILL CT
CRESCENT HTS
QUEENS WY
LINCOLN TER
MARMONT
MONTE
HORN AVE
SHERBOURNE
ALTALOMA RD
HACIENDA PL
OLIVE
FLORES ST
NORMA PL
HAMMOND
HUNTLEY
WESTMOUNT
WESTKNOLL
ALFRED
CROFT
ORLANDO
KINGS
FLORES
RIMPAU BLVD
MUIRFIELD RD
101
2

As much a Hollywood landmark as the famous intersection, **Mann's Chinese Theatre** (formerly Grauman's), at 6925 Hollywood Boulevard, is a combination of authentic and simulated Chinese decor. Original Chinese heaven doves top the facade, and two of the theater's columns are actually from a Ming Dynasty temple. An enclosure in the forecourt was created for the signatures and hand and footprints of the stars, and countless visitors have matched their hands and feet with those of Elizabeth Taylor, Paul Newman, Ginger Rogers, Humphrey Bogart, Frank Sinatra, etc., etc., etc. It's not only hands and feet, though; Betty Grable made an impression, as always, with her shapely leg, Gene Autry with the hoofprints of Champ, his horse, and Jimmy Durante and Bob Hope used (what else?) their noses.

A few blocks north of Hollywood Boulevard is the **Hollywood Bowl**, at 2301 North Highland Avenue (tel: 87-MUSIC), summer home of the Los Angeles Philharmonic and the world's most famous outdoor amphitheater. Every year a pre-dawn pilgrimage is made by Angelenos to the Bowl for Easter sunrise services, which are televised and broadcast across the nation (more about the Bowl in our Nightlife section, coming up).

Dedicated movie buffs might want to visit the **Hollywood Memorial Park Cemetery**, at 6000 Santa Monica Boulevard, between Van Ness and Gower Streets. This is where the mysterious lady in black annually pays homage at the crypt of Valentino on the anniversary of his death. Peter Lorre is buried here, as are Douglas Fairbanks, Norma Talmadge, Tyrone Power, Cecil B. De Mille and Marion Davies. Hours are from 7:30 a.m. to 5 p.m.

Less morbid film fans can view "the cars of the stars" rather than their remains, at the **Hollywood Motorama Museum**, 7001 Hollywood Boulevard, next to the Chinese Theatre. You'll see the sleek black Batmobile, the machine-gun riddled wreckage of Bonnie and Clyde's movie Ford and the Munster Koach, as well as custom-made and antique vehicles. Open weekdays from 10 a.m. to 10 p.m. (weekdays from 11 a.m.). Adults pay $2.50; kids 12 to 17, $1.50; ages six through 11, 75¢; under six free.

The Hollywood Wax Museum

One block east of Mann's Chinese Theatre is Spoony Singh's Hollywood Wax Museum, 6767 Hollywood Boulevard (tel: 462-8860), a last holdout of movie-world glamor. Singh, a bona-fide turbaned and bearded Indian Sikh, took over the barnlike museum some 12 years ago when it was in a state of utter disrepair; Shirley Temple's head had shrunken to the size of a tennis ball and Mickey Rooney's arms had dropped off.

Spoony built up his wax collection to 170 famous figures of the past and present, the most famous of which is Marilyn Monroe in her dress-blowing scene from *The Seven Year Itch*. Though most of the figures are screen stars—Raquel Welch (whose bras, under a shimmering silver midriff, were stolen so often, he finally left her braless), Danny Thomas, Bing Crosby, Barbra Streisand, Steve McQueen, Elizabeth Taylor, etc.—there are also Mother Goose characters, and a Hall of Presidents where first citizens from George Washington to Gerald Ford are on display. Most popular of these is John F. Kennedy at the lectern.

You'll also see tableaux, the Last Supper; a Chamber of Horrors filled with maniacal demons and torture machines, and California's early history depicted in wax.

An added attraction is the **Oscar Movie Theatre**, presenting a film that spans more than 40 years of Academy Award history. The sound track is composed of a medley of award-winning hit songs, and the clips include Vivian

Leigh in *Gone with the Wind,* Bing Crosby in *Going My Way,* Yul Brynner in *The King and I,* and other old favorites.

The museum is open daily from 10 a.m. to midnight (Friday and Saturday till 2 a.m.). Adult admission is $3; juniors (ages 13 to 17), military and senior citizens pay $2; children six to 12, $1 (under six free).

GRIFFITH PARK: To the northeast of Hollywood lies lovely, verdant Griffith Park, at 4,253 acres the largest park within the boundaries of any American city, and second-largest city-owned park in the world (largest is in West Berlin). Home of the Los Angeles Zoo and the Observatory, it offers wide-ranging facilities, including five golf courses, a large wilderness area, a bird sanctuary, tennis courts, picnic areas and even an old-fashioned merry-go-round. Other attractions are the **Greek Theatre** (see Nightlife section); **Travel Town,** where the kids can explore and climb all over retired rail cars and airplanes (admission free, open from 9:30 a.m. to 5:30 p.m. daily); and a **miniature train** ride (50¢ for adults, 35¢ for kids)—for slower locomotion, you can also hire a pony on the same grounds.

Major park entrances are at the northern tip of Western Boulevard (at the prettiest part of the park, **Ferndell,** where New Zealand horticulturists have created a lush setting by planting ferns from around the world); at the northern extremity of Vermont Avenue (leading into the part of the park containing the Greek Theatre, the Observatory, bird sanctuary and Mount Hollywood); and at the junction of Los Feliz Boulevard and Riverside Drive (leading to the municipal golf course, miniature trains, and Children's Zoo). At the junction of the Ventura and Golden State Freeways is yet another entrance to the Zoo and Travel Town, as well as free parking and picnic areas.

From Hollywood Boulevard, you can take bus 91 north on Hill Street to Vermont and Hollywood Boulevard, transferring to bus 23, which will take you to the zoo. If you're going to the Observatory, transfer to the "Observatory" bus at Hollywood Boulevard and Vermont Avenue.

The Los Angeles Zoo

Only in Southern California would a zoo bill its offerings as a "cast of thousands." Here you'll see over 2,000 mammals, birds and reptiles on a 113-acre "stage" divided into continental habitat areas: North America, South America, Africa, Eurasia and Australia. Active in wildlife conservation, the zoo houses about 50 vanishing species, such as the bald-headed American eagle. There's also an aviary with a walk-in flight cage, a reptile house, aquatic section and a children's zoo.

Admission to the zoo is $1.25 for adults, 50¢ for teenagers ages 12 to 15, free for under-11s accompanied by an adult. The zoo is open from 10 a.m. to 5 p.m. (6 p.m. in summer) every day except Christmas.

Griffith Observatory and Planetarium

Atop the hill, closer to the heavens, is the Planetarium, where the "great Zeiss projector" flashes seven shows a year across a 75-foot dome. Excursions into interplanetary space range from moon voyages, to a cosmic search—of vital interest to locals—for the causes of earthquakes, moonquakes and star-quakes. One-hour shows are given daily except Monday; for show times telephone 664-1192. Admission is $1.50 for adults, $1 for ages 13 to 17, 50¢ for ages five to 12. Those under five are not admitted except to the children's programs at 11 a.m. on Saturdays.

At night the Planetarium is the setting for **Laserium,** a cosmic light-show/concert under the stars. Shows are presented Tuesday through Saturday (Monday through Saturday in summer) at 9:15 p.m., with a second show offered Friday and Saturday nights at 10:30 p.m. Tickets cost $2.50 per person.

Also here is the **Hall of Science,** with many fascinating exhibits on galaxies, meteorites and other cosmic subjects. The public can also gaze through the Observatory telescope on any clear night until 10 p.m.

BEVERLY HILLS: A recent cartoon in *Playboy* shows a bunch of glamorous-looking people boarding a bus, with a local explaining to a perplexed passerby, "Here in Beverly Hills, we've got more celebrities than we actually need. We felt the decent thing would be to bus a few of them to the more deprived areas of Los Angeles." Ain't it the truth? Denizens of this star-studded community include Buddy Hackett, Dinah Shore, Doris Day, Lucille Ball, Warren Beatty, Steve McQueen, Walter Pidgeon, James Stewart, Groucho Marx, George Burns and Kirk Douglas, to name just a few. Within Beverly Hills are some of Southern California's most prestigious hotels, restaurants, high-fashion boutiques and department stores—all used to catering to the whims of decades of film personalities.

Douglas Fairbanks and Mary Pickford led the migration of stars to the area when they built their famous home "Pickfair"; today a drive through the glens, canyons and hillsides of Beverly Hills will reveal one palatial home after another. As for "Pickfair," you can drive by and see it at 1143 Summit Drive—it's still owned and lived-in by silent-screen star Mary Pickford and her second husband, Buddy Rogers.

It was once a big tourist trend to visit star's homes, with bus tours and local visitor's bureaus pointing the way. This activity is discouraged these days, celebs demanding privacy—at least in their own homes—from gaping and often inconsiderate crowds. You will see youngsters on the drive going into Beverly Hills hawking "Maps of Stars' Homes"; they're not only expensive, but tend to be inaccurate—many of the occupants pinpointed have not only moved, but have moved to Forest Lawn! We suggest you forget the stars and satisfy your curiosity as to how the other half lives by exploring—

Greystone Mansion

Resting on a hill above Doheny Road and Sunset Boulevard, Greystone Mansion looks like a baronial castle surrounded by 18.6 acres (originally it occupied 410 acres) of formal gardens, orchards, pools, woodlands and lawns. Built in the mid-'20s, Greystone was the $4-million (the equivalent of $20 million today) dream house of Edward Lawrence Doheny, who amassed a great fortune in oil. The servants' quarters alone, for a live-in staff of 36, occupy three floors on one side of the house. The mansion is built in a variety of European architectural styles, the entry staircase stressing Gothic and neo-Classic design. All the oak banisters, balustrades and rafters are hand-carved, the floors in the hallway are marble, and each chimney is handmade in a different design. Greystone had its own fire station, riding stables, kennels, tennis and badminton courts. The 60-foot swimming pool is now a lovely lily pond, its arcades mirrored in the water. The exquisite gardens are lushly planted with avocado trees, eucalyptus, evergreens, banana palms, ferns and flowers.

The mansion is now occupied by the American Film Institute (thus it is no longer furnished), but it is open to the public on a tour basis at a price of $2 per person ($1 for children under 12). Tours are conducted on Saturday and

Sunday at 1 p.m. and 3 p.m. In keeping with the mansion's image, tours are kept small and tickets must be purchased in advance; call 272-4049 for ticket information. The gardens are open to the public daily as a meditation park from 10 a.m. to 5 p.m.

TOURING THE STUDIOS: Want to see what goes on behind the scenes at movie and TV studios? Universal Studios and NBC-TV have both arranged entertaining and informative tours, during which you might even get to see some of your favorite performers. If you only have time for one tour, Universal's is the most elaborate.

Universal City Studios

The largest and busiest movie studio in the world, Universal began offering tours to the public in 1964. Since then, it has been attracting some two-million visitors a year, who want to see the where, why and how of the studio that produced movies from *My Little Chickadee* to *Jaws,* and popular TV series from "Dragnet" to "Baretta." Universal also produces MCA records, handling such big names as Olivia Newton-John, The Who, Roger Daltry and Jerry Jeff Walker.

The guided tour of the studio's 420 acres aboard a "Glamortram" takes two hours, after which you can stay for exciting live shows at the **Entertainment Center.** You'll pass the offices of Alfred Hitchcock, Richard Zanuck and Hal Wallis, stars' dressing rooms and countless departments involved in film production. There's a stop during which you can wander around Lucille Ball's lavish dressing room; at Stage 32 you'll learn about special effects, including those used in monster movies. You'll also see back-lot sets like Six Point Texas—the Western town that has been used since the days of Tom Mix; that's not to mention New York's safest street (though it was devastated for *Earthquake*), patrolled by Baretta, Kojak and Columbo! The reason you don't recognize these streets from movie to movie is that they are constantly undergoing alterations in landscaping and exteriors to prevent audiences from becoming too familiar with them.

The tram encounters countless disasters along the way: a giant rockslide (of foam-rubber boulders); an attack by the deadly 24-foot *Jaws* shark; an Alpine avalanche; the complete collapse of a rickety wooden bridge you happen to be crossing; a flash flood and more.

At the conclusion of this terrifying journey, visitors can wander around the Entertainment Center, where several times each day skilled stuntmen fall off buildings, dodge knife blows and disappear into quicksand pits. In addition, a movie make-up artist transforms two lucky visitors from each tour into Frankenstein and his bride, and a trainer demonstrates the capacities of his trained birds and animals. And each weekend, TV and film celebrities are on hand to sign autographs.

Universal Studios is located in Universal City, just off the Hollywood Freeway at the Lankershim Boulevard exit (tel: 877-2121). Tours are given daily, except Thanksgiving and Christmas, from 8 a.m. to 5 p.m. in summer (from 10 a.m. to 3:30 p.m. the rest of the year). Adults pay $5.95; children ages 12 to 16, $4.95; children five to 11, $3.95; under five free. There are several restaurants on the premises; see also our listings for eating places in the Sheraton Universal Hotel, which is on the grounds.

NBC Television Studios

The largest color studios in the U.S., NBC-TV's Burbank facilities are home for "The Tonight Show," "Little House on the Prairie," "Sanford & Son," "Name That Tune" and many others. A behind-the-camera glimpse at this complex will take you to the sets of the above shows; it's not guaranteed that you'll actually meet a star, but it's not unlikely either—maybe Bob Hope, Dick Van Dyke, McLean Stevenson, Johnny Carson, one of his many guests or substitute hosts.

Aside from the glamor aspect, the tour is most interesting, including an inside look at scenery in production, wardrobe, props, special effects and rehearsal halls.

The NBC Studios in Burbank are located at 3000 West Alameda Avenue, and are easily accessible via the Hollywood or Ventura Freeways or by bus. No reservations are necessary for the one-hour tours, which run from 10 a.m. to 5 p.m., Monday through Saturday. The charge is $1.90 for adults, $1.25 for children ages six to 12, and free for children under six.

Tickets for some shows can be obtained by writing to the address above. However, for "The Tonight Show," tickets are available on a first-come, first-served basis at the studio, starting at 8:30 a.m. on the day of taping (lines begin forming very early in the morning). A few shows offer tickets about two days before the taping. The ticket office is open weekdays from 8:30 a.m. to 5:30 p.m. Call 845-7000 for information.

FOREST LAWN: There aren't many cities where a cemetery is on every tourist's sightseeing agenda, but then, there aren't many cemeteries like Forest Lawn. (Actually there are four Forest Lawns in L.A., but the most famous one is at 1712 South Glendale Avenue, Glendale.)

Comic Lenny Bruce called it "Disneyland for the dead," and Evelyn Waugh wrote a hilarious satire, *The Loved One,* about it. But to founder Dr. Hubert Eaton, Forest Lawn was the cemetery of his dreams that would symbolize the joys of eternal life—"a great park, devoid of . . . customary signs of earthly death, but filled with towering trees, sweeping lawns, splashing fountains, singing birds, beautiful statuary, cheerful flowers . . . a place where lovers new and old shall love to stroll and watch the sunset's glow."

Highlights for the living include: Rosa Caselli Moretti's stained-glass recreation of da Vinci's "The Last Supper" displayed in the Memorial Court of Honor of the Great Mausoleum. Moretti is the last member of a Perugia, Italy family known for its secret process of making stained glass. Thousands of Southern Californians are entombed in the Great Mausoleum, among them Jean Harlow, Clark Gable and W.C. Fields. The art terraces and the corridors are lined with reproductions of great works of Michelangelo and Donatello. In the Court of Honor are crypts that money cannot buy—they're reserved as final resting places for men and women whose service to humanity has been outstanding.

The big draw on the hill—next to the Forest Lawn Museum—is a special theater used for the presentation of two paintings, the "Crucifixion," conceived by Paderewski and painted by Jan Styka, dramatically depicting the moment before Christ is placed on the cross; and "The Resurrection," by Robert Clark, which was conceived by Dr. Eaton. The paintings are shown every half-hour from 11 a.m. to 5 p.m. daily.

Other attractions include reproductions of Ghiberti's "Paradise Doors"; the Court of David, housing a reproduction of Michelangelo's famous masterpiece (with the addition, in the Forest Lawn version, of a figleaf); churches like

Wee Kirk o' the Heather, modeled after the 14th-century Scottish church where Annie Laurie worshiped; and a faithful reproduction of Boston's historic Old North Church of Paul Revere fame.

Forest Lawn isn't just for the dear departed. The six churches have also been the setting for numerous christenings, services, ordinations and some 55,000 or so weddings. It can be visited admission-free from 9 a.m. to 5 p.m. daily. Telephone 254-3131 for information.

BUSCH GARDENS: Just 25 minutes from downtown Los Angeles, Busch Gardens, 16000 Roscoe Boulevard, Van Nuys (tel: 786-0410), is a 27½-acre family entertainment complex in a garden setting, featuring rides, animal shows, live entertainment and special attractions. It's also home to over 2,500 free-flying birds of 184 different species, including peacocks, swans, macaws, penguins, cockatoos, West African touracos and freeloading local ducks who dropped in accidentally and decided to stay.

Opened in 1966 on what had been a flat cabbage patch adjacent to Anheuser-Busch's Van Nuys brewery, Busch Gardens was originally a promotional facility. They still offer a monorail ride through the brewery that turns out Budweiser, Michelob and Busch beers, but entertainment facilities have expanded enormously and over ten-million visitors have come to enjoy them.

The lagoons and tropical gardens are best explored by taking one of the frequently departing boat rides that travel the park's nine acres of winding waterways. The terrain you pass through ranges from simulated High Sierra country, complete with 45-foot waterfalls, to a landscape of tropical palms and bamboo. You'll see birds like the Chinese mandarin duck, the South American king vulture and the scarlet ibis (sacred bird of ancient Egypt).

Seven times a day, beginning with a 1:30 performance, bird shows are staged in the Eagle Playhouse; "Sadie the Vixen" struts around clad only in white feathers, and a heroic winged prince rescues a fragile and feathery Snow White. There's also a penguin, seal and otter show, and a stage spectacular with homo sapiens stars, for a change. Other attractions are the Busch Barrel Flume ride, a self-propelled motorboat ride (kids love it), magic shows, and the recently added Old St. Louis, re-creating the turn-of-the-century St. Louis World's Fair, complete with a fun house, old-fashioned game arcade and a 400-seat replica of the famous Strand Theatre.

Busch Gardens are open daily from 10 a.m. to midnight, June 15 to September 2; the rest of the year they're open weekends and holidays only from 10 a.m. to 6 p.m. (closed Christmas and New Years). The price of general admission includes all rides, shows and attractions. Adults pay $5.25; children four to 11, $4.75 (under four, free). There's parking (50¢) at the Roscoe Boulevard entrance. To reach Busch Gardens, take the Hollywood Freeway to Ventura Freeway, then head north on the San Diego Freeway, getting off at Roscoe Boulevard.

WILSHIRE BOULEVARD: L.A.'s main street—we might call it the city's Champs Elysées, but would that famed Parisian street ever have a section called the **Miracle Mile?** No, that's strictly Americana, and it refers to the portion of Wilshire between Highland and Fairfax. The Boulevard passes through **MacArthur Park,** with its own lake and the **Otis Art Institute,** as well as **Lafayette Park.** Near the eastern edge of Miracle Mile, in the **Hancock Park,** are the **La Brea Tar Pits.**

Los Angeles County Museum of Art

A complex of three modern buildings around a central sculpture plaza, the County Museum of Art at 5905 Wilshire Boulevard (tel: 937-4250) is considered by many to be the finest and most eclectic art museum west of the Mississippi.

The four-story **Ahmanson Gallery** shelters the permanent collection, which encompasses prehistoric art to Andy Warhol. Important recent acquisitions include a sculpture of Saint Scholastica by Ignaz Günther, Germany's most eminent 18th-century sculptor, a monumental tenth-century Cambodian sculpture of the Hindu god Vishnu, and five important Japanese paintings from the Edo period. The museum's collection has been enhanced by considerable bequests, and it's particularly rich in Impressionist and Islamic art. Nineteenth- and 20th-century sculpture is also well represented.

The ground-level galleries are devoted to collections from the Near East, China, Japan, Egypt, Greece, Rome and medieval Europe, plus some rare Assyrian alabaster bas reliefs. Paintings from Spain, England, France and Early and High Renaissance masterpieces from Italy are on the Plaza level. The third level has 19th-century paintings and 20th-century sculpture. The fourth houses textile, costume, print and drawing exhibits, as well as Indian and Islamic art.

In the central building, the **Frances and Armand Hammer Wing**, are permanent and changing exhibits of contemporary art.

The third building, the **Leo S. Bing Center** contains the Bing Theater, Plaza Cafe (with outdoor tables) and an art rental gallery.

The museum is closed Mondays, Thanksgiving, Christmas and New Years. Hours are from 10 a.m. to 5 p.m. Tuesday through Friday, from 10 a.m. to 6 p.m. weekends. No admission is charged except for special exhibits in the Hammer Wing. Free tours covering the highlights of the permanent collection are offered weekdays at 1 p.m., weekends at 1 and 2:30 p.m.

Rancho La Brea Tar Pits

Even today a bubbling murky swamp of congealed oil, the tar pits are a primal sci-fi attraction right on the Miracle Mile. Part of Hancock Park, at 5801 Wilshire, the pits are the largest fossil site inherited from the Ice Age. They date back to prehistoric times (some 40,000 years back), when they formed a deceptively attractive drinking area for mammals, birds, amphibians and even insects (many of which are now extinct), which crawled in to slake a thirst and stayed forever. Other animals, seeing them trapped, thought the victims easy prey and jumped into the mire to devour them. Although the existence of the pits was known as early as the 18th century, it wasn't until 1906 that scientists began a systematic removal and classification of the fossils. In subsequent years, more than half-a-million specimens were brought up: ground sloths, huge vultures, mastodons (early elephants), camels and prehistoric relatives of many of today's rodents, bears, lizards and birds, as well as plants and seashells. In one pit, the skeleton of an Indian—dating, it is thought from 9,000 years ago—was unearthed.

More than two dozen of the specimens have been mounted and placed for exhibition in the new **Hancock Park Page Museum**. And replicas of the original trapped birds and animals stand fully life-sized in their original setting, to spur your imagination.

You can visit the laboratories where scientists are dating fossils: from noon to 3 p.m. Thursday through Sunday, subject to the schedules of the volunteer tour guides. Tours of the tar pits are also available Thursday through Sunday at 1 p.m. Conducted by docents of the Natural History Museum, the tours cover the historical and ecological significance of the excavations, as well as some of the techniques involved in uncovering the remains of prehistoric creatures.

WATTS TOWERS: A little-known American saga is the story of Simon Rodia, an Italian immigrant who came from one of the poorest districts in Rome, grew up in Watts and worked as a tile setter. At the age of 40, he was impressed with the need to create something, to leave something behind in his adopted country. The result of this desire—after 33 years of work with no encouragement, no help and no equipment other than his tile-setting tools—is Watts Towers.

Ignoring the jeers and scorn of his neighbors, Rodia scavenged the city for bits and pieces of iron and tin, steel rods, seashells, broken tiles, old bottles (especially green ones), chips of flowered dishes, etc. With no blueprints, he turned this junkyard of items into the Watts Towers, two of which soar ten stories high (nearly 100 feet), the others averaging 40 feet. Outline designs have been made in the walls with hammers, horseshoes and cooky cutters.

His task completed in 1954, Mr. Rodia suddenly and mysteriously left Watts. He was no longer there to guard his life's achievement, and in the years following, the towers fell into disrepair, attacked for sport by vandals. As it turned out, the greatest danger to the towers was not from vandals, but from the municipal building department, which ordered the towers to be leveled as "hazardous to the general public."

The issue became a nationwide cause célèbre. Art-lovers from all over the world—including New York's Museum of Modern Art, which called them "works of great beauty and imagination"—protested vigorously. And a private Committee for Simon Rodia's Towers in Watts was formed for their protection, demanding that the towers be given a fair test. In front of national television cameras and newspaper reporters, the crucial experiment was performed—the towers were subjected to 10,000 pounds of pull by a derrick. Only one seashell toppled, and the city deemed them safe enough to stand. In 1963, the Towers were designated a cultural monument by the City Cultural Heritage Board.

As for Rodia, he never returned to his towers. He was tracked down in 1959 in Martinez, California, but he seemed not to care about his amazing creation any more. Some speculated that an artist has no further interest in his work after it is completed, others said he was broken by the criticism his work had engendered. Whatever the reason, he died with the secret in 1965, and a memorial service was held for him at the towers.

The towers are at 1765 East 107th Street, Watts, and are open daily from 9 a.m. to 5 p.m. (no admission charge). To reach them take the Harbor Freeway toward San Pedro, getting off and turning left at Century Boulevard. Go right on Central, left on 108th Street, then left onto Willowbrook to 107th Street.

HIGHLAND PARK: When you take the Pasadena Freeway to Avenue 43, you'll find yourself in the great Southwest, that is, at—

The Southwest Museum

Founded by Charles F. Lummis over half a century ago, the Southwest Museum houses one of the finest collections anywhere of American Indian antiquities. Beautifully situated atop a steep hill, at 234 Museum Drive, the museum can be reached via a winding drive or through an elevator in a tunnel at the foot of the hill.

Among the fascinating exhibits here is the Caroline Boeing Poole Basket Collection in the West Wing—over 2,000 baskets from most of the tribes west of the Mississippi. Thirteen dioramas here illustrate the domestic activities and types of homes of the important basket-making tribes.

In the auditorium are examples of handicrafts and other artifacts of native peoples of the Far North and Northwest, including much Eskimo lore. The Plains Indians—the ones most often depicted, however inaccurately, in television and movie westerns—are represented in a hall on the upper floor. These are the Blackfoot, Crow, Sioux, Cheyenne, Arapaho, Kiowa and Comanche, nomadic hunters whose mainstay of existence was the buffalo. The central display here is an Indian camp complete with tanned buffalo- and cow-skin tepee.

On the second floor, the Lummis Hall of Prehistory documents the ancient prehistory of the Southwest, beginning with the rudimentary tools left by early man over 10,000 years ago.

In addition, space is devoted to the cultures of present-day Southwestern Indians.

The museum is open daily, except Monday, from 1 p.m. to 4:45 p.m., although it shuts down completely from mid-August to mid-September. No admission charge.

Also on the premises, at the foot of Museum Hill, is the **Casa de Adobe**, an architecturally correct replica of an early 19th-century Spanish Colonial ranch house. The Casa is open to the public, free of charge, on Wednesdays, Saturdays and Sundays from 2 to 5 p.m.

And you can also visit the home of founder Charles F. Lummis, **El Alisal**, nearby at 200 East Avenue 43. Lummis built this two-story, 13-room "castle" himself, using rocks from a nearby arroyo and telephone poles from along the Santa Fe Railroad. His home was a cultural center for many famous personages in the literary, theatrical, political and art worlds. It's open free to the public every day except Saturday from 1 to 4 p.m.

MAGIC MOUNTAIN: The thrill you've always wanted just might be the Great American Revolution—a huge three-quarter-mile roller coaster with a 360-degree, 90-foot-high vertical loop (that's right, you turn completely upside down). It's just one of over 50 rides and attractions at Magic Mountain, a beautifully landscaped 100-acre amusement park in the green rolling hills of Valencia, 35 miles northwest of downtown Los Angeles. In addition to the above-mentioned roller coaster, the most popular rides (some of which cost as much as $3 million to construct) include the Log Jammer—a log flume ride culminating in a 47-foot plunge into Whitewater Lake; the Gold Rusher—trapped in a runaway mine train, you careen crazily, roller-coaster-style, across hill and dale; and the Jet Stream—the closest you're ever likely to come to crossing Niagara Falls in a barrel. There's also a beautiful turn-of-the-century carousel, an aerial gondola tramway and our favorite, the Spin Out—a circular room that whirls around so fast it forces your body to cling to the wall by supracentrifugal gravity, which is just as well, because the floor drops down a frightening ten feet beneath you.

A new attraction for the tots is Wizard's Village, with rides and creative play equipment specially designed for them. The Wiz personally greets his tiny guests, there are magicians, puppeteers and mimes, and the Animal Farm is right next door.

In the summer, the Showcase Theatre features big-name entertainers—people like Connie Stevens, Bill Cosby, Phyllis Diller, the Righteous Brothers and Tanya Tucker. And year round, variety shows, marching bands, magic acts and local rock groups round out the bill.

You can pack a picnic lunch if you like, but there are many eateries in all price ranges offering everything from Bavarian roast beef to chicken yakitori. Not to mention countless stands selling pizza, hot dogs, burgers, corn on the cob, hot buttered popcorn and other amusement park staples.

A one-price ticket admits visitors to all rides, amusements and special attractions, including the big-name entertainment. Adults pay $7.50; children aged three to 11 pay $6.50 (under three free). The park is open in summer from 9 a.m. to midnight daily. Off-season hours vary, so it's best to call ahead (tel: 805/259-7272) for information.

Magic Mountain is reached from Highway 101 in Ventura by taking State Highway 126 through Fillmore to Castaic Junction, then turning south for about one mile at the junction of 126 and Interstate 5. From either direction, the park is two minutes west of the Golden State Freeway (Interstate 5) at the Magic Mountain Parkway exit.

THE SPANISH MISSIONS: Throughout this book, we've mentioned as sightseeing attractions many of the 21 missions created by Franciscan padre Junipero Serra. Built between 1769 and 1824, they reach from San Diego to Sonoma. In the Los Angeles area is one of the most visited of all the missions—

San Juan Capistrano

Fifty-six miles south of L.A., the little inland town of San Juan Capistrano is known for the swallows that return here every year on March 19th, Saint Joseph's Day. On October 23, the Day of San Juan, the swallows punctually leave for their home to the south, probably somewhere in South America. It's called the "miracle of the swallows", though, in fact, all swallows come and go at regular dates. The mission here dates from 1775. The semi-tropical grounds contain the remains of what is considered the oldest building in California, and the altar, from Catalonia, dates from the 17th century. Unfortunately, most of the mission was destroyed in the 1812 earthquake, so except for the original church (which has been restored) most of what you see here are great piles of ruins.

The mission may be visited from 7 a.m. to 5 p.m., and the admission charge is 50¢ for adults, free for youngsters under 12 if accompanied by parents.

Mission San Fernando

Closer by, at 15151 Mission Boulevard, at the junction of the Golden State and San Diego Freeways in San Fernando, the Mission San Fernando has seven acres of beautiful grounds as well as a convent. Dedicated in 1822, with an arcade of 21 classic arches and adobe walls four feet thick, it was a familiar stop for wayfarers along El Camino Real. The museum and the adjoining cemetery (where half-a-dozen padres and hundreds of Shoshone Indians are buried) are also of interest. Open from 9 a.m. to 4 p.m.; 75¢ admission for adults, 25¢ for children seven to 15.

Mission San Gabriel Arcangel

Nine miles northeast of downtown L.A., at 537 West Mission Drive, San Gabriel, this is one of the best preserved of the missions, tracing its origins to 1771. In the church (with walls five feet thick to withstand the ravages of time), is an oval-faced, sad-eyed "Our Lady of Sorrows"—said to have subdued hostile Indians with its serenity. The museum houses "aboriginal" Indian paintings on sail cloth depicting the 14 Stations of the Cross. Open to visitors daily (except, Christmas, Thanksgiving and Easter) from 9:30 a.m. to 4 p.m. Admission is 50¢ for adults, 25¢ for children five to 12 (under five free).

HUNTINGTON LIBRARY, ART GALLERY AND BOTANICAL GARDENS: At 1151 Oxford Road in San Marino (tel: 681-6601), the 207-acre former estate of pioneer rail tycoon Henry E. Huntington has been converted into a cultural center housing rare books (including a copy of the Gutenberg Bible printed in 15th-century Mainz), original manuscripts and great works of art.

His home is now the art gallery, where paintings, tapestries, furnishings, and other decorative arts are exhibited—chiefly English and French 18th-century works. The most celebrated is Gainsborough's "The Blue Boy," but the art gallery also contains Gilbert Stuart's portrait of George Washington, Sir Joshua Reynolds' "Sarah Siddons as the Tragic Muse," and a collection of Beauvais and Gobelins tapestries.

The library's remarkable collection of English and American first editions, letters and manuscripts includes the original manuscript of Thoreau's *Walden*, a 1410 copy of Chaucer's *Canterbury Tales,* Benjamin Franklin's *Autobiography* in his own writing, and Edgar Allan Poe's handwritten copy of *Annabel Lee*. All told, there are over six million manuscripts and 300,000 rare books ranging from the 11th century to the present.

If all that culture sets your mind aboggle, take a stroll in the magnificent Botanical Gardens: there's a Desert Garden filled with many varieties of cactus; a Camellia Garden with 1,500 varieties; an Australian Garden; a Japanese Garden, complete with an authentically furnished 16th-century samurai's house; a Zen Garden and bonsai court; a Rose Garden; and a Shakespeare Garden of flowers and shrubs mentioned in plays by the Bard. And there are more. Self-guided tour pamphlets of the gardens and the art gallery cost a dime at the bookstore.

The admission-free museum and grounds are open Tuesday through Sunday from 1 p.m. to 4:30 p.m. (closed on major holidays and during the month of October).

THE NORTON SIMON MUSEUM OF ART: Formerly the Pasadena Art Museum, this important collection at Colorado Boulevard and Orange Grove, Pasadena (tel: 449-6840), is situated in a semi-tropical landscape amidst broad plazas, sculpture gardens and a reflection pool. It re-opened as the Norton Simon Museum in March, 1975, with an extensive permanent collection and many rotating exhibits.

Newly installed Indian and Southeast Asian galleries feature works of stone and bronze from India, Nepal, Kashmir, Thailand and Cambodia. Other important areas covered here are Old Masters from Italian, Dutch, Spanish, Flemish and French schools, 20th-century painting and sculpture, Impressionist paintings and Franco-Flemish tapestries.

Some highlights: eight important paintings by Peter Paul Rubens; the most important collection of Chola bronzes outside India; Rembrandt's portrait of his son, Titus; and major works by Rousseau, Courbet, Matisse, Picasso, Corot, Breughel, and Raphael.

The museum is open Thursday through Sunday from noon to 6 p.m. Admission for adults is $1.50, students and senior citizens 50¢, under 12 free.

DESCANSO GARDENS: E. Manchester Boddy began planting camellias in 1941 as a hobby. Today the Rancho del Descanso (Ranch of Rest) that he started contains thousands of camellias with over 600 varieties—making it the world's largest camellia gardens. The County of Los Angeles purchased the gardens when Mr. Boddy retired in 1953, and over the years they have become an attraction that has delighted countless visitors.

In addition to the camellias, there is also a four-acre rose garden, which includes some varieties dating from the time of Christ. A stream and many paths wind through a towering oak forest, and a chaparral nature trail is provided for those who wish to observe native vegetation. Each month different plants in the Gardens are featured—daffodils, azaleas and lilacs in the spring, chrysanthemums in the fall and so on. Other features of the Gardens are monthly art exhibitions in the Hospitality House, and, in the camellia forest, (because the camellia originated in the Orient) a Tea House. The latter, donated by the Japanese-American community, features pools, waterfalls and a rock garden, as well as a gift shop built in the style of a Japanese farm house.

Located at 1418 Descanso Drive, La Canada (tel: 681-0331), the gardens are open daily from 8 a.m. to 5 p.m. (till 5:30 during Daylight Saving Time). Admission is free, though persons under 18 must be accompanied by adults. Picnicking is allowed in specified areas.

ORGANIZED TOURS: If you're pressed for time and want to see a lot, or if you just feel like being lazy and leaving the driving to others, organized sightseeing, offered by a number of companies, may be for you. The largest selection of tours is available from **Gray Line Tours Company,** 1027 West 3rd Street, Los Angeles (tel: 481-2121). In air-conditioned coaches, with commentaries by guides, the tours include such attractions as Disneyland, the movie studios, Farmers Market, Hollywood, Marineland and Movieland Wax Museum.

5. Los Angeles After Dark

The days when Los Angeles nightlife was one glamorous whirl under the scrutiny of gossip columnists is long gone, if indeed it ever really existed outside movie mags and columns. Basically, Los Angeles residents are suburban types, whose idea of a good way to spend an evening is to have friends in for drinks, poolside barbecues and parties. When they do go out on the town, it's usually for dinner at some posh restaurant.

But that doesn't mean there's nothing to do. It's just that Los Angelenos, like New Yorkers, take their abundant nightlife for granted and only bother with it when they have out-of-town guests—then they have a great time and vow to "do this more often." There are comedy clubs where big-name acts appear for a fraction of what you'd pay to see them across the border in Vegas. At any time, you can find top jazz, folk and rock entertainers. And there are always a few hit plays in town along with quality opera, concerts and dance recitals, some of which are presented under the stars at L.A.'s marvelous outdoor amphitheaters. If you have friends in town, take them along—they need to get out once in a while.

LIVE GROUPS: **Doug Weston's Troubadour,** 9081 Santa Monica Boulevard near Doheny, West Hollywood (tel: 276-6168). The management of the Troubadour has a good eye for talent—they often catch great acts just before they rise to national fame and $10-and-up ticket prices. Blood, Sweat and Tears were "discovered" here; it was the scene of Elton John's first appearance in America; and among those who have played here are The Byrds, Judy Collins, the Smothers Brothers, Joni Mitchell, Miles Davis, Loggins and Messina, and Linda Ronstadt. Tickets cost $3 to $5, depending on the act, and there's a two drink minimum (drinks cost $1.25 and up). Two shows are staged nightly, at 9 and 11 p.m. Monday night is hootenanny night, and there's a $2 cover, no minimum, for that evening only. Dress casually.

Filthy McNasty's, 8852 Sunset Boulevard at Larrabee Street (tel: 659-2055). Right in the heart of The Strip, billing itself as "famous since 1971," McNasty's has entertainment and dancing nightly, with performers like El Chicano, Buddy Miles and an all-girl band called Broad Daylight. Some of the audience is even more famous than the people on stage—John Wayne and Evel Kneivel both hang out here. Filthy himself (yes there is a Filthy) sings Wednesday through Sunday nights. There's always a one-drink minimum (about $1.75); weekdays there's a $1 cover charge, Friday and Saturday it's $2. Proof of age (21) is required.

There's another Filthy McNasty's at 11700 Victory Boulevard at Lankershim, in North Hollywood.

O'Shaughnessy's, "C" Level, Arco Plaza, 515 South Flower Street at 5th, downtown (tel: 629-2565). The setting is a medieval Irish castle (well, sort of), and the rollicking entertainment is Irish ballads and drinking songs provided by groups with names like the Mulligans. Needless to say, this is a lively place. You can dine here on Irish and American fare, choosing such entrees as fish 'n' chips ($3.75) and corned beef and cabbage ($4.75), either of which ought to be followed by a traditional dessert—Irish whiskey pie ($1.25). Open from 11 a.m. to 11 p.m. Monday through Thursday (till 1 a.m. on Friday and Saturday). Closed Sunday; no entertainment on Monday nights.

FOR COMEDY: **The Comedy Store,** 8431 Sunset Boulevard, a few blocks east of La Cienega, Hollywood (tel: 656-6225). Prepare yourself for a marathon of laughter at this Los Angeles comedy institution, the brilliant and entertaining creation of owner Mitzi Shore. Twelve to 15 comedians perform nightly—top names like Jimmy Walker, Redd Foxx, Richard Pryor, David Brenner and Gabe Kaplan, along with some lesser-known but still very good acts, the kind of guys (and occasionally gals) you've seen once or twice on the "Tonight Show" who are on their way up. The price: Monday through Thursday and Sunday, a cover of $2 and a one-drink ($1.75) minimum; Friday and Saturday, a $3 cover and a two-drink minimum. Why so inexpensive? This is where the young comedians showcase their acts for producers, agents, managers and talent scouts (they're the ones who aren't laughing as much as you are). And established comedians use the place to polish up their acts for Vegas. The show gets started nightly at 9 p.m. and goes on for five side-splitting hours.

There's another Comedy Store at 1621 Westwood Boulevard, between Santa Monica and Wilshire (tel: 477-4751). If you think you're funny, members of the audience can get up here on Monday and Tuesday nights and do five minutes.

Improvisation, 8162 Melrose Avenue at Crescent Heights, West Hollywood (tel: 651-2583), is a homey theatrical hangout where the comedy segments for TV shows like "Don Kirshner's Rock Concert" and some cable TV

LOS ANGELES: NIGHTLIFE

shows are filmed. Once again, both well-known and up-and-coming professional comedians use the place as a workshop; in the former category are Jimmy Walker, Richard Pryor and Rodney Dangerfield. Even Liza Minnelli has been known to try out new material here. Open nightly; shows begin at 9:30 p.m., with continuous entertainment till 2 a.m. Sunday nights new talent is auditioned, and Wednesday night is songwriters' showcase. Special shows sometimes play from 8:30 to 10 p.m. prior to the regular show on Friday, Saturday and Sunday nights—usually improvisational comedy groups. Dinner is available, and there's a full bar, but you don't have to be 21 to get in. Sunday through Thursday there's a $3.50 drink minimum; Friday it's $5; Saturday, a $5 drink minimum plus a $2 cover charge.

Ye Little Club, 455 North Canon Drive at Santa Monica Boulevard, Beverly Hills (tel: 275-3077), is another, lively place where some big-name entertainers polish up their acts. It's open Monday through Saturday—Monday is amateur night for auditions; the rest of the week live music begins at 9:30 and the show starts at 10:15. The cover charge ranges from $1 to $3 Tuesday through Saturday, the upper figure for entertainers like Joan Rivers, and there's a two-drink minimum (drinks average $1.75 but go up to $2.25 if a name performer is on).

JAZZ SUPPER CLUB: Donte's, 4269 Lankershim Boulevard at Moorpark, North Hollywood (tel: 769-1566), features top names in jazz along with steak and seafood fare in the $2.50-to-$8.95 range. In the past, Count Basie, Morgana King, Benny Carter, Carmen McRae, Sarah Vaughn and the Duke Ellington Orchestra have appeared here. "Jazz dinners" are served from 7 p.m. to 1 a.m.; shows are at 9:30 and 11:15 p.m. and 1 a.m. The cover charge ranges from $2 to $5, depending on the artist performing, and there's always a two-drink minimum (average drink is $1.75). Dinner is in addition to the cover and minimum.

JAZZ ALONG THE COAST: Concerts by the Sea, 100 Fisherman's Wharf, Redondo Beach (tel: 379-4998), features jazz greats like Stan Kenton, Dizzy Gillespie, Ahmad Jamal, Woody Herman and Count Basie. There are two shows nightly, at 9 and 11 p.m., in a concert hall on the lower level of the pier. Tickets range from $3.50 to $6 depending on the artist; Wednesday night it's half-price for everyone (it used to be half-price for women only, but then men got liberated). Under 21 not admitted.

More terrific jazz entertainment at **The Lighthouse**, 30 Pier Avenue, Hermosa Beach (tel: 372-6911). The self-proclaimed world's "oldest jazz and music club" presents mostly jazz, though occasionally there's a good rock group or a very hip comedian. Typically, you might catch Sonny Stitt, Pharaoh Sanders, Kenny Burrell, Cedar Walton or Mose Allison here. Shows are at 9:15 and 11 p.m. and 12:30 a.m. Admission is usually $4 to $5 with a one- or two-drink minimum, depending on who's playing. The Lighthouse is open nightly except Monday, and minors are welcome.

DISCOTHEQUES: Gazzarri's Hollywood à-Go-Go, 9039 Sunset Boulevard, Hollywood (tel: 273-6606), has been go-go-going for years—it's Hollywood's oldest disco, and it's still going strong. The music is provided by top-40 dance bands. Gazzarri's is also well known for the Gazzarri Dancers and its presentation of old-time movies. In addition to records, three groups go full steam Wednesday through Sunday nights. Admission is $3 Wednesday, Thursday, and Sunday, $3.50 Friday and Saturday. On Sunday, students with IDs get in for $1; Thursday nights ladies are admitted free.

The Basement, 4215 Admiralty Way, Marina del Rey (tel: 823-0927), attracts a crowd of affluent-chic young things who know their way around the dance floor. Generally two groups perform nightly, Tuesday through Sunday, and there's always dancing. There's a one-drink minimum every night; in addition, men pay $1 cover on Wednesdays and Thursdays, and everyone pays $2 cover on Friday and Saturdays. But if you dine upstairs, at the Second Story, there's no cover. It happens to be a lovely place to eat, with a wall of windows overlooking the yachts moored in the harbor. Items on the steak and seafood menu range from $5.95 for stuffed dover sole to $8.95 for steak and lobster served with drawn butter, salad and a baked potato. Both parts of this establishment are open seven nights, with dinner beginning at 5 p.m. To get into the Basement, you must have proof that you're over 21.

DANCING WITH A VIEW: L'Escoffier, 9876 Wilshire Boulevard, Beverly Hills (tel: 274-7777), is the Beverly Hilton's award-winning penthouse restaurant. In addition to enjoying the superb continental cuisine, a panoramic view of the city and elegant ambience, you can dance the night away to music provided by a live orchestra. Quite a romantic evening. A la carte entrees are about $10 to $15; Le Menu Classique, a complete prix-fixe dinner, is $17; or you can splurge and order Le Diner Escoffier, a seven-course gourmet feast for $22. Drinks start at $2. Open Monday through Saturday till about midnight.

MIXED BAGS: The **ABC Entertainment Center,** Century City, directly across from the Century Plaza Hotel, offers a variety of nightlife options. For openers, there's the **Shubert Legitimate Theater,** presenting big-time musicals —like *Fiddler on the Roof,* and *A Chorus Line*—often straight from Broadway with the original cast. Evening prices range from about $8 to $16 (matinees are less). Call the box office at 553-9000.

There are two plush first-run movie theaters in the complex (tel: 553-4595 to find out what's playing).

Then there's the **Playboy Club** (tel: 277-2777) for food, entertainment and bunnies aplenty; and **Harry's Bar & Grill** (tel: 277-2333), which looks just like its namesake in Florence, for drinks and dinner nightly and piano bar Tuesday through Saturday.

Across the street at the **Century Plaza Hotel,** there's dancing to a trio Friday and Saturday nights in the **Garden Room** (no cover or minimum; drinks cost $1.85). And finally, in the same hotel, the **Hong Kong Bar** (tel: 277-2000) offers continuous live and recorded entertainment for dancing (light rock and disco sounds) from 9 p.m. to 1:30 a.m. The ambience is dockside-Suzy-Wong-Chinese-cellar-bar-sultry, if you can conjure that one up. A $1 cover charge and a two-drink minimum are levied on Sunday and Tuesday through Thursday. The cover increases to $3 on Friday and Saturday; Wednesday night women get in free. Closed Mondays.

The Hollywood Palladium, 6215 Sunset Boulevard at Vine (tel: 466-4311), provides about as wide a spectrum of entertainment as we can imagine. Traditionally it was the place for big bands, and they still play here on occasion—Les Brown, Ray Anthony, Tex Benecke and of course, Lawrence Welk, who does his famous New Years Eve from the Palladium (actually he plays the last three days of the year). Sometimes rock stars play here—groups like the Average White Band and the Beachboys—or country and western singers. On other nights there are karate exhibitions, Latin dance nights, country and square dance nights, rock award shows, antique shows and closed-circuit fights, among other things. For music, the doors open at 7 p.m.; the show starts at 8:30 and goes till about 2 a.m. Prices vary with the attraction, and are usually within the $5-to-$10 range.

The Hollywood Bowl, 2301 North Highland Avenue at Odin Street (tel: 87-MUSIC), is an outdoor amphitheater with perfect natural acoustics. It's the summer home of the Los Angeles Philharmonic Orchestra (Symphonies under the Stars). The season begins in early July and ends around Labor Day. Internationally known conductors and soloists perform classical programs on Tuesday, Thursday and Saturday nights, but the season also includes many country, folk, jazz and pop events. So you might see anyone from Zubin Mehta conducting Beethoven's Ninth, to Arthur Fiedler conducting Gershwin favorites, to Sarah Vaughn to Waylon Jennings. The last performance of the year usually gets a fireworks finale.

Part of The Bowl ritual is to order a picnic basket from **Pepper Tree Lane** (call 87-MUSIC the day before to order). Or you can reserve a table at the **Patio Restaurant** (tel: 87-MUSIC) which serves a buffet supper.

Seats for classical concerts start at $1 and ascend to $6 for bench seats, to $7-$11 for box seats. For other programs, tickets range from $1 to $10. The box office opens June 1; hours are 10 a.m. to 9 p.m. Monday through Saturday, noon to 6 p.m. on Sunday. Parking space can be reserved for $2.50, though at lots adjacent to The Bowl entrance you can park for $1.

The Greek Theatre, 2700 North Vermont Avenue, Griffith Park (tel: 666-6000). A place where the entertainment ranges from full-scale operatic productions to Neil Diamond to Sammy Davis, Jr. might have been created just to fit into our "mixed bag" category. Such a one is the Greek Theatre, patterned after the classic outdoor theaters of ancient Greece. Dance groups and national theater societies also perform here. The season runs from late June through September. Tickets range in price from $3.50 to $12, depending on whether you want to see the show with or without binoculars. The ticket office is open from 10 a.m. to 10 p.m.

The Music Center, 135 North Grand Avenue at 1st Street, downtown, is L.A.'s most prestigious cultural entertainment facility. It consists of three theaters:

The **Dorothy Chandler Pavilion** is a 3,250-seat hall for opera, recitals, musicals and dance performances, home to the Los Angeles Civic Light Opera and, from October through April, to the Los Angeles Philharmonic. However, it's sometimes used for theater, too—e.g. *Pacific Overtures.* In 1976 the New York City Opera played their Los Angeles engagement here, performing 13 different works over a one-month period.

The **Ahmanson Theatre,** a 2,100-seat legitimate playhouse, is (along with the Mark Taper Forum) home base of the Center Theatre Group, who perform four plays here from mid-October to early May. Last year they were *The Norman Conquests,* starring Richard Benjamin and Paula Prentiss; *The Night of the Iguana,* starring Richard Chamberlain, Eleanor Parker and Raymond Massey; Neil Simon's *California Suite,* and *Same Time, Next Year.* Among the distinguished directors who have worked at the Ahmanson are Sir Laurence Olivier, Mike Nichols and Sir John Gielgud. In addition to the CTG offerings, Broadway productions like *The Wiz* and *Eleanor* are performed here, and occasionally there's a solo performer, like Diana Ross.

The **Mark Taper Forum** is a more intimate, circular theater with 750 seats. Last year's productions included Tom Stoppard's *Travesties,* and *The Robber*

Bridegroom. The emphasis here is on new and contemporary works, though you might catch something like *The Duchess of Malfi,* as well.

Needless to say, with all this diversity, we can't begin to quote prices. There are reductions available to many performances for students and senior citizens. Phone 972-7211 for all ticket information.

SOUTH-OF-THE-BORDER: We're not talking about flying down to Tijuana; we mean Mexican nights right in L.A. Like the festive entertainment offered at **Casa La Golondrina**, 35 Olvera Street, downtown (tel: 628-4349). Located on the city's oldest street, it's housed in the historic Pelanconi House (circa 1850). The cafe itself dates from 1924. You can sit by the fireplace, dine on Mexican fare, or just sip a margarita, while enjoying strolling mariachi troubadours, flamenco guitarists and the like. There's entertainment nightly in summer; the rest of the year the Casa is closed Wednesdays and Thursdays. There's no cover charge or minimum; drinks are $2, Mexican beer $1.25. For $5 you can have a complete meal including a taquito appetizer, guacamole, entree, Mexican beans with cheese, Spanish rice, tortillas, coffee and dessert.

More of the same at **Matador,** 10948 West Pico Boulevard at Veteran Avenue, West L.A. (tel: 475-4949), where you can dine on a delicious paella à la Valencia ($6.25) while enjoying flamenco dancers and guitarists. The entertainment—three shows nightly—begins about 9 or 9:30 Wednesday through Sunday nights. For non-diners there's a $2.50 cover charge plus a one-drink minimum.

El Gato, 7324 Sepulveda Boulevard, Van Nuys (tel: 781-1580), has the greatest variety of entertainment. There's an eight-piece mariachi band for dancing Wednesday through Sunday; the same nights, there's disco dancing in the Cantina cocktail lounge; and Sundays at 6 p.m. there's a marionette show geared to children. We like to dine here (big combination dinners are $4.25 to $7), at the tables overlooking the carp pond. The only extra charge is a $1 cover at the Cantina on Friday and Saturday nights.

VAUDEVILLE: The **Mayfair Music Hall,** 214 Santa Monica Boulevard, (tel: 451-0621), is the oldest theater in Santa Monica. Built in 1911 as an opera house, it later underwent incarnations as a vaudeville house and silent movie theater, complete with organ. Today its decor and entertainment hark back to the Victorian era in London. Patrons find themselves in a setting of plush grandeur, with red cut-velvet seating, gold-leaf rococo boxes, stained-glass windows and glittering cyrstal chandeliers. In the English music-hall tradition, à la "Upstairs, Downstairs," a "chairman" (master of ceremonies) is seated in a box above the stage. With the help of a gavel, he introduces the cast and show, making wry comments throughout. The show consists of a fast-paced collection of songs, dances and sketches.

You can dine elegantly during the show in the **Crystal Palace Dining Pavilion** on the balcony level; complete meals are $4.75 to $8.75. Drinks—beers, ales and spirits—are available from the **Circular Bar;** basket snacks—like sandwiches, hard-boiled eggs, cheese, etc.—from the **Grub Pub.** The hall is closed on Monday and Tuesday. Admission is $5.50, increasing to $6.50 on Saturdays.

FIFTIES NOSTALGIA: Art Laboe's Oldies but Goodies Club, 8433 Sunset Boulevard near La Cienega (tel: 654-6650), is for those of you "hep cats" whose musical consciousness was first awakened to strains of "Earth angel, earth angel, will you be mine?" It's not just the old songs, it's the old groups singing them live—the Coasters, Diamonds, Penguins, Drifters and whoever else is still together after all these years. Polish up your lindy—this music's not just for listening. Open Friday and Saturday nights only from 8 p.m. till 2 a.m. Admission is $3.50 per person, no minimum. Hard and soft drinks are $1.50, and you can order a steak dinner for $5.75. You have to be at least 21 to get in, and at least 33 to sing along.

THEATER: The **Whiskey Theater,** 8901 Sunset Boulevard, West Hollywood (tel: 652-4202), used to be a disco presenting big-name rock entertainers like Stevie Wonder. Nowadays it's a theater showing innovative and offbeat productions like *Coca-Cola Grande,* and *Let My People Come,* both of which came direct from New York, and *The Psycho Sluts,* this from London. Shows are at 8:30 p.m. week nights, 9 p.m. and midnight on Friday and Saturday. All tickets are about $5. Closed Mondays.

The **Huntington Hartford Theatre,** 1615 North Vine near Hollywood Boulevard (tel: 462-6666), offers a wide spectrum of productions. For instance, they've had the Royal Shakespeare Company with Glenda Jackson in *Hedda Gabler,* Sammy Cahn doing *Words and Music,* and San Francisco's excellent American Conservatory Theatre (ACT) performing *Something's Afoot.* Evening shows are at 8:30 p.m. Tuesday through Saturday nights, 7:30 p.m. on Sundays. Ticket prices range from $4.50 to $12.50 (matinees are cheaper).

Theatrecraft, 7445 1/4 Sunset Boulevard at Gardner Street (tel: 876-3575), does serious, classic, avant-garde and comedy productions, all of proven quality. As a professional repertory company staging about six shows per season for the past 15 years, they've even premiered three New York productions. Past productions have included *Rhinoceros, The Balcony, Tiny Alice, Of Mice and Men,* and *A Hatful of Rain.* Performances are Friday and Saturday nights at 8:15 p.m. (there's also a 2 p.m. Sunday matinee). Seats are in the $3-to-$5 range.

The **Company Theater,** 1653 S. La Cienega Boulevard, a few blocks south of Pico (tel: 274-5153), is dedicated to "the exploration of the newest processes, techniques, and materials of today's theatre world and the reinterpretation of classic dramatic works." All of which makes for excellent and vital theater. In its nine years on the scene, the Company has produced over 40 plays, about a third of which were original works. In addition to plays (emphasis on new works) and musicals, the Company is currently moving into other experimental areas (dance presentations, mime and artistic events) and is also opening its doors to traveling companies from around the world. Prices are always most reasonable.

Note: Don't forget the Mark Taper Forum and Ahmanson Theatre at the Music Center, and the Shubert Legitimate Theater at the ABC Entertainment Center; details about them all above under the heading "Mixed Bags."

MOSTLY ROCK: The **Universal Amphitheater,** Universal City (tel: 980-9421), is a 5,200-seat outdoor arena adjacent to the Visitors Entertainment Center of Universal Studios. It's well designed—no seat is more than 140 feet from the stage—and only top names perform here, usually for three to five days. Tickets are often sold out before the concert date, so haunt the box office in advance; it's open Monday to Saturday from 10 a.m. to 9 p.m. (Sunday from noon), with lines forming at dawn. What's all the fuss about? James Taylor, Kris Kristofferson, Roberta Flack, Jose Feliciano, Neil Sedaka, Barry Manilow, Loggins and Messina, Linda Ronstadt, Al Green, Judy Collins, etc., etc., etc. Tickets cost $5.25 to $8.75.

Chapter IX

DISNEYLAND AND ENVIRONS

1. Anaheim
2. Buena Park
3. Santa Ana

THOUGH PHYSICALLY, ANAHEIM, Buena Park and Santa Ana, are among the most unprepossessing towns in California, they are also the ones that attract the most visitors. For if the natural surroundings are uninspiring and the streets lack any vestige of charm, the man-made attractions off the streets are magical and enchanting—transformed by the magic wand of Walt Disney into a wonderful world of make believe. And Disneyland is just one of the spectacular attractions in the area. There's also Knott's Berry Farm, Enchanted Village, The Alligator Farm, Movieland Wax Museum and more. So take the kids, and if you don't have any kids, be a kid.

1. Anaheim

Just 27 miles south-southeast of downtown Los Angeles, reached via the Santa Ana Freeway, Anaheim *is* Disneyland. Once a sleepy little town in the Valencia orange-grove belt, it now has over 50 hotels to handle the masses of visitors who come to visit the world-famed attraction. Disneyland is on everyone's must-see list; even Nikita Khrushchev insisted on seeing it when he visited California.

If you're going by car, just get on the freeway heading south, and you'll be in Anaheim in about an hour. If you go by bus, take the "Freeway Flyer" (No. 800) from the terminal in downtown Los Angeles at 6th and Los Angeles Streets.

DISNEYLAND: Opened in 1955, this $150-million, 74-acre entertainment complex is still unrivaled as "the happiest kingdom on earth." It's split into seven theme lands, each with its own rides and attractions. You might start at the entrance and work clockwise, but our own favorite plan of attack is to arrive at opening time and do all the "E" coupon rides first before the long midday lines form. (Tickets come in A,B,C,D, and E categories—"E" rides are the most exciting and popular, "D" rides the second most, and so on). The themed lands are as follows:

Main Street, the main drag of a small turn-of-the-century American town, is at the entrance to the park. Since most of its attractions are "A" and "B" coupons, we like to save it for the end of the day—particularly the Main Street Cinema (a "B" coupon), where you can rest your weary feet while enjoying silent film classics and cartoons. If you want to tour the entire park, trains (all 1890 or earlier vintage) of the Disneyland Railroad (a "D" coupon) depart regularly from the Main Street Depot and completely encircle the park, with stops at Frontierland and Tomorrowland.

Adventureland is inspired by exotic regions of Asia, Africa and the South Pacific. Here electronically animated tropical birds, flowers and tiki gods present a musical comedy in the Enchanted Tiki Room (an "E" coupon.) Within a spear's throw, a jungle cruise (also an "E" coupon) is threatened by wild animals and cannibals.

New Orleans Square re-creates the atmosphere of that city around the mid-1800s. Of course, you'll take a trip through the Haunted Mansion (an "E" coupon), inhabited by 999 ghosts, always (heh! heh! heh!) in search of "Occupant 1,000." Pirates of the Caribbean (an "E" coupon) takes you down a plunging waterfall through pirate caves, ending in a dynamite explosion set off by a "band of befuddled buccaneers."

Bear Country, inspired by the great outdoors, is the newest area. What better way to see this rugged country than in Davy Crockett Explorer Canoes (a "D" coupon)?

Frontierland, with a log-walled stockade entrance, is America in the early 1800s—a land of dense forests and broad rivers inhabited by hearty pioneers. A Mine Train ("D" Coupon) journeys through the area, where over 200 electronically animated animals, birds and reptiles come to life.

Fantasyland is mostly geared to the very young, with a story-book theme and rides—you can attend the Mad Hatter's wild Tea Party (a "C" coupon) or fly over London to Never Never Land with Peter Pan and Tinker Bell (a "C" coupon). One of the park's most popular rides is in Fantasyland, the Matterhorn Bobsleds (an "E" coupon), a roller-coaster kind of ride past waterfalls and culminating in a big splash into glacier lakes at the bottom of the mountain.

Tomorrowland explores the world of the future. It has some of the most terrific Disneyland attractions: Adventure Through Inner Space (a "C" coupon), which shrinks you to minuscule proportions and takes you into the molecules of a snowflake; Mission to Mars (a "D" coupon); and an atomic Submarine Voyage (an "E" coupon).

And that, of course, is not the half of it. There are costumed Disney characters, penny arcades, restaurants and snack bars galore, fireworks, barbershop quartets, mariachi bands, ragtime pianists, parades, shops, marching bands, etc.

General admission to Disneyland is $5 for adults, $4 for juniors (12-17 years of age) and $2 for children (three to 11). There is no charge for children two or under. Instead of paying separately for each attraction, it's best to purchase one of the ticket books. For example, the "Big 11" ticket book entitles you to 11 adventures as well as your general admission. It costs $6.50 for adults, $6 for juniors and $5.50 for children. Then there's the "Deluxe" book that admits you to 15 attractions and includes the general admission; it costs $7.50 for adults (a $14.60 value), $7 for juniors (a $13.60 value) and $6.50 for kids (an $11.10 value). First-timers may want to take Disneyland's Deluxe Guided Tour, the fee including seven major attractions. Adults and juniors are charged $8, children $5.

During the fall, winter and spring seasons, Disneyland is open from 10 a.m. to 6 p.m. Wednesdays through Fridays, and from 9 a.m. to 7 p.m. weekends. The park is closed Mondays and Tuesdays. During Thanksgiving, Christmas and Easter holidays, Disneyland is open every day on an extended operating schedule. During the summer season, from mid-June to mid-September, the park is open daily from 8 a.m. to 1 a.m., with special entertainment for the entire family. For further information call (714) 533-4456, or (213) 626-8605, ext. 101.

THE ANAHEIM CONVENTION CENTER: Yes, Virginia, there is something else in Anaheim. The Anaheim Convention Center, 800 West Katella (tel: 533-5511), is a $23-million, 40-acre exhibit facility—the largest such complex on the West Coast—located directly opposite Disneyland. Several things are always going on here—they might include a Helen Reddy concert, boxing, an ice revue, antique fair, recreational-vehicles show, or even the circus. Check it out.

WHERE TO STAY IN ANAHEIM: Families and Disney freaks might want to make Anaheim their Southern California base while taking in Disneyland and all the other nearby attractions.

Disneyland Hotel, 1150 West Cerritos Avenue (tel: 635-8600), is just adjacent to the park, and Disneyland's Monorail stops right on the premises. In January of 1976 the hotel completed a $1.5-million renovation and improvement program, and is looking most spiffy. Located on 60 lushly landscaped acres, it offers 1,000 guest rooms, six restaurants and an equal number of cocktail lounges, 16 boutiques, every kind of service desk imaginable, a health spa, two swimming pools, a 50-position driving range and an 18-hole miniature golf course. Six tennis courts are within walking distance, and a baby-sitting service is available. And what other hotel has a panoramic rooftop cocktail lounge that looks out over the Magic Kingdom?

There are two kinds of rooms—those in the main building, and the garden rooms. The former all have one window wall, the latter a lanai area. All are attractively furnished with every modern amenity. Single rooms are $33 to $50; doubles and twins, $38 to $57. Rollaway beds are $5 each, and cribs are free.

The **Sheraton-Anaheim Hotel,** 1015 West Ball Road (tel: 778-1700; 800/ 325-3535), has a Tudor-style turreted exterior that makes you wonder if you haven't wandered into Disneyland's newest theme area. In keeping with this motif, the hotel's dining room (an excellent one, by the way) is called Falstaff Room, and the menu lists items like "M'Lord's Combination Favorite," in this case a steak and lobster dinner, for $10.95. The Falstaff Tavern for wines, beers and spirits adjoins. Facilities include 370 rooms, a discotheque (The Happy Yeoman), a large outdoor pool, free shuttle service back and forth to Disneyland, and free parking.

The rooms are irreproachably modern, with just a few medieval touches; all have color TV, radio, direct-dial phone, dressing rooms, tub/shower bath, and the like. Singles range from $23 to $32, doubles from $29 to $38, and there's no charge for children 17 and under occupying the same room as their parents.

Very nice accommodations, too, at the **Anaheim Viking TraveLodge**, 505 West Katella Avenue, one block from Disneyland (tel: 774-8710; 800/255-3050). The 51 rooms are attractive standard motel units, all with color TV, direct-dial phone, modern bath and in-room coffee-makers. There's a decent-sized swimming pool with a slide and diving board. Rates are seasonal. From May 15 to September 15 singles are $26, doubles $28 and twins $34. The rest of the year singles are $18, doubles $20, twins $24. Children under 17 stay free in their parents' room the year round. In peak season, two-bedroom units that can accommodate up to eight persons are $44 to $48.

Last and least (least expensive, that is), there's a **Motel 6** in Anaheim at 921 South Beach Boulevard (tel: 827-9450). It's 54 air-conditioned units all have TV, and there's a swimming pool on the premises. See the Introduction for details.

WHERE TO DINE: Anaheim is not exactly one of the world's gourmet capitals. If you're just in town for the day, you'll probably eat at Disneyland, and most hotels have reasonable dining facilities. If you should feel like a night out, however, the most prestigious restaurant in town is **Mr. Stox**, 1105 East Katella Avenue (tel: 634-2994), offering hearty steak and seafood dinners in an atmospheric early-California setting. Roast prime rib of beef ($10.50) is the house specialty; it comes with soup or salad, hot San Francisco sourdough bread, horseradish, potatoes and creamed spinach—all served to you by attractive mini-skirted waitresses. Homemade desserts like the chocolate fudge cake Grand Marnier ($1), should not be resisted. Mr. Stox has an exceptional wine cellar, as well. At night there's dancing to a live singer and trio. Open for lunch weekdays (the menu is lower-priced) and dinner nightly.

2. Buena Park

Just five miles from Anaheim is Buena Park, with six major attractions: Knott's Berry Farm, California Alligator Farm, Enchanted Village, Movieland Wax Museum, the Palace of Living Art and Movieworld. Don't even think of doing them all in one day, much less combining them with Disneyland. If you want to see every attraction, it's advisable to stay in the area.

KNOTT'S BERRY FARM: In 1920 Walter and Cordelia Knott arrived in Buena Park in their old Model T and leased 20 acres of land. When times got hard during the Depression, Cornelia set up a roadside stand selling pies and preserves. As traffic increased, she added home-cooked chicken dinners to her offerings. The first day she sold eight, by the end of the year she was selling about 90 a day—today, the world-famous **Chicken Dinner Restaurant** serves up over a million chicken meals a year! But even the first few years, lines were so long that Walter decided to create an Old West Ghost Town as a diversion for waiting customers. That's how it all began. The Knott family is still running the farm, and it has become the nation's third-best-attended family entertainment complex. It's divided into three "Old Time Adventures" areas. They are:

Old West Ghost Town, the original attraction, a collection of authentic buildings, refurbished and relocated from actual deserted Western ghost towns. Guests can immerse themselves in rip-roarin' Wild West lore—pan for gold, climb aboard the stagecoach, ride rickety train cars through the Calico Mine, get held up aboard the Denver and Rio Grand Calico Railroad, or hiss the villain at a melodrama in the Birdcage Theatre.

Fiesta Village is a south-of-the-border environment of open markets, strolling mariachis, re-creations of California missions, wild rides like the "Mexican Whip," and nightly fireworks.

Roaring '20s Amusement Area and Airfield is the latest addition, and it contains the thrilling "Sky Tower," a parachute jump which drops riders 20 stories (over 200 feet) at free-fall speeds. In addition to the 12 chutes, there's an observation car called the Sky Tower, which revolves 360° while traveling up and down the tower. Thrill-seekers will also want to try the "Corkscrew" roller coaster with two 360° loops (this was the world's first upside-down roller coaster). The latest Knott's restaurant is in this section, too—The Airfield Eatery, a replica of a 1920s airplane hangar, where buffet meals are served. And there's even a new discotheque, Cloud Nine.

In addition to the themed areas, there's the **Good Time Theatre,** presenting "America on Ice," a musical ice extravaganza featuring international skating champions daily (except Thursdays) throughout the summer. At night, there's big-name entertainment in the Theatre—people like Frankie Avalon, Phyllis Diller, David Brenner, Rick Nelson and Pat Boone.

Knott's Berry Farm is located two miles south of the Santa Ana Freeway on Beach Boulevard (Highway 39), just ten freeway minutes west of Disneyland and 25 miles southeast of Los Angeles's Civic Center. A Super Bonanza Ticket Book covers admission and ten rides; it costs $5.75 for adults, $4.75 for children 11 and under. Children under three go in free.

There's ample free parking. Open year round except December 25th. Summer hours are 9 a.m. to midnight (till 1 a.m. Friday and Saturday nights); the rest of the year hours are 10 a.m. to 6 p.m. (till 10 p.m. Friday and Saturday nights). For further information call (714) 827-1776.

CALIFORNIA ALLIGATOR FARM: Across the street from Knott's Berry Farm is the Alligator Farm, 7671 La Palma Avenue (tel: 714/522-2615). It's home to over 1,000 alligators and crocs, including one of the largest crocodiles in captivity—more than 15 feet long and weighing about 1,400 pounds. They come from all over—the Nile, the Florida Everglades, South America and India. All branches of the reptile family are represented—snakes, turtles, tortoises, lizards, even the deadly iguana. And some of the inhabitants are movie stars, rented out for jungle scenes.

The Alligator Farm is open daily from 10:30 a.m. to 6 p.m. (till 9 p.m. in summer). There's ample free parking. Admission is $2.50 for adults, $1 for children five to 14; under five free.

ENCHANTED VILLAGE: The newest of Buena Park's attractions, located on a 32-acre site, is the creation of "animal philosopher" Ralph Helfer, who started "affection training," a method of training animals based on love, patience and understanding. The Village offers shows and "happenings" based on a special relationship between man and animal. A "happening" might be a tarantula crawling on, or a python coiling around, a human—not you, a trained employee. On the other hand, it might be the sudden appearance of Tahitian dancers. To enter Enchanted Village, visitors follow a trail that winds through landscaped hills, over bridges and past a waterfall. Once inside, three major entertainment presentations are available.

In the **Gentle Jungle Theatre** a huge elephant and a beautiful girl tell a story, and a single trainer puts ten full-grown Bengal tigers through their paces.

The 3,000-seat **Wilderness Theatre** features a musical extravaganza with horses, eagles, mountain lions, bears, etc., performing alongside human singers and dancers.

The **Lost Island Theatre** uses a jungle setting for land and water animal performances, in which humans and animals meet a mythical swampland creature.

In addition, there are continuous elephant and camel rides, and other attractions including the Tana River Raft Ride through lush tropical greenery filled with exotic birds. And in **The Touching Place** you can pet and feed llamas, 700-pound Galapagos tortoises and other animals.

Enchanted Village is located at 6122 Knott Avenue, about ten minutes north of Disneyland. It's reached by taking the Beach/Artesia off-ramp going south on the Santa Ana Freeway, or via Knott Avenue on the Riverside Freeway.

All shows, happenings and exhibits are included in a single-price admission: $3.50 for adults, $1.75 for children ages four to 11 (under four free). Open daily from 9 a.m. to 9 p.m. in summer; Saturday through Wednesday from 10 a.m. to 6 p.m. the rest of the year. For further information call 523-2381.

MOVIELAND WAX MUSEUM: The glamor that once was Hollywood isn't gone—it's just moved south to Buena Park. Self-billed as "the world's largest and finest wax museum," Movieland creates the illusion of a big Hollywood premiere with a Rolls-Royce forever parked out front and a plush red velvet foyer with crystal chandeliers. It was dedicated in style "to the artists of the entertainment industry" a little over 15 years ago by none other than America's Sweetheart, Mary Pickford.

Over the years, many of the stars have taken an active interest in their wax counterparts. Vincent Price loved to "stand in" for his wax figure and then jump out and terrify unsuspecting visitors. Gina Lollobrigida tugged at the hem of the slip worn by her replica, saying it "showed too much Gina." And, more recently, Tony Orlando and Dawn premiered their figures on network television. All in all, there are 230 stars represented, from Charlie Chaplin perusing his shoe dinner in *The Gold Rush* to Newman and Redford in *Butch Cassidy and the Sundance Kid*. All the most memorable movie scenes are re-created, and to enhance the atmosphere the sets are equipped with kleig lights, microphones, wind machines and cameras ready to roll.

Movie history is further documented by a collection of original movie machines, beginning with flip-card films starring Rin Tin Tin and Tom Mix.

Movieland Wax Museum is located just off the Santa Ana Freeway at 7711 Beach Boulevard (Highway 39). Midway in the galleries is a quick-service restaurant called Commissary of the Stars. The Museum is open in summer Sunday through Thursday from 9 a.m. to 10 p.m. (till 11 p.m. Friday and Saturday). Winter hours on Sunday through Thursday are 10 a.m. to 9 p.m. (till 11 p.m. Friday and Saturday). Adults are charged $4.50 for admission;

children ages four to 11, $2.75; under four free. For further information telephone 522-1154.

Palace of Living Art
For the same admission price you pay at Movieland Wax Museum, you can visit the adjoining million-dollar attraction, the Palace of Living Art. Here sculptures and paintings have been transformed into three-dimensional settings with life-size wax figures. They're all here: Grant Wood's classic Midwest couple, "American Gothic," Michelangelo's "Pietá" and "David," "Mona Lisa" smiling benignly on the scene, while Aristotle prefers to contemplate the bust of Homer.

MOVIEWORLD: Here's some more Hollywood glamor gone south. It's the largest collection of "cars of the stars," movie props and memorabilia outside the studios. If a film has old cars in it, chances are they're from Movieworld. Among the vehicles on display are the Waltons' jalopy, Ma Barker's 1930 Cadillac, the custom-made Pierce-Arrow of Fatty Arbuckle and the custom-built Mercedes-Benz of Al Jolson. Sets and props span 50 years of motion picture history; you'll see Jimmy Durante's piano, the coach from *Gone with the Wind,* Shirley Temple's little candy-cane chair, and a movie set and dinosaur egg from *Planet of the Apes.* The lobby contains a snack bar and a terrific hobby shop of model cars.

Movieland is located at 6920 Orangethorpe Avenue, just a few minutes away from Knott's Berry Farm. It's open year round from 10 a.m. to 10 p.m. Admission is $2.75 for adults (ages 12 and over), $1.25 for kids five to 12; under five free. For more information call 523-1520.

WHERE TO STAY: If you're thinking of staying in Buena Park, you'll find that the **Farm de Ville,** 7800 and 7878 Crescent Avenue, at Highway 39 (tel: 527-2201; 800/854-3380), has a lot to offer. It's located at the south entrance to Knott's Berry Farm, it's convenient to all nearby attractions, and buses to Disneyland (ten minutes away) stop right at the door. The 130 rooms are spacious, immaculate and stylishly furnished; each has a color TV, radio, air conditioning, direct-dial phone, tub/shower bath, coffee-maker and dressing area. Facilities include two swimming pools with slides and diving boards, two wading pools for the little folk, two saunas and a coin-op laundry; a Sambo's restaurant, open 24 hours a day, adjoins.

Summer rates are $18 to $22 single, $18 to $24 double, with a charge of $4 for each additional person. The rest of the year, rates are about $2 less.

3. Santa Ana
Santa Ana lies 35 miles southeast of Los Angeles and ten miles inland from the ocean shore. It's on a freeway that bears its name, connecting Los Angeles and San Diego. Just 15 minutes from Disneyland. in Santa Ana is the—

MOVIELAND OF THE AIR MUSEUM: Launched by Frank Tallman and the late Paul Mantz, this museum traces the history of aircraft from their beginnings through about World War II. It's a $2-million showcase for these aircraft, which skilled mechanics keep in working order. Other planes on display here are "stars" of over 100 movies and TV shows—*Airport '75, Catch-22, Waldo Pepper,* etc.

The museum is located at the Orange County Airport (tel: 545-5021); open daily in summer 10 a.m. to 5 p.m. (closed Mondays in winter). Admission is $2.25 for adults, 75¢ for juniors ages 12 to 17, and 50¢ for kids under 12.

Not actually in Santa Ana, but a few minutes southeast along the San Diego Freeway in Irvine, is—

LION COUNTRY SAFARI: It's the newest kind of zoo, where the animals roam free while the humans are "caged" in cars and chartered buses. The concept was first implemented in 1967 in the Florida Everglades, and it met with such success that a second Lion Country Safari blossomed on this 485-acre tract in Orange County. It's nice to know that wildlife propagation programs are stressed at each Safari park, and the "population explosions" include many rare and endangered species.

Of course, the big thrill is close-up safari-style confrontation with hundreds of free-roaming lions, elephants, cheetahs, rare Bengal tigers, rhinos, giraffes, zebras, buffalo, primates, antelopes and myriad birds—ostriche. cranes, flamingoes, etc. They inhabit six separate areas, the first five named fo African wildlife sanctuaries: Kilimanjaro Plains, Rungwa Forest, Tsavo Park, Amboseli Reserve and Umfolozi River. The sixth is called Bandipur, after one of India's 14 tiger sanctuaries. Native settings have been accurately re-created.

Safety of the animals and their human visitors is stressed, with expert rangers patrolling every turn of the trail. Should you develop any trouble, they'll immediately come to your assistance.

Of course, even the most rugged adventurer has to stop and rest sometimes. So 50 acres of Lion Country Safari are devoted to an African-theme amusement area called **Safari Camp.** It has rides, trained animal shows, a free-flight aviary, a reptile house, a junior jungle of baby animals, an African-cuisine restaurant, cocktail lounge and a bazaar selling African artifacts and curios. In addition, the Royal Continental Circus puts on three performances daily in Safari Camp.

Lion Country Safari is off the San Diego Freeway at 8800 Moulton Parkway, in Irvine Ranch, Orange County. It's a 20-minute drive southeast from Disneyland. Open every day of the year, rain or shine, from 9 a.m.; the last car is admitted at 6 p.m. in summer, 5 p.m. fall and spring, and 3:30 p.m. in winter. One price includes all rides and attractions, plus a taped tour guide: adults pay $4.95; children three to 11, $2.95; under-three free. Needless to say, convertibles are not permitted; if you have one, you can park it (free) and rent a vehicle here for a nominal fee. For further information call (213) 485-8951.

Chapter X

PALM SPRINGS

1. Where to Stay
2. Where to Dine

GOLF, TENNIS, AND SWIMMING-POOL capital of the world, Palm Springs is the playground supreme of the super rich—home to all the Gabor sisters, Kirk Douglas, Lucille Ball, Cary Grant, Elvis Presley, Frank Sinatra, Liberace, Kim Novak, Dean Martin and Jerry Lewis (who, thanks to "old blue eyes" can now be neighborly again). The honorary mayor, by the way, is Bob Hope, and the above list is only a tiny fraction of the stars who live and vacation here.

The sun shines 350 days a year in Palm Springs. More than 100 golf tournaments are held here annually, including the $100,000 Bob Hope Desert Classic and the Colgate Dinah Shore Winners Circle. There are 200 tennis courts in the area, with more under construction, and as for those swimming pools, they number over 5,000—one for every five residents!

Getting to Palm Springs is easy. It's 104 miles southeast of Los Angeles—about a two-hour drive via the San Bernadino Freeway (Interstate 10). And four major airlines service the area: American, Hughes Airwest, Western and Air California. By plane the trip takes 36 minutes from Los Angeles.

Once you're in Palm Springs, it's easy to get around via mini-buses called SunLiners. Typical of the luxurious lifestyle here, they're carpeted, air-conditioned and equipped with stereophonic music; for a quarter passengers can ride around all day.

To gain a birds-eye perspective, take a ride on the **Palm Springs Aerial Tramway,** which travels a distance of 2½ miles up the slopes of Mount Jacinto. It takes you from the desert floor to cool alpine heights in less than 20 minutes; in winter the change is dramatic, from warm desert to deep snowdrifts. At the end of the ride is a restaurant, cocktail lounge, gift shop, game room and picnic area, and also the starting point of 54 miles of hiking trails dotted with campgrounds. The Tramway is located at Tramway Drive–Chino Canyon off Highway 111 (north). Cars depart every half-hour from 10 a.m. to 9 p.m. (closed Tuesday and Wednesday in summer only). Parking is free. Round-trip fare for adults is $4, juniors aged 12 to 17 pay $3, and children four to 11 pay $1.50. You can also get a ride-'n'-dine combination for a sunset dinner at the Alpine Restaurant—$6.95 for adults, $5.95 for juniors and $3.50 for children. For further information call (714) 327-9711.

As elsewhere, we advise anyone planning on a stay in Palm Springs to make a stop at the **Convention and Visitors Bureau,** conveniently located at the Municipal Airport Terminal (tel: 714/327-8411). They can answer all your questions, and provide you with informative brochures and maps.

1. Where to Stay

Poshest of the Palm Springs resorts is the 450-room **Canyon Hotel,** 2850 South Palm Canyon Drive (tel: 323-5656). You might see Flip Wilson, Elton John, Sonny Bono or any of a number of other celebs passing through the lobby. The amazing range of facilities here includes an 18-hole championship golf course and a nine-hole putting green; ten tennis courts (three lit for night play and two air-conditioned indoor courts); a stable of 300 horses for riding; three swimming pools (two of which are Olympic-size); three Jacuzzis; barber and beauty shops; a fully equipped health-club spa offering shiatsu and Swedish massage, facials, sauna and mineral baths. In addition, there are three restaurants, all open seven days a week: L'Escoffier, very "in," for gourmet French/continental dinners; Bogie's for steak and seafood meals—it's open for breakfast, lunch and dinner, and after 10:30 it becomes a lively disco; and Forty Love, a coffee shop serving breakfast, lunch and dinner. You can also have lunch poolside, dance to live music nightly at Raffles, an exotic nightclub, and enjoy drinks and the nightly piano bar in the verdant Greenhouse Lounge.

As for the rooms, they're exceptionally lovely and cheerful, most in pastel blue and yellow color schemes with painted bamboo furnishings and every amenity right down to the extra bathroom phone. Rates for single or double occupancy are seasonal: December 21 to April 20, twin or double rooms are $59 to $75; suites range from $100 to $350. April 21 to July 5 and September 15 to December 20, twins and doubles are $45 to $65. And in summer they go down to a nice, reasonable $25.

The most exquisite rooms in town are at **Ingleside Inn,** a charming hideaway estate at 200 West Ramon Road at Belardo (tel: 325-1366). Each of the 26 rooms and villas is uniquely decorated with priceless antiques—perhaps a commode used by Mary Tudor, a canopied bed or a 15th-century vestment chest will grace your room. Many rooms have fireplaces; all have in-room steam baths and whatever other luxuries you might crave. Once you pass the imposing wrought-iron gates (most of the traffic passing through them is Rolls-Royces, Mercedeses and the like), you leave the bustling world of the 20th century behind and enter an old-world era of luxurious relaxation and fine service. Facilities include paddle tennis, croquet, shuffleboard, a swimming pool and Jacuzzi, and a beautifully appointed backgammon room-cum-library; golf, tennis and horseback-riding can be arranged.

And Melvyn's, one of Palm Spring's most prestigious "in" spots is on the premises. It was here that Frank and Barbara Sinatra hosted an "intimate" dinner for 66 close friends on the eve of their wedding. The food is excellent, the celebrity-watching first-rate, and the decor lovely—an 1895 carved oak and mahogany bar with beveled mirrors, pale beige and chocolate color scheme, lots of potted ferns, wicker and tapestry-upholstered furnishings, and white lace curtains. If you don't stay at the Ingleside Inn at least come by for a meal at Melvyn's. At dinner you might begin with a pâté de foie maison ($2.75), and follow with an entree of escalope of veal with avocado and white wine sauce ($12.25). Your entree is served with soup or salad and vegetable. The wine list is distinguished. For dessert the French pastries ($1.95) are perfection. If that meal sounds a bit disastrous for your budget, come at lunch when you can have a cheeseburger with French fries for $2.95 and hot entrees and cold plates are $3.50 to $5.95. It's also popular for Sunday champagne brunch.

If you do decide to stay here, you'll join the ranks of Elizabeth Taylor, Howard Hughes, Mervyn Leroy, Ava Gardner, John Wayne, Bette Davis, Clare Booth Luce, Salvador Dali, Andre Kostelanetz, Gary Cooper and Rita Hayworth, all of whom have enjoyed the luxurious facilities at one time or another. Rates for singles or doubles from October 1 to June 1 range from $50 to $100 a night; $40 to $80 the rest of the year.

The **Palm Springs Riviera Hotel**, 1600 North Indian Avenue (tel: 327-8311; 800/472-4395) is a delightful 43-acre luxury resort boasting the largest swimming pool in Palm Springs and the largest hydro-therapy pool in the state of California. Facilities also include a nine-hole executive golf course and five tennis courts which guests can use free, beauty and barber shops, as well as boutiques and an art gallery. In addition, guests have use of all the facilities at the Palm Springs Country Club.

A gourmet continental cuisine is served in the Cafe Riviera, a plush dining room overlooking the pool, and there's entertainment and dancing nightly in the Lounge.

The 500 guest rooms have a definite resort feel, with color-coordinated, fern-motif draperies, bedspread and vinyl wall coverings. Color schemes are orange or garden green, and the furnishings are white bamboo. Very pretty. All rooms have color TVs, direct-dial phones, tub/shower baths and outside patios.

Rates from December 16 to April 30 are $38 to $48 single, $45 to $55 double; from May 1 to June 30 and September 15 to December 15, they're $35 to $45 single and $40 to $50 double; from July 1 to September 14, all rooms, single or double, are $24. The year round, an extra person in the room pays $9 and there's no charge for children under 12 in a room with their parents.

One of the more unique choices in Palm Springs is the **Palm Spring Spa Hotel & Mineral Springs,** 100 North Indian Avenue (tel: 325-1461). Formerly the site was a shrine for the Cahuilla Indians, who claimed the springs had magical powers to cure illness. Today vacationers come here to "take the waters" and otherwise pamper body and soul. There are four pools on the premises, one of which is a conventional outdoor swimming pool with sundeck; the other three are filled from underground natural springs brimming with revitalizing minerals. In addition to the outdoor pools, there are 30 indoor sunken Roman swirlpools, also fed from the springs. And that's not all. There's massage, complete gymnasium facilities, a vapor-inhalation room and a rock steam room, where natural mineral waters are turned to three beneficial heat levels of steam. Women can further enhance their healthy new appearances with facials, manicures, pedicures and other beauty treatments. Whatever might be lacking on the premises (like tennis and golf) is available to guests at a nearby country club.

The rooms are luxurious and elegantly appointed; all have refrigerators, direct-dial phones, color TVs, and baths with Travertine marble sinks. And the French cuisine served in the lavish Agua Room, expertly prepared under the careful eye of executive chef Eugene Le Gallo, is *extraordinaire;* Le Gallo's previous credits include the Stork Club, El Morocco and the Waldorf-Astoria. Dinner entrees, served with soup or salad, are reasonably priced, with most under $7.50. Breakfast and lunch are served in the adjoining Cafe Eugene and the Agua Lounge.

Rates for double rooms from October 1 to December 30 and May 1 to June 1 are $38 to $46; from December 20 to April 30, they rise to $50 to $60; and from June 1 to September 30, they plummet to between $22 and $38. Even if you don't stay here, you can come by and use the mineral baths for $5 a day.

Less expensive—and less glamorous—Palm Springs digs at the **Tropics**, 411 East Palm Canyon Drive (tel: 327-1391; 800/528-1234). Though this is a motel, rather than a spa or resort, it still has two Olympic-size pools, two Jacuzzis and shuffleboard. And the 142 air-conditioned rooms are attractively furnished, equipped with color TV, direct-dial phones, and tub/shower baths; many also have refrigerators. The Conga Room Steak House on the premises serves dinner, and a Sambo coffee shop adjoins. Single and double rates are $32 to $44 from January 15 to June 1; $26 to $36 from October 1 to January 15; and $20 to $32 from June 2 to October 1.

Similar accommodations and facilities at the **Westward Ho Motel**, 701 East Palm Canyon Drive (tel: 327-1531). Rates are even lower: in high season, February through April, singles are $21 to $23, doubles $23 to $36. The entire rate structure is too complicated to quote in full here, with mid-week and weekend rates in some seasons; suffice it to say it's a little or a lot less than high season the rest of the year.

And even posh Palm Springs has a **Motel 6**, this one at 595 East Palm Canyon Drive (tel: 327-2044). As usual, refer to the Introduction for details.

2. Where to Dine

Some of the best restaurants in town are at the hotels we've already mentioned—**L'Escoffier** at the Canyon, **Melvyn's** at Ingleside Inn, the **Cafe Riviera** at the Riviera, and the **Agua Room** at the Palm Springs Spa. There are, however, other choices.

Lyon's English Grill, for one, 233 East Palm Canyon Drive (tel: 327-1551), has an almost theatrical woody English-pub ambience comprised of stained-glass windows, old pub signs and maps, Tudor beamed walls and heraldic banners suspended from the ceilings—not to mention waitresses in serving-wench costume. Even the menus were made in England, originally for a restaurant in Hampton Court. The most traditional thing to order is a prime rib dinner, a generous portion of which is $8.95. Less expensive entrees are—in descending price order—roast duckling with wild rice ($7.95), barbecued chicken and rice ($6.95) and filet of sole meunière ($5.95). All entrees are served with a fresh salad tossed tableside (the busboy will offer you pepper from an immense pepper mill), a baked potato and hot sourdough bread. And parents will be glad to know that kids under nine years of age can get a $1 dinner plate. Open daily from 5 p.m. to midnight.

For Italian fare, the place to go is **Perrina's,** 340 North Palm Canyon Drive (tel: 325-6544). The decor somehow evokes New Orleans, with red flocked wallpaper and red tablecloths. There's always lots of action at the bar, where you might see Henry Fonda or Bob Newhart—both frequent patrons. The specialty is veal—piccata, scaloppine, marsala, etc.—served with soup or salad and fresh vegetables, for $7.95, but there's lotsa pasta on the menu, too. Fettuccine Alfredo is $3.95, manicotti $4.25, linguine with garlic, olive oil and anchovies $4.50. A side order of pasta with a regular entree is $1.50. Perrina's is open daily for lunch and dinner.

Chapter XI

FROM MALIBU TO NEWPORT BEACH

1. Malibu
2. Redondo Beach
3. Marineland
4. San Pedro
5. Long Beach
6. Catalina Island
7. Newport Beach

A VISIT TO SOUTHERN CALIFORNIA ideally includes a few days' retreat at one of the many beach resorts dotting the shore from Los Angeles to San Diego. But if you haven't the time for a relaxing seaside vacation, day trips to many of the areas listed below make for very pleasant excursions. You might want to catch "the world's only four-ring sea circus" at Marineland, explore the *Queen Mary*, now permanently docked in Long Beach, browse through the shops at San Pedro's quaint Ports O'Call Village, take a cruise to cove-fringed Catalina Island and see the marine forest from a glass-bottom boat, or just laze in the sunshine at any of the sandy coastal beaches described below.

1. Malibu

Twenty-five miles from Los Angeles Civic Center, Malibu is the stretch of shoreline beginning at Topanga Canyon and extending westward along the Pacific Ocean (West Pacific Coast Highway 101-A) to the Ventura County line. Once a privately owned rancho (purchased for 10¢ an acre) Malibu is now a popular resort city. and acreage has become infinitely more expensive. During the '20s the emerging movie colony flocked here, and Malibu was famous for wild parties and extravagant *Great Gatsby* lifestyles. There are still many famous residents, and though the area is not as celebrated as it once was, a new age of glamor may be dawning—Jean Leon, L.A.'s most chic restaurateur, has just opened **La Scala Malibu** on the site of the old Malibu Shores Motel, 23033 West Pacific Coast Highway. The menu is the same as that of the main dining room at La Scala in Los Angeles (see "Top Restaurants" in Chapter VIII).

ACTIVITIES: Malibu's beaches delight thousands of visitors every year who engage in every activity from nude sunbathing to grunion-hunting. Boating is also a popular activity. **Paradise Cove Sportfishing,** at 28128 W. Pacific Coast Highway (tel: 457-2511), books full-day boat trips aboard its 65-foot *Gentleman* and half-day trips aboard the 100-passenger *Speed Twin*. Full-day fare is $10 for adults, $6 for children 11 or under; half-day fare is $7 adults, $4 children. You can purchase bait here, rent fishing equipment or skiffs ($25 a day) and even get a fishing license (which you'll need) for $4—good for the whole year. And there's horseback-riding and tennis at the aptly named **Malibu Riding & Tennis Club,** 33905 Pacific Coast Highway (tel: 457-9783).

FOOD AND LODGING: For such a wealthy community, Malibu is singularly lacking in glamorous accommodations. The reason is simple: the residents are comfortably ensconced in their own gorgeous houses, and they don't want their quiet retreat turned into a bustling tourist resort. Local ordinances are designed to work against such a contingency.

Best bet is the **Casa Malibu,** 22752 Pacific Coast Highway (tel: 456-2219), a hacienda-style accommodation built around a palm-studded inner courtyard with cuppa d'oro vines growing up the balcony. The rooms are cheerful and attractively furnished—all with private balconies. Each is equipped with a shower bath, oversized beds and color TV (no phone). Steve McQueen and Ali McGraw sometimes stay here, as does Yul Brynner, and Lana Turner rented a Casa Malibu suite for years. Singles or doubles cost $35 overlooking the water, $30 if fronting the patio or coastal highway. Each extra person in a room pays $3; rooms with fully equipped kitchens can be rented for an extra $5 per day (five-day minimum rental). Parking is free.

For dining South Seas style, there's **Tonga Lei,** 22878 Pacific Coast Highway (tel: 456-6444), a thatched-roofed Polynesian restaurant. The decor consists of lots of bamboo, rattan and wicker à la Pago Pago—particularly effective if you sit in the booths overlooking the ocean. The menu is rather extensive; you might order a complete Lanai dinner for two ($6.95 per person), which includes mixed appetizers—spareribs, fried shrimp, rumaki and crab puff, soup, three entrees—chicken with mushrooms, Tai Wan duckling fried rice and ma tai yuke (a pork and vegetable dish), plus dessert. A la carte entrees range from Polynesian-style chicken and rice ($3.75) to broiled lobster tail with drawn butter ($11.95). Potent drinks are, of course, available, and entrees on the very reasonable lunch menu are almost all under $3. Open daily from noon to midnight (Friday and Saturday till 2 a.m.).

Tonga Lei also has six rooms for rent on the premises, all of which have tub/shower baths, color TV and no phones. A single or double is $30 on the ocean side, $24 on the highway.

Nantucket Light, 22706 Pacific Coast Highway (tel: 456-3105), is a delightful weathered-wood seacoast barn that does, in fact, look right out of New England. The interior is a fine example of the "less is more" theory of decorating—elegantly simple and designed so that each table has an ocean view. Chairs and tables are oak, a stone fireplace blazes at night, and plants are suspended from a heavy beamed ceiling. The steak and seafood menu features a seafood brochette for $5.95, a hearty cioppino for $7.95, and filet and lobster combination for $11.25. All entrees are served with salad, bread and butter and rice pilaf. Desserts range from fresh strawberries in cream ($1.25) to a very tasty homemade carrot cake ($1.25).

A relative newcomer on the Malibu restaurant scene is the **Country Wine Cellar (and Continental Delicatessen),** 22853 Pacific Coast Highway (tel: 456-2953). Diners can sit in a lushly planted enclosed cafe area amidst fuschia and fern, with sunlight streaming in through a slatted roof; totally outdoors in a garden area; or inside in the winery. The day begins early, with a wide choice of omelets available at breakfast. For lunch there's a selection of soups, salads and sandwiches, all delicious and reasonably priced, the emphasis being on fresh, natural foods. There are several options at dinner; you might order an entree of beef stroganoff ($6.50), coq au vin ($4.95) or shrimp scampi ($6.50). On the other hand, you could put together a meal of a shrimp and avocado salad ($4.95) and a quiche Lorraine ($2.95) or a pastrami sandwich ($2.50). Either way, leave room for the homemade desserts like apple torte served with cream (85¢). A large selection of wines is available. Open daily from 8 a.m. to 9 p.m. (Mondays till 6 p.m.).

J. PAUL GETTY MUSEUM: A not-to-be-missed Malibu sight, the J. Paul Getty Museum is a spectacular reconstruction of the Roman Villa dei Papyri, which was buried in volcanic mud when Mount Vesuvius erupted in 79 A.D., destroying Pompeii and Herculaneum. Set on ten acres, in the Pacific hills, it houses the magnificent J. Paul Getty collection, which fittingly is strong on Greek and Roman sculpture. The museum is surrounded by a colonnaded peristyle garden with a graceful reflecting pool and replicas of bronze statues found at the site of the original villa. Reproductions of the original frescoes adorn the walls, and 12 different types of marble were used in the halls and colonnades. In addition to the Greco-Roman pieces, the collection is also rich in Renaissance and Baroque paintings from Europe, and 18th-century decorative arts from France. The most valuable painting in the museum is "The Holy Family" by Raphael, which Getty bought for $200 thinking it was a good copy! Millionaires have all the luck. . . .

The museum is located at 17985 Pacific Coast Highway (tel: 459-2306). It's open Monday through Friday, from 10 a.m. to 5 p.m. (Tuesday through Saturday from October to May). There is currently no admission charge. Because of limited facilities, it is advisable to make a *parking* reservation at least one week in advance by calling 454-6541.

2. Redondo Beach

In the 1880s Redondo Beach was the largest shipping port between San Diego and San Francisco. With the decline of commercial shipping, it became

REDONDO BEACH

—and still is—a modest beach resort, just a few minutes south of the Los Angeles International Airport.

The **Fisherman's Wharf** pier is a maze of architecturally attractive restaurants, over 50 shops, galleries, penny arcades, fishing equipment outlets and a concert auditorium (see the nightlife section in Chapter VIII). Though the restaurants concentrate on seafood, there is also Japanese, Polynesian and Mexican cuisine available. For a complete rundown on Redondo Beach facilities, boating, sailing and fishing trips, etc., stop in at the **Chamber of Commerce**, 1215 N. Catalina Avenue (tel: 376-8434).

WHERE TO STAY: Every room at the **Portofino Inn**, 260 Portofino Way (tel: 379-8481), has a balcony overlooking the yacht harbor. And very nice rooms they are, most with grasspaper wall covering, about half with fully equipped kitchenettes, and some with nautical touches like headboards constructed of oars or wood-carved mermaids and Neptunes. All have color TV, radio, direct-dial phone and tub/shower bath. A 10¢ tram stops at the door and takes guests to the beach (a scant block away, in any case), the pier, and all nearby restaurants. Drinking and dining facilities include the Portofino Restaurant, specializing in steak and seafood, and its adjoining cocktail lounge, the Oak Room Coffee Shop and the Crow's Nest Bar. An open-air heated swimming pool overlooks the ocean. Single rooms range from $28 to $36, doubles from $34 to $42.

WHERE TO DINE: Beachbum Burt's, 605 North Harbor Drive (tel: 376-0466), is the creation of Burt Hixson, who bummed his way throughout the beaches of the Pacific, getting potted under the palms and taking thousands of photos along the way. When he returned to California he re-created his South Seas paradise at this famous restaurant. The ambience is lushly tropical, and a section of the palm-thatched roof even folds back for dining under the stars. Most tables overlook the harbor, and the walls are plastered with Hixson's photos and mementoes of his travels through 42 countries. Get into the mood over one of those exotic specialty drinks—like a coconut Willie ($1.75). Dinner entrees include ginger chicken Gauguin ($5.75); at lunch you might order an avocado stuffed with chicken and shrimp ($3.50). For your "tradewind treat" (that's dessert) try Burt's famous American mud pie (75¢). Open daily from 11:30 a.m. to 2 a.m. (Sunday from 10:30 a.m.).

Almost equally extravagant in decor is the **Red Onion**, 655 North Harbor Drive (tel: 376-8813). Only here the ambience and cuisine are not South Seas but south of the border. The ceiling is bamboo, an eclectic selection of chairs leans heavily to bamboo and rattan, ceiling fans whir slowly overhead, and photos of Mexico adorn the walls. Most tables afford a view of the harbor; there's an open brick and tile fireplace, attractive Persian carpeting and ubiquitous foliage. A terrific bargain here is the Happy Hour, 4 to 7 p.m., weekdays. Order a drink, and you can partake of an immense Mexican buffet—easily a full meal. However, if you should decide to dine at other hours, you'll find menu prices most reasonable, with hearty and delicious combination plates ranging from $2.10 to $3.85. Open seven days from 11 a.m. to 2 a.m. (Sundays from 10 a.m.). There's dancing nightly to a live band, except Mondays when it's disco night.

3. Marineland

Right on the Pacific between Redondo Beach and San Pedro, Marineland (tel: 489-2400) is an 85-acre oceanographic park under the management of 20th Century-Fox, with a galaxy of sea-creature stars. Like Orky and Corky, very cutesy names indeed for two killer whales who together total 18,000 pounds of showmanship. Several times a day they put on a 20-minute performance in a 640,000-gallon tank—those sitting up front will get splashed.

Another show—an Olympic competition—is put on by a cast of dolphins. While at the Seaside Stadium, Professor Von Fishbone tries to explain the mysteries of the deep, but pilot whales Bubbles and Squirt and their dolphin friends prove that he's all wet. Other attractions include Sea Lion Theatre, where a tongue-in-cheek competition takes place between two zany sea lions (sounds like a *TV Guide* blurb for a new show). A musical revue of human singers and dancers, featuring sea songs from the 17th century to the present, takes place in the Music of the Sea Pavilion. Rounding out the bill, there's Pirate's Cove (a kiddie playground); a community of animals found stranded on California beaches; a pearl-diving pavilion where beautiful girls dive into a giant tank filled with over 4,000 colorful fish (on request an oyster with a pearl will be brought just for you—satisfaction guaranteed); a walrus pool, penguin pond, flamingo exhibit, otter exhibit; and over 50 aquariums filled with everything from sea horses to deadly piranhas.

For a panoramic view of the proceedings, take the Sky Tower ride, whirling on a spindle 254 feet above the Pacific Ocean.

If you're heading south from Redondo Beach, take the Palos Verdes Drive. If you're inland, Marineland is reached via the San Diego Freeway (take Hawthorne Boulevard to the sea) or the Harbor Freeway to San Pedro, turning left on Gaffey Street and right on 25th Street. You can see all the shows (each presented several times daily) for a single admission price: $5.50 for adults; $3.75 for children four to 11 (under four free). Marineland opens daily at 10 a.m., closing between 5 and 7 p.m. depending on the season.

4. San Pedro

Further down the beach, picturesque San Pedro, the bustling port of Los Angeles, handles an estimated two-million tons of cargo every month. It definitely merits a day's visit, to see a little village-within-a-town created simply for tourists, which is nevertheless charming and fun.

PORTS O' CALL VILLAGE AND THE WHALER'S WHARF: Combining the atmosphere of old California with a 19th-century New Bedford whaling port, the Wharf and Village have 80 international specialty shops and restaurants along winding cobblestone streets. Part of the fun is watching the steady stream of yachts, luxury liners, tankers, freighters, schooners and sailboats cruise past.

The Village itself achieves an early California motif with Spanish colonial-style architecture, archways, wrought-iron enclosed balconies and an abundance of bougainvillea vines and banana palms. Across a graceful bridge the elm-shaded brick lanes of the Wharf evoke New England with shingle-roofed buildings, lantern lights, multi-paned windows and tavern signs. Throughout, there are strolling entertainers and musicians (band concerts on Saturday evenings in summer), and the very browsable shops provide a dazzling display of imported international merchandise ranging from Philippine jewelry to Japanese gunpowder tea.

For an aerial view, take the Sky Tower Crows Nest ride 315 feet upward (75¢ for adults, 50¢ for kids). One-hour sightseeing cruises leave daily at frequent intervals in summer (adults pay $2.75, kids $2.25); from February to April there are special whale-watching cruises ($2.25 per hour)—call 547-2833 for full information on all cruises offered. In addition, helicopter rides leave Whalers Wharf every few minutes for an aerial tour of the inner harbor area ($4.50 per person).

For meals, you can stop off at the **Ports O' Call Restaurant,** (tel: 833-3553)—it's easy to spot because a red Chinese junk is moored in a pond near the footbridge to the entrance, and there's a red rickshaw at the door. The interior looks like a ship. The menu features South Seas specialties like Java seafood curry ($7.25) and filet teriyaki ($8.75), along with steak and seafood "mainland fare" entrees. Luncheon entrees are in the $2.50-to-$4.25 range. Open daily.

If, on the other hand, you're in a New England mood, head for the **Yankee Whaler Inn** (tel: 831-0181). Designed to look like a 19th-century waterside whaling inn, it has a weathered clapboard and shingle facade, and a quaint interior with several working fireplaces, curtained windows and oil lamps on every table. Diners can sit indoors (most tables overlook the water) or outdoors on a brick terrace. "Seafood and grog" dinner offerings include poached salmon Hollandaise ($6.50) and broiled Alaska king crab legs in lemon butter sauce ($8.50). A glass of wine with your meal is 75¢; the same price for a homemade dessert of chocolate mousse. Open daily for lunch and dinner.

To reach Ports O'Call take the Harbor Freeway to its termination, bearing left for two miles after leaving it. The admission-free Village and Wharf are open daily from 11 a.m. to 9 p.m. year round.

5. Long Beach

Continuing south along the shore we come to Long Beach, the sixth-largest city in California that does, in fact, offer a "long beach"—5.5 miles of beckoning sand. It's also well equipped with tennis, golf, sailing, fishing and boating facilities (departures from Pierpoint sportsfishing landing and Belmont Pier), plus the picturesque **Seaport Village** shopping complex at the southeastern edge of the city.

But the principal attraction of this resort town is the **Queen Mary,** docked at the terminus of Pier J (at the southern end of the Long Beach Freeway) since the completion of her final 14,500-mile journey around South America in 1967.

An imposing sight, her black hull and white superstructure a fifth of a mile long, and her three vermilion stacks jutting 150 feet into the air, the former Cunard liner has been inspected by more than four-million persons since the first paying customers trooped aboard. Tourists can explore the ship's engine rooms, boilers, turbines and machinery; the aft steering station (an emergency facility); the elegant three-deck-high Main Lounge; re-creations of all classes of accommodations, and the contrasting GI quarters used when the Queen Mary transported 800,000 troops in World War II. Among the highlights are a 12-minute color film shown in the ship's theater; and the Living Sea exhibits, created by Jacques Cousteau, representing the famed oceanographer's personal view and conquest of the oceans. The newest attraction is The Phantom of the Queen Mary: a spectre rises from the ship's eerie hull to recount frightening adventures and perils of the sea.

Three restaurants on board—all with views of the city's skyline and small-boat harbor—serve lunch and dinner. The Lord Nelson features prime rib, the Lady Hamilton specializes in fish and seafood, and the Capstan has a varied menu. In addition there are many areas for snacks and sandwiches, and the Sir Winston Churchill restaurant for steak dinners—a beautifully appointed room filled with Churchill memorabilia and offering a panoramic harbor view. And as in former days, there are 40 specialty shops on board and a chapel for "at sea" weddings.

Cost of the complete tour is $3.50 for adults, $2.50 for juniors ages 12 to 17, and $1.25 for kids five to 11 (under five free). There's ample parking for $1.

6. Catalina Island

Few tourists know about this quaint, cove-fringed island just 22 miles off the Long Beach shoreline, yet Catalina offers scores of resort attractions. Crystal-clear water makes for excellent boating, fishing, swimming, scuba-diving and snorkeling. There are miles of hiking and biking trails. The beautiful **Wrigley Memorial and Botanical Garden** is here. Camping, golf, tennis and horseback-riding facilities abound. Big-band concerts in summer at the *Catalina Casino,* fabulous undersea gardens and, finally, the picturesque town of Avalon, named for a passage in Tennyson's *Idylls of the King,* round out the Catalina scene.

There are seemingly endless ways to get there. The island is serviced by two airlines— **Air Catalina** (tel: 548-1314 or Avalon 116) and **Catalina Air Lines** (tel: 425-7424), both of which offer daily flights, year round, from Long Beach Airport. **Long Beach/Catalina Cruises** 330 Golden Shore Blvd. (tel: 775-2654), operates 700-passenger vessels from downtown Long Beach, making five trips daily in summer, two in winter. They also have a large ship, *The Monarch,* sailing from San Pedro to Catalina. Adults pay $4.25 each way; children five through 11 pay half-fare, and under-fives pay 25¢.

From Newport Beach, **Catalina Passenger Service** offers daily service in summer months aboard the *Island Holiday.* For reservations and information go to Davey's Locker, Balboa Pavilion, 400 Main Street, Newport (tel: 714/673-5245 or Avalon 451). The boat leaves Newport at 9 a.m. and returns at 7 p.m. Roundtrip fare for adults is $11, $5.50 for children under 12 (no charge under five).

The boat arrives at Avalon; and here the **Catalina Operations Co.,** Sightseeing Ticket Office, Pleasure Pier (tel: Avalon 1111), offers a combination tour ticket that includes a delightful glass-bottom boat ride to see underwater marine life, a drive up a mountain road, and a trip to watch the seal colony along the rocky eastern tip of the island. It costs $6.50 for adults, $3.75 for ages five to 11.

If you'd like to spend the night, or longer, on the island, the **Zane Grey Pueblo Hotel,** Box 216, Avalon (tel: Avalon 966) is a comfortable guest house retreat with a swimming pool. But most important, it's the former home of novelist Zane Grey, who spent his last 20 years in Avalon, enjoying the isolation, the view of ocean and harbor. He wrote many books here, including *Tales of Swordfish and Tuna,* in which he recounted his fishing adventures off Catalina Island. All rooms have private baths, but no phones or televisions. There is, however, a TV in the lounge, along with a piano and an organ. In summer, rooms cost $20 to $40 a night. Winter rates are considerably lower.

7. Newport Beach

Newport Beach is the biggest of the yacht-harbor resorts, and it offers more options to the vacationer than any of the others. About 35 miles south of Los Angeles, it embraces the delightful peninsula town of **Balboa**. The phenomenal growth of hotel and restaurant facilities in the last few years indicates that Newport Beach is fast becoming the most popular of Southern California's coastal towns between L.A. and San Diego. Many tourists now use it as a vacation base from which to visit Anaheim, Buena Park and other Orange County attractions. Convenient bus tours are available—check at your hotel or the **Chamber of Commerce**, 270 Newport Center Drive (tel: 644-8211).

ACTIVITIES: A major focus of activity in the area for nearly a century is the cupola-topped **Balboa Pavilion**, 400 Main Street, which originally served as a bath house. Home of the **Tale of the Whale** seafood restaurant, it is also the Newport departure point for Catalina Island Passenger Service, Harbor Sightseeing Cruises, whale-watching cruises, skiff rentals and a large fleet of modern sportsfishing boats. For information on any of these, call 673-5245. At the Newport Pier you can take a ferry to **Balboa Island**, the ride costing 40¢ for cars, 10¢ for passengers.

The best way to see the bay is to buy a ticket for a harbor cruise. In summer, there are several trips daily leaving from the **Fun Zone Dock** (tel: 673-0240) near the ferry landing. A 45-minute cruise costs adults $3, children under 12, 50¢. In winter the cruise is on weekends only.

WHERE TO STAY: Located on 26 hilltop acres, **Del Webb's Newporter Inn**, 1107 Jamboree Road (tel: 644-1700), is a resort complex par excellence, and an important hub of activity in this beach town. The John Wayne Tennis Club is on the premises, and guests can use its facilities for a nominal fee; they include 16 championship courts, spa equipment, saunas, Jacuzzi and a clubhouse. In addition, the hotel boasts two heated Olympic-size swimming pools, a children's pool and a night-lighted nine-hole golf course. There are several restaurants. Gourmet meals are featured in the Wine Cellar Tuesday through Saturday; dancing and live entertainment are on tap nightly in the Lido Lounge; three meals a day are served in the Café de la Paix and the Bistro; while the Marine Restaurant features gourmet continental fare and a Sunday all-you-can-eat champagne hunt breakfast ($3.95 per person).

Rooms are extremely lovely, decorated in cheerful garden colors with furnishings in bamboo or a French provincial mode. All have balconies or lanai terraces with a view, plus air conditioning, direct-dial phone, color TV (with in-house movies), radio and tub/shower bath. Sightseeing buses depart from the hotel to nearby attractions, and there's bay swimming at the Newport Dunes beach just across the street.

Singles are $32 to $38, doubles $36 to $40. Package plans, including some meals, golf and tennis, are available.

A newcomer on the scene, the 377-room, $10-million **Marriott**, 900 Newport Center Drive (tel: 640-4000; 800/228-9290), opened in April 1975. Built around a nine-story atrium—of which an Italian Renaissance fountain is the focal point—the hotel was designed so that over 80% of the guest rooms would offer ocean views. The rooms are strikingly decorated with rust-color carpeting, cheerful drapes and bedspreads in a fabric sporting an exotic bird motif. Most have balconies overlooking the fountain courtyard hung with ivy and bougainvillea. All are equipped with color TV, radio, direct-dial phone, climate control, tub/shower bath, and a convenient amenity—an ironing board (irons on request). An immense swimming pool and hydro-therapy pool are surrounded by a palm-studded sundeck. Ten tennis courts can be used by guests at no charge on weekdays ($5 weekends), and visitors can play golf at the adjoining Irvine Country Club's 18-hole course.

The Marriott has two restaurants: King's Wharf for seafood dinners and terrific hot buffet-salad-bar lunches ($4.50); and the Mediterranean-style Capriccio, with arched stucco walls, an outdoor cafe area, and Italian cuisine. In addition, there's The Main Brace, a sophisticated disco with a nautical theme, open nightly till 2 a.m.; one of its best features is that the music can be heard only over the dance floor, so when you're not dancing you can talk. The Main Brace is also used for a seafood buffet every night from 5 to 7:30 p.m. Fashion Island, with a theater, playground, 60 shops and ten restaurants, is just across the street.

Rates for single rooms are $32 to $40; twins and doubles are $38 to $46.

A month previous to the opening of the Marriott, a **Sheraton Newport** opened its doors at 4545 MacArthur Boulevard (tel: 833-0570; 800/325-3535). Rooms here are also centered around a courtyard lobby, with ivy-draped balconies reaching upward to a skylight roof. Facilities include two night-lighted tennis courts (no charge for courts or equipment), an adjoining golf course, swimming pool and Jacuzzi, and plenty of free parking. There are two restaurants, Alexander's Banana, offering a steak and seafood menu and live entertainment nightly, and the Festival Cafe, a coffee shop.

Rooms are attractively color-coordinated in three different color schemes —orange and yellow, green and blue, and red and white. All are equipped with every modern amenity.

The Sheraton offers very competitive rates: $28 to $32 single, $32 to $36 double; rates include cocktail party every night, complimentary buffet breakfast, airport limousine transfer, free local calls, and the *Wall Street Journal* delivered with your morning coffee. Package plans are also available, including a Friday-and-Saturday-night plan that gives you Disneyland admission with 11 attractions, a 1976 compact with 200 free miles for Saturday and Sunday, and unlimited cocktails Friday or Saturday night, plus all the above-mentioned regular-rate complimentary benefits; the price is $50.50 per person, based on double occupancy.

Less expensive tha the above superstar accommodations, and our favorite to boot, is the **Balboa Inn**, 105 Main Street, Balboa (tel: 675-8740). A charming hideaway at the foot of Balboa Pier, it was built in the early '30s and had a colorful history throughout the '40s, attracting movie stars like Jean Harlow and Errol Flynn. In 1974 it was renovated and restored to its original state. The architecture is Spanish Colonial, with a tiled roof and rooms looking out onto a potted-palm courtyard, the ocean or swimming pool. An outdoor terrace on the second floor makes a terrific sundeck. Rooms are cheerfully decorated with Indian-print bedspreads—they have no phones or TVs, but a store down the street will rent you a television set and the office takes phone messages. There's an inexpensive Mexican restaurant, Mi Casa, on the premises.

For so much quaint charm at such a convenient location, the rates are extremely reasonable. They begin at $20 for a standard room, and go up to $40 for a large one-bedroom apartment that sleeps up to six people! There are also weekly and monthly rates available.

WHERE TO EAT: **Reuben E. Lee**, 151 East Coast Highway, Newport Beach, is a genuine replica of a famous 19th-century Mississippi riverboat, the *Robert E. Lee*. It's entered via canopied gangplanks, and the promenade decks are elegantly turn-of-the-century. There are two restaurants on board:

The **Sea Food Restaurant** (tel: 675-5790) sports a Victorian motif and serves lunch until 4:30 p.m. Monday through Saturday and dinner nightly till 11 p.m. (till midnight on weekends). The fare includes entrees like New Orleans bouillabaisse ($7.50) and lobster thermidor ($7.95), served with vegetable chowder, salad, potatoes or rice with mushrooms, and fresh-baked rolls and butter. Luncheon entrees are mostly in the $3-to-$4 range, and kids under 12 can eat for $1.50.

At the **Sternwheeler** (tel: 675-5811), located in the stern of the ship, the cuisine is more eclectically continental, with entrees like beef stroganoff ($6.95), Long Island duckling ($7.95) and scampi Italiano ($7.50), served with soup or salad, and rice pilaf or potato. Once again, lunch is in the $3-to-$4 range. Open from 11:30 a.m. to 11 p.m. (from 5 p.m. to midnight on Saturdays and from 4 to 11 p.m. on Sundays).

Le Saint-Tropez, 3012 Newport Boulevard, Newport Beach (tel: 673-7883), is a delightful French inn with logs burning in the brick fireplace, provincial wallpaper on the walls enhanced by art reproductions of Van Goghs, Renoirs, Manets, etc., and freshly cut flowers everywhere. Parisian chef Joseph Viellemaringe turns out classically French specialties like frogs legs provencale ($9.25), broiled salmon in Béarnaise sauce ($9.25), and chicken sauteed in wild mushrooms ($8.75). All entrees include soup and salad. There's a comprehensive wine list of imported French wines and a few domestic selections. Open for dinner Tuesday through Saturday from 6 p.m.

A relative newcomer to the restaurant scene is **Marrakesh**, 1100 West Coast Highway (tel: 645-8384), which adds a Moroccan feast to your Newport Beach dining options. The exotic *Arabian Nights* decor and traditional dining ritual is similar to that at the restaurant of the same name in Los Angeles (see Chapter VIII for a complete description). Intimate dining areas are created by semi-private tents. Full eight-course dinners, priced between $11 and $12 per person, begin with Moroccan soup and follow with a salad that you scoop up with fresh-baked hunks of bread. B'stila (chicken filled pastry topped with cinnamon) comes next, and after that the entree—perhaps sea bass in piquant sauce or baked squab with rice and almonds. The next course is lamb and vegetables with couscous; fresh fruit follows, mint tea is ceremoniously served, and delicious sweet pastries mark the finale.

Diners lounge on cushioned banquettes, Middle Eastern music plays in the background, and the entire dinner is eaten with the hands. It's best enjoyed with a large group of people, though it can also provide a perfect setting for a romantic evening *à deux*. Open for dinner nightly.

About the same time that Marrakesh made the Newport Beach scene, **Chanteclair**, an exquisite mansard-roofed French provincial inn at 18912 MacArthur Boulevard (tel: 752-8001), opened its doors. Styled after a country estate in Normandy, it has several dining areas furnished in original antiques. Authentic Persian carpets and five blazing fireplaces create a warmly intimate ambience throughout. Guests can enjoy drinks in a lounge with hunting-lodge decor, and dine in a bibliothèque, a boudoir, a garden with skylight roof, a veranda with a bamboo ceiling, a grand or petit salon. Weekdays from 5 to 7:30 p.m. a harpist provides background music.

Dinner at Chanteclair might begin with an appetizer of papaya with bay shrimp and house dressing ($4.50), a traditional French onion soup au gratin ($2.25) or—something we bet you never had before—a soup called boula-boula glacé—half turtle, half cream of pea, with glazed whipped cream ($2.25). Entrees range from a very traditional entrecôte au poivre, flamed tableside and served with haricots verts (string beans), grilled tomato and potatoes Dauphine ($10.50), to German-style braised beefsteak with potato pancakes and fresh vegetables ($8.50). For dessert, check out the tray of desserts de maison ($1.75). A wide selection of imported and domestic wines is available. Lunch at Chanteclair (weekdays only) is the in $3-to-$6 range. Open for dinner nightly.

Chapter XII

THE BOTTOM LINE: SAN DIEGO

1. Things to See and Do
2. Where to Stay
3. Where to Dine
4. La Jolla
5. An Excursion to Tijuana

CALIFORNIA HISTORY BEGAN IN San Diego with the arrival of Juan Cabrillo at Point Loma in 1542; later Father Junipero Serra established the first historic mission of El Camino Real here. The city's Spanish heritage is preserved in Old Town, a reconstruction of the first settlement, and the mission has been beautifully restored. Proximity to Mexico further enhances the Spanish flavor. But the most striking note in this coastal city is not its early California overtones. The predominant impression is water—seemingly endless vistas of the blue Pacific, of boat-filled harbors, quiet coves and sparkling bays, fringed with 70 miles of sandy shoreline beaches. And a balmy year-round climate that makes one want to be outdoors all the time. One of the world's most famous natural harbors, San Diego is home base for the 11th Naval District. So many ships and personnel have been sent to San Diego, and so many retired Navy men live there, that it is known as an "unofficial capital of the Navy."

Every sport and activity connected with water is popular. Sportfishing in the ocean is among the finest on the Pacific coast. Charter boats leave from 1551 West Mission Bay Drive (tel: 222-1165) in Mission Bay. You can also fish (for no charge) off the **Ocean Beach Pier** (tel: 224-3359) at the foot of Niagara Street in Ocean Beach, and from the many city lakes (a daily recreation permit is required). For information on lake-fishing contact **City Lakes Recreation,** San Diego Park and Recreation Department, 1222 First Avenue (tel: 460-2944). Sailing, scuba-diving, surfing, swimming and water-skiing are equally popular, as are non-water sports from tennis and golf (there's a choice of 65 excellent courses) to sky-diving.

Facilities for everything are so abundant we can't begin to list them here. The **San Diego Convention & Visitors Bureau** 1200 3rd Ave. (tel: 232-3101), offers visitors to San Diego a one-stop service center for obtaining maps, brochures, sightseeing information and a complete rundown on what to do and where to go in San Diego and vicinity.

GETTING THERE: Only 137 miles south of Los Angeles, San Diego is well served by bus, rail and air (PSA and Air California) lines. And it's an easy trip by car: take Highway 1 and Interstate 5. It's a scenic trip, too—you'll have the Pacific to the right of you much of the way.

1. Things to Do and See

In addition to the beach, a wealth of tourist attractions await the visitor to San Diego. We'll begin at the edge of downtown, at 1,400-acre—

BALBOA PARK: The nation's largest municipal park, this one houses the San Diego Zoo and eight museums, including the **Reuben H. Fleet Space Theater** (about which more below). Inside the **California Building,** with it's 100-bell carillon tower, is the **Museum of Man** (tel: 239-2001), tracing the natural and cultural history of man; emphasis is on the Indian cultures of the Americas. Admission is 75¢ for adults, a dime for those under 17.

The **Aerospace Museum** (tel: 234-8291), off El Prado, the "main street" of the park, displays an outstanding collection of historical aircraft, ranging from an exact replica of the "Spirit of St. Louis" to modern NASA spacecraft. The **International Aerospace Hall of Fame** adjoins. Admission is free.

The **Natural History Museum** (tel: 232-3821), on the east end of El Prado, has a large number of exhibits on plants, animals, birds, fish and minerals of the Southwest. Admission is 75¢ for adults, free to those 16 or under, and free for everyone on Wednesdays.

Along the north side of El Prado are the **Timken Gallery** (tel: 239-5548) and the **Fine Arts Gallery** (tel: 234-7931), both of which house works of many Old Masters, and the latter of which displays many traveling exhibits. Admission is free to both.

The **Hall of Champions** (tel: 234-2544) honors San Diego's athletes who have achieved national or world recognition in sports, among them Ted Williams and Archie Moore. Admission is free.

All of the museums are open from 10 a.m. to 4:30 p.m. daily, except the galleries, which are closed on Mondays.

SAN DIEGO 271

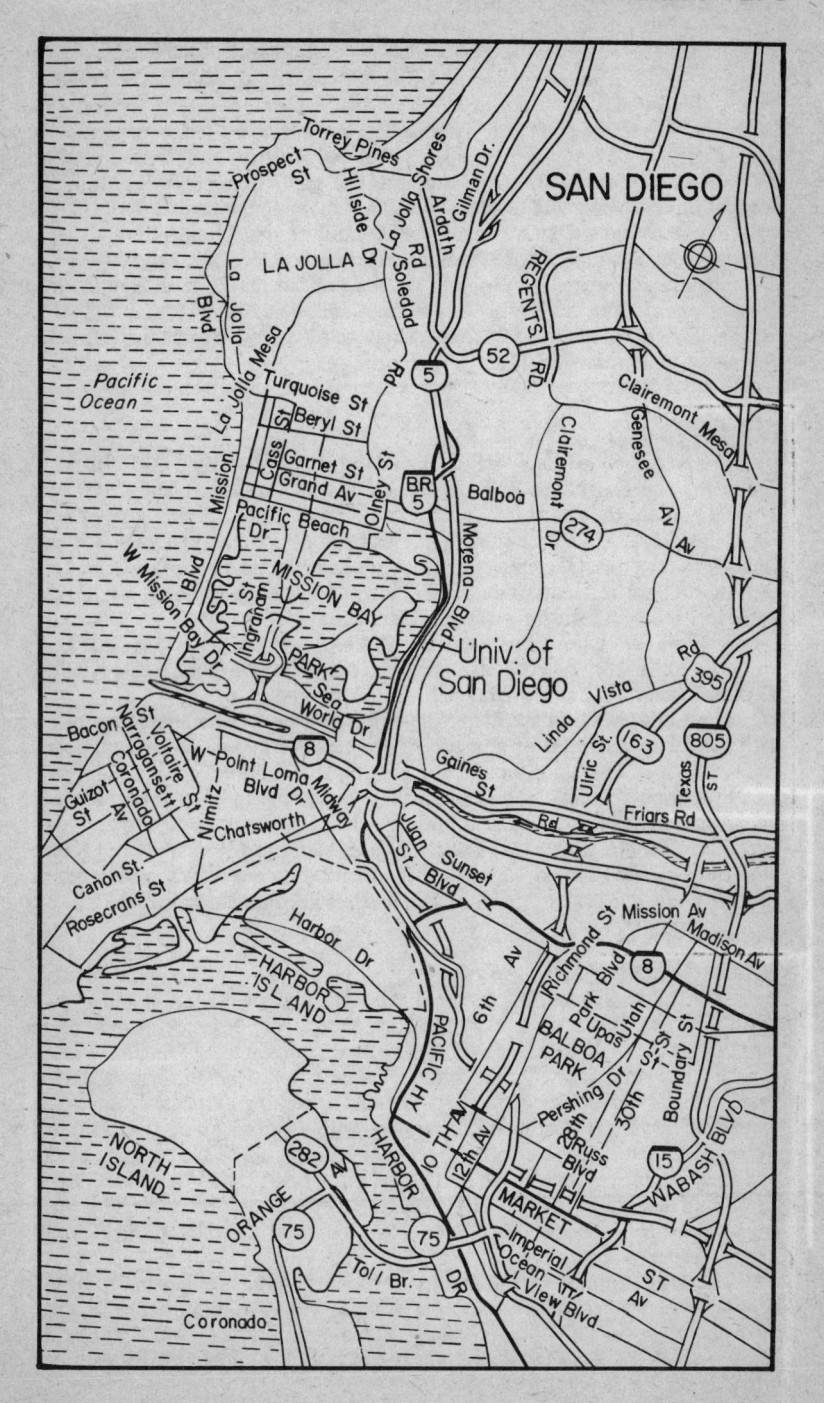

The Reuben H. Fleet Space Theater & Science Center

The largest planetarium in the United States, and the first in the world to have a tilted dome, the Reuben H. Fleet Space Theater takes the viewer out into space to see the stars and planets. The most modern techniques, sophisticated effects and equipment give the simulated journeys an incredible feeling of reality. In addition to space-tripping, the giant dome is the setting for voyages under the sea and inside a volcano. Adjoining the theater is the 8,000-square-foot **Science Center** with over 30 exhibits that blink, blip and beep, ranging from a computerized teaching machine to electronic tic-tac-toe.

The Space Theater is located in Balboa Park at the Plaza de Balboa, just across from the Natural History Museum. Admission is $2.50 for adults, $1.75 for juniors ages ten to 17, $1.25 for ages four to nine. For information on shows and show times, call 238-1168.

San Diego Zoo

The largest collection of wild animals in the world—over 5,000 of them—live at the San Diego Zoo in Balboa Park. Set in a lavishly planted 100-acre tropical garden, the zoo is famous for its rare and exotic species: koala bears, long-billed kiwis, wild Przewalski's horses from Mongolia, pigmy chimps and Galapagos tortoises. Of course, the usual lions, elephants, giraffes and tigers are present, too, not to mention over 3,000 birds. Most of the animals are housed in barless moated enclosures rather than cages.

A 40-minute guided bus tour provides an overview ($1.50 for adults, $1 for kids under 16). Alternately, you can get an aerial perspective via the **Skyfari Tramway** (75¢ for adults, 50¢ for kids under 16).

The **Children's Zoo** is scaled to a youngster's viewpoint. There's a nursery with baby animals and a petting zoo where kids can cuddle up to deer, goats, etc. Adults pay 25¢; ages four to 15, 15¢; under four free.

Free trained animal shows are a daily attraction in **Wegeforth Bowl**.

Admission to the zoo is $2 for adults; children 15 and under are admitted free. From July to Labor Day the hours are 9 a.m. to 6 p.m. Between Labor Day and October 31, and March to June, closing time is 5 p.m. November to February the zoo closes at 4 p.m. For further information call 234-5151.

WILD ANIMAL PARK: An offspring of the San Diego Zoo, Wild Animal Park is an 1,800-acre wildlife preserve and African-style village, 30 miles from downtown San Diego via Interstate 15. Animals from Asia and Africa roam freely in natural habitats, and over 100 birds are housed in an immense aviary. You can lead your own safari along the mile-and-a-quarter **Kilimanjaro Hiking Trail**, which offers many good spots for photographing animals; or explore a jungle *biome* (a natural habitat complete with tropical plants) in **Tropical America**. Other highlights include **Nairobi Village**, a 17-acre complex of native huts, exhibits, animal shows and shops and the five-mile **Wgasa Bush Line**, a five-mile monorail "train" safari through sweeping savannas and veldts, with ample stops for viewing. There's outdoor dining at **Mombasa Cooker** and **Thorn Tree Terrace**.

The Wild Animal Park is open daily from 9 a.m. to 9 p.m. in summer, closing at various earlier hours the rest of the year. An adult ticket package costs $3.75 and includes admission and the monorail tour; those ages four to 15 are admitted free and pay $1.50 for the monorail. Call 234-5151 for further information.

SAN DIEGO

SEA WORLD: **Mission Bay Park,** just north of San Diego on Route 5, is a multimillion-dollar aquatic playground with 4,600 acres of land and water area and facilities for every kind of water sport—sailing, boating, water-skiing, fishing, swimming, etc. But its main attraction is Sea World, an 80-acre family entertainment center where the performers are dolphins, killer whales, seals and penguins. Six shows are presented continuously throughout the day: Shamu, the 5,700-pound killer whale, does high jumps, hurdles and flips, and rides his trainer to the bottom of his million-gallon tank; dolphins participate in "Olympic" events; the creation of the earth and seas are explored by Spunky the dolphin and Max the sea lion; a seal and otter show features trained sea lions, otters, penguins and the amazing "Great Sealini"; in Sparklett's Water Fantasy a colorful rainbow of lights and photographs complement computerized formations of thousands of shimmering jets of water changing patterns to the accompaniment of quadrophonic sound for a magical journey through the seasons; and finally Japanese girls dive for pearl-bearing oysters.

Cap'n Kids World is a new attraction for kids, with nautical-theme rides and adventures. Other exhibits range from the dolphin-petting pool and an alligator pond (the 12 alligators eat 45 pounds of chicken a week), to a collection of over 1,200 water fowl and a Marine Aquarium where 25 separate displays feature hundreds of exotic fish from the world's oceans. Rounding out the bill are shops, band performances, costumed characters, rides and a wide choice of eateries.

One price ($5.50 for adults and $3.25 for children ages four to 12) admits visitors to all shows and exhibits. Sea World is open daily from 9 a.m. to 7:30 p.m. in summer, from 9:30 a.m. to 5 p.m. in winter. For information call 224-3562.

Point Loma

CABRILLO NATIONAL MONUMENT: Commemorating the discovery of California by Juan Rodriguez Cabrillo in 1542, this "Old Lighthouse," located ten miles from downtown San Diego along Pacific Boulevard (U.S. 101), is furnished with period furniture. From the tower, visitors have a sweeping vista of the ocean, bays, islands, mountains, valleys and plains that comprise the area. Open daily from 9 a.m. to 5:30 p.m. Admission is free.

MISSION SAN DIEGO DE ALCALA: While you're experiencing early California history, a visit to the first of Father Serra's missions, at 10818 San Diego Mission Road, takes you back to 1769 with a museum of liturgical robes, books and other relics. Open daily from 9 a.m. to 5 p.m. Continue your historic explorations at—

OLD TOWN: A six-block area northwest of downtown via Interstate 5, Old Town is a traffic-free state historic park that re-creates the setting of early California. Some of the Mexican adobe buildings date from 1825, and in the tree-lined plaza you'll see where the U.S. flag was first raised in 1846. Almost all of its buildings have been fully restored and are open to the public. In addition, there are shops, restaurants, galleries and handicraft centers, including a complex called **Bazaar del Mundo,** on Juan Street, that purports to be a modern version of a Mexican street market.

Since you can't drive into the park, there are three large parking areas at the entrance, right next to the headquarters building at 4016 Wallace Street. Here you can get maps and tour information. A special guided walking tour leaves from Whaley House each Saturday at 1:30 p.m.

THE MARITIME MUSEUM: Located at 1306 North Harbor Drive (tel: 234-9153), this is a nautical museum that consists of three restored historic vessels docked right on the water, near the fish markets. They are the *Berkeley*, the first successful propeller-driven ferry on the Pacific coast, launched in 1898 (she participated in the evacuation of San Francisco following the great earthquake and fire of 1906); the *Medea*, a steam yacht built in Scotland in 1904 (she fought in both world wars); and the *Star of India*, the oldest merchant vessel still afloat, launched in 1863.

You can purchase a boarding pass good for all three ships for $2; 50¢ for children under 12. Servicemen pay only $1.50. Open daily from 9 a.m. to 9 p.m.

BELMONT PARK: This Mission Bay attraction at 3000 Mission Boulevard (tel: 488-0531) doesn't have trained dolphins and killer whales, themed areas or costumed characters. It's just a good old-fashioned amusement park with a big roller coaster and 20 other rides, a kiddyland, midway games, a penny arcade and lots of stands where you can buy soda, cotton candy and crackerjacks. It's open mid-June to mid-September from noon to 11 p.m. (till midnight Fridays and Saturdays); the rest of the year it's open Fridays from 7 to 11 p.m., Saturdays from noon to 11 p.m., and Sundays from noon to 6 p.m. An unlimited-ride pass is $3.75.

2. Where to Stay

The hotel setup in San Diego subdivides into several areas where hotels are clustered. They are as follows:

DOWNTOWN: Little America Westgate, 1055 2nd Avenue, between Broadway and C Streets (tel: 238-1818; 800/522-1564), is a luxury hostelry of the first order. The tone is set as soon as you set foot in the posh lobby, hung with Aubusson and Beauvais tapestries and furnished in priceless antiques. The pattern of the parquet floors is copied from that at Fontainebleau, and the carpets on it are Kermin Oriental. Among the works of art, "The Prodigal Son" by Velasquez is valued at half-a-million dollars.

This is where President Ford stayed when he was in San Diego; so did Nixon before him. Each of the 225 spacious guest rooms is uniquely furnished, though the basic decor combines elements of Louis XV, Louis XVI, Georgian and English Regency periods. All rooms have a phone and a scale in the bath; the color TV is discreetly hidden in an elegant cabinet.

The lavish Fontainebleau Room, adorned with paintings by Boucher, boasts an award-winning French cuisine—chef Roger Jones is one of the world's 15 chefs awarded the "Toque Noir" (black hat) by the Escoffier Club of professional chefs in Paris. The gold-embossed gray suede menu lists items like duckling flamed in Cointreau ($8.95) and glazed crabmeat crêpes in light brandy sauce ($7.95). Open for lunch and dinner daily. In addition, the Westgate Room is open for dining from 7 a.m. to 11:30 p.m., and an exquisite $4.95 buffet brunch—complete with ice sculpture—is served in the Versailles Ballroom every Sunday.

Free transportation is provided to all nearby sports facilities and attractions. Rates are $32 to $46 for singles, $36 to $48 for doubles or twins.

Another palatial downtown choice, the **U.S. Grant**, 326 Broadway, between 3rd and 4th Streets (tel: 232-3121), was erected at the turn of the century by President Grant's sons. A battleship-gray exterior belies the lavish lobby within. Over the years the U.S. Grant has played host to scores of celebrities ranging from Jean Harlow to President Kennedy. The rooms are truly charming and homey, combining old-fashioned spaciousness and substantiality with all modern amenities. There are four eateries, including the oak-paneled, red-carpeted Grant Grill, serving gourmet continental entrees (until a few years ago, it was for men only). A very attractive alternative is the verdant Garden Room, serving breakfast, lunch and dinner.

Rates for singles range from $14 to $25; doubles, $19 to $30.

HOTEL CIRCLE: Mission Valley is the most centrally located resort area in San Diego. Around its Hotel Circle are many restaurants, motels, hotels and the largest shopping complex in the country, Fashion Valley Center. Recommended in Hotel Circle are:

Fabulous Inn, 2485 Hotel Circle Place (tel: 291-7700), a modern four-story, 142-room complex at the extreme western end of the Circle. All rooms have balconies, color TV (with in-house movies), air-conditioning, bath with dressing room, and direct-dial phone. A swimming pool and Jacuzzi are on the premises, a Hungry Tiger Restaurant adjoins, and golf and tennis facilities are just across the street. Rates are "fabulous," considering all you're getting: $17 to $22 for singles, $22 to $35 for doubles.

Town & Country, 500 Hotel Circle (tel: 291-7131), with 1,000 rooms the largest hotel in San Diego, is a super-hotel with seemingly every facility you could want or imagine—even a gas station. There are shops, car-rental, airline and sightseeing desks, shuttle service to the airport and shopping, three swimming pools, a therapy pool, sauna, four restaurants, two coffee shops, a discotheque and a nightclub. In addition, guests can use the Atlas Health Club across the street ($3 for use of tennis courts, $3 for use of all other facilities). Needless to say, the rooms have every amenity as well, right down to in-room movies on your color TV, in-room coffee-makers and daily newspaper delivery. The setting for all this luxury is a 32-acre tropical palm garden. Singles are $32; doubles and twins are $37.

Under the same management, and offering similar facilities, on a smaller and slightly less luxurious scale, is the 271-room **Hanalei Hotel,** 2270 Hotel Circle (tel: 297-1101). There are fewer food and beverage options, and only one swimming pool, but otherwise you get most of what is described above, including use of the Atlas Health Club. Single rooms are $22, doubles and twins $27.

There's a convenient **Motel 6** at 2424 Hotel Circle North (tel: 297-4871). Refer to the Introduction for rates and other particulars.

MISSION BAY: The **Bahia Hotel,** 998 West Mission Bay Drive (tel: 488-0551), has a lovely situation on the peninsula of Mission Bay, with marine views in every direction. Sailboats and paddle boats are rentable at the Bahia dock, and there's an Olympic-size swimming pool, a therapy bath and a health club (tennis courts are under construction). Should you have your own yacht, you can dock it here (we're sure that's a great relief to readers). There's free parking and free airport transfer.

The rooms are pleasant and airy, furnished with attractive modern pieces. Each has a picture window (most with water views), color TV, direct-dial phone, and tub/shower bath with dressing room area. About half the rooms have kitchens and balconies or patios.

Other facilities include two restaurants—a coffee shop adjoining the fireplace lobby, serving breakfast, lunch and dinner; and the plush Mercedes Room. Almost a Mercedes museum, and as elegant as that prestigious automobile, the restaurant has a $50,000, 1902 sports and racing model on stage in the lobby, Mercedes-logo carpeting, Mercedes posters and drawings on the walls. Many seats offer a lovely view of the harbor, and the predominantly blue color scheme enhances the tranquil seaside ambience. Open for dinner nightly, the Mercedes Room offers continental specialties like curried shrimp casserole with grilled banana, fresh pineapple and rice pilaf ($7.25) and broiled filet mignon with mushrooms ($8.95). All entrees are served with soup or salad, homemade bread, potatoes, and coffee or tea.

One other unique offering of the Bahia is a seal pond containing one resident who goes by the name of Otis.

Rates for one or two persons from July 25 to September 12 are $34 for a room with a queen-sized bed, $34 to $38 for extra-large twin beds, and $36 to $40 for double doubles. The rest of the year, queen rooms are $26 to $30, extra-large twins $28 to $32, and double doubles $30 to $36.

Just across the bay from the Bahia is the **Catamaran,** 3999 Mission Boulevard (tel: 488-1081), under the same ownership and offering almost identical facilities. There's a showroom where car-aficionado/owner Bill Evans displays his collection of antique cars, and in place of the Mercedes Room the restaurant here is the Polynesian Room. No seal, however.

A sternwheeler called the *Bahia Belle* cruises the bay, running hourly in summer (less often in winter) and stopping at the Bahia, the Catamaran and Vacation Village. At night there's dancing to live music and cocktails aboard the Belle; fare is $1.50 per person.

Rates at the Catamaran are the same as the Bahia.

HARBOR ISLAND AND SHELTER ISLAND: Man-made Harbor Island is a 1½-mile-long peninsula just minutes from the airport and downtown—a hub of San Diego hotel, nightlife and restaurant activity. It contains the **Sheraton-Harbor Island Hotel,** 1380 Harbor Island Drive (tel: 291-2900; 800/325-3535), with 378 handsomely furnished rooms in a 12-story tower and 122 more in the adjacent "Lanai Village." Tower rooms have balconies, and all accommodations have color TV, air conditioning, oversized beds, etc. The hotel's gourmet restaurant is La Hacienda de Portola, commanding a view of the marina. At the top of the tower, the Butterfield Stage Salon has even more spectacular views; it's open nightly for prime-rib dinners, drinking and dancing. There's also a coffee shop on the premises, serving meals from 6 a.m. to midnight. The hotel's other facilities include two large swimming pools, two children's pools, a Jacuzzi, sauna, shops, beauty salon and barber shop, a game room, laundry room, four lighted tennis courts, a nine-hole putting green, bicycle rental, shuffleboard and volleyball courts, and a boat rental dock.

Rates in either section are $30 to $40 single, $36 to $48 double, depending on the time of year.

There's another Sheraton, the **Sheraton–Half Moon Bay,** 2303 Shelter Island Drive (tel: 224-3411; 800/325-3535), on nearby Shelter Island (also a man-made peninsula)—this one with a lush Polynesian setting. Rates are $26 to $36 for singles, $34 to $44 for doubles.

CORONADO: The grande dame of San Diego's resort hotels, the **Hotel del Coronado,** 1500 Orange Avenue (tel: 435-6611; 800/421-0000), opened its doors in 1888, and was designated in 1970 as a state historical landmark. The last of the extravagantly conceived seaside hotels, it is a monument to Victorian grandeur with its tall cupolas, turrets and gingerbread trim. The register over the years has listed thousands of celebrity guests—five former presidents, Frank Sinatra, Clark Gable, Charlton Heston, Jonathan Winters, Zsa Zsa Gabor and Charlie Chaplin are just a few. Former Secretary of the Interior Stewart Udall was moved to write a poem about the beauty of the early morning in Coronado when he stayed here. Prince Edward met Wally Simpson here and he was moved to abdicate his throne!

The hotel's beach and championship tennis facilities include a large heated swimming pool, children's pool and a white sand beach. There's a health spa for men and women, a championship 18-hole golf course and boat house, as well as six areas for dining and cocktails. The Crown Room is the hotel's main dining room, magnificently unchanged since the turn of the century.

And accommodations are, of course, fittingly exquisite, with custom-made furnishings and all conveniences. Rates begin at $30 for street-side standard rooms (single or double) and go up to $80 for a deluxe lanai double with oceanfront or bay view (many options in between). To stay here is a unique and memorable pleasure; if it's not in your budget, at least come by for a meal and a stroll around the grounds.

3. Where to Dine

Lubach's, 2101 North Harbor Drive (tel: 232-5129), located on the Embarcadero, is an award-winning seafood restaurant with a comfortably traditional decor. The wood-paneled walls are adorned with ship models, wagon-wheel chandeliers are suspended from the ceilings, the tablecloths create a sea of white linen, seating is in captain's chairs and shiny red leather banquettes, and a vase containing a single rosebud graces every table. A blazing fire in a brick fireplace adds a homey touch. The food is delicious—a combination of culinary art and the use of only fresh fish and produce. A specialty is totuava (related to sea bass but firmer and sweeter) sauteed in lemon butter and priced at $8.25; poached salmon in Hollandaise sauce costs the same. Non-seafood entrees include boneless squab with wild rice ($6.50) and beef stroganoff with noodles ($8.50). There's a well-chosen selection of imported and California wines to complement your meal. For dessert you might select one of the French pastries ($1.50) from the cart (baked fresh each morning). Luncheon salads and sandwiches are $2.95 to $5.75. Open for lunch and dinner Monday through Saturday. Jackets are required at dinner.

Another Embarcadero seafood eatery of renown is the Ghio family's **Anthony's Star of the Sea Room,** 1360 Harbor Drive (tel: 232-7408), next to the three-masted *Star of India*. Dramatically set overlooking the San Diego harbor, Anthony's interior is plush, with chairs upholstered in gold suede, gold carpeting, and long-stemmed lamps on every table. Specialties include the cioppino à la Catherine (Catherine is Anthony Ghio's wife) for $10.95, and oven-baked sole stuffed with lobster, shrimp and crab, $19 for two. One can dine less expensively on tasty items like batter-fried fish and chips with vegetables ($5.50) or a sumptuous seafood platter salad ($5.85). It's open daily for dinner from 5:30 to 10:30 p.m.

Adjoining is **Anthony's Fish Grotto** (tel: 232-5103), also run by the Ghio family. The decor is a shade less elegant, though you still have the panoramic harbor view, and prices are lower, with entrees mostly in the $3-to-$6 range. The Grotto is open daily, except Tuesdays, from 11:30 a.m. to 8:30 p.m.

Our award for best ambience goes to **Tom Ham's Lighthouse,** 2150 Harbor Island Drive, Harbor Island (tel: 291-9110), where early California decor and the incredible bay views combine to create an exquisite interior. Not only are the food and decor excellent, you can enjoy a museum as well—a collection of marine artifacts from around the world. At night there's entertainment downstairs in the Harbor View Room, occasionally big names like Cal Tjader or Ramsey Lewis. Seafood specialties include a shrimp brochette with bacon, mushrooms, green peppers and rice pilaf ($6.25), served with New England clam chowder or salad. The menu also lists several Mexican combination plates ($4.95) and steak and prime-rib specialties ($4.95 to $9.25). Luncheon entrees are in the $2.25-to-$4 bracket. Open daily for lunch and dinner.

Like any port city, San Diego boasts an international cuisine. For instance, if you should get a craving for Lebanese food, just direct your camel to **Antoine's Sheik,** 2664 5th Avenue, between Maple and Nutley Streets (tel: 234-5888). It's fittingly exotic, with carpeted walls, a hookah on every table (for decorative purposes only), Arabic music in the background and hushed lighting from cut-brass lamps overhead and candles. Owner Antoine Ghosn is something of a celebrity locally; he occasionally appears on TV demonstrating Arab cookery. Full dinners are served with hommus (crushed chick-pea hors d'oeuvre), taboule (cracked wheat salad) and turnips, green salad, and Lebanese bread. Such a dinner with an entree of lamb shish kabob and rice pilaf would cost $7.50; $6.95 with shrimp curry; $5.95 with stuffed grape leaves and/or cabbage leaves. At lunch most à la carte entrees are under $3. A glass of house wine with either meal is 75¢. Open Monday through Thursday from 11 a.m. to 9:30 p.m., Friday till 10:30 p.m., and Saturday from 4 to 10:30 p.m.

If you are exploring the sights of Old Town, you might as well explore some of the food served here, too—particularly the traditional Mexican specialties at the **Casa de Pico,** in the Bazaar del Mundo. The prices are reasonable, the setting festive.

And for spiritual types or vegetarians, we offer the **Prophet,** 4461 University Avenue, where pictures of gurus line the walls and where healthful organic dishes are priced in the $2-$5 range.

4. La Jolla

On the northern edge of the San Diego coastline, La Jolla (pronounced La Hoya—it means "the Jewel") is famous for its picturesque scenery, beautiful beaches and estates. A serene vacation retreat, the area is dotted with some of San Diego's finest restaurants and hotels. Along Coast Boulevard in La Jolla are natural caves that have been washed out by the action of the ocean over the years, and have fascinating formations and colors. For information about exploring the caves, call 454-6080.

The **Scripps Aquarium Museum,** 8602 La Jolla Shores Drive (tel: 452-4086), is the principal visitor attraction. Renowned for the research it does in the oceans, the Museum invites visitors to see aquarium exhibits of specimens of California and Baja marine life, oceanographic exhibits of typical research done by the Scripps scientists, and a comprehensive collection of oceanographic literature. A new tide-pool exhibit generates waves and tides. The museum is open daily from 9 a.m. to 5 p.m., and no admission is charged.

WHERE TO STAY: La Valencia, 1132 Prospect Street, corner of Hershey (tel: 454-0771), is a gracious old Riviera-style resort that delights the senses at every turn. Dramatically situated on the ocean, it was designed in archetypical early-California-Spanish style by architect Reginald Johnson back in 1926. From the Mediterranean-style colonnaded entrance, to the lush gardens that surround the large swimming pool, to the exquisite mosaic tilework within, it's a beauty.

Rooms are furnished with antiques and reproductions, most overlook the ocean, and each is equipped with a color TV and other modern amenities. A piano player entertains in the La Sala lounge, off the lobby, nightly from 6:30 p.m., and there's a large jigsaw puzzle for guests to work on in the lobby—a Valencia tradition.

Eating facilities include the Sky Room, a cozy rooftop restaurant offering gourmet cuisine and commanding views of the Pacific. A buffet lunch served weekdays is $4.50. At dinner, entrees include roast rack of lamb bouquetière ($8.95) and scampi in white wine sauce ($7.95)—both served with soup or salad, dauphine potatoes or rice pilaf, fresh vegetables and parmesan-cheese bread. Even if you're not staying here, consider a meal at the Sky Room. Reservations are essential.

Another dining choice is the Mediterranean Room, which has an outdoor, flower-bedecked patio on which lunch is served in good weather. It's delightful inside and out, and within there's a wall of windows overlooking the ocean. At lunch salads and sandwiches, in the $2.50-to-$4 range, are featured. The dinner menu consists largely of steak and seafood entrees. Steak and seafood are also featured at the Whaling Bar and Grill, where a New Bedford nautical ambience prevails.

Other facilities include a sauna and whirlpool, a nine-hole putting green and shuffleboard.

Highest rates are charged from July 1 through Labor Day, when singles and doubles are $40 to $49. January 10 to April 1, singles pay $30 to $41, and doubles pay $35 to $46. The rest of the year, singles pay $28 to $39, doubles $33 to $44.

Another elegant Old California accommodation is **Sea Lodge**, 8110 Camino Del Oro (tel: 459-8271), overlooking the Pacific on a mile-long beach. Its 101 rooms are housed in a long and low stucco building with terra-cotta-tile roof, highlighted by fountains, beautiful landscaping and flower beds, open-air walkways, ceramic tilework, graceful arches and Mexican antiques like the 200-year-old cathedral doors leading into the main dining room.

An immense swimming pool gleams jewel-like in the courtyard, where umbrellaed tables are set up for outdoor dining. Other facilities include three championship tennis courts (no charge for use), a sauna, a small putting green and a nine-hole golf course next door at the La Jolla Beach and Tennis Club. The La Sala del Mar Restaurant (that's the above-mentioned main dining room) serves three meals a day, seven days a week, under a peaked beamed ceiling. The decor is richly Spanish and arched windows provide a view of the beach.

As for the rooms, they're large and lovely—all with one barnwood wall (third-floor-rooms—our favorites—have high sloped barnwood ceilings as well), and almost all have an ocean view. All are equipped with carved wooden beds, walls adorned with Mexican bark paintings, large dressing rooms, refrigerators and handsome ceramic-tile baths, as well as balconies or lanais and all modern amenities.

Rates are seasonal: from January 1 to March 31 and September 16 to December 31, singles pay $34 to $42, doubles pay $39 to $47. April 1 to June 15, singles pay $32 to $38, doubles $37 to $43; June 16 to September 15, singles pay $42 to $51, doubles $47 to $56.

WHERE TO DINE: La Jolla has more than its share of good restaurants. Among them we'll single out **El Chalan**, 5621 La Jolla Boulevard (tel: 459-7707), for its Peruvian cuisine. Open Wednesday through Monday from 5:30

to 11 p.m., it is a handsome place, with wood-paneled walls adorned with posters of Peru, and fresh flowers in black Pisco (a Peruvian liqueur) bottles on every table. The food is well prepared and highly flavored. If you can afford the calories, do try the tapas rellenas appetizer—deep-fried meat-stuffed potatoes ($1.35). Entrees range from aji de gallina—stewed shredded chicken in a peanut and cashew sauce ($4.75); to lomo a la huancaina—filet mignon topped with the owner's grandmother's secret sauce and served with Peruvian-style potatoes ($7.50).

5. An Excursion to Tijuana

While you're this far south, you may as well go the extra 18 miles and cross the border to Tijuana, gateway to Mexico. Here you can see thoroughbred-racing at **Agua Caliente** every Saturday and Sunday from 1 p.m.; greyhound-racing is scheduled Wednesday through Sunday.

Mexico's top matadors perform in two different rings every Sunday at 4 p.m. between May and September. In San Diego phone 232-4588 for ticket information.

And then there are jai alai games, often called the fastest sport in the world, played nightly except Thursday starting at 8 p.m. at the **Fronton Palacio,** Ave. Revolucion at Calle 7a (tel: 427-7752 in San Diego; 903-385-1612 in Tijuana).

No passport is needed, and you can shop with American money. For information on **Gray Line** tours to Tijuana call 233-7676. The San Diego Convention and Visitors Bureau can provide you with a wealth of information about Tijuana attractions and tours.

Chapter XIII

LAS VEGAS

1. Getting There
2. Getting Around
3. Food, Fun and Shelter

LAS VEGAS. Disneyland for the 21-and-over set; playground of the rich, the not-so-rich, the tourist from Albuquerque, the sophisticate from New York City. There's something here for everyone, and, more often than not, everyone leaves a little something here. That's the rule of the game, and games are what Las Vegas is all about. Emotion runs high as money runs low, but there is always some place to go to work off those lost-green blues.

Where else could you have your pick of tennis courts 24 hours a day, seven days a week? Get to see Sinatra, Liberace and Elvis all in one week? Dine on the choicest of steaks while watching a three-ring circus directly overhead? Decide to get married and actually do it on the same day—even within the same hour. Only in Vegas, where everything is not just out of the ordinary, but out of the extraordinary.

The funny thing about Las Vegas is that it's never really been any different. From the start, the lure of Nevada was all glitter and gold. During the California Gold Rush, it became a lucrative stopping-off place for prospectors. Gold, silver and other precious metals were mined into the early 1900s, when the rich ore veins were finally picked clean.

The next boom came in on the tail of the Gold Rush, around 1905, when the Union Pacific Railroad built a depot in what immediately and henceforth became known as Las Vegas. As the iron horse flourished, so did Nevada property values. And always there was gambling—finally made legal in 1931—and big-time gamblers, who helped to make Las Vegas a legendary town, while becoming legends themselves. Perhaps the most notorious of these was Nick the Greek, King of Gamblers from 1928 to 1949. In his time he won and lost more than $50 million—and managed to die poor. During his "reign" he was offered hotel partnerships and land in payment for gambling debts owed him. But he spurned these and other offers that would have made him financially independent. Nick preferred to gamble for his fortunes, claiming that he would rather pay and lose. The thrill, for him, was in the betting.

Whether or not you aspire to the big time, Las Vegas will welcome you with open casinos, and enough excitement, thrills and experiences to keep you coming back again and again.

1. Getting There

The information in Chapter I about air, bus and train travel to California applies equally to Las Vegas. All the fares and package options discussed in the air section can be applied, with the exception of night coach: there are no night coach flights between Las Vegas and other cities. There are also some additional "black-out" periods on tour basing fares to Las Vegas. You can check these with TWA or your travel agent, and also find out the full extent of packages available. The minimum price for the land package to Las Vegas is $25.

TWA flies to Las Vegas from the same cities listed in Chapter I, with the exception of Phoenix and the addition of Wichita. One-way coach fare between Los Angeles and Las Vegas is $38; $55 between San Francisco and Las Vegas. The Discover America excursion fare is $61 round trip from Los Angeles and $88 round trip from San Francisco.

TWA's round-trip fares between New York and Las Vegas are as follows: coach, $376; Discover America, $320 peak season, $301 off-peak season; tour-basing, $320 peak, $301 off-peak. Once again, refer back to Chapter I for descriptions of these fare categories.

2. Getting Around

Not only does Las Vegas have the distinction of being the oasis in an otherwise desert state, it is also Nevada's largest city. The sections that will interest you most as a tourist, however, are contained in a fairly compact area.

The Strip (more formally known as Las Vegas Boulevard) intersects **Fremont Street** in the **Downtown Casino Center** area (AKA Glitter Gulch). The major Strip action—and almost all Vegas action is on the Strip—begins at the Sahara Hotel, on Sahara Avenue, and runs south of Tropicana Avenue to the Hacienda Hotel. Though one could, conceivably, walk from the Hacienda to the Sahara, it is only advisable to do so when the sun goes down. Hot or not, it's quite a trek.

Strip buses ply the route from the Hacienda to Fremont Street, stopping at all major hotels. To return to the Strip from Downtown, go to the corner of 3rd and Fremont. Bus fare is 70¢. Taxis cost 75¢ for the first quarter-mile, 80¢ a mile after that.

3. Food, Fun and Shelter

In previous chapters of this book, the questions of where to eat, where to stay and what to do were separate categories, handled, for the most part, independently of one another. In Las Vegas, most of the top restaurants are right in the big hotels, ditto the casinos and the nightclubs. So we've organized

The **Cafe Gigi** serves haute-cuisine continental fare in a Versailles-like setting. Some of the items of decor—like the ornate gold wall panels and mirrors, and the imposing door—are actually from the set of the movie *Marie Antoinette*. The menu is in Frenchified English (in other words, easily translatable) with entrees like roasted rack de lamb ($30 pour deux) and quails en casserole Veronique ($15). You might precede your entree with a lettuce de Boston salad ($1.75), and finish it up with pastries Française ($1.75).

At **Caruso's,** Italian specialties are served in an atmosphere of Venetian elegance. Cobblestone floors, antique iron ovens and classical statuary grace the room, and enormous black and white polka dot menus grace the tables. Pasta dishes range from $4.50 to $6.75; delicious veal, seafood and poultry entrees are in the $8-to-$13.50 bracket, the higher price for an MGM special steak or lobster Fra Diavola. A cannoli for dessert is $2.25.

At the **Barrymore's,** copper and carved-oak accents create a warmly intimate ambience. Seafood is the specialty, with entrees like jumbo shrimps creole in casserole for $9.50. You can also get a prime-rib dinner served with Yorkshire pudding and horseradish ($11.50).

If you don't want to make a big to-do over dinner, try **The Deli,** a replica of a New York Broadway delicatessen, or the **Orleans Coffee House,** a colorful French Quarter cafe with a varied menu.

Another dining option is, of course, the dinner show in the **Celebrity Room,** MGM's headliner theater. Seating 1,200, it features the likes of Dean Martin, Paul Anka, Helen Reddy, Carol Burnett and Shecky Greene. There are two shows nightly: a dinner show starting at 8 p.m. with a $17.50 minimum, and a midnight show for which the minimum is $17.50 to $20, four drinks included.

The **Ziegfeld Room,** ever since the hotel opened, has been offering the musical super-spectacular "Hallelujah Hollywood," which many Vegas regulars opine is the best show in town. It has gorgeous bespangled, ostrich-plumed girls, fantastic scenery, lots of nostalgia, animals on stage, Gershwin and Porter tunes, special effects, etc. The audience is taken to the mysterious East in a number called "Kismet," which is complete with swarming bazaars, minarets and harem houris, not to mention live camels and llamas. Later on in the show a pirate ship sinks in flames and a dolphin does an underwater ballet with an aquabelle, disrobing her in the process. It all ends with a bevy of beautiful girls on stage backgrounded musically by "A Pretty Girl is Like a Melody." There are shows at 9 p.m. and 12:30 a.m., with an additional show on Saturday at 2:30 a.m. A $17.50 minimum is charged at all shows. Don't miss it!

The **Lion's Den, Cub Bar** and **Parisian Bar,** all off the lobby and close to casino action, also offer live entertainment, ranging from comedy to a full orchestra. And the **MGM Theatre** screens old movie greats.

CAESARS PALACE: 3570 Las Vegas Boulevard South (tel: 734-7110; 800/634-6661).

Arriving at Caesars Palace is supposed to be like taking a giant step back in time to ancient Rome, and, more specifically, to Caesar's palace. Caesar should have had it so good! Outrageous, overwhelming, opulence is what this resort complex is all about.

Lining the entranceway are double rows of cypress trees interspersed with magnificent fountains. Marble statues are scattered thither and yon. At night, the hotel bathes itself in a blue-green light that glows and reflects over the entire couple of blocks that make up its facade. The main floor is also dotted with marble statues. In amongst them are marble balustrades, columns, paneling,

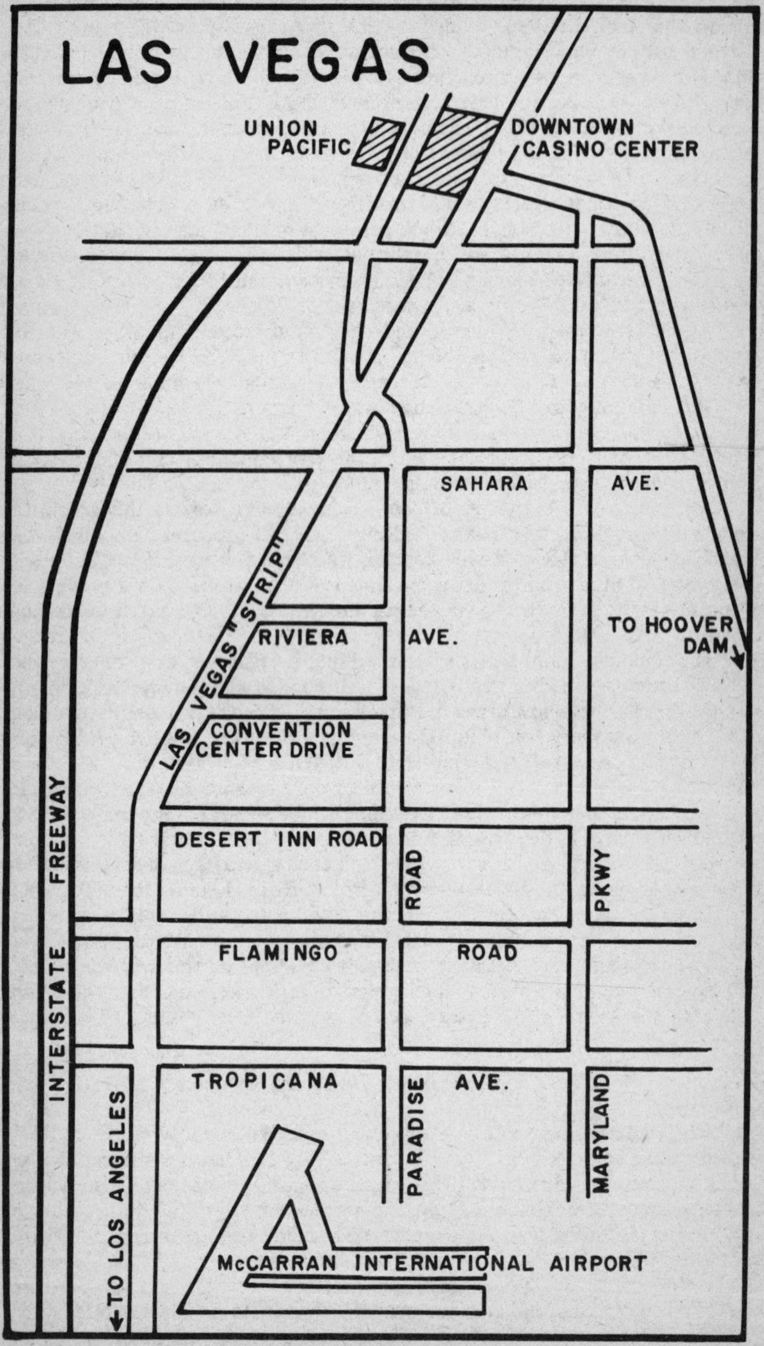
LAS VEGAS
UNION PACIFIC
DOWNTOWN CASINO CENTER
SAHARA AVE.
LAS VEGAS "STRIP"
RIVIERA AVE.
TO HOOVER DAM
CONVENTION CENTER DRIVE
DESERT INN ROAD
ROAD
PKWY
INTERSTATE FREEWAY
FLAMINGO ROAD
TROPICANA AVE.
PARADISE
MARYLAND
TO LOS ANGELES
McCARRAN INTERNATIONAL AIRPORT

gew gaws; in fact, about the only thing that isn't marble in the lobby is the exhibit showing how dice are made (from cotton).

On the premises are five restaurants, a giant 24-hour gambling casino, a nightclub featuring top entertainers, shops and service desks, eight outdoor and four indoor tennis courts (Pancho Gonzalez is the resident pro), golf nearby, an Olympic-size pool and the most fully equipped health club we've ever seen.

The private rooms are every bit as luxurious as the public ones. Rates go from $40 to $60 single or double, and from $105 to $705 for the suites. Add $5 for a third person in the room. The decor is last-days-of-Rome-ornate, with mirrored walls, deep carpeting, and fancy arched dividers separating living area from sleeping area. Some of the rooms even have beds on raised platforms, with steps leading up. Even the drinking glasses are wrapped in gold foil. Of course, all modern amenities are present and accounted for.

The hotel has two gourmet restaurants. **The Bacchanal** continues in the style to which you quickly become accustomed at Caesars Palace. Done up in lavish Roman decor with pillars and statues, it is open from 6 p.m. to midnight, and is "prix-fixed" at $32.50 per person for a banquet with appropriate wines included. Your evening repast will include tidbits, served with your apéritif, followed by more serious hors d'oeuvres, a variety of soups, fish, "a parade of gastronomical surprises," vegetables, desserts, cheeses and coffee.

The second is the new super-posh **Palace Court,** serving classic French cuisine in a mini-museum setting. It's reached via a round elevator with a crystal and bronze car. Works on display here include nine heroic paintings from the school of Peter Paul Rubens and paintings of the 12 Caesars by the Bolognese 17th-century artist Camillo Procaccini. The retractable, domed, stained-glass ceiling in the lounge can be opened to the desert sky. The maitre d' is formerly of Maxim's, and knowledgable *sommeliers* are on hand to assist in wine selection. This is a place to go when you're willing to spend freely—it's easy to work up $50 per person tabs. Open Wednesday through Sunday from 7 p.m. to midnight.

Other dining options include the **Ah-So Steak House,** serving Japanese dinners ($22.50 per person) in an Oriental garden setting; **The Piazza,** specializing in Italian dinners but open for breakfast and lunch weekdays as well; and the **Noshorium,** a 24-hour coffee shop.

For entertainment there's **Circus Maximus,** featuring acts like Johnny Carson, Tom Jones, Steve and Eydie, Andy Williams, Diana Ross, Alan King, Frank Sinatra and Sammy Davis, Jr. There are cocktail shows only—at 9 p.m. and 12:30 a.m.—priced at $15 to $25 minimum, including three or four drinks.

And rounding out the bill is **Cleopatra's Barge,** a replica of Cleopatra's trysting ship, complete with hydraulic mechanism to keep it in constant motion afloat on the "Nile." Open 8 p.m. to 4 a.m., with a live band for dancing.

THE HILTON LAS VEGAS: Paradise Road, adjacent to Las Vegas Convention Center (tel: 732-5111).

Calling itself a vacation spa, the Las Vegas Hilton is the tallest building in the state and has the most rooms in Las Vegas to date. It contains a corps of international restaurants, a grand casino, about 14 shops, and a landscaped 8½-acre recreation deck on the third floor roof with four lighted tennis courts, an 18-hole putting course, shuffleboard, squash and the largest swimming pool in Nevada! There's more. An 18-hole golf course is a mere step away, there are pagoda-style huts for card-playing and snacking . . . well, you get a picture.

The extravagant lobby is hung with tier upon tier of glistening imported crystal chandeliers and boasts a 100-foot reception desk. Extravagance doesn't stop in the lobby. If anything, it is accentuated in the rooms, executed in a continental decor, with one floor decorated in Spanish style, another in Oriental, another in French and so on. The prevailing theme, whatever the floor, is luxury. Singles or doubles go for $37 to $53 per day.

One particularly enticing feature for families is the "Youth Hotel." Supervised 24-hours a day, it even contains a supervised dorm for kids ages three through 18. Every conceivable kind of craft, sport and activity is available to entertain the young while Mom and Dad are out on the town. Rates are about $2 an hour for each child, $8 overnight.

Should you be coming without the kids, however, the ultimate bargain is the package plan called the "Hilton Spree." Three days and two nights, double occupancy, are $76 per person. Included in the package are deluxe accommodations, dinner and show in the main showroom, dancing and two cocktails in the Casino Lounge, a buffet luncheon, unlimited free tennis, tips and taxes.

Now, how about a meal? Most spectacular facility is **Benihana Village**, a complex of five Japanese restaurants and four cocktail lounges set in a life-sized Japanese village complete with lush gardens, running streams and an Imperial Palace. Guests are treated to periodic thunder and lightning storms and pouring rain (not on diners), fireworks displays and dancing waters. And, incidentally, the Japanese fare is superb.

Leonardo's features a vineyard decor with boughs of grapes suspended from the ceiling; the menu is Italian. Then there's the **Bavarian Inn,** for Alpine-inspired entrees like wienerschnitzel and gebratenes rumpfstuck (which translates to a Viennese-style butter-fried New York steak). Right next door is the **Hilton Steak House,** serving immense Texas-style meals in a Southwest setting. The **Barronshire Prime Rib Room,** sporting a bibliothèque decor, is known for its generous portions of guess what; follow it up with the luscious chocolate soufflé. And for refined elegance and gourmet continental fare, the **Imperial Crown Room** has, for openers, table service in 14-karat gold. Finally, there's **Mamchen's Deli Tavern,** for relaxing sit-down or fast stand-up service, and the 24-hour **Market Plaza Coffee Shop.**

Even the entertainment combines with food. The 2,000-seat **Hilton Showroom** (Barbra Streisand was the first act when it opened) features stars like Perry Como, Liberace, Glen Campbell, Bill Cosby and John Davidson. The dinner show at 8 p.m. costs $17 to $20; the midnight show is $12.50 to $15, including three cocktails.

The **Casino Lounge,** used daily for buffet meals, turns into a discotheque at night, offering live and taped music from early evening till dawn. No cover or minimum.

THE TROPICANA HOTEL & COUNTRY CLUB: 3801 Las Vegas Boulevard South (tel: 739-2222; 800/634-6693).

Located at the least flashy extremity of the Strip, the Tropicana replaces the glitter and gaudy razzle-dazzle that is the norm in Vegas with subtle, played-down superiority. This is reflected in the casino, which is done in rich royal blue (as opposed to the usual red on red on red), as well as in the basic facade of the hotel. Instead of trying to be the biggest or tallest, it has been tastefully built in long, low wings of three and four stories.

Currently there are 575 rooms, and another 540 will open when the new $20-million, 22-story addition is completed, some time in 1977. Twin and double rooms rent for $32 to $42 a night. And again, restful elegance governs the decor in attractive, low-key rooms equipped with every modern luxury.

When you call for reservations, ask about package tours—they offer good value.

The hotel is set on lush tropical grounds, which make a nice background for the Olympic-size swimming pool. Across from the hotel is an 18-hole, par-70 golf course with a clubhouse, pro shop and locker rooms. The Tropicana Racquet Club offers 24-hour play on its eight air-conditioned indoor courts, two outdoor courts, handball and racquetball courts. In addition, there's a health club for men and women.

The Tropicana's luxe eatery is the **Tiffany Room,** with a classic French motif and a continental menu. Entrees, such as boneless Colorado trout with toasted almonds and Long Island duckling in orange sauce with wild rice, are in the $10-to-$13 range.

Dinner and cocktails are also served at the **Lord Byron Inn,** designed to look like an English pub and featuring the likes of "olde fashion English chycken and large fluffy home made dumplings" ($7.95), followed, of course by a dessert of "Olde English tryfle au brandy" ($1).

The 24-hour-a-day coffee shop is called the **Brazilian Garden Coffee Shop.**

Finally, there's the **Tiffany Theater,** which is only incidentally a restaurant. It's primarily the setting for the lavish *Folies Bergere,* a dazzling musical extravaganza that has been delighting audiences since 1959. It's racy and funny and spectacular, with French cancan acts, a nostalgic Harlem scene in which a Rolls-Royce pulls up on stage, plus live monkeys (they're wonderful), a horse, acrobats, comedians, magicians and hundreds of semi-clad and/or elaborately costumed lovelies. The 8 p.m. dinner show is $15.50, the midnight show $12 including two drinks.

THE RIVIERA HOTEL: 2901 Las Vegas Boulevard South (tel: 734-5510; 800/634-6855).

Another of the handful of Vegas hotels that projects a refined image, the Riviera attempts to cater "to the carriage trade." The lobby is tastefully arranged, with slot machines discreetly off to one side. Off the lobby is the hotel's promenade, lined with fashionable boutiques, shops and airline offices. In addition to an immense and very popular casino, facilities include an Olympic-size pool surrounded by manicured lawns, and a palm-lined sundeck with piped-in music. There are ten night-lit tennis courts and a Stadium Court with an adjacent grandstand, seating 500; a series of celebrity tournaments takes place here, the most famous of which is the Dewar's Invitational Tennis Tournament. And though baby-sitters are available if you should want to go off sans kids, the Riviera boasts that all its entertainment is suitable for the entire family.

The addition of a 17-story tower in 1975 brought the Riviera's room capacity to 1,000. Tastefully furnished, with bedroom and bath separated by a walk-through closet, rooms cost $32 to $60 a night for double or single occupancy. All rooms have double or king-size beds.

The award-winning gourmet restaurant here is **Delmonico,** patterned after the famous New York restaurant of the same name. Tufted brown and burnt-orange leather chairs are arranged in cozy circles, the hushed atmosphere enhanced by soft lighting from massive chandeliers. A well-stocked wine cellar is on the premises. A meal at Delmonico might begin with an appetizer of smoked Nova Scotia salmon with capers ($4.25). Sumptuous entrees include chicken cacciatore ($12.50) and steak au poivre flamed tableside in cognac ($15.50).

The newest addition to the Riviera's dining facilities is **The Lighthouse,** a seafood restaurant with an elaborately nautical decor patterned after a 19th-century whaling vessel. Most entrees are priced between $10 and $12. And of course, in this 24-hour town, there's a 24-hour coffee shop, the **Cafe Noir.**

In the **Versailles Theatre,** you're likely to see Neil Sedaka, Liza Minnelli, Engelbert Humperdinck, Burt Bacharach, Anthony Newley or Olivia Newton-John. The 8 p.m. dinner show costs $18.50, the midnight cocktail show $17.50.

Finally, in **Le Bistro Bar,** you can enjoy cocktails while viewing your favorite sporting event on a five-foot-square color TV.

THE SANDS HOTEL: 3355 Las Vegas Boulevard South (tel: 735-9111; 800/634-6901).

A Las Vegas landmark since 1952, the Sands's balconied white circular tower (bathed in green light after dark) climbs 18 stories skyward. In total, the hotel offers 777 rooms (a lucky number, perhaps), some of which are housed in smaller units named after famous race tracks; these are grouped around palm-fringed gardens and a putting green.

Facilities comprise two Olympic-size swimming pools, four night-lighted tennis courts, boutiques, beauty salon and barber shop, baby-sitter service, car rental desk and the rest. Complimentary golf privileges are available at the Paradise Country Club, seven miles away. And, of course, there's the ever-present casino, large and plush.

The spacious rooms are softly color-coordinated in lovely hues; furnishings are vaguely Queen Anne. Fully equipped with all amenities, they're among the most attractive rooms in town. Rates, single or double, run from $28 to $46 per day, depending on location.

The Sands boasts two prestigious restaurants: **The Regency Room** and the **Pavilion Club,** both of which serve gourmet continental fare, the latter specializing in fresh seafood. The **Garden Room,** with an indoor-outdoor ambience, adjoins the Pavilion Club bar.

Nightly entertainment in the **Copa Room** (made famous by Sinatra) nowadays features the likes of Wayne Newton, whose recent show drew such a large crowd it had to be moved to the immense Ballroom. Robert Goulet, Doc Severinsen and George Burns also frequently play the Copa Room. Two shows nightly: the dinner show at 8 p.m. is $13 to $22.50; the midnight show is $12 to $17.50, including two drinks. There's also live entertainment in the **Regency Lounge,** off the casino, from 5:30 p.m. to 3:30 a.m.

Throughout 1977, The Sands is offering a tennis package for $84 per person, double occupancy. It includes accommodations for two nights and three days, bellman gratuities, unlimited free tennis and a private one-hour tennis lesson, a gift, health-club privileges, and a prime-rib dinner show or second show with four cocktails.

DUNES HOTEL AND COUNTRY CLUB: 3650 Las Vegas Boulevard South (tel: 734-4110; 800/634-6971).

When the Dunes Hotel completes its $75-million expansion program, it will double its existing 1,000-room capacity and become a tri-tower complex. In addition, the existing accommodations will be expanded and renovated. Present facilities include the 18-hole Emerald Green championship golf course and country club, health club and solaria for men and women, a nursery for the kids, three gourmet restaurants, eight other eateries, nine bars, two immense pools (one Olympic-size), 12 Garden Arcade shops and an opulent casino.

The private guest rooms are spacious and color-coordinated, and have either one king or twin-queen beds. Each has running ice water, a separate theatrically lighted make-up area and brunch table settings for in-room dining. Prices for singles or doubles are from $29 to $45 per night.

Currently there are 11 restaurants at the Dunes. When the expansion program is finished, there will be seven more! One of the three major dining rooms is the exotic, palatial **Sultan's Table.** The motif comes from Kismet, a pleasure palace of the Far East. This one features lots of stained glass, a waterfall and a tented entrance. Diners are serenaded by Arturo Romero's magic violins throughout the evening.

The **Dome of the Sea** is a seashell-shaped seafood restaurant (not by the seashore) with flying fish projected on the walls and a blond mermaid playing the harp from a floating gondola. The basic color scheme is blue and green, with varicolored lights pouring through the domed ceiling. Among the specialties of the Dome are lobster thermidor, pompano en papillote and bouillabaisse Marseillaise.

Atop the 24th floor, offering a panoramic view of the incredible Vegas scene, is **Top O' the Strip.** It opens its doors at noon with a royal Queen Elizabeth luncheon buffet. At dinner, it's famous for succulent duck, prepared, no less, "in the manner of La Tour d'Argent." Other featured items are roast prime rib of beef, stuffed trout and veal scaloppine. Big-name orchestras entertain till dawn.

The big show at the Dunes is **Casino de Paris,** a lavish spectacular with incredible sets and gorgeous plumed and sequinned beauties. Galloping horses and camels appear on stage, and there's comedy, acrobats, lots of nostalgia and a group from Stockholm called "The Stupids." The entire show is imported from Paris with its original cast. The dinner show ($15 to $18.50) is at 7:45 p.m., the cocktail show ($12.50, including three drinks) at 11:45 p.m.

ALADDIN HOTEL: 3667 Las Vegas Boulevard South (tel: 736-0111; 800/634-3424).

Its new 20-story tower bringing the total room count to 1,030, the Aladdin is emerging as a prominent and popular Strip hotel. It recently up-ended the local entertainment scene with the launching, in 1976, of the **Theater for the Performing Arts** for "mega-star" entertainment.

The decor throughout is unrestrainedly Eastern/Arabian, the lobby containing a large scale model of the Taj Mahal on a marble base under more dripping crystal than we've ever seen. Included on the grounds are a bazaar of 25 shops, an exciting casino, nine restaurants, four bars, night-lighted tennis courts, and two swimming pools.

Rooms at the Aladdin are spacious and flamboyant, most furnished in French provincial, with many exotic accents, like minaret-shaped mirrors and ornately jeweled chandeliers. Prices for double or single occupancy range from $28 to $48 per night.

The restaurants here are truly excellent. For dinner, there's a choice of the **Sabre Room,** for American and continental gourmet dining (Elvis Presley's wedding-party dinner was held here), the **Middle East Room,** offering specialties from that area of the world; **Giovanni's,** for terrific Italian food in an exaggeratedly Italian ambience complete with fluted columns, marble statuary and a Venetian gondola; **Fisherman's Mill,** serving gourmet seafood in a quaint New England atmosphere; the medieval-looking **King Richard's,** for carved tender viands; and **Empress Gardens,** for Cantonese fare. That's not to mention

The Oasis, a 24-hour coffee shop, and The Deli, dishing up pastrami on rye and the like.

The big entertainment facility here is the above-mentioned $10-million, 7,500-seat Theatre for the Performing Arts. Neil Diamond, who headlined the inaugural show, was paid $650,000 for four nights. No food or beverages are served here—it's entertainment and entertainment only. Others who have performed here since Diamond include Seals and Croft, Ray Charles, James Taylor and Johnny Mathis; in addition, it's used for Ice Capades, sports events (like the closed-circuit screening of the Ali–Norton fight) and even complete Broadway shows. Ticket prices vary widely, according to the attraction. Showtime is usually 8:30 p.m., with second shows occasionally scheduled.

There's also the Bagdad Theatre, a nightclub offering two shows nightly, at 10 p.m. and 12:30 a.m. Here you might see the Supremes, Lew Rawls, Blood, Sweat & Tears, et al—stars, but not mega-stars. Shows are priced at $5.50 to $10, including two drinks.

And finally, there's the Casino Lounge, charging a mere one-drink minimum to see acts like Don Cherry, the Imperials and the Platters.

FRONTIER HOTEL: 3120 Las Vegas Boulevard South (tel: 734-0110; 800/634-6966).

The horseshoe-shaped Frontier is heralded by a hundred-foot-high sign (frequently emblazoned with the name of show-biz personalities) reputed to have cost over $1 million. The hotel itself is surrounded by beautiful grounds, manicured lawns, fountains and little rustic bridges over a reflecting pool. Within is an enormous and lavish casino, along with 600 guest rooms, shops and services. A broad range of recreational facilities are on the premises: an Olympic-size swimming pool, six tennis courts (half of which are night-lighted) and a putting green; golf is available nearby at the Desert Inn or the Paradise Valley Country Club.

The rooms are decorated predominantly in beige and champagne hues with olive and avocado accents, though there are exceptions with more flamboyant color schemes. They're equipped with every convenience, including remote bedside control of your color TV. Rates are $27 to $43 single or double.

The *de rigueur* epicurean restaurant for continental gourmet fare is the Cabaret, Vegas red-on-red-plush in decor. A daily "Bountiful Buffet" is served in the Steak House from 11 a.m. to 3 p.m.—all you can eat for $3 per person. The ambience is rustic Wild West, with a covered wagon motif. You can also order à la carte, with most dinner entrees (even steak and lobster) in the $10 range.

Also *de rigueur,* the 24-hour coffee shop here is the Pioneer Room.

Entertainment takes place in the 800-seat Music Hall. There are two performances nightly, showing off such stars as Bob Newhart, Wayne Newton, Robert Goulet and Juliet Prowse. The 8:15 p.m. dinner show is priced according to what you order; the midnight show is about $10, including two drinks.

And finally, the Winners' Circle, off the casino, offers live entertainment into the early-morning hours.

DEL WEBB'S HOTEL SAHARA: Las Vegas Boulevard South and Sahara Avenue (tel: 735-2111; 800/634-6666).

Situated at the very start of The Strip, the Sahara sets the tone of things to come with its flamingo-pink facade. The 24-story skyscraper and 14-story tower buildings are set on a 20-acre complex that contains 950 rooms, three restaurants, two showrooms, two swimming pools, a health club for men, smart shops and services. Transportation is available to the nearby Sahara-Nevada Country Club, home of the $150,000 Sahara Invitational, one of the big pro golf tournaments of the year. And, of course, there's an enormous casino with the usual accoutrements.

The rooms are spacious and bright, with neat, modern decor—none of the usual overdone Vegas trappings, but all modern amenities. All have individual dressing rooms, and many have their own private sun patios. Singles and doubles rent for $30 to $39 per night.

Restaurant options range from the South Seas to the "veddy English." In the latter category is the **House of Lords,** done in regal red tones, with beamed ceilings and pewter and stained-glass lighting fixtures. Specialties of the house are more continental than English, however, running the gamut from chicken Kiev with Oriental rice ($11) to frog's legs meuniere ($12). The South Seas fare is at a **Don the Beachcomber** restaurant on the premises, featuring the usual exotic Polynesian decor and live music for dancing nightly.

There's also a 24-hour coffee shop, the **Caravan Room,** which turns out, among other things, huge, heavenly banana splits.

For those who prefer buffet dining, the **South Hall** offers a table piled high at every meal; breakfast and lunch cost $2.45, dinner $3.75. And the popular **Sahara Brunch** is served daily in the Congo Room from 9 a.m. to 2 p.m. for $2.75 ($3.75 on Sunday).

The **Congo Room** is the Sahara's entertainment facility, featuring names like Tennessee Ernie Ford, Vic Damone and Lena Horne. The dinner show costs $17.95 per person, the midnight show $15, including two drinks.

You can also catch shows, ranging from topless revues and vaudeville to once-top musical groups like the Diamonds, in the **Casbar Theatre Lounge.**

STARDUST HOTEL: 3000 Las Vegas Boulevard South (tel: 732-6111; 800/634-6757).

Because the Stardust is so centrally located (right in the center of the Strip) and has such reasonably priced accommodations, it is one of the most heavily booked hotels in Vegas, and its casino is one of the liveliest. It has 1,500 rooms spread throughout seven buildings. There are two Olympic-size pools, four night-lighted tennis courts, five major restaurants, a children's game area and a shopping arcade; there's even a huge campsite.

Accommodations run the gamut from campsite to penthouse, with standard rooms as attractive and well equipped as those costing almost twice as much. Singles are $14 to $24, doubles $16 to $26. Inquire about package plans, which include show tickets, etc.

Among the restaurants on the premises is **Aku Aku,** lushly Polynesian in decor and featuring an immense menu of items like beef in oyster sauce ($7.75) and chicken Hawaiian ($7.95). Exotic drinks here, served in pineapples, coconuts or fancy mugs, are a must. For seafood, there's the nautically themed **Moby Dick,** offering a variety of entrees in the $7-to-$8 range. And the **Palm Room** is a garden-motif 24-hour coffee shop.

The newest eatery is the **Sirloin Room** specializing in prime-rib and sirloin dinners only, for $6.95—the meal includes soup, salad, steak-fried potatoes, rolls and butter, vegetable, strawberry shortcake and coffee.

The big show takes place in the **Cafe Continental**—it's the lavish *Lido de Paris* revue, a Las Vegas tradition since 1958. Like the others of its ilk, it's great fun, with incredible sets and costumes, acrobats and all the rest. This show features an ice-skating scene, the release of live doves, an actual flood and a fire, all on stage. Particularly colorful is a tribute to Carmen Miranda. The dinner show costs $16 to $20, the midnight show $15, including three drinks.

There are also continuous nighttime shows in the **Starlight Lounge,** occasionally featuring big names like B.B. King, Fabian, Fats Domino and Chubby Checker.

THE CIRCUS-CIRCUS HOTEL: 2880 Las Vegas Boulevard South (tel: 734-0410; 800/634-3450).

Among the newer hotels on the Strip, Circus-Circus is shaped like an enormous big-top tent, and its immense sign is clown-shaped. That's because inside there are continuous circus acts going on every day from 11 a.m. to midnight. The entire show—trapeze artists, acrobats, tightrope walkers, etc.—is conducted *above* the casino. The circus theme is carried throughout the hotel, right down to the clown-shaped pool.

Other guest amenities include a sumptuous health spa complete with geisha girls (for men only), a shopping midway, Guinness World Records exhibits, golf, tennis, ice-skating, bowling, six restaurants and an exciting children's arcade from whence the best view of circus acts.

Single and double rooms here are priced from $18 to $34. The distinguishing features are leopard or tiger bedspreads and gaming instruction on closed-circuit TV.

When dining here, you have your choice of the **Pink Pony,** a 24-hour coffee shop; **Cowboy Steak & Bean House,** with ringside views of the circus acts and family-priced meals of steak, prime ribs, "Ranch" breakfasts, and "Wrangler" lunches; **Smorgasbord Internationale,** for all-you-can-eat buffet lunches ($2.50) and dinners ($3.50); **The Bon Vivant,** featuring intimate, opulent dining, away from all the activity; **The Snack Train,** for fast food service; and the newly opened **Italia,** featuring, you guessed it, Italian fare.

In the evening you can visit the **Gilded Cage Lounge,** with live nightly entertainment, or the **Horse Around Bar,** where you watch the circus acts.

Gift shops, boutiques, big-top trapeze acts, a merry-go-round—fun things galore are tucked into the Circus-Circus cornucopia of goodies. This is a sensational Hotel-Casino-Circus-Spa that truly must be seen to be believed.

THE WESTWARD HO MOTEL & CASINO: 2900 Las Vegas Boulevard South (tel: 731-2900; 800/634-6803).

Billed as the largest hotel in the world with its 1,000 rooms and 11, yes 11, swimming pools, The Westward Ho occupies a prime location on the Strip, right across from the Riviera. The amenities here are many: free champagne every night in the casino, a 24-hour restaurant, snack bar and cocktail lounge, game room and fun arcade for the kiddies.

The rooms all have TVs and dressing areas. Midweek rates start at $15 and go up to $24 for a single; $17 to $28 for a double. Rooms up front are the most expensive.

EL MOROCCO: 2975 Las Vegas Boulevard South (tel: 735-7145).

Contemporary in motif, but Moorish in ambience, the El Morocco shares its facilities with its next-door neighbor, the La Concha. These include a nice-size pool, a sundeck, beauty parlor and gift shop. On its own, El Morocco has a casino that offers free shrimp cocktails to guests, and Las Vegas-style-plush rooms, with flocked red and gold curtains painted behind the beds. Priced at $24 to $26, single or double (the less expensive ones are on the outside, not facing the pool), the rooms are spacious and contain two double or two queen- or one king-size bed. Each is equipped with color TV, radio, clock and marble-topped dressers. Water beds are $28 per night.

The two restaurants here are the **Cafe Morocco,** a coffee shop, open 7 a.m. to 10 p.m. daily; and the **Copper Cart,** for steak and prime-rib dinners. There is also a cocktail lounge.

LA CONCHA MOTEL: 2955 Las Vegas Boulevard South (tel: 735-1255).

This hotel, just a dice throw from the El Morocco, has no casino and no dining facilities. It offers, instead, the use of all the amenities at El Morocco, which is under the same ownership.

The 100 rooms here contain either two double or one king-size bed. Once again the only-in-Vegas decor features flocked striped wallpaper, pineapple lamps and gold sparkles on the ceilings. There are dressing areas in each room. Singles and doubles are available at $24 to $26 per night.

MOTEL 6: 195 East Tropicana Boulevard (tel: 736-4904).

Located right off the Strip, about 1½ blocks from the Tropicana, is a branch of this low-priced national chain. We refer you, once again, to the Introduction for details.

Moving away from the Strip, in the Downtown area you might consider the following:

EL CORTEZ: Corner Fremont and 6th Streets (tel: 385-5200).

With only 152 rooms, the El Cortez is one of Las Vegas's smaller, and older, hotels. Built around 1940, and renovated just a few years ago, it has a sparkling coffee shop, the **Carnival Bar,** that is always crowded and always open. Ditto the casino, which boasts "extra-liberal" slot machines.

The rooms, outfitted with black and white TV, direct-dial phones and modern baths, are just $10 to $14 single, $12 to $20 double. There's another eatery on the premises, a steakhouse called the **Cortez Room.**

HORSESHOE HOTEL & CASINO: 128 Fremont at Casino Center Boulevard (tel: 382-1600).

Located in the heart of Downtown, this hotel is frequently thought of as a casino only. Not true. This inexpensive little "getaway" has 85 rooms on three floors. However, the casino *is* the main attraction. There's a restaurant, **The Sombrero Room,** serving Mexican food, to one side of the casino. Adjoining this is a coffee shop. There is also a bar and a gift shop.

The rooms are more than adequate, especially when considering the $13-$20 price tag on singles or doubles. Each has a new tub/shower, and the section that has been refurbished has cheery quilted bedspreads and wallpaper.

One of the Horseshoe's bigger draws is the display of $1,000,000 in cash—a hundred $10,000 bills. You may have your picture taken with the money, free of charge. Another major attraction here is that owner Jack Binion often strolls through the slot-machine area handing out rolls of nickels, dimes or quarters to those playing the slots. You may also be given $1 in nickels to play while you're waiting for your photo to be developed. The casino is also unique in that it allows craps table bets up to $10,000, reputed to be the highest sum allowed in Nevada in any casino for a single bet at craps, which is no doubt of vital importance to many of you.

MINT HOTEL: 100 East Fremont Street at the corner of South 1st Street (tel: 385-7440).

Dominating Glitter Gulch with its 26 stories, flashing lights, and outside glass elevator, the Mint Hotel features one of Nevada's largest casinos, complete with live entertainment from 2 p.m. to 2 a.m.

The rooms here rent for $21 to $31 per night—the lower the floor, the lower the price. All rooms have just been renovated in bright and cheery colors. Each has a color TV with closed-circuit gaming lessons, and other modern amenities.

Two special features at the Mint are the free behind-the-scenes tours of the casino and free lessons in the fundamentals of casino games—it can't hurt, but probably won't help, either.

The Mint's restaurants include a 24-hour coffee shop, a snack bar and the **Top O' the Mint,** (reached by the aforementioned, glass-walled elevator), a gourmet restaurant with live entertainment and dancing nightly.

WESTERN HOTEL: 899 East Fremont Street at 9th (tel: 384-4620).

The Western is a three-story hotel with 115 rooms and a tremendous 1,000-seat bingo parlor. The air-conditioned rooms are cozy, immaculate and pretty, simply but nicely furnished with abundant closet space, black and white TV, direct-dial phones and mirrored dressing alcoves. For a single or double room you pay a mere $10 to $14 per.

"Western Fun Books," which guests may receive daily, are the best around. They entitle you to various free meals, drinks and bingo at the Western and other hotels.

There are snack and cocktail bars on the premises.

ARTHUR FROMMER, INC.
380 MADISON AVE., NEW YORK, N.Y. 10017   Date_____

Friends:
Please send me (postpaid) the books checked below:

$10-A-DAY GUIDES
(In-depth guides to low-cost tourist accommodations and facilities.)

- ☐ Europe on $10 a Day $4.95
- ☐ England on $15 a Day $4.50
- ☐ Greece on $10 a Day $3.95
- ☐ Hawaii on $15 & $20 a Day $4.50
- ☐ India (plus Sri Lanka and Nepal) on $5 & $10 a Day $3.95
- ☐ Ireland on $10 a Day $4.50
- ☐ Israel on $10 & $15 a Day $3.95
- ☐ Mexico and Guatemala on $10 a Day......................$4.95
- ☐ New Zealand on $10 a Day $3.95
- ☐ New York on $15 a Day $3.95
- ☐ Scandinavia on $15 & $20 a Day $4.50
- ☐ South America on $10 & $15 a Day $4.50
- ☐ Spain and Morocco (plus the Canary Is.) on $10 & $15 a Day $4.50
- ☐ Turkey on $5 & $10 a Day $3.95
- ☐ Washington, D.C. on $10 & $15 a Day $3.95

DOLLAR-WISE GUIDES

(Guides to tourist accommodations and facilities from budget to deluxe, with emphasis on the medium-priced.)

- ☐ England $4.50
- ☐ France $4.50
- ☐ Germany $3.95
- ☐ Italy $4.50
- ☐ Portugal $3.95
- ☐ California $4.50

THE ARTHUR FROMMER GUIDES

(Pocket-size guides to tourist accommodations and facilities in all price ranges.)

- ☐ Athens $1.95
- ☐ Boston $1.95
- ☐ Honolulu $1.95
- ☐ Ireland/Dublin/Shannon ...$1.95
- ☐ Las Vegas $1.95
- ☐ Lisbon/Madrid/Costa del Sol $1.95
- ☐ London $1.95
- ☐ Los Angeles $1.95
- ☐ New York $1.95
- ☐ Paris $1.95
- ☐ Rome $1.95
- ☐ San Francisco $1.95
- ☐ Washington, D.C. ..$1.95

By the Council on International Educational Exchange

☐ Whole World Handbook $2.95
(A student guide to work, study and travel worldwide.)

☐ Where to Stay USA $2.95
(A guide to accommodations in all 50 states costing from 50¢ to $10 per night.)

Enclosed is my check or money order for $_____

NAME_____

ADDRESS_____

CITY_____STATE_____ZIP_____